HORSE SENSE
of the Carolinas

MORE THAN A
MIRROR

Horses, Humans, and Therapeutic Practices

by Shannon Knapp

More than a Mirror: Horses, Humans, and Therapeutic Practices
Copyright © 2013 by Shannon Knapp

Cover Photo by Coco Baptiste

Cover design by elWray Design, elwraydesign.com

Interior Design & layout by Crowboat Creative, crowboatcreative.com

Editing by Emily Koenig, emilykoenig.com

Notice of Rights

All rights reserved. Except as permitted under U.S. Copyright Act of 1976, no part of this publication may be reproduced, distributed, or transmitted in any form or by any means, or stored in a database or retrieval system, without the prior written permission of the publisher.

Notice of Liability

This purpose of this book is to inform and educate its readers as to the opinions and experiences of its author and contributors on the subjects covered, and encourage readers to consider that information in light of their own experiences.
Nothing contained in this book is to be considered therapeutic, safety, legal, business, or other professional advice for any specific situation.

Nothing contained in this book is a substitute for the diligent exercise of sound judgment, especially as to matters of safety, the selection, training or use of any particular horse in equine assisted therapy, the conduct of any equine assisted therapy session, or the selection, training or use of any person as an equine specialist.

Although reasonable care has been taken in the preparation of this book, the author, contributors, publisher and Horse Sense of the Carolinas, Inc. make no representations or warranties of any kind and assume no liabilities of any kind with respect to the accuracy or completeness of the contents and specifically disclaim any implied warranties of merchantability or fitness of use for a particular purpose. The information in this book is distributed "AS IS".

Neither the author, contributors, publisher and Horse Sense of the Carolinas, Inc. shall be held liable or responsible to any person or entity with respect to any loss or incidental or consequential damages caused, or alleged to have been caused, directly or indirectly, by the information contained in, implied by or omitted from this book.

Purchase or use of this book shall constitute the voluntary assumption of any and all risks that may arise therefrom.

The presentation of information from contributors does not imply an endorsement of that information by the author, publisher or any other contributor.

Printed in the United States of America
First Edition: March 5, 2013
ISBN: 0-9794041-8-5
ISBN: 978-0-9794041-8-4

— ⊞ —

To Richard,

My hero, my best friend, my biggest supporter, my honest partner.
Thanks for all you do and are.

Contents

FIGURES & ILLUSTRATIONS

Acknowledgements

It takes a village to do many things; writing and completing a book is most definitely one of them!

I'd like to thank all the wonderful folks who took the original online questionnaires, and those who have attended conference presentations and workshops I've offered through the years. Every comment has contributed to my thinking on the subject. We have such a wealth of experience together. I'd also like to thank the *Horse Sense Trailblazers*, and the Mastermind groups: Working Together Works!

I'd also like to thank the interviewees for the book, who helped me tease apart the questions and took time out of their ever-busy schedules to talk with me: Rhiannon, Liza, StarrLee, Amy, Patti & Randy, Carissa, Paul, Linda & Z. I'm humbled by their collective and individual knowledge and experience, and am grateful to be a contemporary and a colleague.

Thanks also to the many, many contributors of guest segments: Leif, Kris, Tanya, Kendall, Lynn, Tim, Bettina & Laura, Lillan, Annick & Elizabeth, Michelle & Cami, Harriet, Ashley, Jayna, Tracy and Lisa. Linda Parelli and the folks at Parelli have been gracious in reading through and approving drafts, allowing permission for me to share what has influenced me so very much. Thanks also to Coco, for her wonderful cover photo, her smile and her kind spirit. Linda and Pat Parelli have been enormous influences on my work and our practice; thank you for the guidance and leadership!

There are many who helped in the research, writing and production of this book. Among these stars are Josie Mosser, Emily Koenig and Eleni Dines. Josie Mosser **is** the flying octopus, doing so many different things at the same time and doing them well, as always (almost perfect!). Emily Koenig jumped in and said "I can" when we needed her most, and has been an ever-present force behind *Horse Sense* for years now, keeping things running smoothly, allowing me time to disappear into the book. Eleni Dines showed up just in time to make sense of chaos; many emails, much detective work and several late nights later, it all makes sense! Emily Wray has done her usual bang-up job on the cover design and all things visual, often within less than twenty-four hours! RL Adams offered sage legal advice. Brenda Dammann and Lisa McElmurry were part of the original team, transcribing, researching and contributing to initial drafts. Thanks!

Finally, Eleni, Tim & Bettina, Richard, Lori, Michelle, Cami and Kris were all excellent readers with keen eyes, who patiently read through these drafts and offered wise commentary. Richard, you have been your usual fussy, difficult and troublesome self throughout the process (not!). Lori Araki, you have inspired me with your kindness, humor, and wisdom, and I'm grateful to have you as a co-worker and a friend. Lastly, I'd like to thank Ellen Hearne and Sue for bringing me on this journey in the first place, as well as Dreamer and Scout, two horses who have taught me multitudes about what I don't know! There isn't space nor thanks enough for all the other horses who have taught me, nor for the many, many clients whose paths have crossed mine and allowed me to be enriched by them. All errors, omissions and mistakes are, of course, mine!

Foreward

BY LINDA PARELLI

There is something about horses that opens your heart, your soul, that accesses your inner being. I am privileged to teach all over the world and it never ceases to amaze me how the love of horses crosses all boundaries and borders, at every level - mentally, emotionally and physically. And everyone seems to say the same thing... "Horses are such good therapy."

When you're with a horse, you forget about your troubles and pressures, your everyday life, and you are transported into a world of childhood dreams and adult realizations. Of course things don't always go as planned, there are ups and downs, but that undying passion for horses keeps you deeply committed to the relationship.

I first encountered Shannon and her husband Richard in 2004 when they attended my 2-week Riding with Fluidity course in Florida. Then green but eager to learn, they have become regulars in Colorado, Florida and at tour stops through the years, as both are on the journey of never-ending self-improvement, for themselves, their clients and their horses.

Shannon and Richard have taken their work with horses and humans to an extraordinary level. In their unique program of equine-assisted psychotherapy they transform the lives of troubled humans, teaching self-belief, respect, responsibility, communication, leadership skills and engaging horses using the relationship principles of natural horsemanship. They integrate the 7 Games™ and much of the Parelli philosophy into their work with youth involved in gangs and those who are incarcerated, among many other groups of people. There is no-one horses cannot touch!

I'm amazed as well by the work pursued by others who are Parelli practitioners in the equine-assisted field, like Lillan Roquet and her co-workers in Australia who offered "HorsePlay" to adolescents, Harriet Laurie with her work in British prisons applying Horsenality™ as a character development program for inmates, and Ashley Edmonds Hayes, who has taken Horsenality™ and applied it to facilitating humans in ways that best match their Humanalities™. Each of these exciting programs is encapsulated in this book, bringing together how Parelli–overtly–develops humans, making it the first of a kind!

When my husband, Pat Parelli, was approached in 2010 to write a segment in an equine-assisted counseling book (*Harnessing the Power of Equine Assisted Counseling: Adding Animal Assisted Therapy to your Practice*, Routledge, 2011), I knew Shannon would be a great source of information as to how Parelli fits into the equine-assisted therapy and learning framework. We ended up inviting her to write some segments of that chapter, as she was an expert in the field!

I'm delighted that Shannon has authored this book, sharing what she knows and helping to make the world a better place for horses and humans.

Linda Parelli
Wellington, Florida, February 8, 2013

Introduction
A NEW FOCUS

There have been many changes in the years since publishing the book *Horse Sense, Business Sense* – both at *Horse Sense* as a business and within the Equine Assisted Practice/Equine Assisted Learning (EAP/EAL) industry. And, while I've always known there would be much more to write about in the future, it wasn't clear what the topic of that "Next Book" should be. Where do we go next? In what direction is the field heading? What information would be most helpful for people currently working within the field and those considering entering the field?

In Volume I of *Horse Sense, Business Sense*, I focused on the start-up equine-assisted practice, addressing the questions and issues raised through the many phone calls I received, as a whole industry of non-business people tackled starting their own profit and non-profit programs. I spent hours helping people from all walks of life with questions on insurance, business formation, marketing, and other aspects of running an EAP/EAL program. It seemed the greatest need for guidance centered on starting, running, and surviving the practical tasks of actually operating a business.

Even as *Horse Sense, Business Sense* provided insight on managing these common situations, the questions being asked began to shift. People became more interested in the deeper work of developing their own core philosophy and applying principles to the roles of the various professionals in equine-assisted sessions. These questions were harder to answer and, as our own philosophy at *Horse Sense* developed, it was the answers to these questions that provided the direction for the "Next Book."

I've always been very passionate about understanding how horses and clients interact in equine-assisted work. The role of the Equine Specialist (ES) in supporting this interaction is especially important if the interaction is to be effective for the client. Too many times, I have witnessed practitioners attempting to support clients in session when it is apparent they barely know which end of the horse to put the halter on. I've also witnessed Equine Specialists who had little or no ability in reading the body language of their horses offer "interpretations" of what the horse was thinking. Ultimately, it's the client who loses out. Therefore it is critical for there to be a discussion that identifies the essential criteria for an Equine Specialist to be considered a true professional.

This discussion is made more complicated because the skillsets required for an ES to be considered a professional aren't necessarily tangible. It's not like other areas of the horse world, where some people measure competency by time in the saddle or trophies and ribbons. What makes an Equine Specialist excellent is far less concrete and, in my opinion, has everything to do with demonstrating competency in understanding equine psychology, communication and behavior, and becoming highly proficient at reading body language of both horse and human. Bringing this concept of raising the professional standards of Equine Specialists to the forefront of the discussion has become a true passion for me. And, judging by the questions which I have received since publishing the first book, it's also where passion meets need.

Similarly, the care, selection, and assessment of the horse(s) has become an oft-overlooked part of the EAP/EAL process. As the most important element distinguishing this work, there appears to be a lack of time, attention and critical thought applied to the process of selecting, assessing, and supporting the EAP/EAL horse. EAP/EAL work isn't an appropriate field for every horse, although almost any horse **can** be successful, under the right circumstances and for the right client(s).

So, while a follow-up book to *Horse Sense, Business Sense* will be forthcoming, the time seems right to focus attention on a different aspect of EAP/EAL: taking a closer look at the vital roles of the Equine Specialist and the horse in equine-assisted client sessions. And, in the process of seeking answers to these questions, we'll be taking a look at the practice itself. We've learned a great deal during the past decade of performing this work at *Horse Sense*, and are eager to share this knowledge and experience.

THE MAKING OF A HORSE PROFESSIONAL

To me, being a true horse professional in any capacity is about being a student of the horse. I've seen how the role of Equine Specialist can be so much deeper and richer than most practitioners suggest. Do Equine Specialists really understand the significance of prey psychology as it applies to the horse? Are many aware of the deep differences in personality between different horses, and how those differences play out with clients? How many study the intricate subtleties in the way horses respond—subtleties which can yield layers of meaning to the client interaction? There is tremendous opportunity here to enrich and build our understanding and to make equine-assisted work even more powerful than it already is.

It's important to note that I'll be approaching most of this discussion from the perspective of an EAGALA practitioner (EAGALA referring to the Equine-Assisted Growth and Learning Association, www. EAGALA.org). Equine-assisted work in the EAGALA model today takes place on the ground and always utilizes a team approach with two professionals in the arena with the client and horses in each client session: a mental health professional and a horsew professional/ Equine Specialist.

In my opinion, it's this dual-facilitator aspect of the EAGALA model which gives the Equine Specialist an especially important role in equine-assisted work. The Equine Specialist has an important and specific focus in this model that doesn't exist in other models. An ES focuses his/her eyes and knowledge predominantly on the horse in the session, while the mental health professional monitors the mental and emotional health of the client.

No matter how many sets of eyes are in the arena, there's always opportunity to miss something or for the facilitators' "stuff" (their own personal opinions, agendas, and so forth) to get in the way of a successful session between the client and the horse. But, the chances are greater for something to be missed, overlooked, or lost when only one individual tries to monitor both client and horse in session. In the same way putting a client in the saddle adds another layer of processing (whether informative or white noise) between the client and the issue(s), having only one professional facilitating a session gives that professional two layers of information to process. And while this doesn't necessarily translate directly into a disadvantage for the client, it does mean there is a greater likelihood that some information may not be captured and utilized. Although I don't think a team can capture everything that happens in a session, that capture is far more likely with a team approach than when only one professional is involved. Team facilitation also greatly simplifies basic tasks necessary to operate a session.

Each of the various training and certifying organizations have their own preferred terminology to identify the work they do: EAGALA refers to their work as Equine Assisted Psychotherapy (EAP) or Equine Assisted Learning (EAL). Practitioners of PATH International (formerly called NARHA and EFMHA; more on this in chapter 2) generally refer to their work as Equine Facilitated Psychotherapy and Learning. The Equine Guided Education Association (EGEA) obviously prefers the term "guided" to "facilitated" or "assisted." Even here at *Horse Sense*, we sometimes apply a learning model we call Equine Interactive Learning, or EIL, with our clients. And the list goes on and on.

With deference to all the many models out there, throughout this book I'll be using the term "equine-assisted practice" as an all-encompassing definition to describe the many different models used when horses assist humans in learning or therapy situations.

WHO IS THIS BOOK FOR?

There have been seismic shifts in how we relate to horses in the past one hundred years; our understanding of the horse has changed alongside those shifts. So first and foremost, this is a book for people who love horses and understand the potential horses have to teach us and to help us create change in our lives. There are many of us out there who are deep into the practice of learning from horses and into the theory of what is happening as we learn from horses. There are people paying attention to nuances of the field of EAP/EAL as well as learning the broad brushstrokes, people who, like me, want a forum for a richer discussion. I hope this book provides a starting point for that discussion.

Many of us who've come to this field as horse professionals have also thought about the life skills we're learning from our horses. At some point, we recognized we are working on ourselves as much as playing with our horses. We started to recognize we are getting a great deal more out of playing with horses than just a really neat relationship (or a really challenging relationship—whatever the situation happens to be!). We also began to realize the skills we learn at the barn carry over to our real lives. Magazines are full of stories about life lessons learned at the barn. T-shirts proclaim, "All I need to learn, I learned from my horse." And many of us know for a fact that hanging out with horses saved our lives and kept us from getting into trouble.

After, and perhaps because of, our own personal experiences living these lessons taught by horses, it's really exciting to think about bringing the power of horses to others in need of support. These people may or may not have any deep affection for horses or may not even want a long-term relationship with one. Though we differ from our clients in these sentiments, the power of horses is still available to them through the work we do.

This book is also, of course, for equine-assisted professionals—mental health professionals, horse professionals, educators, and others—and those interested in becoming a part of the field. I've spoken before about what I call "the horse and the curry comb" syndrome: "I've got a horse and a curry comb. Come on! Let's do some therapy!" There's so much more to it than that! Great things can come just from hanging out at the barn and being with horses. However, those same activities, carried out carelessly and without thought, have the potential to become meaningless snake-oil salesmanship and possibly dangerous interactions for both horses and humans, both of which can damage a young field immeasurably.

As EAP/EAL professionals, if we are busy providing services and working with actual clients (as opposed to only teaching others how to work with actual clients), we don't often get the opportunity to talk with each other about our own practice at a deeper level. Annual conferences and workshops reveal how many new folks are coming into the field, and the focus (rightfully) is about teaching fundamentals. A side-effect of this, however, is that sometimes this focus leaves those of us who've been doing it for a while wanting more. Practitioners who've been working for a decade or more don't have as many available forums in which to explore advanced skills and advanced principles. For them, I hope this book will provide several launching-points for discussions.

I believe a tremendous amount of specialization and skill goes into becoming an Equine Specialist. Like many highly skilled professions, there's an art to it. The more we recognize and talk about developing skills, developing a deeper understanding of what assists the client, what gets in the way of the client, what assists the horse, and what gets in the way of the horse—the more meaningful our work will be. This book is about those deeper concepts, and how they work in session and out for the horses, the horse professional, and the clients.

The research I've conducted at *Horse Sense* indicates most people come to the field of equine-assisted work with their own horses and/or a deep desire and longing for horses. At some point, they've recognized what horses do for them or for others they encounter. They've heard about equine-assisted practice and they want to bring it to their community. Many programs start as backyard practices and stay that way, and their community benefits. No matter the size or scope of the practice, I want this book to encourage everyone to aspire to a higher level of professionalism and proficiency in equine-assisted practice.

KEEPING AN OPEN MIND

There can be as much politics involved in the equine-assisted industry as in any professional field. In reading this book (or *any* book, for that matter!), an open mind will be essential. No matter what your persuasion, your flavor of equine-assisted practice, or what brand of horsemanship you practice, remember all information has the potential to further your knowledge. Ultimately, the best advice is to keep what you can use and leave the rest.

OUTLINE OF THIS BOOK

As we move through the concepts of this book, we'll start in Section 1 by exploring some necessary background. First, we'll talk about the history and core principles of Natural Horsemanship and how they've been defined and refined since their early inception. Then, we'll look at some of the main organizations leading the field of EAP and EAL work, and the principles which helped shape current forms of practice. Next, we'll move into explaining, as clearly as possible for an experiential form of practice, how this work happens in real time in the field. After that, we'll consider utilizing Natural Horsemanship theory, practice and principles as learning tools in client sessions, with special attention paid to Parelli Natural Horsemanship™. We'll close out Section 1 by reviewing some of the scientific literature and thought-leaders from other fields, and how those impact our work in EAP/EAL.

In Section 2, we'll look more closely at the horse and the role of the horse in EAP/EAL, including choosing and assessing the herd for your equine-assisted work, identifying and dealing with burnout in EAP/EAL horses, and developing and supporting the EAP/EAL horse. Finally, we'll spend some time examining the current field of horse professionals in equine-assisted practices: what skills are present, what skills may need development and ongoing support, and the role of the horse professional in EAP/EAL practices.

There is value in each of the different approaches out there. I invite you to explore your own calling in regards to this work, as well as to the established models we'll be discussing here. Through self-questioning, collaboration and renewed commitment to the horse, hopefully we can continue to elevate the equine-assisted profession as a whole.

Welcome!

Section One

Horses Changing People

RESCUING HORSES, FINDING PARELLI, AND FINDING EA WORK

Perhaps the best way to demonstrate how horses can create change in people is to tell you a few stories of my own. If you're into horses long enough, eventually that One Horse shows up in your life: the one who gives you fits, the one who challenges all your supposed experience. The one who makes you realize you don't know *anything*. This horse becomes what I call a "Waterloo Horse" unless we seek help and grow beyond our current boundaries. And, sometimes, this is the horse who leads us to unexpected places.

This is the story of my "Waterloo Horse".

After taking a few years off from horses for college and grad school while in my 20s, I moved to Texas and officially got back into horses. Susan Denero—or 'Black-Eyed Sue'—came to me the summer of 1998 as a 4-year-old registered dun paint broodmare. When I saw her for the first time at a horse show, I thought she looked great. Her owners were there to help her acclimate to the show environment. I was so excited to see her that I didn't stop long enough to consider the twisted-wire snaffle bit they were using—and why they might be using it. It should have been my first clue; it's the classic "normal" bit for the hard-to-control horse.

The more important thing to know, however, is Sue was actually my second Waterloo horse. I had sold her predecessor, named Brandy, because I kept hitting one wall after another until finally, out of sheer frustration, I sold her. Of course, I was convinced the issues were Brandy's fault, not mine. In the back of my mind I suspected differently, but everyone around me knew more, so I listened with relief to their suggestions that I sell her and get another horse more suited to me.

I really wanted this relationship with Sue to be different—I was tired of leaving the barn crying—but in no time at all I started having the same issues. How interesting! An unhappy truth started to surface: Maybe it wasn't the horse; maybe it was me.

Around the same time a significant event developed in my life, where a family crisis swiftly evolved into a personal crisis. I became painfully aware of the disconnect between who I was and who I wanted to be, and knew these were far bigger issues than anything I could resolve alone.

I decided to stop my life to seek help and, once I made the decision to take action, I also made a clear decision to stop trying to ride my horse until my issues were resolved. I just simply went out to the pasture and sat with Sue for hours on end (what I know now as Undemanding Time). Without knowing it, my horse became the most visible element in my recovery, helping me see I could never change the things that felt wrong in my life without changing me.

*This period of growth marked a really difficult time in my life, and there were moments when I wasn't motivated enough to get better for myself, but I **was** motivated to get better in order to have a good relationship with Sue. She motivated me when nothing else did.*

And so Black-Eyed Sue—along with her predecessor, Brandy—became the first examples in my life of how horses create change in humans. Sue's response to me became a powerful reflection of my issues and an even more powerful catalyst for healing.

Sue is now a wonderful EAP/EAL horse: great with kids, great with ground-work. She still has significant challenges under saddle, but her gifts to clients and to me have been innumerable.

My experiences with Sue were only the first steps toward realizing how horses generate change in people. I was still a long way from finding equine-assisted practice as a form of work, much less developing a concrete system for working with horses as professionals. My belief system and principles manifested through a combination of incidents, experience, intention, and osmosis to become a natural extension of *Horse Sense.*

In fact, I didn't actually plan to operate an equine-assisted practice at all. My husband Richard and I finalized our decision to move from Texas to North Carolina in 1999. Ten months, multiple trips, and thousands of details later, we were there. After our move, the original intention was to become a rescue and rehabilitation farm. We'd spent the Texas years doing rehab for large dogs, and wanted to do the same for horses in North Carolina. We found horses through the local horse rescue organization, Hope for Horses, and the North Carolina Equine Rescue League (which is now the United States Equine Rescue League) and worked to bring each horse back to health before finding them a new home.

As we assessed each horse who came to us, we would also often receive a laundry list of issues from those involved: the owner, the vet, the barn manager or whomever. This caused me great frustration. Humans were subjective; we needed something objective to measure horse behavior, but I had yet to find anything reliable, and there was no way to do so in the timeframe I needed, given my age and the hours necessary to become a true "outlier" (a la Malcolm Gladwell in his book *Outliers*, who asserts that the key to success in any field is, to a large extent, a matter of practicing a specific task for around 10,000 hours). And, while I could see what the horse's body was doing, I recognized I couldn't understand the mental and emotional picture that body presented.

Another point of frustration was seeing the rescue facilities fill up with healthy but unrideable horses who couldn't be placed. Few people wanted a horse they couldn't ride. It was fairly easy to place a young, rideable horse who only needed some training or retraining, and the additional groceries. It was also fairly easy to place a retirement-age horse. But a young, healthy, unrideable horse? There were very few good options for placing that horse.

There wasn't anything truly "wrong" with these horses; it seemed arrogant and species-centered to judge them worthless simply because they couldn't be "used" for riding. The question of how to help them began to plague me, perhaps because I've always somewhat questioned the philosophical appropriateness of riding. In my early years, I'd debated with myself: Is riding kind? Is it necessary? Is it demeaning? I have questioned human dominion over horses, and I suppose that uncertainty impacted my thinking here. Was there a way for a horse to have purpose and value in a new home while retaining his or her innate nature and dignity?

My husband Richard and I had one significant crisis during this time that really brought the question of the horse's dignity to the forefront, albeit in a different way. I volunteered us to transport a rescue horse to Tennessee for proud-flesh removal surgery. Although Richard and I were not very experienced, we felt that all we had to do was get there safely and drop off the horse. However, upon our arrival, the clinic rejected the horse for surgery because he was too unmanageable; the vets deemed him unsuitable for stall-bound recovery. So I had to load him in the trailer for the drive back to North Carolina. There was only one problem. I couldn't reload this horse; he absolutely refused to go back in the trailer. I had to go get help. The vet finally took a chain and slid it over the horse's gums to subdue him and then used a butt-rope to force him into the trailer. It was revolting, and yet I didn't have any other answers. As I watched the horse be man-handled and painfully forced into the trailer, I vowed never again to put myself in a situation where my ignorance caused a horse in my care to be treated inappropriately.

After this episode, I began to realize how easy it was to get into trouble with an unknown horse. I was lucky I'd never had a more serious incident working with rescues—having a horse run through a fence, climb through the hay manger in a trailer, or trample someone. Since then, I have seen how ill-equipped many horsepeople are to respond to these kinds of contingencies, much less recognize or avert them in the first place.

During our first year in North Carolina, this growing frustration on the rescue horse front began to intersect with frustrations in my personal horse journey. Settled into our new home, I was finally in a place where I could start giving my attention to Black-Eyed Sue and begin working with her as I'd planned. However, I was in for a host of surprises as I really began to understand the depth of the problems she had.

Moving from a large herd environment in Texas to a pasture of two horses was a big shift for herd-bound Sue. Her issues became more apparent, her behavior more pronounced. And her long layoff from training of almost two-years didn't help.

Issues began right away. Kept in a 4-acre pasture instead of her Texas boarding stall, Sue was elusive and virtually uncatchable. Her first reaction to pressure of any kind was to panic and run. She reacted violently to cinching. She ran through the bit. She was suspicious, highly reactive, and emotionally explosive; upon losing confidence she would kick, buck, and bolt. In short: life with Black-Eyed Sue quickly became miserable.

Finally, a girlfriend and fellow horse-rescue person suggested Parelli™. I was against it. I had studied with several natural horsemanship clinicians and was familiar with Tom Dorrance and Ray Hunt. But I'd always resisted learning more about the work of Pat Parelli because of their polished marketing. Without ever having seen Pat or Linda, I'd decided that Parelli™ was all flash and no substance. But, I was at my wit's end, and my friend pestered enough that I finally relented and agreed to attend a Parelli™ tour-stop.

At that Parelli™ tour stop in Atlanta over a decade ago, I saw something I'd never really, truly seen before: people enjoying their horses without dominating them, and horses enjoying being with people. When I saw the "warm-up" team at the opening morning of the Parelli™ tour stop, I saw people young and old, men and women, playing with horses. I saw horses unafraid of tarps and tractor tires and all sorts of crazy items. I saw play and humor in the eyes of the people; I saw understanding and connection in the body language of the horses. Perhaps I *had* seen it before, but for whatever reason I couldn't or wouldn't recognize it. But, on that day, I finally saw it—horses and humans enjoying just being together.

That Parelli™ tour stop in Atlanta was a real catalyst for change for me, and therefore for Sue. I came away from that first real exposure to Parelli™ realizing that, while Sue hadn't necessarily been the most mistreated horse in the world, her response was a natural, "normal" response for *any* horse when faced with more traditional horsemanship methods. That weekend represented a systemic shift in my relationship with horses.

And so, Sue became my gateway to change once again, this time to a whole new way of thinking about horses and my own personal horsemanship. In Parelli™, I experienced instant recognition that the skills being taught were the pieces I was missing. I also saw that, not only was Pat good with horses, an "outlier", he apparently was capable of teaching humans too, as evidenced by the many students I saw play with their horses through that initial weekend. Eventually, as I learned about and became more involved with Parelli™, I began using my knowledge and experience to assess our horse rescues from a very different place, making me more effective in handling and working with them, and keeping both them and myself safer in the process.

While this thought process was incubating in my head, I continued working almost exclusively with horses on the ground, helping them recover physically. I paid more attention to what I was doing, and slowed down the processes I was using. I would go sit with a horse and just observe. I became focused on the process, curious about my actions and the horse's response, noticing how simple and clear the job was of cleaning stalls, how meditative it was to groom. In that noticing, in paying attention, I experienced a satisfying, "chop wood, carry water" aspect to being around horses, which encouraged patience and presence.

I shared these experiences with my friends, who would then ask how they could work toward experiencing the same feelings. They had surprisingly little desire to ride, just a desire to take part in the activities that were bringing me so much awareness about myself and the world around me. I began to invite these friends to the barn, and I tried to set up their time, both with and without horses, so they could experience what I was feeling. Friends came away focused in the moment, being more present, having "aha" moments. Unbeknownst to me, I was in the beginning phases of offering equine-assisted sessions.

These new experiences reminded me of my volunteer work at a therapeutic riding facility in Texas. Even then, I remember being more interested in the psychological and emotional outcomes for clients than the physical or the riding outcomes, amazing though those were. Putting those memories together with these new experiences, I felt closer to an answer about my own needs. Now I knew what I was looking for: a way to help people learn about themselves and incorporating horses in the process. I could pair unrideable horses with people who didn't necessarily need to ride in order to learn from them.

> **SHOULD WE RIDE?**
> If the question of whether or not it is appropriate to ride horses is of interest to you, check out Stormy May's video *The Path of the Horse* for an intriguing take on one person's approach. Also visit the website of Alexander Nevzorov, whose program advocates taking at least one year off from riding.

Then an internet search for "horse psychotherapy" led me to EAGA-LA—the Equine-Assisted Growth & Learning Association, and I learned for the first time what I was searching for actually had names: Equine-Assisted Psychotherapy and Equine-Assisted Learning. In short order, I was at my first Equine-Assisted Growth & Learning Association training.

Now I had a path! I initiated deeper exploration, checking out nearby programs and learning all I could about other models and organizations. I volunteered at the Pavillon International equine program in Mill Spring, NC. I attended a workshop on the "Epona Approach" with Linda Kohanov & her then-facilitation partner Kathleen Barry Ingram. I even returned for a week-long retreat as a client of the Epona program in Arizona. Before I was finished, I also studied the academic and intellectual approach of Adele and Deborah McCormick, authors of *Horse Sense and the Human Heart*. I explored the Equine Facilitated Mental Health Association (EFHMA) approach, under the umbrella of the North American Riding for the Handicapped Association (NARHA), by attending one of the first ever Equine Specialist trainings offered (now referred to as PATH Professional Association of Therapeutic Horsemanship). Since then, I've participated in hundreds of hours of trainings, workshops and offerings by EAP/EAL professionals, famous and obscure, and learned from every one of them.

Each experience, whether it occurred long ago or more recently, provided me with additional perspectives toward equine-assisted work and helped me recognize distinctions and examples of treatment teams, individuals and horses at work. I was able to sort through the aspects I resonated with and perspectives I didn't; it became clear which approaches were in alignment with what I wanted to deliver as a practice.

Finding EAGALA at that point in time was significant. As I read and explored, I felt like EAGALA practice most represented the way I wanted to partner with horses, because the model allowed the horse to maintain value, dignity, and integrity regardless of rideability. I returned to several more EAGALA trainings where, armed with a better vocabulary and a more well-rounded perspective, I could now compare things and clearly define the differences and similarities for myself. I was most interested in a clear mental health approach to this work, as opposed to riding, stewardship and other practices. This is why I resonated so heavily with EAGALA.

More than a Mirror, by Shannon Knapp

During this same time that I was learning about all these methods and approaches to EAP/EAL, I was also digging into Parelli™, thanks to a badly broken foot (courtesy of a bunk bed, not a horse!) which literally forced me off my feet for several months. I had nothing to do except sit around and study every video and manual I could find. My wheelchair and I also attended a couple Parelli™ clinics, where a friend participated with Sue, while I watched and learned. This observer's perspective gave me the opportunity to spend plenty of time watching without doing.

Once I was back on my feet, I attended my first in-depth, two-week course at the Parelli™ Center in Florida. It was a pivotal time. With all I'd learned by reading books and watching videos, and with all I thought I understood of Parelli™, this first course truly blew me away. While I was (and still am) enormously grateful for my time in wheelchairs and on crutches and the sheer amount of observation time afforded me by my injury, I was struck by how much more powerful my learning was when I was actually having the experience instead of reading about it or watching it.

So, as a result of timing, I immersed myself in both equine-assisted practices and Parelli™ during the same general period of time, making it hard to miss the parallels between them. Here were two separate systems, each based on the principle that the most effective way for people to learn, grow, and change was to allow them the space to figure out solutions for themselves. The realization of a philosophical connection between equine-assisted practices and Parelli™ started to develop quite naturally at this point.

In Florida, I experienced Parelli™ instructors applying a learning model to their teaching which empowered their students, moving them from a place of dependence to independence using a consistent set of principles. They didn't rush in to fix problems. Rather, they provided support by helping students solve puzzles for themselves. This was so different from what I had encountered anywhere else. As a former college professor myself, I found their learner-center method challenging and provocative. In my English classrooms, you'd often hear me say: "Show, don't tell." What I was learning through Parelli™ & equine-assisted practices was just the next level—that neither showing nor telling got the whole job done—experiencing it did!

In practice, equine-assisted work and the EAGALA-model in particular put the client in the center of his/her own experience, with practitioners facilitating the learning by providing observation and feedback instead of instruction. It's the student who experiments, discovers, and adjusts, drawing from the moment to answer questions for themselves. In comparing EAGALA's approach to other equine-assisted philosophies, and as my own years of experience as a teacher illustrated very clearly, I was more interested in developing a learner-centered approach for my own practice.

When I started *Horse Sense* as an EAGALA-based business, I chose to implement Parelli™ at our barn out of pure practicality. I was keenly aware of the many philosophies and attitudes people brought to the horse world, differences which could (and did) create a lot of passion, drama, and politics in a barn. I didn't want a multitude of competing philosophies among staff at *Horse Sense*. The horses would already be exposed to a variety of knowledge and experience levels from our clients; they didn't need it from staff members too. The least I could do was mandate a baseline of consistency in how we haltered, handled, and treated each horse. It was important to have a philosophy to guide us through the different challenges of the different horses, one that fit the bigger picture.

For example, if a horse was having an issue with running off while being unhaltered and turned loose in pasture, it was helpful to rule out inconsistent handling and turnout procedures as a possible factor in the behavior. With Parelli™ in place at our barn, I could assume the horse person was standing at the horse's left shoulder, tipping the horse's nose to him/herself, and asking for a soft "give" to pressure before turning the horse loose. If all that was happening, i.e., if the handling was consistent, and the horse was being asked for a give and the undesired behavior was still occurring, we could move on to consider other variables in solving the puzzle.

During the first year or so of *Horse Sense*'s existence, a Parelli™ instructor came to our farm to teach Parelli™ Level I for the whole staff. For very practical reasons, I wanted both Equine Specialists and Mental Health Professionals to understand the Parelli™ philosophy in regard to handling the horses, and as a way to build awareness of each other's roles within the treatment teams. Interestingly, it wasn't long before the teams began to develop their own awareness that the Parelli™ process of helping horses was not so different from an experiential approach of helping people; they were parallel. I now think this Parelli™ Level I course at the farm was really the start of integrating Parelli™ into our program beyond the practical horse-handling and horse-care aspects at *Horse Sense*.

On another note, my husband Richard's exposure to Parelli™ during that same Level I training course piqued his interest. He remarked that he learned more about horses in those two days than he had in ten years of riding. We were off and running—we began taking Parelli™ courses whenever our schedules permitted, both together and separately, at Parelli™ centers in Florida and Colorado, and in workshops and events by Licensed Parelli™ Professionals in barns near and far.

From that point forward, Parelli™ knowledge has become a cornerstone in my continuing horse rescue efforts, and in Richard's burgeoning interest in the work of starting and restarting horses. What we both saw in the horses we played with in those early years (and into current day) was that the Parelli Games™ are both a tool to shape behavior and a gauge to measure each horse's progress. They are also a way to assess a horse for EAP/EAL work.

The Parelli Liberty and Horse Behavior course became the next major "aha" moment in my thinking, and an especially important element in shaping and developing the *Horse Sense* philosophy. Its emphasis was on a serious study of equine body language, and on the development of a deeper understanding of the horse's non-verbal communication as it manifested in his/her behavior. In this course, we were also exposed to the early beginnings of defining and naming horse personalities— which later became known as "Horsenalities™." The whole two-week course elevated my understanding of horse psychology to a new, much higher level. For me, it rewrote the rules on how to interact and build relationships with horses.

The work of an Equine Specialist is all about understanding the horse and reading the horse's response in session. The primary way to interpret this is through the horse's outward manifestation of behavior and body language. After attending the Liberty and Horse Behavior course, I recognized the perfect fit for its application in equine-assisted work. So profound and provocative was my own learning, I became passionate in making sure every Equine Specialist at *Horse Sense* took the same course, either in person or in its boxed version.

Yet, I reached a point where it became clear to me that I could not continue on the path to becoming a Parelli™ professional while simultaneously running a full-scale, full-time equine-assisted practice. It was Richard who became dedicated to pursuing Parelli™ as a profession. So, we eventually decided to split paths: I would follow my passion of developing *Horse Sense* as a practice, and Richard, who has a much better natural feel with horses than I do, took the Parelli™ route. Several years later, I'm an EAGALA Advanced Practitioner, a Parelli™ Level 3 student, and *Horse Sense* is a leader in the field of EAP/EAL. Richard is a Licensed Parelli™ Instructor and Parelli™ Level 4 student, having spent a great deal of time both at the Parelli™ centers and at other horse farms, learning from many professionals. Ultimately, the reason we integrated both Parelli™ and equine-assisted philosophies at *Horse Sense* is that both are very much about human development as well as horse development. As the Parelli™ Principle #7 says, "Horses teach humans...and humans teach horses." (More about Parelli™ Principles in the next chapter!)

So that is how one horse led me to experience my own personal change and to Parelli™, and then how Parelli™ came to be such an important part of *Horse Sense*. And where is Black-Eyed Sue these days? Because of her extreme sensitivity and reactivity in the saddle, she eventually found the best fit at *Horse Sense* almost exclusively in our EAP work, where her sensitivity is not a drawback, but a gift.

Natural Horsemanship

PARELLI AND EQUINE ASSISTED PRACTICE

It was a very personal journey that led me to discovering how horses act as agents of change for people, a serendipitous set of circumstances starting with my own transformation, which led to rescuing horses, which led to discovering a much larger purpose for my life and the lives of horses we "rescued." But after those initial serendipitous occasions, development and growth became very intentional. As a teacher and a student of learning, once I found the trail leading to equine-assisted work—I became a devoted researcher.

Part of that journey—and the rationale we've used to integrate the multiple disciplines of Natural Horsemanship and equine-assisted practice into our work at *Horse Sense*—comes from first understanding the underlying principles and concepts inherent in both disciplines. We established our equine-assisted practice at *Horse Sense* based on these principles, and use them to continually evolve the skills of our Equine Specialists. But before we delve into those aspects, it seems appropriate to pause here and take a closer look at both the history and formation of equine-assisted practice and Natural Horsemanship in general, and Parelli™ concepts in particular, as part of our "groundwork" for future chapters.

How do equine-assisted practices and Natural Horsemanship merge? Do the principles overlap? How might Natural Horsemanship skills serve to enhance the Equine Specialist beyond the limits of "normal," or traditional horsemanship? The similarities are deeper than you might expect. Not only do I believe recognizing these common overlaps makes us better Equine Specialists, I believe the evolution of Natural Horsemanship itself was a catalyst which resulted in the field of equine-assisted practice being even conceivable in our time.

NATURAL HORSEMANSHIP
From Equipment to Leisure Activity

During the past century, the status of horses in our culture changed drastically. Their primary roles evolved from those of essential field equipment and transportation to leisure and expensive hobby assets to valued therapy partners—quite a spectrum! In each case, their essential value developed from, and corresponded to, a cultural mindset.

The "horses as equipment" mindset came from a very traditional and practical time in our country's history. Horses were necessary for getting work done, crops planted, wars won. Therefore, it was a matter of economic and physical survival to train a horse for these duties in a quick and expedient manner, with little consideration for the horse. This old method of training was efficient, singularly-focused, and could be brutal. During that period, it was quite unusual for people to even consider the horse as an emotional, thinking being. Therefore, horses who were unworkable in serving as either equipment or as breeding stock for more equipment, were expendable.

If you think about it, most of our equine pleasure activities evolved from these earlier, more utilitarian uses: the tactical maneuver training of war horses became the sports of dressage and show jumping; cow work became the sports of reining, cutting, penning, and roping. And the "get 'er done" practice of horse breaking became the sport of bronc riding and rodeo. We spend little time thinking about it, but even the way we groom, saddle, and mount horses today developed from centuries-old military traditions grounded in very practical considerations.

Once the mechanical engine prompted development of other modes of transportation and work production, the role of horses in society changed. The role shifted from one of utility to pleasure, entertainment, and sport, perhaps revealing that first glimmer of possibility where a horse's value would be considered from another perspective. Up to that point, the average person in our society spent very little time questioning the rather unfeeling methods for training horses.

Yet, from the time of Xenophon, there were people taking the horse into consideration, and thinking about what was in the best interests of the horse-human relationship. Led by Antoine de Pluvinel (b. circa 1552), dressage and other English trainers like Walter Zettl, Alois Podhajsky, and Nuno Olivera were thinking about the horse as a partner, as were cowboys like Tom Dorrance (born in the early 1900's), Ray Hunt and others. Whatever style of saddle they used (English, Western or none at all), "Natural Horsemanship" practitioners sought to utilize a horse's natural instincts, psychology, and herd behavior rather than using pain, dominance, and fear to develop the horse for human endeavors.

THE EARLY INFLUENCERS OF AMERICAN NATURAL HORSEMANSHIP

While some contemporary camps ostracize Natural Horsemanship as soft, faddish, and ineffective, its roots are, in fact, very deep. The Greek mercenary soldier, historian, and writer Xenophon (c. 430 – 354 BC) was among the first to document and advocate sympathetic horsemanship in his writing, *On Horsemanship*. Centuries later, Natural Horsemanship proponents trace roots of the concept to the California vaquero tradition, which in itself was influenced by Native American methods, Spanish and even Hungarian traditions. A parallel tradition of "horse whisperers" has roots in the British Isles and Eastern United States.

Using today's pop culture terminology, the early Natural Horsemanship advocates in the U.S. would be called "Early Influencers." Most practitioners today reference Tom Dorrance as the earliest modern practitioner, who then influenced Ray Hunt and a whole host of others, including Troy Henry, and Ronnie Willis in the 1960s and 1970s. Veterinarian Dr. Robert M. Miller brought a new level of credibility to the practice through his books, the most important of which are *Understanding the Ancient Secrets of the Horse's Mind* and *The Revolution in Horsemanship*. The circle then grew to include the likes of contemporary practitioners Mark Rashid, Buck Brannaman, John Lyons and Pat and Linda Parelli, among many others.

In the earliest days, the number of people interested in practicing Natural Horsemanship was small, and advocates were far-flung, with little to unite them but a sparse handful of random clinics and little communication. Slowly, clinicians developed more sophisticated marketing techniques. Some, like Parelli™, created student curricula enabling people to learn, explore, and make progress on their own between or in place of clinics. Today, the internet has contributed greatly to the Natural Horsemanship revolution, increasing reach, awareness, and community, and allowing students to communicate and interact more easily with other horsepeople. Natural Horsemanship is now within reach of nearly anyone who has the desire to participate. There are a host of students who have become instructors in their own right, teaching and expanding the circle further.

During this period, the educational understanding of the Natural Horsemanship student and the number of students greatly increased. We're able to communicate with other like-minded souls easily, and can even reach across oceans and continents to Australia, Africa, or Iceland. Natural Horsemanship today is no longer a trend; it's the rare horseperson who hasn't heard of it.

FOUNDATIONAL IDEAS & BASIC PRINCIPLES OF NATURAL HORSEMANSHIP

What distinguishes Natural Horsemanship from "normal" horsemanship? What are the key concepts? Natural Horsemanship has served to create some major shifts in the awareness and understanding of horses and horse behavior, even for those not following the practice closely.

As I see it, there are five key principles:

1. ***Horses are prey animals; humans are predators.*** Prey animals' natural characteristics allow them to detect the most seemingly insignificant incongruency in their environment and flee before danger strikes. For horses, this incongruency can be either emotional or environmental. Prey animal psychology differs greatly from predator psychology, and this creates many of the fundamental misunderstandings between humans and horses. Horses, as Parelli says, are "cowards, skeptics, claustrophobics and panic-a-holics by nature and varying degrees." That defines the term "prey" in just one sentence!

   By disregarding or under-acknowledging this significant aspect of the horse, or by understanding this but primarily using it against horses, humans tend to interpret everything only from a predator mentality, and have little patience for understanding the prey animal's unique point of view. It is the nature of predators to exploit the weaknesses of another creature to survive. If you extend this into human nature, this translates into "might vs. right," exploiting another creature because it's expedient, because the human needs to get something done, because it needs to be my way.

   Understanding the predator/prey relationship is key to understanding why horses do what they do. Interestingly, it's also part of what makes horses effective as therapy animals; the horse's innate ability to detect incongruency (shifts, changes, conflicting information all constitute a kind of incongruency) makes him or her ideal for recognizing it in the client during session. Horses have to be able to tell, from a great distance away, the difference between a lion who is sleeping and one who is stalking: both present as hunched down in the grass!

2. ***Cause your idea to become the horse's idea.*** Simple, right? Again, the human tendency toward direct-line thinking is

in complete contrast to this concept. The process of causing your idea to become the horse's idea, putting how we get there ahead of how fast we get there, and putting the relationship ahead of the task, is still a revolutionary concept because of its non-linear, inclusive aspect in a traditional, direct-line world.

Before we can cause our idea to become the horse's idea, we need to first understand his or her idea. To do that we need to understand the horse's priorities: safety, comfort, and play/food, usually in that order (although some argue, with some merit, that food is part of comfort).

Taking time to set up a situation in which a horse can succeed and naturally engage with you is the central process to creating harmony, and yet it's one of the most difficult concepts to apply successfully. Understanding those triggers which intrinsically motivate another creature requires being process-oriented, not goal-oriented. It also requires one to be ready to abandon the original plan for what's best in-the-moment. But the results can be much more remarkable, permanent, and far-reaching when horses relate to humans as partners.

3. **Pressure and release:** The idea that when the horse is not doing what we want, we apply pressure, and that when the horse does do what we are asking for, we release. This includes the corresponding concepts of approach and retreat, "as gentle as possible, yet as firm as necessary," and "love, language & leadership vs. force, fear and intimidation." Again, this is a major shift away from the more direct-line mindset of traditional horsemanship. To detect the smallest change and slightest attempt takes more time and requires a far more nuanced mindset along with greater emotional intelligence on our part. In our horsemanship past, time was deemed a luxury when it came to preparing a horse to perform a task.

4. **Work from the ground before working from the saddle.** The

More than a Mirror, by Shannon Knapp

most effective Natural Horsemanship practices put emphasis on building progress in a logical sequence, taking time to set up the basic foundation before asking for refinement. We're only now recognizing the damage caused by the old methods. Some of the damage is physical, caused by moving the horse to advanced levels too quickly. And some of the damage is mental, seen too often in performance horses pushed to the point of mental breakdown. It's a rare practitioner who can help a horse more quickly and gently from the saddle than from the ground. It's also a huge shift for many to think that riding isn't the only or even the main goal in connecting with horses. When I was attending a training at the Parelli™ ranch in Florida, there was a presentation by a dolphin trainer. She had a wonderfully interesting perspective on the work we were doing, telling us that dolphin trainers usually had to log thousands of hours with dolphins before they ever get an opportunity to ride. How interesting!

5. **You're not working on the horse; you're working on yourself.** For the human fully engaged in the process, Natural Horsemanship is the ultimate personal growth experience. Even in the earliest context, from the writings of Ray Hunt, Henry Blake, and Tom Dorrance, we find the articulation of this concept. We also see an inherent learner-centered approach, an approach which now permeates through the organizational culture at Parelli™ and also through some equine-assisted models, where learner-centered teaching is a basic principle. This, for me, is one of the most provocative points of intersection of Natural Horsemanship with equine-assisted practice.

CULTURAL SHIFTS

We can probably tie the acceptance of Natural Horsemanship philosophy to a few additional shifts within our culture as well. Dr. Robert

M. Miller lays these out more cleanly and concisely in *The Revolution in Horsemanship*, but we'll touch on some ideas briefly here:

1. The shift in the horses' role from utilitarian to hobby. With few exceptions, most people who have horses now have them as a hobby or a pleasure pastime.

2. The rise in our cultural awareness of behavioral psychology as a field of study. Once human psychological theory was accepted, the possibility of applying psychology to animal behavior developed as well. And, just as getting counseling help went from being considered taboo to mainstream in the matter of a few decades, the study of equine behavior is likewise taking a similar arc. As people become more aware of animal behavior and recognize animals as capable of emotions, awareness, and pain, there is an increase in animal rights activism against violence, which has naturally extended into the horse world. Natural Horsemanship is a part of that process.

3. Significant changes in the profile of the horse community itself. As our culture's view of horses changed from work to pleasure/pastime, and as horse sports evolved from the world of the upscale and wealthy to being accessible to the middle class, significant numbers of women became involved, to the point where women dominate many horse events today. Although I dislike generalizations, women usually do tend to approach horses with a different set of sensibilities, a much more relationship-oriented approach. It's not difficult to see a corresponding influence/acceptance of a more natural, non-linear approach to being with horses—one that differs from the traditional means of dominance, submission, and force. This more relational approach naturally translates into a decreased acceptance of aggressive and sometimes violent training methods. Another change in the profile of the horse

community corresponds with the rising education level of the average horseperson.

4. As I was in the late stages of writing this book, the Cambridge Declaration of Consciousness was made, which has bearing on the conversation here. Reprinted in full in the Appendix, the Cambridge Declaration concluded:

> The absence of a neocortex does not appear to preclude an organism from experiencing affective states. Convergent evidence indicates that non-human animals have the neuroanatomical, neurochemical, and neurophysiological substrates of conscious states along with the capacity to exhibit intentional behaviors. Consequently, the weight of evidence indicates that humans are not unique in possessing the neurological substrates that generate consciousness. Non-human animals, including all mammals and birds, and many other creatures, including octopuses, also possess these neurological substrates. (Low, n.d., p. 2)

All these concepts together form a significant "reframing" of traditional or normal horsemanship methods. Indeed, reframing itself is a key component of Natural Horsemanship. The awareness of the horse, first from the perspective of a prey animal, and second from an awareness of the horse as an emotional being, is certainly a big shift from the "horse as object" mentality from our history. Take, for example, a situation where horse and human are in disagreement with each other. In normal horsemanship, the person often automatically labels a horse as the one with the problem: having a bad attitude, being difficult, or being stupid. Natural Horsemanship first looks at the situation, and more often and more readily takes into account a point of view of the horse which is broader than the human point of view. Isn't that one definition of emotional growth?

Early practictioners of Natural Horsemanship started asking themselves if it might not be more productive to work with the horse rather than against the horse. How much more effective could the process be when we develop the horse as a partner and work in relationship to his or her motivation and inherent nature? These questions, along with the corresponding shifts in our society, were all big steps toward opening the door to this latest development in horse/human relations: the advent of equine-assisted practice.

PARELLI™ NATURAL HORSEMANSHIP

A Brief Introduction

As I developed in my personal horse practice, Parelli™ became my Natural Horsemanship method of choice for a variety of reasons. I responded to it as a horseperson, a learner, and as a teacher. And it's a program that continues to earn my respect the deeper I get, continuously growing as I grow. Basic concepts can be further explored so that not only do student and horse advance to greater levels of skill and ability, the theoretical aspects advance as well, becoming more complex and complete.

Another reason I remain a devoted student is that the Parelli™ team of professionals never stops evolving as individuals or as an organization. The Parelli™ organization is as dedicated to continuous self-examination as the most devoted self-improvement student. It continues to advance, accessing the latest principles in human development while simultaneously evolving advanced concepts in equine psychology and behavior.

Because we'll reference Parelli™ concepts throughout the remainder of this book, an overview of basic principles is appropriate. To be as congruent, correct, and accurate as possible, the material in this chapter borrows heavily from the official language and teaching of the Parelli™ organization. In no way am I attempting to teach you Parelli™; my goal is to illustrate the basic concepts and principles driving the effectiveness of Parelli™ as a Natural Horsemanship system, and to examine the basic Parelli™ elements at the heart of how we practice our equine-assisted work at *Horse Sense*. I believe these elements are

More than a Mirror, by Shannon Knapp

capable of advancing the professionalism of Equine Specialists in the field and hence the field as a whole. You'll also find commentary directly from Linda Parelli throughout this chapter, material which came from an interview I conducted with her in 2011. (Thanks, Linda!) For a biography of the Pat and Linda Parelli, see the Appendix.

PARELLI LEVELS & SKILLS

Foundation before Specialization or, Walk before you Run

From his days studying martial arts, Parelli recognized that there are levels of proficiency in any endeavor, including Natural Horsemanship, with different skillsets developed at each level. Parelli utilizes this concept to set up his horsemanship program into levels as well. Over the years, the Parelli™ organization has created several sets of the Parelli Levels curriculum, all of which I enjoy, as I like to see the development and progressive distillation of the ideas. The first level package I trained with in 1999 included a VCR tape, pocket guides and an audio CD, which I still watch and listen to today. I am particularly a fan of the "red" Level 1 materials from 2004 and the "blue" Level 2 materials from 2005. These particular sets contain a wealth of theory and other information contributing to the learning process, material I reference often when working with new Equine Specialists or mental health professionals. The newest version is a combination of the Level 1 and 2 pack (2009) The Parelli™ home study material has evolved over the years. Any of these packs, old or new, can improve your knowledge, skills and effectiveness as a horseperson.

Parelli's Level 1 material focuses on basic safety with horses and deconstructs traditional beliefs and approaches to horsemanship. Level 2 focuses on developing confidence with horses, and reworks and reframes basic principles, marrying it to deeper, more intangible theory before bringing knowledge back to wholeness. As students finish the more definitive skills in Level 1 and enter the more theory-based aspects of Level 2, the adult-learner information provided by Dr. Stephanie Burns in the 2004-2005 versions explains the different ways people access and assimilate information, from beginning to middle to end. Dr. Burns' learning theory helps students anticipate and survive this critical "middle" portion of the learning cycle.

Key ideas addressed in the Parelli/Burns system, such as supporting the learner in the "beginning, middle and end" of the learning process, and "crossing the 'silly' bridge" (getting past how inept we appear during our learning phases and our accompanying self-consciousness), were missing from other Natural Horsemanship programs. Not only is there a plan to help students progress, there's also an integration of deep thought into how Parelli™ instructors, videos, written materials and live events help people through the learning process. Other practitioners have started putting these same kinds of levels, systems and processes into place for their methods, but they seem to lack this deeper awareness of the adult learner and the potential impacts of varied learning styles.

From transforming concepts and theory into memorable material, i.e., the Seven Games™, the Eight Principles, and Horsenality™, to providing this material in a way that supports various learning styles—auditory, visual, or tactile—Parelli™ sets people up for success in a manner that has not been accomplished by anyone else.

Groundwork Before Riding: Four Areas of Savvy & Skill

A unique aspect of the Parelli™ system is a focus on developing skills in four distinct areas of horsemanship: 1) Online, 2) Freestyle, 3) Liberty, and 4) Finesse. Parelli calls this the "Four Savvys" and applies every aspect of the program to them; once students master a skill in one Savvy, the program starts integrating that skill into the next. In this way, the Seven Games™ and all the other Parelli™ concepts build upon themselves, becoming seamless, versatile tools while thoroughly embedding critical skills.

Parelli's starting point is for the learner to be unmounted; doing online groundwork before work in the saddle. This is a key component of the program. Most people and many clinicians in the "normal" horsemanship world put their emphasis on work under saddle. The process of getting people into the saddle is usually very fast, and everything from that point on is about riding. In contrast, Parelli™ spends a substantial amount of time de-constructing the traditional approach to horses, and doesn't re-introduce riding until after the Level 1 skills of online work have been presented. This isn't to say that students can't ride while undergoing Level 1, but riding is not a foregone conclusion with Parelli™. Before putting people in the saddle, the program first spends time taking apart old paradigms and going back to the basics to help people reverse and "un-learn" years of traditional habits and teaching. Simultaneously, people are learning skills (like thinking from the horse's point of view) often glossed over in other programs.

Level 1/"Online Savvy" is all about safety, as it applies to skills and habits utilized on the ground while being attached to the horse with a 12-foot (for Level 1), 22-foot (introduced in Level 2), or 45-foot line (Level 3 & beyond). During Online Savvy, horse and human remain connected, via halter and lead rope and, as the distance between them increases, the human's level of communication, influence, and skillful body language also needs to grow, as does his or her ability to read the body language and interpret communication from the horse.

During this online groundwork phase, Parelli™ introduces a critical aspect to its program: horse psychology and body language. This foundational knowledge plays a part in every aspect of Parelli™ teaching that follows, on the ground and in the saddle. Knowing your horse, and knowing how to recognize your horse's shifts from day to day, and even from moment to moment or situation to situation, becomes part of each student's ongoing assessment. It helps determine if your horse is even rideable from one day to the next. You are also getting to know yourself: How's your feel? How's your timing? How do these translate from your head to your hands?

The Level 2/"Freestyle Savvy" takes place in the saddle, but on a loose rein and without contact. When students do get back in the saddle, Parelli™ teaches seat, balance, positioning, hands, direct and indirect reining, and other mounted skills. (There is also considerable teaching involving appropriate and supportive mounting techniques, for the good of the horse and rider, including proper saddling and saddle fit support). Riding on a loose rein enables the student to establish these basic skills while staying out of the horse's way. Parelli™ in the saddle usually begins with only a halter and a lead line. Giving humans, as predators, two reins (often referred to as split reins) encourages us to pull back, jerk, and contract, which encouraged the horse to brace. Riding with only a single rein, we learn how to present a different demeanor when tense or anxious. Students graduate to a continuous rein, but are encouraged to go back to one rein when the tendency to clench and grab returns: One rein for control, two reins for communication.

Many people outside the Parelli™ program see little value in this emphasis on groundwork, or even the emphasis on the Level 3/"Liberty Savvy" portion of the program. And it's not surprising; where else do you see people interacting with horses at liberty, except maybe at the circus? What value could it have? But for those of us doing psychotherapy and learning in equine-assisted practice, work at liberty encapsulates a great deal of what takes place with our clients in session. As Parelli says, "When you take off the halter and lead rope, what you are left with is the truth." And indeed, it's what horses show our clients every day in session. Horses at liberty are free to express themselves, and they will not hesitate to show us very clearly where we stand in relationship to them.

For that reason, Parelli™'s Liberty portion of the program has been invaluable for us at *Horse Sense*. It fine-tunes our psychology and body language sensibilities, helps us recognize the subtle ways horses can connect and disconnect from humans, and helps us learn how to re-establish that connection. In short, it enhances our development as both Equine Specialists and as horsepeople. Liberty work is also incredibly useful and meaningful in herd environments, which is often how we function in equine-assisted practices. Becoming accomplished at Liberty skills with one horse, and then with more than one, is a key skill for our field.

Level 4/"Finesse Savvy" is where focus on Refinement takes place by adding the fourth Savvy: Finesse riding and the fundamentals of performance. Under Finesse, riders establish contact with the bit and add specialization (such as dressage, reining, etc.) to the foundational work. Here again, Parelli™ theory first constructs and teaches skills such as contact, collection, and other advanced concepts within the context of putting relationship with the horse first. While the student returns to more "normal" riding activities associated with an area of sport or specialization, the challenge to work within this perspective remains.

Is it a challenge to develop competence in each of the 4 Savvys? Definitely. Most people practicing "normal" horsemanship never gain fluency or competency in anything but some form of specialized riding. Parelli™ challenges us to see how much more is possible with our horses when we give equal weight to relationship in all four areas.

THE EIGHT PRINCIPLES

A foundation of eight core principles underscores the entire Parelli™ system. These Eight Principles constitute the original material taught by Pat Parelli over thirty years ago in his very first Natural Horsemanship presentation, and are a distillation of the teachings Pat learned from his mentors. Contributors to the founding philosophy behind the program, you'll see echoes from the writings of Tom Dorrance and Ray

Hunt, carefully preserved and honored. The order of the Eight Principles is very deliberate; the program uses them as a touchstone challenging each Natural Horsemanship student in his/her journey. Let's take a brief look at each of these eight principles, as they figure both in horsemanship and in equine-assisted practices.

As Parelli has said at many a tour stop I've attended, "Natural Horsemanship is not something you do instead of a particular horse sport, it's just a different approach to achieving those same goals with your horse." It puts horsemanship first, and sports/specialization second, as in "foundation before specialization." Perhaps more than anything, Parelli™ is unique in the Natural Horsemanship world for developing and packaging a curriculum allowing students to learn at a pace suitable to both horse and human where they can achieve goals no matter what form they take:

> [Parelli] teaches you to become so good with horses that whatever you choose as your ultimate specialization is an easy transition. It's easy because you know how to communicate with your horse in an intricate way, with feel and finesse, mentally and emotionally, not just physically. It's only hard when you don't have the right foundation, or the qualities of a real Horseman. I want you to know how to teach your horse everything, no matter what "costume" you end up wearing. (Parelli, 2000, p.20)

Principle 1: Horsemanship is natural.

Parelli not only believes horses and humans are made to be together, he believes they accommodate and stimulate growth and change in each other. In his words:

> With a Horseman, a horse learns to be calmer, smarter, braver, and more athletic. With a horse, the Horseman can be fleet of foot, more powerful, and more perceptive...he can learn to develop all the qualities of a leader: to have endless patience, become more assertive, less aggressive, less feeble, to have emotional stability, to be responsible for direction and decisions. (Parelli, 2000, p. 16)

This first principle acknowledges the power of horses to create change in humans, a concept embedded in the very early teaching methods of

Natural Horsemanship, a cornerstone of equine-assisted practice.

In discussing equine-assisted practice with Linda Parelli, it becomes evident the organization has always been very aware of how their work with horses generates change in people; it's something the organization has intentionally managed. "All our work with horses is 'equine-assist-ed,'" says Linda. "Horses provide lessons for life; they make us better people. You can't separate horses and humans; if you learn to be this way with horses, you will change. You realize that you're responsible for the behavior of the horse; the horse was fine until you showed up." (Personal communication, February 21, 2011)

Another aspect of this principle recognizes horses as prey animals. It emphasize we don't try to make them something that they're not; any application of coercion or force taking away from a horse's natural character and dignity is outright impermissible. In other words, you're never to do anything to a horse you wouldn't want your mother to see or, in our case as equine-assisted professionals, anything that we would flinch at a client with a trauma background watching. At the same time, one should not construe "natural" for "wimpy." Horses are strong and bold with one another in the herd!

Principle 2: Don't make (or teach) assumptions.

Horses are a precocial species, which means they're highly adept, "full faculty" learners at birth, able to stand, run, and adapt within hours of hitting the ground; if they don't, they're not going to make it. They are naturally fast learners. As such, we have to be much more mindful of what information we "put into" a horse. Parelli expands on this con-cept beautifully:

> People assume all the time. They assume horses are safe and simple. They assume if a horse has been ridden, he's rideable no matter what. They assume the same training technique will work for every horse. They assume it's the horse's fault whenever something doesn't go right. They assume if the horse did it one day, he'll automatically do it the next. They assume horses think the same way as people do, and that they value the same things. They assume a prey animal will not

hurt people, things, other horses, or himself in order to save himself.

Un-savvy people also teach horses to make assumptions—good and bad. They'll trot home to the barn three or four days in a row and then expect the horse to walk back in a relaxed way the next time. They teach horses to assume feeding time is at 6AM and 5PM every day, causing all kinds of mental, emotional, and physical stress in the horse when they're late. They teach horses to assume that they can run over people, invade their space, and behave disrespectfully. So, make no assumptions and teach no assumptions. (Parelli, 2000, p.16)

Linda speaks to how humans make numerous assumptions in mis-reading the energy and intention of horses:

[Those who] don't really know horses assume 'that horse is out to get me' or 'he loves to flip over;' it's a kind of anthropomorphic thinking. [The horse] wasn't out to get you; he was either having fun or he was defending himself. I think that's what people get down to as well, personally; we have a lot more masks we can put on and an ego, whereas horses don't have an ego. It's just survival of the species.

Pat Hanley has a saying: 'We judge ourselves by intention and others by their behavior.' I think we do the same thing with horses. When you look at what a horse's intentions are, it's more about survival. It's safety-comfort-play. And then Horsenality™ gives you another filter in the domesticated horse. I think when you can really feel horses and you really know them, you know what they're up to and what they're thinking. You almost know what they're going to do before they do it. That's real mastery. (Personal communication, February 21, 2011)

Humans, like horses, are pattern animals as well. When we talk about patterns horses develop with clients, we rarely blame the horse for developing the pattern. We can see the many influences conspiring to create this pattern in the horse. They also observe how challenging it can be to change patterns. All this impacts the client's understanding of his or her own challenges, usually in a positive way.

Principle 3: Communication is two or more individuals sharing and understanding an idea.

How often do we stop horses from, or punish them for, expressing themselves? How often do we punish them without figuring out what they are telling us? Parelli used to say communication is mutual. Now he gets more specific:

More than a Mirror, by Shannon Knapp

...communication is two or more individuals sharing and understanding an idea. If you just give a horse orders without listening to him, this is not communication. If you can't listen to a horse, and if the horse won't listen to you, you don't have communication. If you're both "shouting" at each other you don't have communication.

In order to listen to horses you have to learn how to read them, how to play with them, how to observe their behavior and expressions. You also have to allow them to express themselves, which is where The Seven Games™ and Freestyle riding can be so valuable; they allow a horse to play. (Parelli, 2000, p.17)

One of the beautiful principles behind equine-assisted practice is how we deliberately engage and utilize the horse's natural instincts and behavior to help us. In the best case scenario, equine-assisted practice is its most powerful when we allow horses to be what they are: horses. Where I believe we most often fall short is that we don't fully develop our skills learning to read them.

Principle 4: Horses have responsibilities and Humans have responsibilities.

Here's Parelli's list of these responsibilities:

For the human:

1. Act like a partner, not like a predator. Become more mentally, emotionally, and physically fit.

2. Have an independent seat.

3. Think like a horse-man.

4. Use the natural power of focus.

For the horse:

1. Act like a partner, not like a prey animal. Become more mentally, emotionally, and physically fit.

2. Don't change gait.

3. Don't change direction.

4. Look where you are going.

When you take over the horse's responsibilities instead of teaching him to uphold them, and when you don't take care of your own, there can be no partnership. It will be something more like master and slave. The human becomes more domineering and less effective and the horse becomes mindless. (Parelli, 2000, p.17)

Interestingly, the number one responsibility for both horse and human is to simply not act like what we are: we are called instead to expand, to act like a partner. Natural Horsemanship asks us to see things from a different perspective, which is what "playing" with horses in the Seven Games™ is all about. The journey toward trusting your horse at a deep level is the true journey of a horseman; earning enough respect from and having enough respect for the horse requires our highest skill and efforts.

The natural power of focus is all about being present, and having a plan. One of the gifts predators have is the vision and ability to judge depth, yet even with this kind of vision we are often unfocused in what we're doing, mindless as opposed to mindful. One of the biggest challenges with one of my horses is about focus—if I wasn't looking at the horizon instead of his ears, he'd stop in his tracks!—and using focus to show him where I want to go. Parelli's discussion around focus has implications way beyond the barn. People really working on this principle start learning that focus not only impacts where our horse goes, it impacts where we go, what we get, and what we accomplish in life. What you focus on, you attract.

Linda Parelli takes the concept one step further,

> Horses cause you to be really present, so you can't bring the anxiety of the future, and you can't bring the baggage of the past and be effective. You have to be one hundred percent present, to be this open book, and open to what happens. You learn how to have a plan but still be absolutely present. The emotional fitness that it gives you is phenomenal." (Personal communication, February 21, 2011)

The power of the client's focus in EAP/EAL, as well as the focus of the facilitation team, greatly impacts the session work. Clients often get a chance to see where their focus has been, negatively or positively, in 3-D with the horses, and then understand the significance of that focus on their outcomes. Similarly, if the facilitation team's focus is compromised, the session work suffers.

Principle 5: An attitude of justice is effective

Being effective in communication, which is related to the "attitude of justice" in Principle 5, is often one of the most challenging issues for our clients. To support them in learning about effective communication, we use the Parelli™ language of Phases, a key concept we use with horses, equine-assisted horsemanship interns, and with clients as well. One way to think of phases is to compare it to volume. Phase 1 is a whisper. Phase 2 is speaking normally. Phase 3 is speaking with intention and some increase in volume. Phase 4 is just short of shouting. If we begin speaking at Phase 4 without having started at Phase 1, we are not communicating well or effectively. Ideally, I only want to have to use Phase 4 once or twice.

Justice in behavior and communication is a challenge for many. Parelli explains:

> There should be small consequences for small mistakes and big consequences for big mistakes. The Four Phases help us be just, to neither overreact nor under-react. You just have to become savvy enough to know which is which, and to gain control over destructive emotions such as fear, frustration, and anger. Horses respond to positive and negative reinforcement, but they don't understand punishment. (Parelli, 2000, p.17)

This principle is a challenge for many people, and sometimes especially challenging for women. Just as "lightness" can be a big challenge for men, "firmness" can be very difficult for many women. Principle 5, along with Parelli's Four Phases, are about being as firm as necessary while also being as light as possible. It's a duality we must learn to grasp when we are with horses. The attitude of justice is a concept about what it really means to have clear boundaries and implement consequences—appropriate consequences—for actions. Many of us don't necessarily learn how to be "firm and fair without being mean or mad," or how to be "particular without being critical." These and many other "Parelli-isms" can be found in Parelli's Natural Horsemanship book, part of the Western Horseman series.

The attitude of justice is where we enter into a discussion involving "cause and allow" vs. "make or let." Some people let their horses get away with things. Others make their horses do things, and this is where women especially can misconstrue older cultural concepts of force and intimidation with effectiveness. Being firm doesn't include being mean; being firm is being fair. "Cause and allow" shows more respect than either "make" or "let."

In practice at *Horse Sense*, we spend a great deal of time helping clients find that line between passive, aggressive, passive-aggressive, and assertive. The Four Phases are enormously helpful in bringing the concept to life.

Another component of the attitude of justice is to trust your horse to respond when asked while being ready to correct. The caveat: don't expect—or anticipate—one action more than the other. I remember struggling with this concept at a clinic early on. The Parelli™ instructor could see I was anticipating a certain response (because I'd seen it several times in my horse). It was a challenge for me to allow my horse to make the mistake, then correct it and move on without getting hung up anticipating it again the next time around. Too often we don't allow learning to take place in our efforts to avoid making mistakes at all costs (or looking silly). If we sincerely want a partnership—with our horse or our kids or in any relationship—we need to allow learning, in the form of mistakes, to happen.

Principle 6: Body language is universal.

A common denominator of all our clients, and one we have with all animals, is body language. We can't not communicate, and humans sometimes even use words!

> Horses do not understand English, German, Italian, Japanese...they understand 'horse.' Horses communicate through body language more than anything else. Body language crosses any language barrier. We need to close our mouths and use our body and expressions to communicate with horses. (Parelli, 2000, p. 17)

More than a Mirror, by Shannon Knapp

Everybody has body language, even despite our individual cultural differences. Dr. Paul Ekman has many books on the subject of macro-expressions and micro-expressions. He's identified specific facial muscles, expressions, and their meanings across cultures. He also has characterized certain facial structures for key emotions that are universal.

Likewise, horses communicate how they think and feel through their body language, perhaps more than through any other mechanism. Not only do Parelli™ students spend a large amount of time developing their understanding of equine body language, but learn to discern the subtle (and not so subtle) ways different Horsenalities™ express themselves in their bodies.

When it comes to working as an Equine Specialist, this particular principle of body language is an important one to me. Simply knowing equine body language is not enough; understanding the differences in the body language expression of a Left-Brained Introvert vs. a Right-Brained Extrovert is also important. Some Horsenalities™ express themselves in strikingly different ways, and it serves to be relatively fluent in each Horsenality™.

Human body language is something we don't study nearly enough, either in regard to our own or those of our our clients. In our EAP sessions, clients often learn that how they see themselves is often very different from how others see them. In EAP/EAL, clients can come to understand the two don't always line up. For example, I might think I'm walking toward my horse with an attitude of friendliness. Yet when I see myself on videotape, I realize my strong shoulder, hard eyes and direct, brisk pace do not appear friendly at all. Or, I may understand this when the horse runs to the next county whenever I approach. Perhaps I wasn't looking so friendly after all!

Principle 7: Horses teach humans and humans teach horses.
Here again we see the concept that horsemanship is as much about

human development as horse development, a concept recognized by the earliest Natural Horsemanship teachers. It is the core of equine-assisted practices, and of Natural Horsemanship. Parelli (2000) wrote:

> An experienced horse can teach you a lot; he can fill in some of the gaps for you. Even if you don't own this horse, see if you can ride him to experience how it should feel. The same goes for when you have savvy. You'll be able to offer the horse your skills, experience, and confident leadership. You'll be able to set him up so doing what you want is easy for him. (p.17)

Linda Parelli speaks to the experiences she's witnessed while teaching Natural Horsemanship to students over the years:

> People are here for a week or two weeks and it's exciting to see them change. It's also interesting to see people that are around for ten years and then all of a sudden, a light bulb goes off. I've seen people that have regained self-respect. I've had people screaming at me and then in the middle of it going, 'My husband wants to leave me.' The question is not the question; the problem is not the problem. It's not the horse; it's the person. (Personal communication, February 21, 2011)

Linda says her work with horses has transferred into other areas of her own life "in every single way. It's not an act. It shapes your character. I started to really accept people, where I was quite judgmental before. I started to be able to see the beauty in people. I became more able to converse with all different humanalities—and love them for what they are." (Personal communication, February 21, 2011) She expands on this in a blog entry: "I believe that what we make of life is our own, to understand that we have choices and we can choose to be enriched by the experience" (Parelli, 2010, para. 5).

If you were to draw the horse's comfort/knowledge zone as a really small circle and the human's comfort/knowledge zone as a really big circle, that would represent a scenario in which the horse can learn from the human. (B in Figure 2.1) Likewise if the horse's comfort/ knowledge zone is a big circle and the human's comfort/knowledge zone is a little circle, that's an opportunity for the human to learn from the horse. (A in Figure 2.1) The worst scenario is that in which both horse and human have small zones, both horse and human are lacking in experience and/or knowledge. (C in Figure 2.1) This is the scenario in which people and horse alike get hurt, physically, emotionally, and mentally. At the opposite end of the spectrum, when you have a large comfort zone from both human and horse (D in Figure 2.1), you get a magic partnership, like Pat and his stallion Casper, Linda and her horse Remmer, or John Lyons and his horse Zip. That's where amazing things can happen.

In EAP/EAL, horses are teaching humans. They are teaching humans how to feel, how to focus, how to communicate, and how to be in harmony with the environment, amongst a myriad of other things. The horse will teach that which the human most needs to learn. That is the simplest expression of EAP/EAL I know.

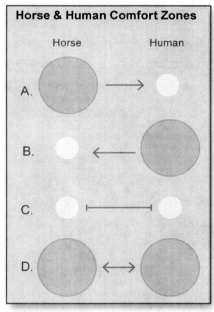

Figure 2.1
Horse & Human Comfort Zones

Principle 8: Principles, purpose, and time are the tools of teaching.

What is it that motivates your path as a horseperson? What guidelines inform how you solve issues? How do you measure progress for you and your horse? Is it all about how far you can go in the shortest time? What provides meaning for you? And do you often consider what provides meaning or purpose for your horse? As both predators and humans, we often fail to remember our purpose is not the same as a horse's purpose. How often do we think about each play session from the horse's point of view?

Principles combined with Purpose give us the road map. Principles and Purpose are our responsibility; our job is to stick to Principles and maintain Purpose around what we're doing so it's not just mindless repetition. The timeline, as Pat often says, is up to the horse:

> You need to take the time it takes so it takes less time. Putting time into your horse is an investment. You can't hurry a horse's development or you'll end up using force (even resorting to artificial aids) that causes resistance and develops underlying problems that diminish potential. Treat your horse like the finest thing you've ever owned... He is nature in its finest form. (Parelli, 2000, p.17)

Principles drive *how* we do *what* we do. If our Principle is to "cause the right thing to be easy and the wrong thing to be difficult," to put it in Natural Horsemanship vernacular, it changes what we do and how we approach puzzles (not problems) with our horse. It dictates a method of taking the time to search for and find that which creates a "cause and allow" situation instead of a "make and let" situation.

As Pat once said at one of many tour stops I've attended, it's easy to figure out how to achieve a "cause and allow" situation with your horse: figure out the predatory tactic everyone else is using, then do the opposite! The simple principle of "doing the opposite" usually puts us in the right frame of mind. This is about learning to think laterally, learning the power of approaching in arcs rather than in straight lines.

The principles of positive and negative reinforcement are much more effective than punishment and reward. EAGALA recommends a book called *Punished by Rewards* by Alfie Kohn, subtitled "The Trouble with Gold Stars, Incentive Plans, A's, Praise, and Other Bribes." Daniel Pink describes much the same thing in his book, *Drive*. If motivation does not come from an intrinsic and internal place, it's going to be fleeting and forever dependent on renewing an external factor. Internal motivation is far more effective, whether you're talking horse or human.

Ultimately, we are also helping reinforce these ideas for people in EAP/EAL sessions. What are the principles they wish to live by? How are they enacting those principles in their daily lives? If they aren't doing this already, what tools do they need to be able to do so?

THE SEVEN GAMES™

Now that some of the basic background is in place, it's time to move into the Main Event—Parelli's Seven Games™, the most visible aspect of the Parelli™ program. The first reframe and shift is in calling them "games" rather than jobs or tasks. This is both deliberate and significant. These seven elements, packaged as games, not only make the concepts easy for the human to remember, it also puts us immediately into a more appropriate mindset. Play vs. work serves to start disengaging the traditional, direct-line, predatory approach many folks typically have toward their lives, and hence toward our horses, even if our horses are recreation for us. It's important to remember that the early part of the Parelli™ system is about "un-learning" old mindsets—much like EAGALA promotes in their "Untrainings." The Seven Games™ are a system of understanding, assessing, and building a new foundation for understanding the horse. And it's one of the most important signature tenets of the Parelli™ system.

The framework for each of the Seven Games™ is also significant in that it hinges on the natural behaviors horses display in a herd. Putting these Games into the context of horse psychology makes it both understandable to the human and frames our efforts in a language horses can decipher without forcing them into operating in ways only humans understand.

Even the basic tools for the Seven Games™ are metaphors, including a rope halter, a 12-foot lead line, a Carrot Stick™, and a Savvy String™. Parelli™ utilizes many different mnemonic devices (ways to help us remember things) in his programs, and the Carrot Stick™ and Savvy String™ are no different. The name Carrot Stick™ is very intentional. Parelli (1999) writes, "I named it the Carrot Stick™ to forever keep in mind that it is somewhere between the 'carrot' and the 'stick' methods that are so commonly used with horses." (p.23) It becomes too easy for a person using only the "carrot" method to end up bribing and enticing the horse; others use the "stick" method as a means of force. The term

Carrot Stick™ reminds students to strive for the middle of the road.

The Parelli™ curriculum speaks directly to our cultural perception of sticks as tools of punishment, and reframes the Carrot Stick™, not as a whip, but as a method of communication. In fact, using the Carrot Stick™ to convey no harm to the horse becomes one of the first tasks for students. Many instructors first teach students to use the stick without the horse until they achieve some degree of control with it and learn to apply it appropriately without emotional involvement. Another aspect of the Carrot Stick™ is that it becomes an extension of our arm, allowing us to become the same length as the horse, so we can reach where we need to reach, and influence different zones of the horse while staying safe.

Here's a brief overview of each of the Seven Games™. The first 3 Games are the Foundation or the Principle Games, and Games 4 through 7 are the combination or Purpose Games. If something's not working right with Games 4 through 7, it's a result of something being "broken," misinterpreted, or misread in Games 1 through 3. So foundational are these first three, you can trace virtually every problem a horse has to issues accepting or not accepting some aspect of your relationship via these first 3 Games.

Game 1: The Friendly Game™

The Friendly Game™ is about desensitization and relaxation in the presence of stimuli. Some of the things we at *Horse Sense* look for in our horses include: Can I touch you with a Savvy String™? Can I touch you with a Carrot Stick™? Can I touch you with my hands? We're asking, "Will you allow me to touch you here?" And that gives us information about how guarded, tense, or nervous a horse might be and how curious he or she might become. At *Horse Sense*, we've dealt with many horses who have barely been touched beyond what it takes to groom, saddle, and bridle them. The Friendly Game™ is a key way to build trust, and becomes a grounding point as the relationship progresses. Whenever the horse loses confidence, returning to The Friendly Game™ can restore connection.

Similarly with clients, we want to build a sense of not moving beyond what a client can tolerate, respecting the boundaries they need to have in place as we deepen the therapeutic relationship.

Game 2: The Porcupine Game™

The Porcupine Game™ is a game of steady pressure with a corresponding release from pressure that teaches. This is where the Parelli Four Phases, which were described earlier, becomes a significant concept. The human applies pressure to the horse in an intentional progression of phases: Phase 1 being the lightest (hair only—or lighter!), Phase 2 applies pressure to skin, Phase 3 applies deeper pressure to muscle, and Phase 4 applies pressure as if to touch the bone. Similar phases correspond to exercises when the Carrot Stick™ is used. The human starts with Phase 1 pressure, gradually applying greater and greater pressure in intervals of three seconds per phase, which helps to slow us down, until we feel the horse respond. The moment the human feels that response, pressure is immediately released. As Parelli clarifies:

> These phases take comfort away in increments until the horse is motivated to respond in order to find comfort again. As soon as he does the right thing, the discomfort is released. He learns what he did in order to get that release, and next time does it again for the same result. Every communication with a horse involves affecting his comfort in some way, and the timing of the release is a critical factor. (Parelli, 1999, p.17)

As the program progresses and the horse understands more, the human moves through the Four Phases more quickly, with a longer Phase 1 and a quick Phase 2-4; it becomes a game in itself for the horse to respond appropriately and quickly before the human applies greater pressure. And through the Porcupine Game™, which starts as a game on the ground and progresses through the levels to a game under saddle, the horse ideally becomes very responsive and sensitive.

From the horse's point of view, the Porcupine Game™ is about moving away from steady pressure. From the human's point of view, it's about being specific and about being present. This is one of the most challenging aspects for humans, because the "release" is what ultimately teaches the horse. We as humans often get caught up in the moment and forget to release, until we practice it enough that it becomes second nature. Without being specific and ready to release at the slightest try from the horse, the Porcupine Game™ loses its meaning. Ultimately, we'd like the horse to give to pressure all over his body with trust and lightness, keeping in mind "light as a feather and as firm as another horse" presents an incredibly wide set of parameters. If you've ever watched horses in the wild (or even in your backyard!), they can be quite disconcertingly firm with each other. As we will see in the next chapter, the Porcupine Game™ can bring many client issues to the surface.

Game 3: The Driving Game™

The Driving Game™ adds rhythmic pressure to the language (as opposed to the steady pressure applied during the Porcupine Game™). Again, the Four Phases come into play here, along with a more pronounced focus on another element: using our body language and positioning to maneuver and influence the horse, the way horses do in nature. In Parelli™, there's more emphasis placed on human body language than on voice commands. When I first visited the Parelli™ Center in Florida, we were encouraged not to speak to our horses at all. This invited us to examine if our body language was in sync with our emotions (congruency), something we also address with clients in session.

Game 4: The Yo-Yo Game™

The Yo-Yo Game™ begins adding complexity, which involves asking the horse to back away from rhythmic pressure before bringing the horse back with steady pressure. Simple in theory, the Yo-Yo Game™ asks the horse to come forward and backward with responsiveness. It becomes even more meaningful when you start asking for Yo-Yo over and around obstacles, which increases difficulty. The game becomes a form of approach and retreat. The Yo-Yo Game™ becomes a foundational element for the advanced skills of lengthening and shortening stride under saddle, improving stops, and developing a sliding stop.

Game 5: The Circling Game™

The Circling Game™ introduces the aspect of "neutral" to the program, requiring the human to add more nuance to his/her repertoire. The Circling Game™ is often mistaken initially with longeing, which is utilized in a different way for a different purpose, and too often becomes a mindless exercise for both horse and human. The Circling Game™ is a three-part game: Send, Allow, and Bring Back. It's one challenge to get the horse out onto the circle, then it's a second challenge for the human to stay mentally engaged, quiet, and neutral while the horse circles. The human only comes out of his neutral position when the horse disrupts the pattern or when he wants to bring the horse back from the circle. In this way, the horse learns to influence the human's behavior (remember: cause your idea to become the horse's idea). As long as the horse maintains his responsibility within the circle pattern and at the speed requested, the human leaves him alone. It is only when he disrupts the pattern that the human takes action. As you progress through the levels, the Circling Game™ becomes a foundational exercise for mental focus and connection, and the patterns progress later to become serpentines, figure eights, and a host of other patterns under saddle. Parelli™ likens clucking to the horse while he or she is circling and following the horse around with a whip or crop as "nagging." The Circling Game™ can become a great visual way to represent this to clients, if applicable!

Game 6: The Sideways Game™

Sideways movement isn't normal as a survival or escape tool for a horse in the wild; it's not a position which allows them to run very fast, far, or effectively. Therefore, it isn't as readily used. The Sideways Game™ adds this challenging (and important!) element to the mix and gives human and horse a whole new range of movement to finesse. The ability to send a horse sideways is especially effective in engaging Left-Brain thinking because of the significant coordination it requires. More than that, it becomes an important tool increasing athleticism, suspension, maneuverability, and coordination, foundational work for later, more lateral maneuvers like lead changes, turns, spins, leg yields, and half passes for dressage, reining, and other sports. Unusual movement, such as lateral movement, can provide the opportunity to discuss lateral thinking with clients. What is another way to reach a goal, one that might seem counter-intuitive at first? What's another way to accomplish an end?

Game 7: The Squeeze Game™

The Squeeze Game™ is all about addressing the horse's innate claustrophobic tendencies. Prey animals instinctively avoid small or tight spaces, and yet we put horses in claustrophobic positions all the time, from the insides of trailers and stalls to trail riding in tight spots. Even halters, cinches and show jumps can have a claustrophobic aspect for a horse. It's an important skill-building exercise with enormous practical implications, to help horses approach these situations in a calm, Left-Brained way. The Squeeze Game™ gives us quite a bit of information about a horse, and speaks to his/her mental and emotional state. The same is true for clients. Where are their "squeeze spots?" When/where/with whom do they feel the need to squirt out and away? What has helped them to not feel the need to do so?

HORSENALITY™

Perhaps the most significant Parelli™ concept translated by Linda has been the definition of the Horsenality™ horse psychology matrix. Horsenality™ is a major tool for us at *Horse Sense*, and has become a constant point of reference and discussion in working with our herd.

The advent of Horsenality™ elevated the Parelli™ program to a whole new level. According to Linda, the theory of Horsenality™ solidified for her only after years of trying to puzzle out Pat's varying responses to horses in countless clinics and demonstrations. The Liberty and Horse Behavior course, a series of DVDs encapsulating the ideas and teachings from the original two-week onsite workshop from the early 2000s, related early concepts in terms of different horse "personalities" and responses, but the pieces didn't coalesce as "Horsenality" until 2007. In a personal interview in February 2011, Linda spoke about how the whole paradigm came together for her in the middle of the night. The basis for the concept of horse "personalities" came from a paradigm created by her mentor Glynn Braddy, and resulted in an elegant profile chart making the basic theory easy to understand.

Horsenality™ not only clarifies and explains a multitude of horse behaviors, it completely re-frames our understanding of why certain horses act and respond the way they do. The two main axes of Horsenality™ are introvert/extrovert—relatively self-explanatory—and left-brained/right-brained, which I simplify for myself as confident/unconfident. Hence there are four core combinations to remember: left-brain introvert and extrovert and right-brain introvert and extrovert. Ideally, I'll have all of them present in a herd I'm working with while doing EAP. I think of Horsenality™ as a simpler Myers-Briggs Type Indicator (MBTI), with only four quadrants rather than the 16+ MBTI possibilities. Myers-Briggs is based on how people perceive the world and how they make decisions, and much the same analysis is at work in Horsenality™, which represents, to the best of our ability, our assessment of these things, not being horses ourselves! (You can download your own Horsenality™ chart from the Parelli™ website, and map a chart for each of your horses, and then map each of your horses in a variety of circumstances. There is also an excellent DVD with demonstrations and information available on each Horsenality™ to help you in your assessment.)

The idea is not so much to label or pigeonhole a horse strictly in one quadrant, although each horse expresses an inherent Horsenality™. A horse can move into other quadrants when under stress, or when expressing fear or entering a situation which causes him or her to feel unconfident. In each quadrant, horses express themselves in specific ways, ways often misinterpreted by their humans. And each expresses varying levels of behavior: mild, moderate, or extreme. What we are looking for is a "default" behavior when under stress of any kind.

Why does one horse overreact while another one shuts down? Why does one horse express himself or herself by becoming animated and spooky while another remains stoic and unflappable? The answer lies in Horsenality™, and an effective response on our part as horsepeople also lies in understanding their Horsenality™. One horse might need constant stimulation while another needs us to slow things way down. One Horsenality™ may be very expressive in response to stimulus, while the other end of the spectrum may show only extremely subtle signs of acknowledgement. Horsenality™ can also tell us how to motivate a particular horse—one horse needs play and becomes mouthy around food; another becomes bored by repetition but responds well to food-based rewards. Certain horses shut down when unconfident, then explode when becoming overloaded. Others can't stand still at all.

With an understanding of Horsenalities™ comes the deeper, more sober understanding of the many ways we mislabel and constantly misinterpret horse behavior. The Left-Brain Introvert isn't necessarily stubborn and willful but, instead, is a thinking horse who's easily bored. The Right-Brain Extrovert isn't crazy, but over-emotional and unconfident.

Knowing that one Horsenality™ is very expressive while another demonstrates only the most subtle changes in body language is huge for us in client sessions, as is the knowledge that Horsenality™ can shift as a result of environment and circumstance. Without this piece of horse psychology, it would be very easy to miss a key moment or important pieces of information.

To use Horsenality™ effectively means to know each horse at an entirely different level. At *Horse Sense*, we track our horses' Horsenality™ from how they show up in the herd versus when they're in an arena learning something new. Do they become unconfident quickly or are they confident and three steps ahead of us? What degree of confidence do they show? Are they bored easily? What are their default responses?

Another way we've integrated Horsenality™ into our work at *Horse Sense* is when we have a lot of new staff or interns with varying skill levels with horses. As a group we select a horse and each fill out a Horsenality™ on that horse., Then we come together with that horse in the pasture to talk about what was learned, who we think this horse might work well with, or with whom there might not be an ideal fit.

Four different aspects further influence the Horsenality™ chart: the horse's innate characteristics, the spirit level, environment, and learned behavior.

- Innate characteristics remain unaffected by learning or our influence; they're hard-wired.
- Horses have different spirit levels, from low to high. And many breeds have an innate spirit level as a whole, with certain individuals being exceptions. For example, draft horses often have a low spirit level, while Arabs are typically more high-spirited.

- Like humans, environment contributes to the make-up of individual horses. Did the horse grow up stall bound? Were they in the wild? Are they used to being in a herd? Are they used to being isolated? So much of a horse's personality is defined by environment, and how artificial or natural it is.
- Learned behavior: what has been part of their process? What assumptions do they make based on their past, their training, how humans have handled them? What bad habits do they have?

Once we understand a horse's Horsenality™, it sets the pace for how much new information can be given at any particular time or in what kind of novel situations we would expect this horse to respond in a positive fashion. It also gives us information about how much pressure each horse is likely to be able to handle. It clues us in to an idea of what rewards they enjoy and provides us with a way to measure progress, from extreme, to moderate to mild.

MORE PARELLI™ CONCEPTS FOR THERAPEUTIC HORSEMANSHIP

Aside from the Parelli™ concepts referenced above, there are additional attributes to Parelli™ that swiftly captured my attention. As both teacher and student, these concepts are just a few examples of aspects of Parelli™ that, for me, cross over beautifully into equine-assisted practice.

Learner–Centered Philosophy

One of the most interesting intersections of equine-assisted practice and Natural Horsemanship is the learner-centered approach, which is evident in the writings of very early Natural Horsemanship practitioners like Tom Dorrance and Ray Hunt.

When asked how such a concept became part of the teaching within Parelli™, Linda Parelli comments, "Those guys [Dorrance and Hunt] were doing it naturally, so Pat [came about] it naturally. Then it just developed as a culture" (Personal communication, February 21, 2011). Linda goes on to state that, as a student of Tony Robbins and Robert Kiyosaki, she recognized the methodology when she walked into her first Parelli™ clinic. She also recognized one important place where it was missing: "I was already studying with all of those guys before I met Pat...and then I walked in and realized I wasn't [applying] any of that with my horses" (Personal communication, February 21, 2011).

In the 2004 and 2005 Levels, Dr. Stephanie Burns was brought in to more fully develop the adult learning theory in Parelli™ home-study materials. Dr. Burns is a pioneer in the study of adult learning in deep skill development and transference. Her examination of the learning process, and what affects human motivation in the process of change, helped enhance the Parelli™ curriculum for both student and instructor courses. And again, its intersection with equine-assisted theory is significant in that both advocate the experiential, learner-center approach to change.

Dr. Burns acknowledged learning takes place outside each person's comfort zone and this, by necessity, involves discomfort. In 2004, the Parelli™ curriculum began to include material designed to help students build resilience for the learning process and taught them to reframe and manage the intensity of their discomfort. By recognizing that learning was taking place rather than letting discomfort become a barrier to change, Parelli™ introduced the concept of each student's responsibility to make sure he not only ventured outside his comfort zone during the program, but stayed there long enough for discomfort to change. As Burns put it in one of her lectures on the Parelli™ campus I attended, "Learning doesn't happen in neutral."

Instructor John Baar, at one point Parelli's faculty leader and head of on-campus education, explains:

> Our teaching system is the opposite of a typical education environment in a lot of ways. As with our horses, we strive to empower people with a more hands-on, problem-based learning strategy. The truth

is, the more problems a student experiences, the more she's going to learn. We don't just feed people answers; we teach them how to think, to become puzzle solvers. As a student, you still have to go through the trials and tribulations yourself. You must be able to experience the frustrations and have the time and patience just to hang in there and get the feeling for yourself...you can't rob the student of her journey. (Espinoza-Sokal, 2010, p.53)

Acknowledging Fear

Another significant aspect of Parelli™ theory, for me, revolves around the discussion of fear and the part it plays in our horsemanship development. Again, Linda Parelli has opened the door on an important and oft under-discussed topic.

Working again with Dr. Burns, Linda developed curriculum elements integrating awareness around the various zones encountered by students in their horsemanship, what we have called "the Comfort Zone, the Learning Zone, and the Fear Zone." The Comfort Zone is not a place for learning and change; a student needs to be outside the Comfort Zone to learn. In contrast, the Fear Zone is the opposite end of the spectrum, the deep end of the pool. If you're in the Fear Zone and can't swim, there's no opportunity for learning to happen. In such a place, the student goes from a learning response to a threat response (more on the threat response in the next chapter). Once we feel threatened in a significant way, all learning ceases. We move into pure survival mode, like horses.

As a student, knowing which zone you're in and learning to self-regulate your response to it is important. The discussion around fear, alone, is a significant and necessary piece of human psychology in the horsemanship world. Too often, horse people experience pressure from other riders to "just get over it" or "just get back on the horse." At a minimum, a rider trying to push blindly through fear only serves to undermine safety and erode confidence even further. Sometimes, the person gets back on and gets lucky: nothing more damaging happens. Other times, something totally disastrous happens; the horse interprets the rider's fear response as incongruent—and therefore suspicious—and reacts accordingly.

In session, the theory around the three zones has many applications in helping clients interpret, respond, and build skills in response to their own fear and perceptions of fear. If you're interested in learning more about the topic of dealing with fear, read Dr. Stephanie Burns' *Move Closer, Stay Longer*. While you're at it, check out her other book *Great Lies We Live By* for additional provocative material.

Other Parelli Concepts for Equine-Assisted Practice

These concepts, first introduced to me in the hands of Parelli™ instructors, have become deeply ingrained in my horsemanship practice. I mention them here because I find myself drawing upon these concepts time and again in my practice with humans at *Horse Sense*.

- "Take the time that it takes, so it takes less time." It takes time to think like a horse instead of a predator. And short cuts don't work; in fact, they often backfire. If our objective is to achieve a certain behavior in such a way that the horse responds with complete affinity, willingness, and enthusiasm, we're sometimes talking about a lot of time. And the result can be spectacular. So in those moments if we stop, slow down, and take the time it takes up front, we actually spend much less time back-tracking and re-doing. This principle applies to clients as well.

- "Exaggerate to teach, refine as you go along." This is one reason the Games™ often look regimented and regulated when people first begin with Parelli™. Until the sequence and feel become second nature, the student has to proceed with slow deliberation until she reaches a point where the movement becomes fluid. The concept of "exaggerate to teach" is a great concept for clients in session for the same reason; doing something different than you've always done is going to feel awkward and clunky the first few times!

- Drift: Prey animals—and some people—naturally distrust confinement, physically or emotionally. The tighter and more rigid our control in whatever guise, the more we trigger the horse's flight instinct. By allowing some "drift," we avoid triggering an unnecessary and unproductive response, in both horses and clients. If I'm holding a horse's lead rope at the snap, for example, and this horse gets frightened and needs to move his or her feet, the confinement of my hand so close to his or her head—and the common predator response of not letting the horse move when he or she is spooking and needs to move—will cause even more of a prey response in the horse. Hence we have twelve-foot lines, and often lead our horses while holding that line at the six or seven foot mark.

- "Praise, recognition, and pork chops" (or material things, for humans) work for predators, but not for horses. What's important to people is not what's important to horses; blue ribbons don't mean a thing. Parelli™ defines the four things most important to horses as prey animals, in this order: safety, comfort, play, and food. Understanding this hierarchy goes a long way toward addressing issues and complications, especially when dealing with rescue horses. As herd animals, horses find both comfort and safety being in the herd; it's part of their most base instinctual drive, and carries enormous psychological implications. A multitude of vices and issues stem from being unable to fulfill this most basic need. When you consider this needs hierarchy, it becomes a useful construct for problem-solving, i.e., if a horse doesn't feel safe, she probably won't eat. Again, we've certainly seen this in rescue horses; it's not unusual to see a horse refuse to eat for several days until she feels more comfortable in the new environment. When she returns to eating, it's a sign of progress in the rehabilitation journey. As clients interact with horses and perhaps learn about this hierarchy, they can view themselves and their own lives in similar fashion.

- Approach and Retreat is another important concept in terms of equine psychology. As predators, humans have a tendency to go straight to what we want. Horses often need to approach and retreat in a situation until they feel safe. Linda Parelli discusses the concept of "thresholds" in play with horses, the natural, invisible "stopping points" of horses we've all encountered. Blow through too many (or some might say any) of your horse's thresholds, and you create a problem. Recognizing, respecting, and giving proper emphasis to a horse's thresholds is an Approach and Retreat technique designed to manage those thresholds and build confidence, both in the horse and in the horse's relationship with the human (or the client's relationship with the treatment team, for that matter).

- Opposition Reflex: Biting, kicking, rearing, bolting, and bucking are horse actions humans usually describe as naughty instead of recognizing that other elements might be at work. Certainly boredom is one element, defense is another. Opposition Reflex is the third. From the horse's point of view: "If a predator wants me to do this, there must be something wrong with it. Therefore if I do the opposite, I can survive." Parelli™ encourages us to concentrate more on the principle, or the Game™, and on the quality of the horse's response rather than on the trailer, the clippers, or the cinch. The more you try to catch horses, the more they try to escape. The challenge is to rewire ourselves a bit to think about this from a different perspective. When we become afraid—we get tight, we dig in, we become paralyzed, we contract. Opposition Reflex is a prey animal's reaction to a predator as the prey is dragged to its death. I've given several presentations on this single topic of horsemanship and its importance in EAP/EAL. This concept will be discussed more fully in the upcoming chapter on the horse in equine-assisted practices.

We now offer an equine-assisted horsemanship field of study at *Horse Sense*. I told our first herd of students that I couldn't teach them about horsemanship for equine-assisted practices without also talking significantly about Parelli™. The same has been true here.

HORSES TEACH PEOPLE
Equine–Assisted Practices and Therapeutic Horsemanship

This field wouldn't exist without Natural Horsemanship in our culture. Equine-assisted work in all its forms wouldn't exist if we still used horses as machinery. So much would be different.

This is not to say horses haven't been therapeutic for people even back in the day when horses were used for plowing fields, transportation, and warfare. But people of those times likely would have scoffed at any attempts to make this therapeutic benefit tangible and credible.

Like Natural Horsemanship, equine-assisted practice, as an activity, has deep roots. References from as early as 600 B.C. speak of the early Greeks utilizing horses not only for people with disabilities, but for general health and well-being. Jump forward to the 1800s, where European physicians found horseback riding helpful in the treatment of certain neurological conditions to improve balance, posture, and strength. Physicians used riding therapy during a Scandinavian outbreak of poliomyelitis (a kind of polio) in 1946. In a famous case from that time, horsewoman Liz Hartel used daily riding sessions to recover from the disease, and later went on to win a silver medal in Dressage in the 1952 Helsinki Olympic Games. Her story brought attention to horseback riding for the disabled, and she later partnered with physical therapist Ulla Harpoth to bring equine therapy to patients.

Therapeutic riding began in the U.S. and Canada in the 1960s; in 1969, the North American Riding for the Handicapped (NARHA) formed in the U.S. Therapeutic riding practitioners were able to catalogue a range of beneficial aspects, including physical, psychological, social, and educational outcomes: improved balance and strength, decreased spasticity and increased coordination, emotional control and self-discipline, and improved hand-eye coordination. Hippotherapy evolved as a separate focus in therapeutic riding, with a direct application toward achieving functional outcomes as part of a physical, speech, and occupational therapy treatment strategy under the supervision of a professional therapist. Hippotherapy is also often viewed as another form of rehabilitation. In Therapeutic Riding, the focus is instruction to ride, with a goal towards independent riding, along with all the intangible benefits. In EAP/EAL, the end goal is not about horsemanship or instruction to ride or competence to ride. To learn more about the history of Therapeutic Riding and Hippotherapy, visit the PATH website and peruse PATH's *Strides* magazine. Much of the preceding information was gleaned from those two sources.

During the following decades, the beginnings of equine-assisted practice for psychotherapy and learning formed. Equine-assisted activities evolved from the focus on special needs and physical and occupational therapy to include a focus on therapeutic benefits in the realm of mental health professionals. Practitioners realized the implications of expanding equine-assisted work into other areas. They started working with different populations and focusing on adapting equine-assisted work to include mental health issues, complex social problems, skill-building, behavioral, and motivational psychotherapy aspects in their work with at-risk youth, family therapy, and personal growth therapy.

The first professional associations for equine psychotherapy and learning work showed up in the 1990s, with the formation of the Equine Facilitated Mental Health Association (EFMHA) by NARHA in 1996 (now PATH), and the Equine-Assisted Growth & Learning Association (EAGALA) in 1999. Both created slightly different approaches to the field and, through the years, developed standards for professional development.

As a volunteer for a Texas therapeutic riding program back in the 1990s, it was the emotional and mental shifts in therapeutic riding clients that first caught my attention. Therapeutic riding was my entrance to the equine-assisted field; even then, volunteering as a leader and side-walker, my attention was captured far more by the psychological aspects rather than the physical aspects.

When investigating the field of equine-assisted practice, examining the philosophical distinctions between the various organizations became very important to me. As a teacher and learner, I wanted *Horse Sense*'s approach to equine-assisted practices to be informed by both theory and practice, with equal weight in both areas. And now, as an Equine Specialist, I continue to explore and observe. Each of the equine-assisted organizations continues to evolve their philosophies to this day, in part because the industry is still quite young. All of us are still discovering, examining, quantifying, and documenting the many nuances horses bring to our practices. As in many areas of life, our own education—as practitioners and as horse people—is never finished.

FOUNDATIONAL IDEAS & BASIC PRINCIPLES WITHIN EQUINE–ASSISTED ORGANIZATIONS

Each of the equine-assisted organizations has their own philosophical approach and guiding principles in practicing psychotherapy and learning. Below is an overview of today's equine-assisted landscape, circa 2012.

PATH International

When it emerged in the early 1990s, PATH International (the Professional Association of Therapeutic Horsemanship, previously known as NARHA) was among the first to provide guidance and oversight in the field. Much of this early thinking was influenced by the work of Barbara Rector, who partnered with horses in facilitating her own recovery from devastating injury in 1973. Based on her experience, Rector went on to explore and implement the psychological aspects of what was to become equine-facilitated practice. In the early 1990s, Rector started the first official equine-facilitated psychotherapy program at the Sierra Tucson addiction treatment center, utilizing horses as a treatment method.

Under the banner of EFMHA (Equine Facilitated Mental Health Association), a subgroup of NARHA, Rector was part of the team formulating the early guidelines and principles for Equine Facilitated Mental Health in 1996. Those guidelines have undergone change since 2010, when NARHA moved to more formally integrate EFMHA into its organization and merge the two entities while also renaming itself PATH Int (Professional Association of Therapeutic Horsemanship International). This integration is significant in the industry in that it "reflects the recognition that equine facilitated learning and equine facilitated mental health and wellness achievements take place in every situation in which humans and horses are partnered." PATH (n.d.) further states, "this step forward is a commitment by the association to approach the equine-assisted activities and therapies environment in a manner in which the whole person is being served through partnering with the whole horse" (p. 1).

This integration and the PATH International approach to EFP/EFL is perhaps best explained by Leif Hallberg, M.A., LCPC, LPC. Leif is a pioneer and expert in the field of equine interactions and her book, *Walking the Way of the Horse: Exploring the Power of the Horse-Human Relationship* is used as a classroom text across the United States and internationally. She is an active volunteer for PATH Intl. and served as past board member of EFMHA and past chair of the PATH Intl. EFP and EFL membership task force.

— ⌗ —

An Introduction to PATH International
By Leif Hallberg, M.A., LCPC, LPC

For fourteen years the Equine Facilitated Mental Health Association (EFMHA) functioned as a subgroup of NARHA. Although the two organizations co-existed under the same non-profit 501(c)3 status, each retained their own board of directors, code of ethics, committee structure and membership base. NARHA primarily served professionals interested in therapeutic riding and hippotherapy, and EFMHA served professionals interested in equine facilitated mental health and equine facilitated learning.

In 2010, the two entities recognized the similarity of their work and the power of integration. They came together as one united association, better able to address the needs of their membership with increased resources and knowledge. Simultaneously, it was clear the association had outgrown its name. It no longer provided support only to professionals who were teaching riding and working with a physically disabled clientele in North America. Rather it had grown to an internationally-based membership of professionals providing diverse services for an equally diverse clientele. The name change from NARHA to PATH Intl., coupled with the full integration of EFMHA, fundamentally changed the association. Professionals around the world are now able to interact, learn from one another and mutually support the development of professionalism within the field of equine-assisted activities and therapies.

As a part of the integration, a new code of ethics was developed which melds together the beliefs and values of both organizations. All members of PATH Intl. now adhere to the united code of ethics. As a part of this code, the role of the equine has become more pronounced, with PATH Intl. fully supporting the concepts of partnership between equines and humans and equine sentience. This outlook promoted the creation of a new equine welfare committee and new equine welfare guidelines.

Mental health, education, coaching and a myriad of other professionals can utilize the resources offered through PATH Intl. The PATH Intl. code of ethics, the Standards for Certification and Accreditation manual and the Equine Facilitated Psychotherapy Guidelines provide members with useful information to consider when starting and operating an equine program. The Equine Facilitated Psychotherapy Manual guides mental health professionals through the step-by-step process of adding equines to an existing private practice or working with a PATH Intl. center. The professional certifications PATH Intl. offers continue to expand and new certifications are being designed to meet the emerging needs of mental health and learning professionals.

The association still has tasks to accomplish before the integration of the mental health and learning professions is final. The center accreditation process must be evaluated and potentially adapted to fit the needs of a more diverse membership. New standards need to be created for equine-facilitated psychotherapy and equine-facilitated learning and outreach needs to be conducted to help the public understand the new direction of the association.

As a part of the integration, there is mental health and learning representation on every committee throughout the association. This ensures the needs of a mental health and learning membership are heard and attended to. Many members enjoy participating in committees where tasks are accomplished and new ideas generated. Others may not have the time to volunteer, but choose to vote on important issues like standards and association-wide decisions. Either way, members are the voice and guiding force behind PATH Intl. and thus as the mental health and learning community has grown, so has its impact on the organization.

PATH Intl.'s approach to equine-facilitated psychotherapy begins with the foundation of equine partnership and includes the belief that equines are valuable and sentient members of the treatment team. This orientation supports methods of practice in which both the equine and the client are supported through educated, safe and respectful approaches to human-equine interactions. PATH Intl. views equine-facilitated psychotherapy as a "specialty area of practice" which is governed first and foremost by the ethics and standards put forth by the licensing boards and membership organizations which oversee the field of mental health. The ethical codes governing mental health professionals require that a licensed professional is educated, trained, supervised and experienced in any new method or specialty area of practice they provide. PATH Intl. believes that by setting competency standards for mental health professionals which align with those required for other specialty areas of practice, the services provided will be safer for clients and equines alike.

Equine Specialist-Specific Certification of PATH
by Kris Batchelor

PATH International currently has a single level certification available for the Equine Specialist in Mental Health and Learning. There are several requirements that must be met prior to application, including sixty (60) hours of experience in a mental health or special education setting, twenty (20) hours of education in equine psychology and behavior, an online test and recommendations from professionals in the field. Candidates must then attend a three-day instructional workshop, which is taught jointly by a mental health professional and Equine Specialist. Through both lecture and experiential format, the workshop explores the finer points of vital ES skills like curriculum development, creation of a therapeutic environment, the art of co-facilitation and the importance of equine welfare within this field. Following the didactic portion, on the final day, participants may elect to take a horsemanship skills test that allows them to demonstrate basic proficiency in safe horse handling. Certification as a PATH ES is subject to annual compliance requirements, including eight hours of documented continuing education and commitment to the PATH code of ethics.

(See Contributor Biographies to read more about the authors)

Equine-Assisted Growth and Learning Association-EAGALA

EAGALA and the EAGALA Model is perhaps one of the clearest, most crystallized "model" in all of equine-assisted practices. Lynn Thomas, co-founder and Executive Director, explains this more fully.

The EAGALA Model
By Lynn Thomas, LCSW, Co-founder/Executive Director, EAGALA

The Equine-Assisted Growth and Learning Association (EAGALA) was founded in 1999 to establish professional standards and provide education, resources, innovation and support for professionals providing Equine-Assisted Psychotherapy and Learning (EAP/EAL) worldwide. The association provides training and certification with its basis being the EAGALA Model.

The EAGALA Model provides a standard and structure for providing EAP/EAL sessions. Practicing within a model establishes a foundation of key values and beliefs, and provides a basis of good practice and professionalism. The EAGALA Model provides a framework of practice, but within that framework, there are infinite opportunities for creativity and adaptability to various therapeutic styles.

The EAGALA Model
There are four key standards to the model:

- **Team approach**—A licensed Mental Health Professional and a qualified Equine Specialist* work as a team with the clients and horses. This level of care is provided in all sessions whether EAP or EAL. (*Note: EAGALA has set a minimum standard to be a qualified Equine Specialist which includes 6,000 hours of hands-on work with horses, 100 hours of continuing education in the horse profession including topics covering ground work, horse psychology and reading horse body language/nonverbal communication, and at least 40 hours of that continuing education completed in the last two years)

- **Ground-based**—No riding is involved. Instead, effective and deliberate techniques are utilized where the horses are metaphors in specific ground-based experiences.

- **Solution-oriented**—The basis of the EAGALA Model is a belief that all clients have the best solutions for themselves when given the opportunity to discover them. The facilitation and experiences provide opportunities for clients to explore, problem-solve, take risks, employ creativity, and allow their own story and solutions to unfold.

- **Code of Ethics**—EAGALA has high standards of practice and ethics and an ethics committee and protocol for upholding these standards.

THE EAGALA TEAM

The Horse: Horses have many characteristics which lend them to being effective agents of change, including honesty, awareness, and ability with nonverbal communication. The role of the horses in an EAGALA session is to be themselves.

The Equine Specialist (ES): The ES chooses the horses to be used in sessions, works with the MH to develop the structure/activities of sessions, keeps an equine log to document horse behaviors in sessions, stays aware of safety and welfare of clients, horses, and team, and makes observations of horse SPUD's (see below) which can bring in potential metaphors.

The Mental Health Professional (MH): The MH is responsible for treatment planning, documentation of clients, and ensuring ethical practice. The MH builds on the ES's horse observations, bringing in the metaphoric and therapeutic/learning relevance of the session.

KEY POINTS OF THE EAGALA MODEL
- It is **experiential**. Learning occurs through the experience in the pro-

cess. The Principles of Experiential Practice apply (see http://www.aee.org/about/whatIsEE).

- **Safety** is part of the experiential process.
- Observation and facilitation are from a **clean language** perspective.
- **Metaphor** is a foundation—the clients are sharing their life stories symbolically through their experience with the horses.
- **Activities** are created to provide a structure of parallels to real-life—every intervention, horse, prop, decision and intervention is decided based on the potential metaphor it can become in the client's story and need.
- Focus on the **nonverbal** of clients and horses. Listen to the **verbal** to compare it to the nonverbal and to use their language to reflect on their stories.
- Use **SPUD'S** to help focus observations and key in on the potential metaphors.
- **Ask guestions** and **make observations** with genuine **curiosity** to invite reflective thought rather than direct to our biased solutions.
- **Focus** on the **horses**! This work is about the power of horses to impact the change.
- Keep aware of our **'S ("My Stuff")**—our own responses, beliefs and emotions can be informing us, and also can impact our sessions with less favorable outcomes when we choose interventions without this awareness.

EAGALA Model sessions are designed to be experiential, incorporate the horse as an active facilitator for change and create a parallel to the clients' lives. Facilitators invite clients to participate in experiences which accomplish this design and address the clients' treatment plan, goals and needs.

The key view is to think of the session as providing an opportunity for the clients to experience/tell their stories. Activities provide the structure through which their stories begin to emerge.

FACILITATION
In experiential models, observing the nonverbal and behavioral actions occurring through the experience provides information which may be

used in processing (discussion) with the clients. Processing provides the space for clients to bring meaning, reflection, understanding and applicability to the equine experience on a conscious level when it fits to do so.

SPUD'S™ (trademarked EAGALA) is a framework developed by EAGALA to assist facilitators in determining where to focus observations since there is so much to observe.

S—Shifts: Watch for any shifts that occur in behaviors, including actual physical placement, of both horses and humans. For instance, the horses were standing, now they are running. Shifts are especially important to note because they indicate change.

P—Patterns: If a behavior occurs three or more times, it is a pattern, and these patterns tend to parallel other patterns in the clients' lives.

U—Unique: When observing, if the horses do something out of the ordinary, like kick up, or something dramatic or unusual, or if the humans do something that is quite Unique, note that moment—what the Unique behavior was, and what was happening in the entire arena with humans and horses.

D—Discrepancy: While the primary focus in the EAGALA Model is on the nonverbal, another area of focus is what the client is saying verbally, but key in this is comparing the verbal to the non-verbal. For instance, the client says she "doesn't want to do this," but at the same time she is walking towards the horses. Discrepancies are important because they indicate an opportunity for change—a motivation—and a potential metaphor.

'S (apostrophe S)—Self-awareness or "My Stuff": While observing the experience of the clients and horses, facilitators constantly observe their own countertransference, i.e., observing themselves. 'S influences planning, observations and processing by leading to agenda-filled observations and questions which are more about the facilitators' needs and solutions instead of the clients'. The EAGALA Model focuses on 'S as a key aspect influencing the outcomes of sessions. As such, facilitators utilizing the EAGALA Model must be open and focused on ongoing self-awareness and evaluation.

OBSERVE WITHOUT INTERPRETATION
Observing without interpreting is a key foundation in the EAGALA Model, and one of the biggest challenges for facilitators. When watching

through the framework of SPUD'S, observations must be specific, objective, behavioral actions of clients and horses seen through an unclouded lens. In other words, observations without judgment, biases, beliefs and assessments about what it all means. This is done so clients can express their perspectives and discover their own solutions—the solution-oriented standard of the model.

In EAGALA, this is referred to as "Clean Language." Clean Language is a term developed by David Grove in the 1980s. It is about the facilitators keeping opinions and advice to themselves, while listening and observing attentively, asking clean questions, and exploring metaphors being brought out by the client and in the client's language. Through this process, clients naturally change by their own direction, instead of someone trying to "force" change. In the arena with horses, it allows the clients and horses to "be" and truly experience the moment.

One of the most important qualities of an EAGALA Model facilitator is the ability to be sincerely and genuinely curious: curious about what the client really thinks and believes, curious about what the horses are doing and what it might mean to the client, curious about what the clients and horses might do next, curious about what one's team member is thinking and doing, and just overall curious about everything. It is through this place of curiosity that facilitators are able to keep their language cleaner and be open to learning and accepting others rather than placing judgments and expectations on them.

(Recommended reading on Clean Language and metaphor: Clean Language: Revealing Metaphors and Opening Minds by Wendy Sullivan and Judy Rees and Metaphors in Mind: Transformation through Symbolic Modelling by James Lawley and Penny Tompkins)

TRUST THE PROCESS

The phrase "trust the process" is used in EAGALA to remind facilitators that it is the horses and clients which direct the process and know best what is needed, and it is the facilitator's role to listen and not block this process from happening by inserting personal agendas. When observing the EAGALA Model, it is easy to wonder what is going on. Yet the power of the interaction between horses and clients continues to manifest itself

More than a Mirror, by Shannon Knapp

time and time again when providing this opportunity and following the model.

SUMMARY

In summary, the EAGALA Model provides professional standards and a framework for structuring and facilitating powerful sessions focused on mental health and human development goals. The model helps facilitators team together on the same page philosophically and provides for an approach that can be researched and replicated worldwide. And through the ground-focused approach, it provides an exciting and rewarding niche for horses of all types in all stages of life to have a role and let their personalities shine by being themselves. (Learn more at www.eagala.org) *(See Contributor Biographies to read more about the author)*

An exciting, up-and-coming model is presented by Tim Jobe and Bettina Shultz-Jobe, of Natural Lifemanship. Called Trauma-Focused Equine-Assisted Psychotherapy (or TF-EAP for short), this model has both an unmounted and a mounted component, blending both worlds to serve the client. More about this new, rigorous model is presented below.

Trauma-Focused Equine-Assisted Psychotherapy
By Tim Jobe, B.S., Bettina Shultz-Jobe, MA, LPC, LPCC,
and Laura McFarland, M.Ed.

Trauma-Focused Equine-Assisted Psychotherapy (TF-EAP) was developed by Tim Jobe and Bettina Shultz-Jobe, the co-founders of Natural Lifemanship. TF-EAP is a comprehensive model of equine-assisted therapy that employs both the physiology and the psychology of the horse to address specific therapeutic goals with children, adults, and families who suffer from trauma-related mental health disorders. It is driven by the beliefs that a good principle is a good principle regardless of where it is applied, and that all mental health issues result in dysfunction of intrapersonal and/or interpersonal relationships. Because TF-EAP is based on principles rather than techniques, clients are able to readily transfer their progress in the arena and in the round pen to the venues of their daily lives. Likewise, family members of traumatized youth as well as other professionals who work with them (e.g., teachers, caseworkers) benefit by learning and applying the principles of TF-EAP, even if they never have the opportunity to work directly with a horse.

A PARADIGM SHIFT

Many therapists and equine professionals who have learned the Natural Lifemanship model describe it as a paradigm shift. The focus of the model and the principles that drive it offer a completely new perspective on horse and human relationships. An underlying belief is that humans and horses are capable of emotionally intimate partnerships, which does not come naturally to either. Both naturally gravitate toward a hierarchy in which one is either the leader or the follower. Likewise, clients who have been victimized often assume the role of either victim or persecutor, both of which have grave effects on the individual's ability for authentic, safe relationships. It is in the context of emotionally intimate partnerships that the greatest potential for health and wellbeing is found. The only chance a horse ever has of relating in a partnership is with a human. Natural Lifemanship teaches a form of applied horse psychology that was developed with human relationship principles in mind, and with the belief that if it is not good for both the human and the horse it is not good for either.

IT'S ALL ABOUT RELATIONSHIPS!

Trauma, by definition, has lasting effects on its sufferers regardless of the age(s) at which it occurs. At the core of traumatic stress is a breakdown in the ability to regulate internal states. When a person is repeatedly exposed to traumatic stress, their brain changes to accommodate an environment in which survival is the overriding concern, affecting their ability to regulate emotions and behavioral impulses. The compromised ability to self regulate on a physiological level combined with the psychological scars of trauma result in pervasive problems in relationships at home, at work, at school, and in the community at large. The effects of traumatic stress are thus manifested most dramatically in the realm of relationships, including the relationship with self and with others.

Combining mounted work and groundwork, TF-EAP utilizes every aspect of the horse to address the client's physiological and psychological responses to trauma. Horses are not used metaphorically nor simply as a tool for healing; rather, they are partners in healing as clients connect and build real relationships with them. Two primary activities comprise the TF-EAP model: Relationship Logic and Rhythmic Riding.

RELATIONSHIP LOGIC

Relationship Logic is the foundation of Natural Lifemanship. It consists primarily of groundwork during which each client builds a relationship with a horse that is truly based on a partnership—not coercion, appease-ment, or submission. Relationship Logic joins clients with horses who have varying levels of experience. While well-trained horses are excel-lent partners for this work, so are horses with very little understanding of human relationships or horses who have experienced trauma. Every principle that applies to building a relationship with a horse must transfer to healthy human relationships. The horse is not a metaphor for other relationships—it is a real relationship in which patterns play out. Objects are often used as metaphors, but living beings are not. Because the client and the horse are engaged in building a real (as opposed to metaphor-ical) relationship, real relationship patterns surface and are transformed during TF-EAP sessions.

The client's reaction to life experiences determines how they create their relationships. Trauma sets in motion ways of coping and interacting in relationships that frequently become a pattern. Even after trauma has been processed cognitively, a client's relationship patterns are often still in place. These coping mechanisms and relational interactions, while once necessary for survival, become detrimental in situations where survival is no longer the overriding concern. Clients will naturally follow this developed pattern when creating a relationship with a horse. Horses respond honestly to clients' behaviors and internal states, so clients can easily recognize the problems they create in the relationship with the horse. Clients can then identify how they create those same problems in relationship with themselves and others, and also identify the problems for which they are not responsible. Relationship Logic facilitates a process whereby clients are able to address and move through past or present damaging life circumstances, understand how those circumstances affect their current interactions, and make the personal changes necessary for healthy, fulfilling relationships in the present and future.

Mounted work is often utilized in the Relationship Logic component of TF-EAP to allow clients to further recognize relationship patterns and deepen intimacy. The nature of relationships is that the place with the most potential for reward is also the place with the most potential for loss. The most intimate and vulnerable a person will ever be in a relationship with a horse is on its back. Horseback riding requires a higher degree of trust than groundwork from both the human and horse, and it is also where the greatest potential for conflict in the relationship lies. When building a relationship with a horse, if this place of intimacy is forced before each party is ready, it will damage the relationship and have the potential for emotional and physical pain. However, healthy relationships are always moving forward in some way. If the horse and human reach the point where it is time to take the next step, and either party is unwilling, the relationship will suffer. When clients try to move toward this level of intimacy too quickly, there are consequences, and poignant therapeutic work abounds. The same opportunity exists when the client is unwilling or fearful of moving to this level of intimacy. In either situation, this is a pattern that causes problems in their relationships. Therefore, riding, when it is appropriate, is a very important part of the therapeutic process.

RHYTHMIC RIDING

TF-EAP incorporates horseback riding into the therapy process in order to address very specific therapeutic goals related to the client's ability to regulate his or her physiological responses to stress and their accompanying emotional states. Studies show that brain functionality in people who have experienced trauma such as abuse, neglect, combat, or natural disasters, is often compromised due to disorganization and/or lack of neurological connections in the brain. Trauma victims often struggle with emotion and impulse control, which results in the inability to appropriately handle even minimal stress. TF-EAP utilizes the rhythmic, patterned, repetitive, bilateral movement inherent in riding a horse to increase and reorganize the connections in the brain, thereby increasing the brain's ability for emotion and impulse control. The horse is able to provide the rhythm required to effectively heal the traumatized brain until the client is able to independently provide that rhythm. In effect, clients passively learn to self-regulate through the use of the rhythmic, patterned, repetitive movement of the horse.

Music and other somatosensory interventions are often incorporated into Rhythmic Riding to capitalize on the sensory integration it provides. When we tap into the areas of the brain responsible for the senses, we tap into and activate the areas of the brain most affected by trauma. Rhythmic Riding not only activates the sub-cortical regions of the brain providing passive self-regulation, it also requires the client to problem solve (e.g., ride in rhythm with the music; direct the horse along an established path), thus activating the areas of the brain responsible for planning and impulse control. Therefore Rhythmic Riding offers the ideal conditions to establish and strengthen the cross-brain neuronal connections necessary for self-regulation.

As with other therapeutic modalities, clients are taught specific skills to enable them to self-regulate in stressful or emotional situations. However, unlike office-based counseling sessions in which the therapist discusses with the client how to use the learned skills in more stressful situations, riding provides a medium through which clients can learn and practice these skills. During Rhythmic Riding, horses provide a mildly stressful environment that is safe and predictable (eustress) in which to practice these skills. Before the horse will appropriately control herself, the client must first be in control of his/her own thoughts, emotions, and actions. Riding affords clients who live in chaotic, dysfunctional environments, the opportunity to practice skills that will help them control the chaos inside them when they can't control the chaos around them. Many clients are unable to do deeper, insight-oriented therapeutic work until they are able to bring their level of arousal to a place that allows them to gain and retain insight, and benefit from higher-level learning. This level of regulation is most profoundly experienced and learned on the back of a horse.

QUALIFICATIONS FOR EQUINE SPECIALIST IN TF-EAP

Currently, Natural Lifemanship is a training, rather than a certifying organization. In order to effectively utilize TF-EAP, it is imperative that the Equine Specialist have extensive knowledge and an intimate understanding of Natural Lifemanship relationship- building principles and horse psychology. These core competencies will be outlined as Natural Lifemanship continues to develop an academic certification through The Institute for Human Animal Connection at The University of Denver.

SUMMARY

Trauma-Focused EAP is a potent and innovative therapeutic solution for a population of clients who are often deemed "treatment resistant." Clients with a history of trauma often come to therapy with a compromised ability to benefit from strictly cognitive approaches. The physiological responses and relationship patterns set in place by adverse life experiences need to be effectively treated for true healing to occur. TF-EAP facilitates such healing by utilizing the physiology and the psychology of the horse. Clients benefit from the horse's physiology through riding and the rhythmic, patterned, repetitive motion it affords, thus building the neural connections that enable the client to regulate his or her internal states. Relationship patterns are directly identified, processed, and transformed through the process of creating a progressively intimate relationship with a horse. The principles learned in therapy sessions immediately apply to human relationships in the client's life as well. (Learn more at www.NaturalLifemanship.com)
(See Contributor Biographies to read more about the authors)

Other Equine-Assisted Trainings, Certifications & Models of Interest, based in the USA
- **EGEA**: The Equine Guided Education Association was formed in 2003, with the main priority to provide a membership community and foundation for the growing field of Equine Guided Education and all of its components. EGEA's mission is to encourage a unified discourse of the horse as a respected "guide" in human growth, learning and devel-

opment. EGEA further provides information, resources, education, networking opportunities, an annual conference, and a membership community.

In defining the horse's role in the learning process, the word "guide" has a specific meaning and most appropriately describes the horse's amazing gift. The horse does more than facilitate or assist the learning process. The horse literally "guides" the process. The certified EGE professional follows and listens to the horse's input, considering it to be of paramount importance. The word "guide" was carefully chosen because it means, "one who can find a path through unknown or unexplored territory." This describes the profound and magical aspect of horses in the learning process. Learn more at www.EGEA.us.

- **EponaQuest**: Founded in 1997 by author, lecturer and horse trainer Linda Kohanov, Epona Equestrian Services has received international attention for horse training and breeding innovations, as well as educational programs that employ horses in teaching leadership, assertiveness, personal empowerment, relationship, intuition, and emotional fitness skills to people. Amateur and professional equestrians, families, counselors, artists, educators, and business leaders travel from around the world to attend workshops and private sessions with the EponaQuest herd. Since 2002, Kohanov and her staff have also trained over 150 EponaQuest Instructors who now offer EponaQuest-based programs on five continents. Learn more at www.EponaQuest.com.

- **HEAL**: Human-Equine Alliances for Learning: Human-Equine Alliances for Learning (HEAL) is a non-profit organization that promotes, supports and studies Equine-Facilitated Psychotherapy (EFP). EFP is an experiential therapy in which horses are employed to facilitate emotional growth and learning for humans. HEAL founder and lead therapist Leigh Shambo, MSW, LMHC has developed the HEAL Model™ of EFP, based on scientifically validated principles from the fields of neuroscience and psychology (human and animal). The HEAL Model™ teaches core skills for navigating and enhancing relationships, while strengthening autonomy and awareness of self. The horses are respected as sensitive and intelligent communicators who may guide the process in unique ways! Learn more at www.HumanEquineAlliance.org.

- **GEP**: Gestalt Equine Psychotherapy: Founded in 1969, The Gestalt Institute of the Rockies provides the most comprehensive Gestalt Equine-Assisted Psychotherapy™ training program currently available.

Participants gain an understanding of the therapeutic relationship between therapist-horse-client, and competency in the essential theoretical concepts and experiential process of Gestalt therapy, development and horsemanship. Training provides basic knowledge of horses including: safety, herd behavior, groundwork, riding, health care, theory and history of horsemanship, and other relevant areas of horse management. They also provide extensive training in Gestalt Theory and Practice as well as interweaving developmental theory into all of their work. Gestalt Equine-Assisted Psychotherapy™ is an existential and experiential psychotherapy where horses partner with people to facilitate their experience in the present moment. Awareness, relationship and healing is cultivated through the therapist-client-horse relationship, the exploration of self within the environment, and the dynamics of contact. Learn more at www.GestaltEquineInstitute.com.

- **OK Corral**: The O.K. Corral Series educates, promotes, and supports professionals in the practice of authentic equine-assisted work. Authentic equine-assisted work honors and integrates natural horse and herd behavior as a model for human mental and emotional health using the equine-assisted philosophies developed by Greg Kersten. The O.K. Corral Series teaches ground (95%) and mounted exercises for use in the practice of Equine-Assisted Psychotherapy and equine-assisted learning. There are multiple trainings offered, focusing in on specific areas, such as Family, Business, Crisis, Military and more. Learn more at www.OKCorralSeries.com.

- **The Equine Experiential Education Association**, or E3A, is an international professional membership organization offering training, certification, business development and resources for the implementation of Equine-Assisted Learning (EAL) programs by educators, coaches, professional development trainers and other facilitators. They provide the necessary resources for the promotion and implementation of quality, successful, professional equine experiential education programs and businesses. E3A provides a home for professionals who want to facilitate experiential learning experiences with horses outside of the special needs, therapeutic, and/or mental health models. It provides a more traditional training approach to the corporate, educational, coaching, and personal development fields through learning experiences based on the horse/human connection. Learn more at www.E3assoc.org.

Several colleges and universities are also offering significant education and training in the field of EAP/EAL:

- **Carroll College** in Montana has an undergraduate degree in Anthrozoology, also known as The Human-Animal Bond Program. This major explores the unique relationship between humans and animals, both canine and equine. Carroll College's unique experiential approach provides students with both scientific and academic rigor and the hands-on application of the knowledge gained. Learn more at www.carroll. edu.

- **Prescott College** in Prescott, Arizona offers a Master's Degree in Counseling and a Master's Degree in Education, one with a concentration in Equine-Assisted Mental Health and the other with a concentration in Equine-Assisted Learning. Both are offered as low-residency programs and have internationally-renowned presenters teach the "intensives" that Master's students attend four times a year. Learn more at www.prescott.edu.

Several people are advancing higher education work and approaches in equine-assisted practice, including Dr. Tracy Weber from Kaleidoscope Learning Circle in Frankenmuth, Michigan (www.MyKLC.com) and Dr. Paul Smith, who teaches at Prescott College and runs Centaur Leadership Services (www.prescott.com). Pam McPhee of the Browne Center at the University of New Hampshire, is another leader in the field of equine-assisted practices, at a corporate level as well as for youth and students (www.BrowneCenter.com).

There are also practitioners adapting equine-assisted work to include the fields of coaching and other variations. Ann Kerr Romberg and Lynn Baskfield of Wisdom Horse Coaching (www.WisdomHorseCoaching.com) and Lisa Murrell of Equine Alchemy (www.EquineAlchemy. com), are such coaches incorporating an equine-assisted approach in their coaching work.

There are new applications, specializations and organizations springing up all the time, and these are just a few of those currently available.

PRINCIPLES THAT HAVE SHAPED EQUINE-ASSISTED PRACTICE AT HORSE SENSE

Many people approach me asking for advice on which certification and/or organization is right for them, or which one they should attend. My best answer is to attend any and all trainings and certifications, as one can learn from anyone. However, without unlimited resources and time, I believe understanding where they stand on some key concepts will identify which of the organizations they most closely align with philosophically.

Although *Horse Sense* has offered predominantly EAGALA-based services since inception, all the people and organizations I've studied with and under have taught me and have added something to how *Horse Sense* approaches EAP & EAL. I've included extended discussions of PATH, EAGALA and TF-EAP in this section because of the influence they have either with me or in the field as a whole, or both.

Since 2010-2011, *Horse Sense* has evolved its offerings to include mounted work with clients in the form of limited Therapeutic Riding and Trauma-Focused Equine-Assisted Psychotherapy, which includes both riding and unmounted work. We have very specific and clear distinctions among the methodologies in our toolkit. We feel we can meet 75% of our clients' needs utilizing solely groundwork, and we've begun offering these other modalities to address the other 25% of needs we feel are best treated with some form of mounted work. Our overwhelming commitment is to the client, not to a specific methodology or model. That said, we strive to be "clean and clear" about what, how and why we employ different modalities, and constantly challenge ourselves and each other in this process to articulate the reasons that drive what we are doing.

Below are some of the key ideas informing the *Horse Sense* philosophy, as they have crystallized for me throughout the years.

1. Concept of what promotes change

Pain is a very strong motivator; with sufficient discomfort, one becomes open-minded enough to start seeking answers. Pain and discomfort are the walls most people run into before they become ready to change. My experience is that people create, cause, and seek out change in their life when they get into enough discomfort or recognize the ineffectiveness of the approach they've employed to make something different in their life. Without enough need to change, there's no motivation to do it and to follow through. As Stephanie Burns says, "Learning isn't fun." In my experience, neither is change.

2. Process-focused vs. goal-focused

In some definitions of EFP, "goal-focused" is part of the description. While I recognize that anytime actual therapy is taking place there are always treatment goals and hence there is an unavoidable focus on the goals, the description of EFP as "goal-focused" causes me to flinch a bit. I'm concerned this description causes practitioners to think more about short-term solutions rather than long-term ones, and focuses too much on outcomes rather than the process. Goal-focused programming can create much benefit and relief temporarily, but does not produce the lasting change necessary for long-term recovery from ineffective and/or destructive behaviors. I find that when an agenda is set more for what clients "should" or "need to" experience, or there is more attachment to how something should look—then, the less true learning actually happens. The efforts become (and are felt by the clients as), at best, forced and often condescending. I find the effects of being goal-driven and agenda-focused causes problems for horses as well.

3. Learner-centered, experiential approach

Part of what we strive for at *Horse Sense* is creating a learner-centered environment for the client. People learn more effectively as they find their own answers from within instead of seeking answers from the outside, from an "expert." The horse supports this learner-centered approach by providing the client with a means to see their behavior reflected, to change that behavior in real time, and to experiment with alternatives.

As the website for the Association of Experiential Education (AEE) states: "Experiences are structured to require the client to take initiative, make decisions, and be accountable for results. Throughout the experiential learning process, the client is actively engaged in posing questions, investigating, experimenting, being curious, solving problems, assuming responsibility, being creative, and constructing meaning." (www.AEE.org)

4. *Power dynamics & gurus*

Through my personal experience, my background as a college teacher, and in my experience with other equine-assisted practice and training programs, I like how a team approach decentralizes power; no one person has "the right answer" from the traditional teaching paradigm. Whereas the normal classroom sets up the right and wrong answers as known a priori, the learner-centered model is open-ended; there is no right or wrong.

A treatment team also reduces the possibility of what I call the "Guru Effect," in which the therapist or facilitator is set up to be idealized, creating dependence rather than independence. This is certainly something I see in the EAP/EAL field.

5. *Team approach*

In addition to de-centralizing power the two-person team model also brings two sets of eyes to each client session, a dynamic I feel is critical. Each professional has a focus, one on the client and much of the verbal communication, the other on the horse and the non-verbal communication. A single facilitator has to concentrate on everything, leaving room to miss nuances and details. As an Equine Specialist, I really appreciate the many layers of information coming from the horse's body language alone. The mental health professional, likewise, is deeply engaged with the client, the intellectual process of the client, and the level of understanding of the client. They occupy a very different space and perspective in the session. As an aside, the two-person EAGALA team also presents an opportunity for modeling communication, interaction, and other key life-skills for clients. Also, in terms of safety and legality, I find two sets of eyes is preferable.

There is also what I call the "Shoulder-to-Shoulder" effect in the team approach. Instead of being in the front of the classroom, teaching what clients "need to know," the facilitators are more often "shoulder-to-shoulder" with the client, examining the challenge and being curious and inquisitive about possible solutions, in just the same manner as the client.

6. Value of and Purpose

EAP and EAL offer a great opportunity for horses who don't fit in the traditional or normal horse world. It gives them a chance to develop, thrive, and give their many gifts to others.

All of my experiences in the EAP/EAL world, as well as our Parelli-based, Natural Horsemanship approach at *Horse Sense* helps us serve clients. We continually practice "un-training" ourselves from direct-line thinking and the linear approach utilized with horses. It also helps us more clearly recognize what is happening with the horse in client sessions, something we'll be exploring in the coming chapter. Additionally, after all these years integrating Natural Horsemanship into our equine-assisted practice at *Horse Sense*, the intersection of the two disciplines is incredibly clear to us. This will also be explored more in the next chapter.

It is highly likely, if not outright apparent, that early Natural Horsemanship practitioners recognized the horse's capacity to heal and teach humans. They certainly recognized their work as equal amounts of training/teaching/playing with the horse and teaching the human counterparts. But, while these early practitioners might have articulated the concept in the arena, they left the conversations behind in the arena as well.

Perhaps now there is an opportunity for us, as equine-assisted professionals, to bring Natural Horsemanship back into our client sessions with deliberate intention and respect for what it can teach us as horse people, helping horses create change in humans.

From the Inside Out

DISCOVERY, SKILL BUILDING, AND REINFORCEMENT IN EAP

One of the greatest challenges we have in equine-assisted practice is making our work understandable to the outside world. While we understand something significant is happening when our clients work with horses, what we think happens and how we think it happens varies from practitioner to practitioner. Equine-assisted practice is a field with a highly experiential dynamic, making it a challenge to explain. How do you describe something designed to be felt? Understanding involves the whole body: head, heart and gut.

There really is no singular definition that fits all expressions of equine-assisted psychotherapy and learning practice. Although more and more people now understand that equine-assisted practice is not simply riding lessons or participating in horse shows, most people still have only a vague understanding of what actually occurs during an equine-assisted session. In response to this challenge, the language and messaging around our practice has slowly evolved.

Ariana Strozzi captured the essence of this evolution nicely in a private communication back in 2008: "If you said you were a 'coach' twenty years ago, people assumed you were coaching Little League, soccer, or football. Nobody knew what a 'business coach' or 'personal coach' was or, if they did, that wasn't their first thought upon hearing 'coach.'" However, today, if someone says they're a "coach," many interpret the duties through a much broader definition: life coach, business coach, or weight loss coach. We are in this same process of evolution with equine specialists and equine-assisted practices.

It's difficult to explain the theory, interaction and outcomes that are such a large part of equine-assisted practice to the public. But, in this same vein, I wonder just how well those of us in the field really understand all the different layers and how they work together. While we might understand basic aspects of the horse/human dynamic, new research on social and emotional intelligence is evolving, and emerging science is building a much bigger picture to deepen our understanding. This same science might eventually help us develop more credible, definitive language and support regarding what we already know happens in the arena between horse and human.

First, before we explore these behaviors and emotional concepts, it seems most practical to move our journey forward by taking you, the reader, through the steps of a typical client experience. By establishing this basic understanding, we can then step into the deeper aspects of what takes place when horses become involved in human therapy and learning. Before you can fully understand the ability and insight an equine-assisted practitioner should have in order to be successful, everyone would benefit by having a rough idea of what takes place in client sessions at *Horse Sense*: how we shape a client's progression, and how a client can move through the learning and therapy experience to a greater understanding of his life and choices.

So, I'll offer a glimpse into what typically happens at *Horse Sense*, reminding you that the practice we've evolved from our years of experience is only one snapshot of what happens globally at centers throughout the industry. We'll review a fairly typical progression of treatment from a high-level perspective.

As my own understanding matures through both practice and study, I believe that horses truly excel at teaching and modeling social and emotional intelligence. Within their own natural behavior and by attuning to the human client in session, horses create the ideal context in which our clients can—no matter the issues—adapt and enhance their own emotional and social intelligence as it relates to their self-awareness and self-management in the human world.

What does our practice look like? How do we progress with a "classic" client (if there is such a thing)? How would we introduce activities that promote awareness and then use that awareness to build new skills? Let's step through the process together. Keep in mind the following anecdotes represent a composite profile from hundreds of client experiences; care has been taken to obscure identifying details. It's also helpful to remember that the kind of intervention described in this chapter is predominantly intended for clients over the age of eight years old, whether developmentally or chronologically. Our approach with younger clients would be different.

There are three distinct stages in the client process: Discovery Phase, Skill Building Phase, and Reinforcement Phase. When we provide equine-assisted psychotherapy at *Horse Sense*, much of our time is spent in the first two Phases: Discovery and Skill Building. In the Discovery phase, the client is focusing on discovering identity, what's happening in his world, and how he feels and reacts to circumstances. Equine-assisted practice is a wonderful discovery tool to access information about one's thoughts, perceptions and emotions without needing the cognitive and language skills necessary to share this information with another person. It's also a great way for more holistic learners to integrate information. Equine-assisted work allows the client access to this information cleanly, without the interpretive lens of someone else's experience or thoughts. It also allows the client to better see the "filters" on his own lenses.

THE CLASSIC CLIENT SERIES, SESSION ONE TO COMPLETION

The Discovery Phase: The Client and Her World

In session, we begin in Discovery, and may stay in that phase for a long time. As a client develops awareness and insight, we'll likely move on to more Skill Building-type activities. The beginning of the Discovery Phase, for us as facilitators, is also an assessment phase, where we seek to discover what is presenting itself as the most pressing issue(s). But first, before any arena/horse time, an office intake/assessment is completed.

Most of our individual clients begin the therapy process in our office with a mental health professional, working through some form of intake procedure. Before coming into contact with the horses, we try to determine if equine-assisted work is a good fit and an appropriate strategy for helping a particular client with his issues. Although there are a number of reasons why we might suggest that EAP is not a fit for a client, some of the situations under which we've actually referred a client out include: clients who were actively delusional and not taking prescribed medications, clients who were actively using drugs or alcohol, or clients who had a pattern of arson or of assaulting their therapist. Oddly enough, a pattern or indication of past animal abuse perpetrated by a client is not, by itself, grounds for referral out of our program. To some degree, if such a person is not working with a group of professionals like us, then this important interaction may never take place. Of course, I don't want to put my horses in harm's way, but I also believe horses might be the most viable opportunity for a client facing these challenges to experience a shift in perspective.

The assessment/clinical intake process determines what the issues are, what's stuck, and what brought the client to our door. After this initial session, subsequent sessions take place at the barn. Oftentimes, the initial office visit will end with a brief tour around the farm, an introduction to the Equine Specialist, and a time for questions from the client.

OBSERVATION

Once we move on to horse session work, the full team takes shape: the mental health professional, the Equine Specialist, and the horses. Virtually every client will start out with the same initial activity: Observation. The client is invited to observe several (often 2-3) horses loose in an arena on one side of a partition while the team and the client watch from the outside.

Although the mental health professional and the ES have already shared fundamental information regarding the client and the client's issues/challenges, this initial Observation session is a great opportunity for the ES to evaluate what's happening with the client with his or her own eyes. With limited information regarding potential diagnoses or the client's "story," this "clean read" can create the foundation for supporting change for the client. The ES takes note of anything observed during this exercise, documenting it for use in future sessions.

Instructions for the client during Observation, and often throughout the entire treatment process, are extremely simple and open-ended. The client is asked to observe the horses. We may or may not offer a lens through which to observe, such as, "Watch how the horses interact with one another," or "Notice what you can learn about them by watching how they communicate." We'll encourage silence from the client during this Observation activity by maintaining our own silence (sometimes for a couple of minutes, or for a whole session, or more). Sometimes we'll invite the client to carry out this activity using "horse rules," which we explain as not speaking to the horses, to herself or to us. Sometimes we invite the client not to touch the horses unless the horse touches her first—which is much more difficult to do than it sounds!

This simple Observation exercise reveals an incredible amount of information to the trained treatment team, and sometimes creates an epiphany for the client as well. Through silence and simple observation, this activity allows everyone to become present to the moment in the arena, to their senses and to their environment. The client has the opportunity to get used to the horses from a comfortable distance, so she is not thrown into the middle of the action with 1,000-pound prey animals at liberty. For some clients, this might be their first exposure to horses. If this time of silence and observation proves to be a challenge for a client, even this information gives the team some direction for future treatment/sessions. At this point, both the non-verbal language of the client and the behavior of the horses in response to the client are being noted. The client's level of engagement in the observation process is also evaluated. During this Observation session, a bit of a baseline about the physical presentation of the client is often established; this baseline may be helpful in later sessions.

People ask me, "How do you know the horses are responding to the client, and not to you or the mental health professional, or to the weather?" It's a great question, and points to the need for the horse professional to know her horses really well, having observed them in lots of different circumstances and in all kinds of weather. Similarly, if treatment team members are calm and centered, chances are high that the horses are responding to the client, not to the team. More will be said about team members, their presentation and their impact on clients and horses later in this book.

In this initial activity, having a barrier—a fence, a panel, whatever—between the humans and the horses is something we find really important because many, many clients are uncertain or outright afraid of horses. During this first activity, we're careful to create a generous degree of space between horse and human so people don't feel that we have thrown them "into the deep end." As we move further into our work with the client, we adjust this degree of space—from the "comfort" zone, which is fully relaxed, to the "learning" zone, characterized by a degree of discomfort, to the "fear" zone, where nothing matters beyond survival (See Figure 3.1). In the Learning Zone, the client is awake, present, and paying attention; this is the optimum zone for change and learning to take place. In contrast, little, if any, learning takes place in the Fear Zone; we don't want to push a client into that

Fear Zone during this initial encounter with horses or, arguably, at any point during her time with the horses. With that in mind, having a barrier between horses and clients during the Observation session with the horses is key to creating an environment where there is little concern for client safety. So much of this early process is about creating a safe space for the client, not by actively trying to build rapport, but by listening deeply to what she has to say and to what she notices during the experience.

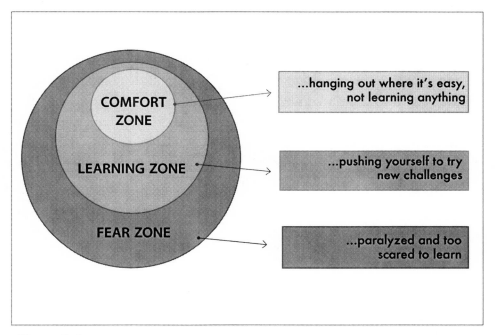

Figure 3.1
Learning Zones

The great thing about this first exercise is that we get to learn about the client's world through her own eyes. In asking the client to describe what she sees, the language reveals a great deal about what's going on and how she is interpreting the world. We look at both what the client is saying and what the client is not saying, noticing also the body language of the client while speaking and whether she is moving around, etc. What does the body language reveal about the client's internal state? This discussion with the client about what she is noticing during observation of the horses opens a big window revealing what's going on inside the mind of the client. If the client isn't inclined or interested in sharing perceptions at this point, we don't push.

At some point, the timing will be right—often when there is a long lull in activity or during a flurry of activity—to ask the client what she is noticing, about the horses, herself or both. Often we'll encourage her to remain facing the horses while responding to our inquiries, so she stays connected with the horses instead of turning her eyes and attention to us and her back to the horses. Or, we'll join her along the fence-line, shoulder-to-shoulder, as she responds to our inquiries. For many clients, they pick up quite quickly on the idea that perception is reality, and that we tend to see the world as we are, not as it is. At this point, some clients will recognize the pattern in their own responses/observations and experience a valuable 'aha' moment. Others may be unable to participate at that level of listening yet, which is just fine. Regardless, what clients notice about the horses during this initial activity usually reflects more on their own experience rather than on the actual behaviors of the horses.

During this initial activity, I've had clients immediately relate very insightful remarks, saying something like, "Those two horses are biting on one another. That's my mom and dad. And that third horse in the corner, looking out the window? That's me. I just want to get out." This kind of deeper information is less likely to be shared by the client in an office environment. Other times, clients notice that all their observations relate to how the horses see them, rather than to how they see the horses. Even in our youth groups, Observation is an activity we do every time, every session, if only for the first few minutes. There are still other clients who remain fairly shut-off during this initial session; sometimes a bit of coaxing is appropriate; sometimes we'll simply move on.

More than a Mirror, by Shannon Knapp

We may move further into the process, asking additional questions like: "Which of these horses would you choose to interact with right now? What draws you to this horse?" We've led group activities where we assign each person to be the voice of one of the horses, asking the group to put human language to the herd's actions. With other groups, we'll invite everyone to close their eyes, and have each group member take a turn describing what the horses are doing. Then, we'll invite them all to open their eyes. We'll ask, "Are the horses where you thought they would be, based on the descriptions/observations you heard?" Again, we gain tremendous insight by what the client says, and can adjust this activity in a variety of ways to better suit the client or group.

However, this is also one activity that, if facilitated poorly, can "out" clients in a manner that overexposes them. This is not the way we wish to meet our clients and support them in their growth. At its core, we use this first activity to allow a client to get his bearings and get used to the environment and also to get used to being around horses. The insight gained by the treatment team through observation of the client and his initial interaction with the horses is invaluable.

Throughout the entire Discovery phase, periods of intense dialogue with the client are unlikely. We will respond to most questions by the client with open-ended answers, continually referring him back to himself and the wisdom that comes from his personal insight. We will be looking for gaps in his perception or in his process. For example, a client might read an interaction between two horses as "loving" when it's actually the exact opposite. If we observe a client reading his world through a particular lens, like all behavior from horses as loving or all behavior from horses as dangerous, we'll take note of that interpretation for future exploration.

If the treatment team fields a lot of questions from the client about the horses, we'll encourage the client to continue observing, often inviting him to behave as a detective in regards to the horses. Reminding the client that he will have plenty of opportunities to observe a horse's particular behavior or body posture, we invite him to gather evidence of when the behavior occurs and what appears to be going on at that moment. We also encourage the client to note when the behavior does not occur. In this way, we position the client to become "a person gathering information towards a hypothesis" rather than "a person seeking answers from others." It's a philosophy comparable to the adage "teach a man to fish" instead of "give a man a fish." If we provide answers to questions like: "Why does the horse bite the wood?" or "Is that horse angry or sad?"—we remove the opportunity for the client to practice this detective-like approach. The detective exercise also removes the shame that some clients may feel for not having all the answers; this shame can often impede client progress. Finally, asking questions is often an indication that the client feels outside his comfort zone. When a client asks many questions, we believe the client is engaged, there is a high probability that he is already outside his comfort zone, and there is curiosity. These three elements combine to create a great opportunity for learning! Allowing the client to experience this form of discomfort leads him to practice a key concept: being comfortable with discomfort, and learning how to gather information and determine his own answers when there is no one else to ask. This is a fundamental element of our approach in equine-assisted practice and, from the early stage of therapy, just one way our work begins to parallel life.

SAFETY

Before we move clients into the next activity, usually the "Meet and Greet," safety issues are discussed. Safety is always a big topic in the field of equine-assisted practices. Whenever there are 1,000-pound prey animals wandering around "at liberty" (without halters or lead ropes), a very interesting dynamic is created. In addition to not being

More than a Mirror, by Shannon Knapp

naturally comfortable when around horses, most people have little or no means to interpret equine body language at this stage.

We don't present a long list of "do" and "don't" rules which might be found at many horse barns. We, quite deliberately, leave this aspect open-ended. In our experience, specifying an extended list of safety rules creates a dynamic that potentially inhibits the process. Especially for our oppositional clients, which we encounter often given our focus with youth, the more rules that are presented to them, the more opportunities they have to focus on rules they can try to break.

In saying that, however, we don't take a completely hands-off approach either. "Let's just throw everyone together and see what the natural consequences are," is not a theory we espouse. Rather, it's the job of the horse professional to know each situation well enough to anticipate the likelihood of something undesirable developing, and to circumvent such dynamics in the least intrusive way possible. It is important to remember what Greg Kersten said at early EAGALA trainings, "The answer to a 'could' question is always, 'Yes'" (Could the horse kick me? Could the horse run over me?). As an Equine Specialist, the actions I can take to mitigate the negatives of a possible "yes" answer today is always on my mind.

As we prepare to enter the arena with a client or a group for the first time, one of the ways we introduce the idea of safety is to ask, "While we're in there, if you should feel unsafe or uncomfortable at any time, what are three things you can do to take care of yourself in the moment?" We then highlight the three things, visually, by counting off the ideas and holding up the corresponding fingers for each one. This often elicits suggestions such as "I'll stand by you" or "I'll step outside the arena" and so on. There is often conversation among groups as they discuss whether an idea is a good one or not. We've had people recommend, "Run full speed and jump over the fence!" We're happy to have discussion around that idea, and may also interject comments about the merit of other particular ideas, although usually we don't need to: the clients and groups usually arrive at useful conclusions themselves.

Since we emphasize coming up with "three things" to do in such a situation, we ask the client or group **why** we might be keen on having them list three items. The exercise of coming up with multiple resolutions to a situation is often fruitful, in itself, for clients who haven't had this modeled for them before, who are impulsive and reactive, or are not likely to think through various possibilities before acting. Important territory can be covered in this introduction to safety, not least of which is that it encourages the client to take ownership of her own safety. This "three things exercise" is covered on the Brainstorming Options Skill Card (more about Skill Cards later in this chapter).

When we discuss safety options with the client or a group, we also offer a fourth option—what we call the "Time Out." We are careful to explain that a Time Out doesn't mean anyone is in trouble; it simply means we're hitting the "pause button" on the game and the client or group should gather near where the therapy team is standing in the arena. If we observe something that causes us to be uncomfortable, we can call a Time Out; if a client sees something or feels uncomfortable about something, either with regard to herself or to another horse or human, she can call a Time Out. We explain that Time Out applies to everyone, and does not apply just to the person who feels uncomfortable. We then circle up and take a minute to discuss what's going on, beginning by asking, "So what might have caused us to call that Time Out?" This simple question ignites wonderful discussions about situational awareness. Sometimes, everyone knows exactly why the Time Out was called. At other times, half the group isn't aware of a possible safety situation, or that someone in the group might "read" a situation differently from the rest. Again, it's a great opportunity for discussion.

When we do have a particularly good reason for concern over physical safety, we will often first remove the client from the situation

More than a Mirror, by Shannon Knapp

without highlighting it as a safety issue. We might ask the client to "come over here for a second," or to "circle up over here real quick" and then ask her to talk about the situation she just left. We may or may not explain anything we noticed in great detail. While our goal is to maintain safety, we also don't want to lose the potential for additional insight to be gained by the client. How aware is the client of her own world? How aware is she of the physical environment, "situational awareness," and safety? If we provide too many rules on the front end, we limit access to information that could help the client later. For example, if the client starts to go marching into the middle of a situation where two horses are getting rowdy and playful, with no awareness of the potential safety issues, that's information for us and for her. We might draw the client's attention to this and ask if it bears any resemblance to real-life situations in which she has been involved.

Before entering the arena for the Meet and Greet, we will often invite the client to identify, using a scale of 1-10, the current level in terms of comfort and relaxation, or nervousness and anxiety (or outright fear) when she thinks of going into the arena with the horses. The 1 on the scale represents feeling "very calm" and 10 means "I'm probably too close to the horses where I'm standing right now." (Depending on the situation, we will sometimes do this scale exercise before we introduce the idea of safety.) Many times, in groups of youth, we might hear a bunch of 1's, or even negative numbers. We recognize the peer pressure of the moment pushes youth clients to report feeling "cool and calm." When we're faced with a group of 12-year-olds who all report being at 1, we'll circumvent the "cool factor" by reporting where we are on the scale as well. Lori Araki, who's been an Equine Specialist with *Horse Sense* since 2009, came up with the following explanation, "Well, I'm actually at about a 5 or 6 now, since all of you are at 1 or below. I'm that high on the scale because I worry that you're so calm that you are no longer paying attention to your own safety." This invites wonderful discussion from the group about the difference between being cool and being safe, and about the relationship between excitement and anxiety: "What's the difference between excitement/anticipation and anxiety? Does excitement turn into anxiety? What is that progression like for you?" We also ask the group to identify what we (as a group) could do to help each of them come down on their scale if they reported being at a 5 or higher.. Finally, we invite them to tell us if/when that number spikes for them at any point while they are in the arena. At this point, we have fully covered issues of safety. We reiterate the Time Out concept and proceed into the arena.

MEET AND GREET

The next activity a client is likely to engage in at *Horse Sense* is Meet and Greet. As in previous activities, this exercise develops at the client's speed, not the speed of the therapy team. This is especially true if the client has deep fear issues with horses. With the Meet and Greet, we invite the client to meet the horses in whatever way feels comfortable. Again, we intentionally leave this activity as open-ended as possible. By using this strategy, we see a lot of variance between clients. We see how the clients show up in their world rather than hearing how they think they show up. There's not a meta-conversation going on about the process; we are witnessing the process itself.

When we invite the client to "meet the horses in whatever way feels appropriate and/or comfortable," we might tell him that this is an opportunity to learn something more about each horse and to allow the horses to learn something more about him. Some will hear this as an instruction to walk straight up to the horses, shoulders back, petting each one on the nose. Others might hear an instruction to spend twenty minutes with one horse, cautiously circling around his field of vision. Or, still others might wait for the horse to approach him by putting himself in the horse's field of vision and then waiting for the horse to close the gap. Not only are there many different ways for the exercise to progress, the exercise also reveals many things about the client.

For the client and for us, it's a process of observing reflex responses, reactions and skills.

As we begin the Meet and Greet, we don't provide the client a whole lot of information on the front end about how to introduce himself to horses; we don't want to limit his interpretation and expression of this action. We're not as concerned with ideas of success or successfully connecting with the horses at this point as we are with examining the tools already in the client's "toolkit." What choices does the client make? What is the default behavior?

Usually, if one approaches a horse laterally rather than squarely from the front, the horse is more likely to stand still and allow contact. But we're not providing that kind of information to the client at this point, because that would impact his natural approach. This would affect the kind of information we obtain from how the client approaches the horse, which we associate with how he approaches his world. We want to know how the client shows up in his own life right now, and this kind of activity provides a strong indication of that. We create scenarios where this type of information comes to the surface in ways that illuminate how the treatment team can help, or how a client can see and understand these issues for himself, perhaps for the first time, or in a new way.

During this exercise it's not unusual for a client to admit, "I've known this about myself (that I'm quiet, that I'm shy, that I'm angry) in my head for so long, but I didn't understand how that impacted people's response to me until now." The horse's response provides evidence in a non-biased manner, allowing a client to get a chance to learn and assess things about himself at a level he usually hasn't understood before. The experiential aspect of equine-assisted work shifts this awareness to the whole body rather than just in an intellectual capacity, and sets the stage for this awareness to become part of the process of change.

At this point in our classic therapy client series, there might be all sorts of conversation. "What was that like?" or "How was that for you?" are among the questions we might ask after the client finishes introducing himself to the horses. The client's interpretation of what happened reveals volumes about how the client shows up in his world, and provides insights into how he is reading the world. This is often where our first EAP session will end.

As much as we're paying attention to the client in these initial sessions, we're also paying equal attention to the horses and their response to the client. How does the horse respond to a client's approach? What actions does the horse allow and what does the horse reject? Is the horse indifferent? Intrigued? For example, we once had a young man who was doing Meet and Greet and one of our kindest, sweetest horses literally turned her nose up at him and walked away. We'd rarely, if ever, seen her respond this way, so that kind of information was really significant to the treatment team, a unique occurrence to be sure. We might not know exactly what the horse's response meant, but we know it's unique and worth acknowledging and tracking. Of equal importance is the client's interpretation of the horse's response: are all actions read as negative bordering on aggressive? As loving and positive?

Our clients engage in the Observation and Meet and Greet process almost every time they come to the farm. We'll either expand or shorten that time based on what the treatment goals are, and what we're seeing from the horses and client. We'll use our assessment from these two exercises to move the treatment series forward. As we often say to the client, "It's never the same river twice," as nothing is ever exactly the same as the day before, the month before, or the minute before. This acknowledges the concept that change is constant. Taking time, if only for a few minutes, to check in with ourselves and the horses in this moment on this day, is an important opportunity to model taking one's own emotional temperature and awareness of change.

MOVE A HORSE

Our first two activities in equine-assisted psychotherapy tend to be fairly passive and reflective in nature. Upon completing these, if we feel we have a pretty good chunk of information about the client, we may move toward something that's a little more active, assessing skills in motion. Observing the horses can be a very outside-in sort of process and, while we're not asking much of the horse, these exercises can sometimes ask a lot of the client. There may be many weeks' worth of material here, especially when dealing with issues of trauma and anxiety, where these first three exercises may be the bulk of a client's treatment.

After early observation-type exercises, we have a much better sense about the most beneficial kind of "Skill Building" activities for the client. There's no magic in these activities; these are just activities designed to create scenarios where behavior patterns show up and come to the surface for examination. We design activities to "draw the poison"—the life challenges or issues—to the surface and highlight areas that seem significant.

One of our favorite next activities for a session is to ask the client to choose a horse and then move him from one side of the arena to the other, or to bring a horse to the therapy team. While some clients may be very comfortable and confident performing this task, others may be completely overwhelmed. Once again, we specifically refrain from providing more than basic direction; the more rules, the more props, the more direction we provide, the more we limit what happens, and subsequently, the more we limit what the client learns during the process.

As clients undergo the trial-and-error process of each activity with the horse, we begin to see how the client reacts when she lack skills, knowledge, or information to get a job done. How does she respond to the challenge of not knowing? What tools does she bring out? We design each scenario in the arena to mimic real-life situations, situations the client may be facing in the world. As the client demonstrates how she currently responds to these challenges, more conversation takes place between the mental health professional, the horse professional, and the client about how well that approach is working and what she might like to do differently.

The exercise "Move a Horse" begins significantly changing the dynamic in the arena. The client goes from not asking anything of the horse to asking for something definitive and specific. Think about it this way: if you're going out to dinner with a group of friends, you can relax and just enjoy the company and the food. But if you're going out to dinner and you want to sell something to your friends, like a product or a service, oftentimes your whole approach to the situation changes. The same thing happens when you start asking something of the horse in the arena. How the client changes in this process often tells us where to spend time as we move forward.

During the Discovery stage, one of the most common thoughts shared by clients is that all the horses' actions are a direct result or response to them (the client). To some degree this is true, and a lot of equine-assisted psychotherapy is based on this principle, but the way our clients articulate this is what causes it to be a problem area. For example, if she is approaching a horse, and the horse suddenly raises her head and runs off, individuals and some groups will often say "the horse doesn't like me". At this, we'll likely ask them to, "Name three reasons the horse moved away that doesn't have anything to do with you." We'll then count them up on our fingers, for all to see, making a point of having three answers, such as: "He was frightened by something," "He wanted to be with his friend over there," or "He wanted to scratch his butt on the fence." Rather than directly challenging the client's opinion about the cause of the horse's behavior, we open the door for other interpretations. I find this to be extremely effective with broadening a client's perspective beyond herself.

More than a Mirror, by Shannon Knapp

One side note in regard to some of the activities commonly used in EAGALA-model equine-assisted psychotherapy: I've seen many instances where professionals are tempted to use these activities as a "gotcha" tactic with clients, i.e., "If you'd only realized you could use the lead rope to do this, you could've been done ten minutes ago." This activity should not be used as any kind of weapon to make the client feel foolish or stupid for not knowing better. That tactic is not at all beneficial for the client. That's the ego of the facilitators getting in the way of the client's process. Shame and humiliation are never a part of good therapy, whether equine-assisted or not.

At its best, this activity is not about looking for definitive "right vs. wrong" thinking, answers, or skill sets. We're looking for clues into the client's coping patterns, no matter what solution she devises. What alternatives does the client think of? In what phase of the problem-solving process does the point of breakdown occur for the client? What options does the client not think of?

Anne Wilson Schaef, author of *Living in Balance: Truths for Living the Path of the Soul*, has a wonderful quote, now tacked to my bulletin board: "Insight and understanding are interesting; neither heals." With equine-assisted practice, we see how understanding and awareness can be a part of the process towards healing but how they, by themselves, are not necessarily what provides healing for many people. So much of traditional therapy is about accessing and understanding insight and awareness. But we know it goes beyond that; understanding the problem doesn't guarantee a solution.

Equine-assisted therapy and learning takes the typical practice of "insight and understanding" and adds other elements: experience and practice. Imagine if your therapist not only talked with you in session, but then shadowed you during a restaurant dinner with your husband or while you were interacting with people throughout the day, listening in on your conversations, observing others' reactions to you. Indeed, the therapist may learn a great deal about your relationships and how you show up in your world. Those scenarios are comparable to the process of equine-assisted therapy—observing people in a real-time interaction instead of discussing that interaction during an office visit.

However, if being shadowed in your daily routine by your therapist sounds mildly uncomfortable, it probably would be. And that dynamic of being "watched" in equine-assisted psychotherapy sometimes triggers reflexive self-consciousness in clients, if not actively mitigated by the facilitators. This requires flexibility and sometimes creativity on the part of the facilitators, and can present a very real impediment to therapy. We work to create an environment in the arena in which everyone is able to observe the dynamics in a neutral setting where there's far less at stake, "shoulder-to-shoulder" with the treatment team, rather than face-to-face. Shoulder-to-shoulder is a "we" perspective; face-to-face is more confrontational and oppositional: I vs. You. We are mindful of our physical presence and location in relation to the client as a treatment team in circumstances when self-consciousness has been triggered. Similarly, a treatment team chatting while a client is in process can push a self-conscious client over the edge!

Another area that can be especially (and rightly) troubling for clients and needs to be actively managed by the treatment team is the use of shaming language. I've seen one too many equine-assisted professional explain an activity to a group poorly and then blame that group for not following the rules or understanding the directions. It's a trap for the treatment team, one that tends to be encouraged by some models or ways in which activities are set up.

When possible, I believe a treatment team is at its best when the mental health professional and the horse professional all but blend into the background. I call it "going 2-D" or "flattening out"—while still being very much available to the client in time of need, concern, or distress. In Parelli™ Natural Horsemanship, this is called being in neutral. We want to blend into the background and allow the client an opportunity to learn about himself as much as possible through interacting with the horses.

There's no right or wrong in any of these initial activities (indeed in virtually any activities in the Discovery Phase), although many clients have an attachment to the idea that there is only one right way. As a treatment team, we work to de-construct the idea that, if the client just knew the one "right way," all would be well.

As we move into the next phase, which is more about Skill Building, if the team feels it is appropriate and/or necessary, we'll explain how the treatment team is going to show up in this part of the treatment process. That conversation might sound something like this:

> We're moving into a new phase of our time together, and during this, we'll be asking you to try out new things without necessarily having a rule-book or a set of instructions about how to do them. You might turn and ask us how to do something, and we may not answer. The reason we're doing that is that out in the world you may find yourself in a situation where you don't know what to do, and you won't have someone there to ask. We're recreating that to some degree here, to help you develop problem-solving skills.

This next period in treatment represents a transition period: in one session we may be in Discovery, and in the next, working in Skill Building. We're acutely aware of how the client is responding to his environment, and how the horse is responding to the client, and this directs our approach at any given time.

The Skill Building Phase: What's in the Toolkit?

There are no hard and clear lines between the Discovery Phase and the Skill Building Phase of the process at *Horse Sense*; it's about knowing when there is enough information and when is the appropriate time to begin developing tools together to add to the client's toolkit. In an average eight-week equine-assisted psychotherapy series, we might spend four to five sessions in Skill Building.

For many clients, there comes a time when the Discovery Phase offers diminishing returns. Clients need a transition to concrete skill building, and then ample opportunity to practice those skills. There's only so much awareness that one person can hold at a time and still expect to integrate and move forward with changes. Too much Discovery can become unproductive.

"Pure" EAGALA—Anti–Skill Building?

There are those who would say any kind of skill building is the opposite of the EAGALA process, that all time and attention should be spent in the Discovery Phase. Certainly there are clients and populations for whom this is true.

And yet, even in traditional therapy, there is a fair amount of psycho-educational and skill building work that takes place, and the same is true in equine-assisted psychotherapy. During this Skill Building phase we might teach about life skills, coping skills, or communication styles. I believe there is room within the EAGALA model for teaching skills.

Some professionals believe that skill building is inherent in the EAGALA model, feeling clients learn experientially by participating in an activity in an EAP/EAL session. Perhaps the difference is not so much on what happens, but the language we use for it: skill building, or some other term. Clients often discover their own new skills through the activities in session.

I understand the need for having a model and also value the benefits of having a model; it clarifies the practice and provides structure and guidelines. But over-reliance on any model at the expense of a client can be damaging. Sacrificing the horse or the client to serve a model is not part of our process; our priorities at Horse Sense are to meet the client where they are, not where a model might want them to be.

Oftentimes, when adults approach us for equine-assisted learning (as opposed to therapy), they are asking for work in the Skill Building Phase: they have a sense of what's wrong and what they want to work on, and are looking for another way to do so, but aren't looking for therapy. With this type of client, we often won't do an intake, but will discuss goals and the circumstances bringing the client to our door. We often have life and business coaches, along with our mental health professional and Equine Specialist, conduct the initial session or two with his client out with us and the horses, to help everyone better understand the challenges facing the client. For example, a client may be aware that his interpersonal style is overbearing, which creates problems at work. He may come to us trying to find ways to soften the delivery and be more relatable to people. In this scenario, we'll spend a brief amount of time in the Discovery Phase, determining if the horses and the client still feel that what the client reports as the issue initially is really the challenge, and then move relatively quickly into a skill building component. We are also mindful that we may need to slow down at any given point, if suggested by the horses!

What if the issue the client perceives isn't the one the identified by the horse? What might the suggestion from the horse look like? Let's take that example client who reports self-awareness of being overbearing in the work environment. Our initial Discovery Phase with the horse may bear this out. Yet, as we move into Skill Building, we may find that the horses are not picking up as much on "overbearing" tendencies as on a "lack of self-confidence," a bravado that can present as being overbearing. Some of our horses might respond to an overbearing client by moving away, and respond to a client lacking self-confidence by doing nothing. In such a circumstance, we would slow down the exercise and ask the client what he sees in the exchange, if he could find another explanation for the horse's behavior. A phrase you might hear in our barn is: "The question isn't the question; the problem isn't the problem." What first presents as the question or the problem may just be the surface!

Overall, though, our goal with the EAL or the Skill Building Phase client is to move relatively quickly into activities that draw forth the skills to affect the change clients are seeking, whether they are self-awareness, interpersonal, or leadership-based. Our work with this client helps him create additional tools to put in his toolkit. This client can see us for an eight-week cycle of sessions, or for just a few sessions. It's all up to what the client needs.

Skill Identification

Part of the *Horse Sense* process includes identifying necessary skills for success. For example, if assertiveness is an issue, we strive to set up opportunities in which the client can experience and practice this skill with the horses. We want the client to identify and demonstrate what the behavior looks like and feels like in herself and to talk about the impact this behavior has on the horse.

For many clients, the first hurdle is reading the non-verbal and social cues from another being, or in trusting what they are reading. Horses provide an ultra-large canvas for reading body language and learning how our self-presentation registers with another being. We then invite the client to experiment with different variations of any given skill's body language (like assertiveness, for example) while noticing how the horse responds. Once the client understands the skill and has experienced it in action with her own body, it becomes a matter of practicing it and refining it over a number of sessions.

Another hurdle for a client might be understanding how her own physical presentation affects the response of the horse. If the skill to be addressed is assertive leadership, inviting the client to "embody" (mimic) an assertive leader she admires and then to approach the horse as if she were that person might generate some positive shifts in presentation, and a shift in response from the horse. We might then discuss what was different about how the client initially presented, and what changed when embodying someone else who is a good leader. Was there something different about her eyes? Her shoulders? Her speed in walking? What were the elements that shifted?

Utilizing Additional Skill building Tools: Horse Sense's Skill Cards

Over the years, our work revealed a standard set of issues being worked on by many of the clients we were encountering. Through our experience with these clients, we developed *Horse Sense Skill Cards*, which we now use regularly to support our work in the arena. For example, our experience with adjudicated and at-risk youth revealed they (as a group) were consistently lacking a very specific set of skills. So, borrowing an idea from the Parelli™ curriculum—a set of pocket-size laminated cards that could be used in the arena as a reference— we developed a deck of "Skill Cards." I loved this idea; cards that helped teach students to teach themselves (rather than teaching students to chase down an instructor).

The Skill Cards help those clients who can benefit through the use of a tangible teaching component to reinforce life skills. Each card identifies a skill and correlates that skill to human and horse, showing the parallels between them. We might start a session by selecting three Skill Cards and letting the client choose which one she would like to work on. (See Figure 3.2) The

Figure 3.2
Example of a Skill Card

more common Skill Cards we utilize with clients include: Observing my Environment, Knowing What My Body is Telling Me, Brainstorming Options, Problem-Solving, the Anger Scale, and Assertiveness (vs. Passive/Aggressive). Once we, as a team (client, therapist and Equine Specialist), decide what skill to work on, we'll develop a simple activity that helps the client practice that skill.

If the skill decided upon is Observing my Environment, we might ask the client to approach the horse in the pasture, giving us a "play-by-play" of what he is noticing as he is noticing it. This might sound like, "The horse is not looking at me, but his ear twitched when I stepped on that stick...," or "It's raining, and my rain pants are making a strange sound every time I step, and the horses are moving away from me...." If the client doesn't notice anything, we might ask him a few questions, such as, "What do you hear? What do you smell?" and so forth. We might utilize a skill like Problem-Solving in the "Move a Horse" activity (mentioned previously), inviting the client to walk through the six stages of problem-solving, determining where he is in the process and where he is getting stuck. Then, we might "Brainstorm Options" for getting unstuck. It's quite a fluid process!

The Skill Cards are a tactile tool for learners, some of whom aren't as adept at intellectualizing intangible concepts. The Skill Cards also draw attention to the fact that everyone is a learner, that we're not necessarily expected to know how to do everything without help. The Skill Cards remove a bit of the stigma from a client's challenge and normalizes whatever he is trying to learn, i.e., "If they have a Skill Card for it, I must not be the only person to have this challenge!" The Skill Cards are just one tool we've developed to help clients process information and address challenges. The Skill Cards are also a reference tool for the client when away from the farm.

One question that is often asked is: "What activity is best for X group?" There are plenty of activity guides available at EAP/EAL con-

ferences these days, many of them helpful in the planning and organization of groups or in creating a series of experiences for clients, or
for addressing particular populations, such as *Horse Sense*'s own *Body
Sense* for clients with Eating Disorders or *Running with Mustangs* for
At-Risk Youth. But there's a trend in the field among practitioners that
the "meat" of the work lies in the activity, when in fact it lies in the
experience with the horses. A metaphor I like to use to describe EAP
is that the therapist, the Equine Specialist, the arena, and the activity
serve as the table setting for a meal; they are the fork, the spoon, the
drinking glass. None of these, however, are the meal. The activity is a
vehicle driving the client to learn something or experience something
or understand something with the horses. Activities are constantly
designed by Equine Specialists to meet the immediate needs of the
client; hence I hesitate to put too much stock in any one activity.

Much of my inspiration for activities derives from playing the Parelli's Seven Games™ with horses. And the Seven Games™ themselves can
be activities for clients!

The Parelli Seven Games™ as Skill Building
Invoking Parelli's Seven Games™ in EAP/EAL is not about teaching
horsemanship; it's specifically about accessing and assessing the client's skills and process. Our purpose in utilizing the Seven Games™
changes in our EA practice depending on the stage we're working in
with the client. Each stage has its list of caveats. I do not want to put
a client in the position of being horse trainers. Horse training for me
is a particular skill, with a different process. I try to be aware of these
considerations when utilizing the Seven Games™ (or any activity!) in
sessions:

- It helps to let go of preconceived notions of how each Game or Natural
  Horsemanship task is supposed to look. Just as we un-train ourselves
  when learning specific aspects of equine-assisted practice, horse professionals have to set aside how they think a particular activity should
  look, and allow the client to make it his/her own. For example, a Parel-

li™ student follows very clear steps in order to execute the Circling Game™. With a client, however, it's likely we're not going to outline those specific steps. In fact, this same activity can take many forms. We would encourage a client to try out a few things rather than just giving him/her the steps. We want the client to determine what the steps are, then discuss whether the steps chosen are useful or effective after playing around with the process.

- I encourage leaving behind the "Name Game." We don't use the language of the Friendly Game™, or the Porcupine Game™ when playing the Seven Games™ at this stage. Later, when we get into Reinforcement, we might introduce the names. If we reference the specific games by name in these earlier phases, the client often senses a system, and therefore searches for right and wrong ways to work within that system. We're also concerned about prejudicing the experience of the activity by giving it a name. For example, "Porcupine" has a very specific visual and physical connotation along with a representative meaning. This reasoning is similar to those supporting the practice of not revealing the horses' names to clients.

- Like all elements in the Discovery & Skill building phases, the name assigned by a client to the Seven Games™ or the activity or task at hand can be very illuminating. We worked with a client who called the Friendly Game™ "Painting" because for him it evoked images of touching the entire horse as if to "color him in," This is a wonderful visual that would have been stifled had the activity been introduced with the title of "Friendly." As one of our clients pointed out, the words themselves have very little meaning with horses; it's how we say them. The same can be said for the names of activities!

- We need to be aware of how we match horses with humans when utilizing the Seven Games™. Think back for a moment to the concept of comfort zones in the learning process (see figure 2.1). Since learning takes place outside the comfort zone, we need to carefully manage the comfort and learning zones of both horse and human parties. We don't want to place a "green" horse, with his small comfort zone, alongside a human with a small comfort zone. Both parties can too easily step far enough outside the individual comfort zones to create a real problem, putting one or both into the fear zone. The phrase, "green on green makes black and blue" references the dynamic of this fundamental mismatch. A green horse and green rider both have small comfort

zones, and are prone to finding trouble that can often be counterproductive to the session work.

Clients come to us because circumstances in their lives are causing
disruption, or they've recognized change is necessary; to some degree,
they're already outside their comfort zone. I want to make sure that
my horses are comfortable being with people who are uncomfortable
and outside of their comfort zone. If the human has a small comfort
zone, we really want the horse to have a big comfort zone. Later, as we
get into the Seven Games™ as a Reinforcement Tool, we'll broaden our
focus more. At that point, the horse with the small comfort zone might
be matched to a human with a big comfort zone.

The Games in Session

In Chapter Two, I mentioned that Parelli™ Games 1-3 are considered
the Principle Games. The Principle Games are foundational; if something is "broken" or not functioning well with your horse, you can
usually trace it back to a problem with one of the first three Games.
Games 4-7 are considered the Purpose Games, where the Foundational
Games are put to use. If we've decided to implement the Seven Games™
with a client, we will likely start at the very beginning, the Principle
Games. However, each client comes to us from such a unique place that
flexibility is paramount in deciding what is necessary and appropriate. So even though we'll discuss the Seven Games™ in order here, you
may encounter a non-linear scenario, i.e., a parent who would be best
served developing fluency with the Yo-Yo Game™ before learning the
Porcupine Game™.

It is key to know that we are not teaching clients steps to "make"
a horse do something so much as we are helping clients make fundamental changes within themselves that affects how they show up
in the world, and how others respond to that behavior, i.e., the horses. In reference to the Parelli Games™, and to many Parelli™ concepts,
we've had clients who have taken the multiple lessons from the arena
back to the juvenile lock-down facility. It's particularly rewarding to

know Pat's saying, "Be passively persistent in the proper position," and other sayings can become mantras helping a kid manage his behavior in other areas of life.

The Friendly Game™

As you may recall, the Friendly Game™ uses touch and rhythmic motion to build trust between horse and human. Touch comes in the form of using the Carrot Stick™ and Savvy String™, the lead rope, or even the hands.

We approach the Friendly Game™ from an extremely simple perspective when using it with clients. Our instructions: "This is an opportunity to touch your horse all over. Notice when and where you have permission—and don't have permission—to touch the horse." We may have groom kits around and invite clients to use the tools as part of the activity, or we may tell them that each horse has a special scratchy spot where he loves to be scratched, challenging them to find it. A client may start out using the Carrot Stick™ and the Savvy String™ or he may start out using his hand; it depends on the client, the client's issues and the horses. There are many clients, specifically those who have been subjected to abuse, for whom the Carrot Stick™ is a big trigger. For these and certain other clients, the Carrot Stick™ usually needs to be introduced quite mindfully, if at all.

Generally, the treatment team or the Equine Specialist will not demonstrate this or any of the other games. Just like any other activity in this phase, the team is going to leave the instructions very open-ended, and see what manifests. We choose the Friendly Game™ when we're working to assess the client's ability to read social cues and body language. We've also used it for clients working toward understanding empathy. We sometimes structure the activity so it progresses from the Carrot Stick™/Savvy String™, to the lead rope, to hands.

As we move into more Skill Building, we might invite a client to "turn up the volume" on the Friendly Game by doing a "helicopter" with the Carrot Stick™ and Savvy String™, or doing Friendly by rubbing the horse all over with a tarp. This form of the activity draws attention to the client's body language, energy, and presentation, or the horse's body language or both together. As the emphasis switches, the Friendly Game presents multiple opportunities to talk about and to practice ways to build trust, rapport, and connection. This experience can be the pinnacle of a session or the pinnacle of a treatment series for clients with significant fear issues and abusive pasts. Using the Friendly Game™ to get close to the horse, to touch him, and then to touch him all over, has the potential to move some clients through really significant issues.

The Porcupine Game™

The Porcupine Game™ is a game of steady pressure, using touch on the chest, the nose, the shoulder, the hips, etc. to ask the horse to move away from pressure. We may set the situation up as, "Using as light a touch as possible, ask the horse to cross his back legs three times—moving his hind end away from you—while keeping his front legs inside a hula hoop on the ground," or "Ask the horse to back four steps."

This game is helpful for clients dealing with assertiveness, issues of fear, or lack of focus. When a client is struggling with focus, inducing movement from the horse can help her learn to bring attention back to a specific, particular task or situation. If a client's focused on what's happening on the other side of the barn, the horse tends not to listen; the response for focused vs. unfocused is very visible.

With the Porcupine Game™, we also might incorporate additional concepts, such as the idea of "Rub-Press-Rub." The Porcupine Game™ isn't just about applying pressure; there's a rub before and after the pressure that re-establishes "friendly." We also use this to reinforce the concept of the "Rewarding the Slightest Try" from the horse with the "Release that Teaches." The Porcupine Game™ is all about learning to time our interaction to provide release effectively; in this way, we can provide just the right amount of pressure with a release that rewards. We can also "rub" to show appreciation. The implications of each of these ideas on human relationships is often part of the discussion with clients.

The Driving Game™

The Driving Game™ is about moving a horse using rhythmic pressure. This can be a great game to address a variety of client issues: learning how to be consistent in behavior, learning how to follow through effectively, or learning how to establish boundaries. Asking a horse to stay out of your personal space is a powerful metaphor for other areas of life.

In session, we might set up the Driving Game™ by asking the client to move the horse four steps without touching. This is a very provocative idea for many clients who are convinced that the only way they can get something done, especially with a horse, is to use their hands or other tools in the arena. Some people can't imagine how they can influence a horse without hands or rope.

We worked with a 12-year-old who was dealing with issues of bullying at school. We gave her the opportunity to play the Driving Game™ with one of our more left-brain introvert "you and what army?" horses. Being on the small side, you can imagine her surprise when, after some trial and error, she successfully turned a 1000-pound horse 360 degrees just by wagging her finger at him. She looked at her finger as if it was a magic wand, astonished at her own power and ability to influence the world around her without "doing" anything. It was a pivotal moment for her. It's important to note that none of our horses are "push-button" horses, in that they don't know the Games™ so well that they do them without needing much from the client. Our horses are present enough and savvy enough that, if the client doesn't embody and mean it, they won't do it!

The Porcupine Game™ and the Driving Game™ also offer opportunities to bring up the concept of Phases. As referenced earlier, Parelli™ has students start with Phase 1 pressure, gradually applying greater and greater pressure up to Phase 4 until the horse responds. The very instant the human feels a response from the horse, the human releases pressure. In the Discovery Phase, we may learn that a client is ineffective disciplining her children because she only utilizes a Phase 2 pressure. Another client may go straight to Phase 4 pressure as a default setting. In the Skill Building phase, we can actually help clients find more effective answers on their own by using "Phases" with the horse's response as feedback. The client who is often passive can learn to become more effective; the client with aggressiveness issues can learn to modulate pressure. Learning about, practicing and playing with Phases are significant learning opportunities.

The Yo-Yo Game™

The Yo-Yo Game™ asks the horse to back away and then return to us in a straight line. This game can be especially effective for a client dealing with issues of respect, personal space, communication, and boundaries. Learning to be "firm and fair without being mean or mad"—like utilizing the four Phases—can be very hard for a predator/human.

When we utilize the Yo-Yo Game™, we may begin by having a client practice using the lead rope tied to the top of the fence, feeling the effort required for each of the Phases, getting comfortable with gradually increasing the pressure and practicing the release. Many clients are loathe to try tasks with the Carrot Stick™, Savvy String™, halter, and lead rope attached to the horse because they are afraid it's going to hurt the horse. It's a great door into the client's world, if the Carrot Stick™ should be an object of concern.

Simulations with inanimate objects are very productive with clients, and we'll use the fence with clients who are afraid to go to Phase 4 with the horse—or with a human—as they don't know what their Phase 4 looks like, or they only know their Phase 4 as an emotional outburst and it scares them. We may start with a fence, progress to doing the simulation with the therapist or the Equine Specialist playing the role of the horse, and culminate in doing Phases with an actual horse. We often see clients progress through a pendulum pattern. Before someone who is stuck at one end of the pendulum can access a middle ground, they almost, by necessity, have to swing completely to the other end of the pendulum first. Because of this pendulum dynamic, we often choose to do simulations without the horses, which saves time and anxiety (and horses!).

We have found the Yo-Yo Game™ useful for parents struggling with interacting with their child as a friend while also trying to be a parent. For example, we had one parent who was struggling with being effective with her kids when disciplining. She was afraid to go beyond Phase 2. We took the Carrot Stick™ and the Savvy String™, set out a plastic chair, and invited her to practice getting a really clear idea of what each phase looked like and progressing through the Phases from 1 to 4, then dropping rapidly back down to Phase 1. In her first few tries, she was stuck in Phase 2. However, when she was finally able to move past Phase 2, the flood gates opened and she jumped past Phases 3 and 4, beating the chair within an inch of its life, literally destroying it.

By first providing an opportunity to simulate the Phases with an inanimate object, this parent was able to break through and find both ends of the pendulum—and then her center—without hurting anything except a chair. The exercise succeeded in helping her safely access the extreme end of the pendulum before finding the more appropriate center, something we would never want to happen with a horse, much less her child.

The Circling Game™
The Circling Game™ is a game about responsibilities, one that can help clients learn how to avoid micromanaging. In the Circling Game™,

there's the Send (asking the horse to move away to the outer perimeter of the circle), the Allow (allowing the horse to maintain the circle, with no interference or nagging from us) and the Bring Back (disengaging the hindquarters to stop the circle and bringing the horse back to facing in). When the horse is doing what we've asked, our job is to Allow (to remain quiet and in neutral).

The Circling Game™ is among the more complex games, and invokes mutual responsibilities for both horse and human, which is often how we utilize it with clients in session. The Circling Game™ is a dance—the client has a role and the horse has a role—and the human only leaves the neutral position when the horse fails to fulfill his responsibilities by changing gait or stopping. Both horse and human have a part in this activity, and a responsibility not to overtake or micromanage the other.

We might use the Circling Game™ as a way to define this concept of mutual responsibility. It's also an especially powerful way to bring visual attention to the concept of nagging. If the horse is going around a client in a circle, and the client is constantly tapping the Savvy String™/Carrot Stick™ behind him, or continually clucking or kissing to him to keep him moving eventually becomes a form of noise to the horse, i.e., nagging. It's not much different than asking your child to take out the trash and following behind him as he is doing it, repeatedly saying, "Take out the trash! Take out the trash!" The propensity to nag is information; it exhibits a form of distrust, and doesn't allow the other partner an opportunity to follow through on his responsibilities.

In the Circling Game™, we find that many of our clients don't have a "neutral." They only experience nagging, either as the giver or the receiver. The idea that they can ask for something, and trust a partner to do it, is a really interesting concept. The Circling Game™ allows for a physical, visual, somatic representation of a sometimes-nebulous concept like "neutral."

The Circling Game™ can also allow us to talk about having a true attitude of justice, or follow-through when a polite and reasonable request is ignored. In the Circling Game™, coming out of neutral when the horse fails to hold up her responsibility is a consequence. The horse learns that by maintaining her responsibility, she can influence the human to remain neutral.

There are consequences for our behavior, whether positive or negative, and sometimes the consequence means going to Phase 4. Although there can be a Phase 4 in any game, I've found the Circling Game™ offers the most clear-cut opportunity to talk about it and find the appropriate circumstances in which to invoke it. Having an attitude of justice is something we discuss as the client sorts out the use of Phases. We examine the concept that, while Phase 4 is the most extreme response, it can be applied without being accompanied by over-the-top emotion. Threats, tears, and anger are not a part of an attitude of justice.

The Sideways Game™

Sideways is a wonderful opportunity to talk about synchronization, or how to put a plan together. Like Problem-Solving, there are multiple steps involved in putting a plan together, and Sideways is a great representation of that. From the horse's point of view, the Sideways Game™ involves a lot of thought and coordination. Moving sideways isn't common in the wild. It involves synchronizing legs, feet, and bending the body without falling over oneself.

During this exercise, clients often end up thinking about how to set up a situation for success by helping the horse understand what they are asking. It involves clear communication, organization, and breaking down an activity into steps. The Sideways Game™ is also an opportunity to practice the concepts of "slow and right beats fast and wrong" and "take the time it takes." For many of our clients (and possibly for humans in general), the general disposition is towards obtaining fast

More than a Mirror, by Shannon Knapp

results. Success at the Sideways Game™ requires the opposite of this. Often the faster we try to get somewhere without developing a good foundation, the more things fall apart.

What we ask of the horse in the Sideways Game™ is to "Think; Don't just react." Sideways is a wonderful opportunity to discuss how to de-escalate a problematic situation. "Sideways" becomes verbal shorthand in our sessions for "How can you center yourself and regroup?"

The Squeeze Game™

We often describe this in EAP/EAL as the "between, over or through" activity. The Squeeze Game™ is a visual, physical representation of spending a little bit of time in a difficult circumstance and then coming back out, with a goal of being able to be in challenging situations without responding poorly. Many times the object of the squeeze is the trailer, but it can also be a gate, backing in and out of a stall, or even going over jumps and obstacles. Each of these "squeeze" circumstances can be claustrophobic situations for horses. Clients get to observe the horse experience this process, and can then consider how they can apply lessons learned to their own circumstances.

Additional concepts that accompany the Squeeze Game™ include the ideas of Touch and Go. Pilots use Touch and Go when they practice coming in for a landing: touching the wheels down to the ground, and then taking back off immediately. We have a Skill Card specifically covering this topic, as we find it to be a common challenge. We also liken this game to Dr. Stephanie Burns' concept of "move closer, stay longer." When fear is a prime motivator, often the most we can ask—of ourselves, others, and our horses—is to move just a little bit closer than the previous time, and then stay just a little bit longer before moving away from the situation, i.e., "move closer, stay longer." This concept is especially useful for clients when approaching difficult emotions. Big emotions create big fear for many clients. They can "touch and go" or practice "move closer, stay longer" without feeling like they have to stay mired in the emotion forever.

In a Squeeze Game™, we might set up the activity where the horse is asked to go between the client and a wall, progressively narrowing the space. Or we might ask the horse to proceed into a trailer or over a jump. The Squeeze Game™ is a wonderful opportunity for the client to see the horse's reaction to a potentially claustrophobic and scary situation, and for the client to realize how unfounded that fear might be. We've all heard of horses who won't cross small creeks, although we know that the creek won't hurt them. Who has the "right" perspective on the situation? What can the horse tolerate? How can the client help the horse see the scary circumstance in a different way? Clients can experiment with a situation in their own lives, one that may be similarly frightening. Who in their lives might have a different perspective on their situation that they might talk to? We don't suggest that clients' fears aren't founded; we're suggesting that those fears may have gotten out of proportion. That's the opportunity in the Squeeze Game™ for some clients.

After a period of time we and the client may find there are now a lot more tools in her toolkit, and may decide to close out treatment at this point. How do we close out treatment with a client? The end of treatment may be as clear as a horse coming over and nuzzling a client, or a horse backing up calmly and confidently at the suggestion of the client. We may simply reach a point at which the therapist suggests reviewing the original treatment goals and determining if it feels appropriate or necessary to continue work. Many times we invite clients to take a break between "rounds" of EAP, to live in and with the changes they have made in their lives and their behavior a bit before taking on a new round of issues/challenges. We will often take a picture of the client with the horse who had the most significant impact and give her a certificate of completion with the photo. We also invite the client to say goodbye in the same way she said hello: in whatever way feels comfortable.

In sum, many of the skills that clients are working on in session directly connect with their treatment goals. Again, during this Phase, the goal is not to teach horsemanship. We do introduce the halter, lead rope, Carrot Stick™ and Savvy String™, among other tools, but when we present the Games™ as activities to clients, we are very open-ended about them, offering very little instruction. A more instructional approach will take place in the next phase: Reinforcement.

THE REINFORCEMENT PHASE
Practice, Practice, Practice

Whether you call this Reinforcement or Refinement—either is correct—this Phase is about creating lots of practice opportunities for clients, about spending time in and moving a client from Conscious Competence (having to think and focus on a skill) to Unconscious Competence (where the skill becomes so natural they're not even aware of doing it). This phase is a life's journey!

There are many schemas and models for moving clients from a place of not knowing to knowing, including the Conscious Competence model. Although more time will be spent with this and other models in the next chapter, the stages in the Conscious Competence model are as follows:

1. **Unconscious Incompetence:** "I don't know what I don't know."
2. **Conscious Incompetence:** "I don't know a *lot*!"
3. **Conscious Competence:** "I am actively trying to do this skill."
4. **Unconscious Competence:** "I don't know when it became second nature for me to do it this way!"

In the Discovery Phase, we're usually spending a lot of time in the first two stages. In Skill Building, we're definitely in the third stage, and in Reinforcement, we're providing the time and opportunity to move clients from stage three to four. Read more about this in the next chapter.

At *Horse Sense*, the Reinforcement Phase is where we move into Horsemanship as the primary teaching tool. Reinforcement comes from the intersection of practice and knowledge, so when we're in this phase with clients, it becomes about practice, practice, practice—doing similar activities in new ways, sometimes with multiple horses and with a variety of horsenalities.

So why is more of a horsemanship-based approach appropriate for Reinforcement of life skills? It is appropriate for all the same reasons that we utilize horses in EAP/EAL: playing with horses provides multiple learning methods for understanding, including kinesthetic, auditory, and visual. The Reinforcement Phase is in-vivo, in the moment, allowing for correction and adaptation in real time, with real feedback about what's actually happening. Horses, unlike people, respond to us in the moment; often, people respond to us based on experiences from days, weeks, sometimes months in the past. We don't start in the past because if we did, we'd be putting ourselves, as facilitators, in the position of being the "experts" who simply need to teach a set of techniques to clients. While potentially fun and quickly rewarding for clients, this approach does not often yield long-term change.

As Tim Jobe and Bettina Shultz-Jobe say in their Natural Lifemanship™ program, "This is not designed to provide a metaphor for a relationship; what the client and the horse create together **is** a relationship." When we talk about providing Reinforcement skills with horses, our approach switches from inviting and exploring metaphors for life to providing practice in life.

At *Horse Sense*, we work more with Discovery and Skill Building than activities in the Reinforcement Phase. However, when we have long-running clients or groups, such as in our *Running with Mustangs* curriculum or residential therapeutic boarding school clients, we will transition to more of a Horsemanship approach. The ideal program we developed recently for longer-term residential clients follows this progression:

1. Two-three months of weekly EAGALA-model Group/Ground experiences

2. Two-three months of weekly TF-EAP: Relationship Logic and Rhythmic Riding (both each week)

3. Two-three months of weekly Parelli™ Natural Horsemanship

As we move through Discovery and Skill Building into Reinforcement, we're aware that issues may still surface for the client. We do not shut that down; but, we're not necessarily going to redirect the focus of the session to pursue those issues at this time. We're looking less at what comes up for the client while practicing a particular skill, and focusing more on developing Conscious Competence around a skill that's already been identified as necessary and lacking, and has already been examined and mined for significance and meaning to some degree. Reinforcement is about developing feel, timing, and balance, about creating muscle memory and creating new neural connections to set new patterns in place. If significant new issues were to surface during the Reinforcment process, the team would consult to decide on the proper course of action.

Horsemanship in the EAP/EAL Setting

How do we bring Horsemanship into session with clients? One model we've offered utilizes the complete treatment team comprised of a mental health professional and an Equine Specialist. In such cases, the client, the mental health professional and the horse professional each have a horse they are playing with in each session. At least one of the team members—typically the ES—is skilled at the activity; the team and the clients then practice/play together. This often looks like a "Can you..." play session, similar to the basketball game called, oddly enough, H-O-R-S-E, in which one of the team members does something with the horse, like weave through cones, and the others are invited to do the same. This is often a very fun and playful experience!

The triad of client, mental health professional (who's not necessarily good at the horse activity!) and horse professional (who is hopefully pretty good with the activity!) can be really effective in that it provides a shoulder-to-shoulder approach to problem-solving. This is a wonderful opportunity for the client to see persevering behavior modeled in someone else, either the mental health professional or the ES, in a positive way. The ES may play with a particularly young or green horse in such a session, while the client and mental health professional may play with more polished horses. With the whole-team approach, the client has an opportunity to feel less scrutinized and more included.

Another method involves transitioning the client to work with a completely new horse professional (not the same ES from the therapy session work), without a mental health professional present. In such situations, the new ES plays with horses and supports clients in doing the same "Can you..."-type games and activities. Sometimes, the new ES assumes a more formal teacher role, instructing on specific Natural Horsemanship ideas and principles to be applied with horses. My husband, Richard, is a Licensed Parelli™ Professional, and he steps into this role to teach formal Parelli Natural Horsemanship and the Seven Games™ to groups who've transitioned with us from group EAGALA-Model Group/Ground sessions, to Trauma-Focused EAP sessions (both Relationship Logic™ and Rhythmic Riding™).

A third method uses a combination of these first two methods. A new ES is introduced and assumes a leading role in the sessions with the client, but the original treatment team is present to provide a period of transition time. This can help ease any concern during the change-over, and can provide the client with an avenue to continue discussing personal issues and challenges with the treatment team or with the mental health professional from that treatment team outside of horse time. This is particularly appropriate in those situations where we are collaborating with mental health professionals from some of our partner organizations, rather than when we are providing both members

More than a Mirror, by Shannon Knapp

of the treatment team.

It's important to mention that the new ES in this situation still needs to be a skilled and savvy facilitator, ready for what comes up and able to redirect the client to the appropriate support, as necessary. This ES is also responsible for helping the client make the connection between what may feel like learning techniques to life circumstances, often done in a debrief at the end of each Natural Horsemanship session.

Transitioning from EAP into Horsemanship is akin to transitioning from EAP to Therapeutic Riding. The needs of each individual client are kept in mind, knowing that one size does not fit all.

Spending long periods of time in trial-and-error learning-by-doing, perhaps a hallmark of the Discovery Phase, is not a fundamental component of the Reinforcement process. Where the bulk of a one-hour session might be an appropriate amount of time for a client to spend in the trial-and-error process of the EAP Discovery Phase, less than half of a session is an appropriate amount of time to spend in the Skill Building phase, and even less time is spent in the Reinforcement phase.

Unfortunately, we've seen practitioners expand the use of this concept of letting trial-and-error take place without any support to the extreme, allowing the client to spin in endless circles. After a certain point, it's difficult for the client not to interpret that as shameful or humiliating. While this "spinning around the drain" can be instructive for some clients, for others it can become counterproductive, especially if the pattern needing intervention is the pattern of spinning around the drain!

As horse professionals in Natural Horsemanship, we're going to offer more information and provide more instruction during the Reinforcement Phase, just like we do during Therapeutic Riding. We'll be doing more to suggest ideas, affirm and support the client. This phase is about practicing skills, not about learning them for the first time or discovering what skills aren't in the toolkit.

— ▦ —

Having an EAGALA Model Program in a Combined Equine-Assisted Activities & Therapies Organization
By Michelle Holling-Brooks & Cami Murnane

For those of us who have been in the field of equine assisted therapies for a while we have had the pleasure and sometimes pain of watching this field grow, stretch itself, and find new ways to serve even more populations through the healing power of the horse. At Unbridled Change we are constantly asked by other providers in this field how we manage to have a wide spectrum of services while still staying true to the EAGALA model. The answer is pretty simple – we understand and respect the purposes of the different EAAT models and what populations we can serve with them. Above all ethics guide our program to ensure that our clients' emotional safety, needs, and treatment goals are at the top of the decision making process as we place clients in our different programs. Hopefully after reading this article you can start to see what possibilities are out there to help grow your client base. If you pre-plan and put the policies and procedures in place, you too can have multiple programs.

First a short little background on Unbridled Change (UBC) and why we feel so strongly that you can have EAGALA, PATH, Natural Lifemanship, and so on living happily under one roof. As the founder of UBC, I set out from the beginning to create an organization that has both a strong EAGALA EAP/EAL program and a strong PATH International therapeutic riding and now Natural Lifemanship rhythmic riding program. I have been in the EAAT field since college and a certified professional in this field since 2001. I have been program director for multiple PATH Premier Centers and also helped bring EAGALA model EAP to residential and locked detention facilities. I also have a background in working as the Child Services Coordinator at a domestic violence and sexual assault shelter and as a Juvenile Probation Officer. This diverse background with at-risk populations and diverse background in the different models of EAAT has shown me that the different populations can benefit from crossing over and so can EAAT programs. It not only helps the clients but it helps diversify your funding streams and client pools. As UBC enters its 5th year we have grown to a 6 day a week over and 8 hours a day of client time – serving more than 80 clients a week and around 300 plus clients a year. We have a 3 to 4 month waiting list on all sides of our programs and in the next 3 years plan to expand to building another indoor arena and a larger covered outdoor space.

How do you put the different worlds together?
The glue that holds UBC together is the EAGALA model. We have found that for our staff and the clients we serve the EAGALA model fits with about 80% of them. Even on the PATH side the philosophy and basic components of the EAGALA model apply:

- Client and solution focused—we believe our clients hold the answers to their own problems/obstacles; it is our job as the treatment team, instructor, coach to help provide the space and guidance for them to find it. Our clients will constantly amaze us if we just allow them too!

- Relationships come first—the EAGALA model is unmounted to allow the focus to remain about the relationship the horse and client. We model that our relationship with the horse is based on mutual respect, trust, and personal responsibility.

- Ethics—do no harm. This principle drives our policies and procedures on which side of our program we refer clients to, and if we transition clients from one side of our program to another.

You will need to start with a very clear and real conversation with yourself and your organization about what you believe are the benefits and goals for the different sides of your program. If you skip this step, you will run the risk of making unethical decisions. For UBC we believe the following are the goals of our different programs:

- EAP—true outpatient mental health therapy. Clients enrolled is this program are working on developing coping skills and changing thought/behavior patterns. A few examples of the presenting issues we see are: Reactive Attachment Disorder, Oppositional Defiance Disoder, anger management, parent/family reunifications, and trauma/PTSD. There are treatment goals and a start date and end date to this program. Typically clients are with us for 12-24 weeks.

- EAL—group learning and skill development that focuses on communication, relationship, and problem solving (non-violent conflict resolution) skills.

- Therapeutic Riding (TR)—teaching a rider how to ride a horse as independently as possible is the main goal. Clients enrolled in this program are working on secondary goals as well such as: fine and gross motor skills, posture and balance, processing and sequencing skills, and some social skills. There is no end to this program at UBC. Riders can stay enrolled as long as they are able to benefit from TR. This program runs in 6 week cycles year-round.

- Rhythmic Riding—fine tuning of relationship, trust, and self regulation skills through a combination of coaching while riding in rhythm to music. Clients enrolled in this program can be referred from other programs within UBC. This program is focused on both riding skills and self regulation skills and runs in 6 week cycles.

Based on the above goals, when a client is first referred to our program, staff will sit and chat with them about their goals. We will then develop a treatment plan and place them in the program that best fits with their needs.

How do you transition clients from one side to the other?

The next most asked question for us is, "Do your EAP clients ever ride?" The answer is no, they don't. However we do move clients from one program to another *if* it matches a treatment goal. So the question then is how and when you as an organization can ethically move clients around.

The ethical problem with moving clients from one side of the program to another or putting a client that has been in true EAGALA model EAP treatment are:

- You are changing your roles and your structure with the clients— there is no right or wrong, only what works. When it comes to riding there are some basic rights and wrongs if you want to maintain safety; the ES is going to have to start "teaching, guiding, instructing" (whatever you want to call it).

More than a Mirror, by Shannon Knapp

- Different emotional/physical risk for the client—are they ready to be on the back of the horse and have that increase in intimacy and vulnerability that comes with that transition? How are you going to manage this transition?

- Long term and dual relationships—if you come from the horse world this is a foreign concept. As a horse trainer or riding barn it is our goal in life to keep and grow with our cliesnts. We want to take then from beginner riding lessons, to helping them purchase their first horse, to lessons, clinics, shows, and boarding their horses–you have a friend that wants to learn to ride, great–bring them on and the cycle can start again! On the TR side this concept is perfectly fine since our relationship with them is one of recreational therapy not mental health therapy. On the EAP side of our program this same approach is not ethical. The treatment team serves a purpose to help our clients address certain treatment goals. Once those goals are met it is the responsibility of the therapist to close that relationship and allow the client to move forward into their lives with their new skills.

side note – why are we not including EAL? Typically we do not transition EAL clients because they are usually at UBC for a one time teambuilding activity.

UBC's policies for transitioning a client

From the EAP to RR or TR—As a client is approaching the end of their treatment at UBC, the treatment team meets with the client to review the progress they have made toward their treatment goals. If they have met their original goals but we all feel that the client is looking to refine a goal such as trust, self-regulation, and/or communication skills, riding might be an appropriate next step for them. For 90% of our clients riding is not the appropriate next step; the EAP sessions have given them the skills they need and they are discharged from our program. For that other 10% (typically these are clients with dual diagnoses such as RAD and Autism spectrum or RAD and impulse control) we will look at RR or TR and if they would be beneficial. If the therapist believes will be beneficial once the EAP sessions are complete, that client is closed from the EAGALA model EAP sessions and reopened as a PATH model EFP client. For the first few sessions (typically 4-6) the therapist and ES remain in the arena during the lessons to help provide emotional support and processing if required. Once the client is able to self-regulate to the point of dealing internally with anything that might be triggered during a riding lesson, the client is closed out from the EFP model and opened as a TR/RR client. At this last transition the client is passed off to a totally different TR instructor.

Transitioning from the old EAP/EFP treatment team to a new TR instructor is the piece that UBC feels strongly about if you are going to maintain the highest ethical standards in your program. It is not ethical for the EAP/EFP treatment team to remain the instructor for the client at this point. They are not longer receiving mental health therapy; instead they are working on self confidence and their own self-regulation through riding lessons—learning to ride as independently as possible. As the EAP/EFP treatment team you have a pre-existing relationship and knowledge of the client that would potentially blur the lines, therefore if your organization does not have a separate person to teach riding then you should not try to transition clients until you do, in our opinion. We have ensured there is no cross over even further in our program by placing our RR & TR lessons on separate days than our EAP sessions so that staff does not cross paths with past clients.

TR side to EFP—On occasion we have moved a TR client to the EFP side of our program to help with mental health issues that have popped up that the clients/parents wish for our help with. The same protocol applies to them as to opening and closing them from one side and moving them once their treatment goals are met.

A key item to remember in all transitions is that the mental health therapist and the client are the main decision makers on when and if transitioning a client is appropriate.

EAP to volunteer for barn help or therapeutic riding volunteer—to volunteer, past clients must be closed out of the program for at least 6 months prior to being able to apply to volunteer at UBC. Prior to volunteering, the past client will meet with the former EAP treatment team and volunteer coordinator to review the differences in the relationship of a client verses a volunteer and their roles and responsibility as a volunteer. Again the EAP treatment team does not have supervision or interaction

More than a Mirror, by Shannon Knapp

with the past client during their volunteer time.

Nuts and Bolts of what the organization needs to offer a combined EAAT program

Staff—at UBC the TR/RR instructors are required to be at least PATH cert. Instructors, EAGALA certified ES's, and have attended a Natural Lifemanship training. Our mental health therapists are at least EAGALA certified MHPs. We believe this provides the clinical and professional excellence to ensure both physical and emotional safety.

Horses—traditionally EAP horses have a bit more personality quirks than traditional TR horses. So if you are going to be offering riding, your horses will need to be evaluated to ensure they are sound and trained enough to provide safe riding lessons. UBC follows PATH standards for screening and training our riding horses.

Facilities—ASTM approved helmets, mounting ramps and/or blocks, and an enclosed arena free of hazards and with footing appropriate for mounted activities. Again UBC follows PATH's facility standards for all mounted work areas around our farm.

We hope that this article has sparked ideas to "lick and chew". It is our testimony that in following the above policies and procedures your clients and organization will be able to benefit from a combined EAAT program. *(See Contributor Biographies to read more about the authors.)*

As clients move through the Parelli Seven Games™ in Reinforcement, they can also submit tapes to qualify for official Level 1 status within the Parelli™ organization. In this phase, riding may take place, if appropriate, as deemed by the client, the horse and the horse professional. This is not about guaranteed riding time for clients, but is about moving through a series of activities together, continuing to progress. This can culminate in bareback riding in a halter and lead rope (a starting point for us in Natural Horsemanship) and culminate in trail rides with saddle and bit, and more.

Lillan Roquet, in Australia, offers another perspective on working with youth using the Seven Games™. Here's more about that:

— ⌗ —

Playing Around with Horses:
Helping young people to re-engage in Australia
by Lillan Roquet, Annick Maujean, PhD., and Elizabeth Kendall, PhD.

Background

Our innovative program in Queensland, Australia is using Parelli™ techniques to connect with young people who have disengaged from school and society. The "Horse Play" Program emerged from a Riding for Disabled Program that focused on using horses to help young people recover from serious injuries and disabilities. This initial program was started in 1998 by John Wright who, after sustaining a hemiplegia in a farm injury, used his own horses as a form of therapy supervised by his physiotherapist mother. Key volunteers and horses in the program were trained in basic natural horsemanship techniques and the value of this approach was immediately clear. The next year, John visited the Parelli™ Ranch in Colorado and returned even more inspired. The program runs out of Woodstock, a 300 acre property near the base of Mt. Tamborine that was originally donated to the community by the Hancock family who owned large tracts of pine forest in the area.

Although its origins were in rehabilitation, the Horse Play program is now used to help all young people explore and discover their personal strengths and abilities in a positive environment. Rather than making these young people sit in counselling offices, the program uses the outdoor environment, horses and the innovative Parelli™ Program to improve their levels of self-esteem and self-efficacy (i.e., one's belief in the ability to perform in ways that give one control over events that affect one's life). The ultimate aim of the program is to support the translation of the Parelli™ techniques to other parts of their lives, such as their friendships and families as well as their schoolwork or employment.

Program

Sixteen adolescents participated in the Horse Play program and they attended the weekly sessions for ten weeks. Participants were recruited through a local community organisation (Youth and Family Services) which offers a wide range of services and programs for young people, including those who have disengaged from school and are considered "at-risk" of juvenile detention. Our participants were selected by their case managers to deliberately represent young people of all ages who had failed to respond to previous traditional interventions.

In each session, participants were taught the Level One program of Parelli Natural Horsemanship, basically consisting of the Seven Games™ and the first two Parelli™ Patterns (Touch it, and Figure-8). At the end of each weekly session, the participants discussed their progress and strengths with the team of horse facilitators, the Parelli™ Instructor, their case managers from YFS, and a clinical psychologist. In these sessions, they discussed how they could apply these skills they had learned in their everyday life. Every week, the young people identified one new quality they had learned about themselves and were encouraged to practice this skill in their everyday life before the next session.

Case managers described Horse Play as being central to the development of skills the young people needed to overcome difficulties they faced in their lives as well as gaining greater insight into their own personal capabilities (see Maujean, Kendall, Roquet, Sharp, & Pringle, 2012). After participating in the Horse Play program, there were significant positive changes in the participants' levels of self-esteem and self-efficacy, as well as significant positive changes in their attitudes and behaviours (e.g., a reduction in smoking, an increase in positive thoughts, re-engagement at school, healthier relationship with family members and an increase in their social interaction). These changes, which are described in detail elsewhere (see Maujean et al., 2012), were not found among a similar group of young people who did not participate in the Horse Play program. Most importantly, the positive results for the Horse Play participants were sustained well beyond the expected duration, making this program a potentially important investment in long-term wellbeing.

In designing the program, it was thought that the Parelli Natural Horsemanship (PNH) skills would provide the opportunity for young people to connect with their horses, but also to connect with people in better ways. The Parelli™ program was pivotal in helping the young people make changes in their lives because it offers a balanced approach that is unique in two main ways. First, it offers a useful combination of structure and freedom, ingenuity and imagination that can easily be mirrored in addressing the challenges of daily life. The way in which Parelli™ breaks the program into levels, tasks, requirements, savvys and principles enables young people to see the necessity of strong foundations and values, responsibility, timing, and performing the routine tasks of daily life that can be seen as mundane and easily disrespected, especially by teenagers. This balance, in combination with PNH's respect for imagination and free flowing responsiveness highlights the necessity of unique ideas and embracing life in order to be successful. This combination creates a program that allows young people to make the leap between the relationships they are creating with their horses and those they should be striving to create with teachers, peers, and superiors in a range of other contexts.

Second, the Parelli™ approach is unique in its requirement of the balance between respect and boundaries, friendship and care. When working with horses, the students are required to develop strong boundaries and ask the horses to respect their personal space as well as being responsive to their requests. They are also asked to balance their demands on their horses with rest, reward, and a commitment to developing a friendship bond. Learning this balanced leadership style is priceless for learning how to positively relate to everyone in their lives and to creating healthy relationships with others in their future. Due to the balance the Parelli™ approach promotes in these crucial areas (foundations and structure versus imagination and freedom, and respect and boundaries versus friendship and care) students are enabled to find similar balance in their own approach to life. Once this balance is achieved in their relationship with an equine partner, it is easier for these young people to see a pathway towards creating similar positive and healthy relationships and patterns in the rest of their lives.

(See Contributor Biographies to read more about the authors.)

HORSEMANSHIP IDEAS FOR ALL THREE PHASES

Time and again, I find myself reaching for concepts I learned through Natural Horsemanship and within the Parelli™ curriculum, seeing easy parallels between what I've been taught as a student of horsemanship and how I approach the client in EAP/EAL sessions. I often see a clear connection between these concepts and what I feel is happening in the arena with clients. Here are some of the "back-pocket" ideas I keep with me when working with others through all three phases, gleaned primarily from my time at Parelli™ Study Centers and with Parelli™ instructors.

Horsenality™/Humanality™ in Client Work

Horsenality™, the horse analysis chart created by Linda Parelli™ and described in Chapter 2, supports just about everything we do with horses at *Horse Sense*. And we have found multiple applications for using it in our work with clients. The questions I might ask about a horse when trying to assess Horsenality™ are the same questions I might ask about a client: What is his/her default behavior in a pinch? Does that behavior serve? If not, what are the opportunities to grow beyond that behavior? How can the treatment team facilitate that happening?

Ashley Edmonds Hayes of Shepherd Youth Ranch (www.shepherdyouthranch.org) has done a great deal of work more deeply in this area, developing a chart that applies Horsenality™ to Humanality™. The following diagrams and discussion explain further.

Humanality™ in EAP
by Ashley Edmonds Hayes

Background
Shepherd Youth Ranch Inc. is a non-profit 501c3, faith-based organization that provides restoration and hope to youth and families

in need by pairing them with horses that are rescued from abuse and neglect. During the past eight years Shepherd Youth Ranch (SYR) served over 3000 youth and families in need and provided over 50,000 hours of EAP, EAL and Equine-Assisted Therapeutic Services.

Throughout its history, SYR has forged long-standing relationships with local school counselors, court counselors, mental health professionals, teachers, parental associations and community groups which served as a valuable referral base. During this time, the majority population served were referred by local court counselors associated with the Juvenile Crime Prevention Counsel in our county or from our Local Mental Health Entity. A child referred to our program from either of these agencies could meet one or more of the following criteria: adjudication and court-ordered to complete our program, assigned a juvenile court counselor, presenting with a mental health diagnosis, step-down from group home or considered at-risk by a professional or caregiver.

The EAP programs offered addressed one or more of the following: clinical mental health issues or diagnosis, substance abuse, and juvenile sex offender treatment. EAL programs focused on interpersonal skill building, coping skills, cognitive-behavioral patterns, anger management, strength-based learning and healing from grief and loss to name a few. Each child referred attended several group, individual and family sessions paired with horses and our professional therapy team over the course of several months to a year. Our staff was privileged to witness many incredible changes in the lives of these youth and their families.

Equine–Assisted Skill Building (EASB)
A service added to SYR's programming in more recent years is coined by ranch staff as Equine-Assisted Skill Building (EASB) where a greater amount of focus is placed on developing horsemanship (including riding) or a partnership with a horse that translates into life skills building. This mentoring-based program is offered to anyone in need, regardless of financial ability. The EASB program is growing rapidly and will eventually become a primary focus of our program development.

The foundation for horsemanship in all our programs whether it is EAP, EAL or EASB or rehabilitating rescued horses is Parelli Natural Horsemanship. Thanks to Linda and Pat Parelli's program, the blueprint for horsemanship, which is really a partnership between man and horse, is easily translated to youth. The same skills in Parelli Natural Horse-Man-Ship™ employed to partner with a horse are the basis for many human-learned

More than a Mirror, by Shannon Knapp

life skills. Take for example the Parelli™ concept of Horsenality™. This is a fabulous resource for identifying a horse's needs, motivators, responses, conditions, limitations and strengths. In addition, the strategies for humans interacting with a particular Horsenality™ prove to be invaluable. Shepherd Youth Ranch is currently developing a philosophy and training based on Horsenality™ and Humanality™ that can translate across EAP, EAL and EASB modalities. The charts below represent a glimpse of some of the educational materials Shepherd Youth Ranch will offer in the future and are based on Parelli's Horsenality™ concept intertwined with eight years of professional observations of youth involved in our programs.

The Youth Humanality™ Attributes chart (figure 3.4) reflects observations of over 150 youth referred either by a court counselor or community professional. The Strategies for Humanality™ chart (Figure 3.3) provide some ideas for capitalizing on strengths and responding to the four Humanalites™. A brief synopsis of each Humanality™ is provided here for reference:

Humanalities™

- Left-Brain Extroverts (LBE) can present as quick learners who are easily bored and ready to "pounce" (play) on a peer or staff member. They can be funny, quick witted and show leadership and/or dominant qualities. These are the youth that when presented with a set of rules or boundaries in an EAP/EAL activity, will also choose to come up with their own rules and boundaries which may or may not be to the liking of the horse or other peers. The LBE youth derives great joy in coming up with a plan that can sometimes lead to chaos. These are the kids who if ever wanted to curse will curse and at every opportunity. When given the opportunity, tools and skills to capitalize on their strengths, these youth can be great leaders, creative inventors, visionaries and just plain fun!

- Right-Brain Extroverts (RBE) need to move their feet which is sometimes mislabeled as disrespectful behavior or fidgeting. These are the youth who need to have their energy channeled in a direction so that they feel confident. When RBE youth feel nervous in a session, the fidgeting may get worse and they can start asking a lot of questions about a task. When it comes to taking personal responsibility, these youth may make excuses or flat out deny a behavior, feeling or thought. When given rules in a session, these youth may forget them or not even remember hearing the rules. Confidence is what these kids are after and therefore need to learn skills that help them create direction and structure. When given the opportunity, they are very perceptive, sensitive and display great empathy.

- Left-Brain Introverts (LBI) can be very clever, witty and sometimes argumentative or stubborn. You may hear an LBI use the popular phrase "whatever" frequently. These youth are intelligent and can be easily bored or check out of a session. As far as rules, they simply may chose to ignore them. Youth that fall into this category love to ask "why" questions sometimes in an effort to avoid the task or question presented and to get staff and peers off track. These youth may need help with anger management and coping skills as their tendency is to get stuck in a quiet anger or avoidance. These youth may present a "better than you" attitude and could use help developing empathy skills. The key to helping LBI youth is to find what motivates them and their passion and then reward them with those things that give them purpose.

- Right-Brain Introverts (RBI) can present as very shy or insecure. This could be representative of the child hanging out in the back of the group or the child of few words. These children may have difficulty trusting staff and other peers. The question commonly asked of an RBI whether verbalized externally or internally is "what if". The fear of the unknown can be very paralyzing for these youth. However, once trust between child and horse is established, an intense very therapeutic bond is forged. The RBI child may be somewhat of a chameleon as they will take on the characteristics of those around them. It should be noted that when these youth take on the characteristic of extroverts it can be very draining for them in the end. These are also the youth that like to shirk responsibility by blaming others or circumstances. Because these youth are very obedient, they crave rules and boundaries and will almost always follow them. When these youth are able to establish comfort and trust, they can be very loyal to people, values and causes.

(See Contributor Biographies to read more about the author.)

More than a Mirror, by Shannon Knapp

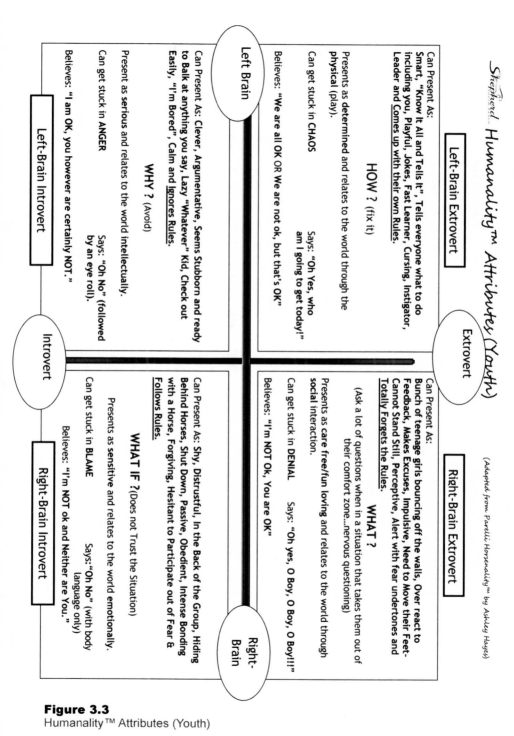

Figure 3.3
Humanality™ Attributes (Youth)

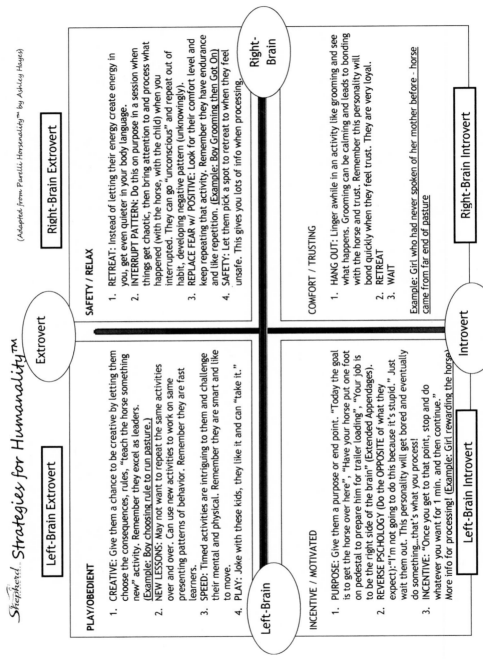

Shepherd Strategies for Humanality™

(Adapted from Parelli Horsenality™ by Ashley Hayes)

Right-Brain Extrovert

SAFETY / RELAX

1. RETREAT: Instead of letting their energy create energy in you, get even quieter in your body language.
2. INTERRUPT PATTERN: Do this on purpose in a session when things get chaotic, then bring attention to and process what happened (with the horse, with the child) when you interrupted. They can go "unconscious" and repeat out of habit, developing negative pattern (unknowingly).
3. REPLACE FEAR w/ POSITIVE: Look for their comfort level and keep repeating that activity. Remember they have endurance and like repetition. (Example: Boy Grooming then Got On)
4. SAFETY: Let them pick a spot to retreat to when they feel unsafe. This gives you lots of info when processing.

Right-Brain

Extrovert

Introvert

Right-Brain Introvert

COMFORT / TRUSTING

1. HANG OUT: Linger awhile in an activity like grooming and see what happens. Grooming can be calming and leads to bonding with the horse and trust. Remember this personality will bond quickly when they feel trust. They are very loyal.
2. RETREAT
3. WAIT

Example: Girl who had never spoken of her mother before - horse came from far end of pasture

Left-Brain Extrovert

PLAY/OBEDIENT

1. CREATIVE: Give them a chance to be creative by letting them choose the consequences, rules, "teach the horse something new" activity. Remember they excel as leaders. (Example: Boy choosing rule to run pasture.)
2. NEW LESSONS: May not want to repeat the same activities over and over. Can use new activities to work on same presenting patterns of behavior. Remember they are fast learners.
3. SPEED: Timed activities are intriguing to them and challenge their mental and physical. Remember they are smart and like to move.
4. PLAY: Joke with these kids, they like it and can "take it."

Left-Brain

INCENTIVE / MOTIVATED

1. PURPOSE: Give them a purpose or end point. "Today the goal is to get the horse over here", "Have your horse put one foot on pedestal to prepare him for trailer loading", "Your job is to be the right side of the brain" (Extended Appendages).
2. REVERSE PSCHOLOGY (Do the OPPOSITE of what they expect):"I'm not going to do this because it's stupid." Just wait them out. This personality will get bored and eventually do something...that's what you process!
3. INCENTIVE: "Once you get to that point, stop and do whatever you want for 1 min. and then continue." More info for processing! (Example: Girl rewarding the horse)

Left-Brain Introvert

Figure 3.4
Strategies for Humanality™

More than a Mirror, by Shannon Knapp

The work Ashley Edmonds Hayes is doing has clear applications in EAP/EAL, among them adapting communication and leadership to fit the Horsenality™ in both a professional and a therapeutic environment. A parent may struggle with one child who's introverted and one child who's extroverted; Humanality™ helps illuminate that, as well as helps clarify best approaches. For other people, Horsenality™ can inform their pattern of life choices. Although we are not yet utilizing Humanality™ charts in session work with clients, we often ask them to reflect on what they think their Horsenality™/Humanality™ is, and the Horsenality™/Humanality™ of significant people in their lives. Horsenality™ work in the arena can help humans understand that their next step in growth and development is learning to make better choices. When they can see the consequences of choosing the horse who is a good fit vs. the horse who will push all their buttons, it can help them make better choices in other areas of life as well.

The concepts of Horsenality™/Humanality™ also provides multiple opportunities for learning with corporate clients and in the workplace. During their time with us, our management-level clients seek insight on the common challenge of dealing with different types of workers. Horsenality™ becomes a natural fit for a corporate audience who encounters a mixture of personalities at the office or in the workplace. We'll utilize Horsenality™ to illustrate the crossovers and similarities with Myers-Briggs or the DISC inventory. We will offer skills to identify the personality types and how to work with each one, then give human leaders and corporate teams a chance to adapt their communication and leadership styles to fit the horses in the arena. This provides an excellent, present-moment skill building format for practice and pattern development. Moving from one Horsenality™ to another increases flexibility and adaptability, setting the client up for fluid behavior later in the office. The human can apply the Horsenality™ leadership style needed to each horse before transferring that to their human world.

The framework of Horsenality™ also gives us the opportunity to talk about diversity and equality; not everybody is a Left-Brained Introvert, and they shouldn't be more valued than Right-Brained Extroverts. If all of us fit into one category, we would miss the gifts and opportunities brought by each personality. Recognizing both the strengths and challenges inherent in personality types is an important skill.

When illustrating the concept of how different Humanalities™— as Ashley refers to them—can utilize their particular gifts and skills in the workplace or at home or school, the metaphor of rescue horses becomes a great example. The "traditional" horse world has designated rescue horses as often useless, inappropriate, troubled, or crazy. Once we get the rescue horse comfortable in his own skin, he often becomes the perfect portal through which certain clients can learn a life skill or communication style.

Another exciting application of Horsenality™ in a therapeutic setting comes from Harriet Laurie, in England. She is doing significant work in Britain building off Horsenality™ with prisoners. An explanation of her work and some excellent preliminary results follow.

— ▦ —

TheHorseCourse (THC)
by Harriet Laurie

TheHorseCourse is an equine-assisted 'offending behaviour program' delivered in prisons in the UK focusing on the most disengaged and disruptive of violent offenders within the system—those who are usually excluded from behaviour interventions. The project began at HMP Portland in 2010 and replicated into HMP Oakwood, HMP Verne and HMP Eastwood Park in 2012, with three further facilitators delivering the course with their own horses.

There are three strands to TheHorseCourse:

- The specific THC structure and approach;
- Participants learning positive behaviour patterns as a 'by-product' of

learning Parelli Natural Horsemanship (PNH)

- Instructors treating participants in a similar way to horses, using non-verbal interactions based on PNH horse-training strategies.

The specific THC structure and approach

TheHorseCourse is a short intense course focusing on fundamental life skills as detailed in the 'Star' (Figure 3.5). The course is delivered using Parelli-trained horses to provide motivation, feedback and structure. The Instructor relies on Parelli Natural Horsemanship (PNH) as the context for the work and is not necessarily a professional therapist or educator. The course takes place outdoors.

Key features:

- Seven sessions of 2 to 2.5 hours, two participants, 2 horses, over 4-5 days (following Pat Parelli's advice that it takes 7 repetitions to create a habit).

- Participants work towards a horsemanship goal of Parelli™ Level 1. In order to achieve the horsemanship goal, they work on the 8 skills outlined in the THC Star. Tasks are guided by the Instructor to address behaviour problems via horsemanship tasks. The horses provide clear and easily observed feedback which participants cannot attribute to an interpersonal agenda. Hence shifts are made 'in the moment', in response to difficulties. (Parelli™ horses have the advantage that their natural sensitivity is carefully retained and built upon).

- Participants are awarded a THC Certificate, usually by a Governor or visiting dignitary. Often they will show off their horsemanship in front of a small crowd, or teach a horsemanship task to a prison staff member or visitor during the 8th 'certificate session'.

- A ten minute 'audition' is submitted to Parelli™ USA for external assessment—participants normally receive a Parelli™ Level 1 certificate

- Participants receive a DVD of the assessment, showing themselves performing successfully with a horse—many share this with family.

- Both the Participants and the Referrer receive a copy of TheHorse-Course Star—showing 'before and after' growth in life skills. This is completed by the Instructor and Participant together in an exit interview, based on observations during the course.

- Feedback from the Instructor outlining challenges and progress during the course goes to the Referrer after discussion with the Participant.

Participants learning positive behaviour patterns as a 'by-product' of learning Parelli Natural Horsemanship (PNH)

A key feature of TheHorseCourse is to train participants in horsemanship using PNH-training methods. Participants are unmounted handlers, learning to communicate with the horses on the ground, to Level 1 of the Parelli™ programme.

As is widely recognised, PNH places responsibility on the human to gain mastery not only of technique but of their own emotional and mental controls. In striving for quality in PNH Level 1 tasks (and beyond), the participants are obliged to practice crucial life skills, including those detailed in the THC star (Figure 3.5).

Using high level horses allows the instructor to task students at a more demanding level where appropriate. For the participant it may seem that the course is all about the horsemanship, but for the instructor it is clear that the horsemanship is merely a vehicle for teaching life skills.

The role of the instructor is to:

- Ensure safety
- Teach excellent horsemanship
- Enable learners to read the horses' feedback for themselves
- Set ever-increasing challenges, sufficient to provoke frustration—testing and developing the 8 skills defined by the THC Star
- Coach for improvements in those skills, in the moment, to create success, providing a learning experience that is based on rehearsal rather than intellectualisation.

The horses help to engage and motivate participants. They are selected as much for their daunting and attractive presence as for their training. The demands of the horsemanship create an immediate and visceral learning environment where the participant is drawn forcibly into the 'here and now', and engaged by the opportunity to work with a horse as a willing partner to achieve results that both look and feel impressive.

More than a Mirror, by Shannon Knapp

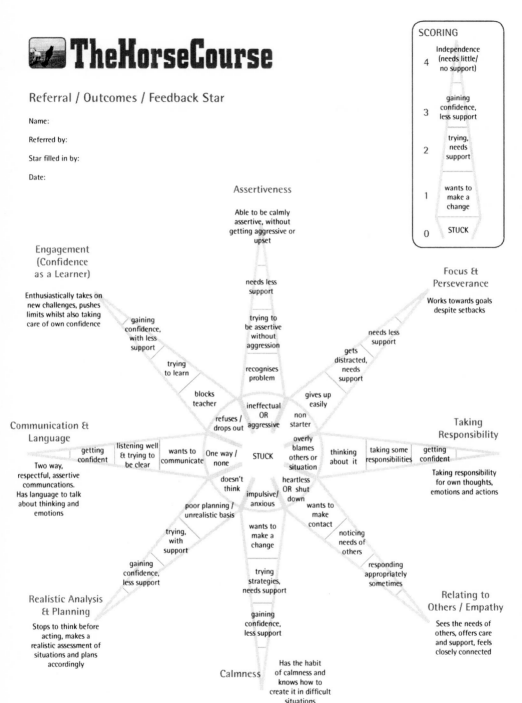

Figure 3.5
TheHorseCourse Star

The horses are, crucially, PNH Level 3+, ensuring that their understanding of the PNH patterns and games are sufficiently secure that they will provide reliable and clear results at all times. A key function of the horse is to offer feedback in the moment as to whether the participant's communications are calm, assertive, focused and clear. They reward improvement by offering success since they are trained to respond to subtle changes in energy and body language in a way that most horses are not.

In striving for perfection in Level 1 tasks, participants have to practice THC Star skills. Some examples:

- setting and maintaining a strong focus to lead from zone 3 or to play 'touch it';
- showing patience and empathy in scary Squeeze Games;
- planning carefully to orchestrate a Fig 8 or a flowing audition;
- finding the difference between assertive and aggressive to get smooth departures and transitions on a circle;
- finding a genuine neutral (calmness) to achieve the extreme friendly game;
- dropping to neutral 100's of times to say 'yes' to the horse in all games;
- taking responsibility for all their communications because the horse is never wrong.

As Parelli™ people fully appreciate, the horses will give accurate feedback, in the moment. It is honest and unbiased and it seems that people who have become entirely closed off to feedback from a therapist, educator or probation officer, can still accept the truth from a horse. Part of the instructor's job is to empower the participants to read the horse for themselves. Another part is to prove that a failed task is never the horse's fault; we do this by coaching for success and/or demonstrating that, with appropriate communication, the horse is ready and willing to comply. The art of the instructor is to set challenges that are at the edges of what the student can do, allow them to feel anger or frustration just long enough to be uncomfortable, and then coach a new habit of behaviour that will bring success. As with training a horse, the instructor must judge when the participants need consistency to consolidate the learning and when they are ready to progress. To run this particular course with lower level horses or non-Parelli™ horses would be impossible.

The pressure of aiming for a strong PNH Level 1 audition within 7 sessions keeps sessions highly progressive and creates accountability for the instructors.

Instructors treating participants in a similar way to horses, using non-verbal interactions based on PNH horse-training strategies

TheHorseCourse approach takes PNH methods and asks instructors to treat participants as if they were horses themselves. Instructors are trained to read participant body language as the primary source of information and feedback, rather than focusing on verbal interactions with the participants.

What is critical about TheHorseCourse approach is the extent to which instructors rely on non-verbal forms of communication throughout the program—all horsemanship tasks are taught through simulation and rehearsal, not through verbal explanations or written materials. But more than that, participants are often moved around like a horse—indeed the instructor will usually revert to non-verbal interactions to manage or deal with problem behaviour, rather than get into a discussion. For example, a well-understood PNH technique such as "let me help you" might be used on a fidgety participant simply by running the participant around, using numerous changes in direction, until the body softens and the participant 'offers' to be still. What is key is that the instructor's verbal communications are kept to a minimum, offering simple practical directions based in the present moment, and avoiding any discussion of personal histories or psychology. Only at the end of the course is there discussion of past offending and the impact of new skills learnt on the course.

The purpose and theory underlying this extension of PNH 'simulations' is that it allows the instructor to make behaviour modifications directly, avoiding encounters with the individual's well-practiced verbal blocks, distractions and confusions. Using PNH strategies on humans in the same way as with a horse to alter thoughts and emotions, and therefore behaviour, through physical interactions seems to create remarkably swift and solid changes to behavioural habits. In this way, the training seeks to work 'under the radar', engaging centres of the human mind which are often overlooked by verbal methods, but with which, as Parelli™ horsemen, we are highly trained to engage.

Another extension of the PNH-system used in TheHorseCourse is a modified version of the well-known PNH "Horsenality™" chart. The modified chart (Figure 3.6) divides the four PNH quadrants further into behaviours that are dysfunctional (depicted as amber [middle gray] or red [dark gray]), and functional (depicted as green [light gray]); the behaviour descriptors are also human-focused rather than horse-focused. These modifications achieve a couple of goals: first, the new vocabulary allows the instructor to apply appropriate strategies directly to modify human behaviours (which flows from the above-noted method of treating humans as horses); second, it provides for heightened objective measurability in terms of rating outcomes.

This modified chart is used by the instructors for session notes and to guide course content rather than as a feedback tool to students. It has also been used as part of an academic study by Dr. Hemingway of Bournemouth University, UK, to track observable behaviour shifts in participants.

One principle behind the modified chart is that fully functioning human beings are able to move to any and all of the 'green [light gray]' areas at will. For instance, to do taxes, a person should be operating at bottom left; to get the house clean, it might be better to be operating at top right. Very successful individuals are able to move freely throughout the green areas of the chart, thus 'getting themselves in the mood' appropriate to the situation or task presenting itself. And overall, the trick is to learn how to decrease the likelihood of going amber [middle gray] or red [dark gray], and at the same time have access to a greater repertoire of green [light gray] states and behaviours.

Findings include statistically significant changes in behaviour whilst in prison, as well as impressive feedback from staff, participants and observers. Amongst the findings by Dr. Rosie Meek:

- The numeric data is positive: Adjudications post course down 74%, Negative Entries down 72%, Positive Entries up 168%, drop out rate nil.

- Qualitative data is also positive: exit interviews consistently report

More than a Mirror, by Shannon Knapp

TheHorseCourse

Observation Chart (read the body rather than face and totally ignore what is being said)

Edge descriptors:
- **won't listen**
- smooth movements, loose muscles, forwards
- jerky movements, tight muscles, moves backwards/away
- soft muscles, calm stillness, easy posture, present
- tight muscles, awkward postures, holds breath, invisible
- **can't listen, can't think**

Energy markers: neutral · high energy · draw · allow · ask · zero energy · neutral · fight / flight

	dominance	play	confidence	curiosity	fear
won't listen (red)	fast, calm aggression, destructive	slow and deliberate aggression, destructive	hostile, refusing, "try and make me"		calm, determined, immovable, "you can't hurt me"
(amber)	destructive, rough, won't keep still	pushy, dominant	moves slowly, lazy, resistant, makes you work harder		won't move, unyielding
(green)	exuberant, fast, fun, play, loose muscles	experimental, brave, investigative, assertive	persistent, calm, planning, dependable		patient, slow, analytical, at ease
(green)	fast, efficient, athletic, vigilant, focused	responsive, perceptive, doing, speedy, curious	bonding, sensitive, connected	gentle, compliant, empathic	peaceful, connected, tranquil
(amber)	can't keep still, frenetic, running about, reactive	hyper vigilant, tense, jerky, often backwards, messy energy, displaced behaviours	weak messy energy, ineffective, pleading, tight body, retreating		can't move, fixed
can't listen, can't think (red)	overly sweaty, panicking, manic		quivery, shut down		frozen in fear

Figure 3.6

TheHorseCourse Observation Chart (Original chart is in color and corresponds to the grayscale as follows: red = dark gray; amber = light gray; green = middle gray)

increased confidence and new skills in self-relaxation. Many participants express the benefit of learning self-efficacy in the moment rather than attempting to learn through classroom work. ... Participants consistently gain observable skills in: Calmness, Attention span, Planning, Perseverance and Confidence.

- This intervention ... seems particularly appropriate for those who have failed to engage with interventions, learning and activities and are medium to high risk.

- We would also recommend this course for those with entrenched aggressive behaviour within the prison.

It is important to acknowledge the extraordinary work of Pat and Linda Parelli in devising and communicating the PNH programme. It has been a continuous source of inspiration and information. There is no other horsemanship programme in the world that demonstrates the elegance, simplicity and completeness seen in PNH, and I believe it provides concepts that go beyond horsemanship to inform the human condition. I am extremely grateful for the generosity and goodwill that Linda Parelli and others within the wider Parelli™ community have shown towards this experimental work and I sincerely hope the results will be a source of satisfaction to them.

(See Contributor Biographies to read more about the author.)

More Parelli-inspired Ideas

Many Parelli™ ideas and activities that have found a home in *Horse Sense* equine-assisted practices include "Me and My Shadow," "Stick to Me," "Herd of Two," "Mosey," "Undemanding Time," and "Thresholds." We'll take a brief look at each one and how we might apply it in session work.

"Me and My Shadow" is a game we often use to develop social empathy skills. An unmounted client walks side-by-side with the horse, mirroring the horse in speed, movement, and activity. This activity puts the client in a position to see the world from another's point of

view, and can evoke a tremendous amount of curiosity—or boredom! Why is the horse moving this way? What does the horse look at? What is she interested in? Me and My Shadow initiates a process of listening to what matters to someone else.

Additionally, since horses are really good at stopping and grazing, this exercise is a wonderful activity to help a client slow down and move into the present moment. It is also an opportunity to play with equal partnership. I think of playing with my horse as having 51% of the leading role while she has 49%. Sometimes that 51% flips back and forth between us, depending on what we're doing. Me and My Shadow can be an opportunity to play with handing off leadership roles; when the client lets go of or takes the lead, what is the default percentage? Do they take 10%? 90%? Are they generous or possessive? Playing with this exchange can be a metaphor of how we behave in relationship with others, work, or our families.

"Stick to Me" is an activity from the Parelli™ centers in which the horse is invited to stay with the person, even though the horse is at liberty. This is not the same as Monty Roberts' "Join-up," however. Perhaps the client has developed a relationship with one horse, who is now loose in an arena. We'll invite the client to "get back in relationship" with the horse, or to re-forge the connection. It becomes a puzzle for the client to set up the situation so the horse is invited to "catch" her. We can utilize this process to observe Horsenality™, and explore how to "cause your idea to become the horse's idea." It becomes an exercise useful in helping a parent learn to cause her idea to become her child's idea.

Another concept we apply in session is the "Herd of Two." If my horse and I are connected, and another horse or another person tries to break into our time together, I'm in a position of protecting and defending my Herd of Two. Good parallels to this can be found within the parent-child relationship: if I've put my trust in you as the leader of this Herd of Two, my expectation is that you're going to protect me against all comers, and I will do the same for you. What does that look like? How can the client be effective without actively chasing those "comers"—horses or people—away? How quietly can the client get this point across?

We also use the concepts of "Mosey" and "Undemanding Time." As predators, we tend to be good at direct-line thinking (goal- or task-oriented), a concept that horses don't engage with very well. Depending on what issues they're presenting with, we help clients disengage their direct-line behavior and encourage them to spend twenty minutes casually moseying with their horse back to the pasture. With Mosey, we may invite the client to see how many ways he can get to the pasture gate without making a beeline for it.

We had one client who did an enormous amount of personal work with us. When we asked him what he most wanted to do in his last session, his answer was Undemanding Time. He wanted to simply hang out in one of our shelters next to a couple of horses who were quietly munching hay. Mosey and Undemanding Time can be extremely hard to grasp for those used to showing up with an agenda and a timeframe. For horses used to this type of predator/human, this same activity can really shift behavior and generate tremendous curiosity, i.e.: "Who is this human that doesn't want to demand something from us?"

As you may also have noticed, we integrate Simulations without horses into a lot of our work with clients as well, because practicing with horses or people right away can be too highly charged for many clients. Parelli™ integrates a good deal of simulation into their coursework, and we do the same in our EAP practice. An inanimate object, like a fencepost or a chair, provides a great opportunity to learn without worrying that someone will get hurt. We might simulate the Phases with a client in the role of the horse and the ES as the client practicing the Phases, then switch and practice the Phases with a member of the treatment team in the role of the horse. This way, the client can feel the sensations for himself first, then feel how to do it with someone who can talk to him about it, before moving onto the horse.

This ties in with another concept, that of "Energy Management." "Bring up your life" or "Bring up your energy", i.e., come out of neutral and "mean it" when you communicate is a skill we'll invite clients to practice throughout their time with us, with the horse offering feedback. We'll ask: "How much energy do you have to bring to this situation to cause success?" "Can you bring just a little bit, or does this situation require 'more': more intention, more focus, more life?"

"Reframing" is a common skill clients practice throughout EAP and EAL. Take, for example, "Make vs. Cause." Helping a client move from, "I'm going to make this horse do this," to, "I'm going to cause this idea to become the horse's idea" is a significant shift. The same is true for "Let vs. Allow." There is a subtle but important difference between, "I'm going to let my horse do this," to, "I'm going to allow this to happen." Another reframe is the idea of turning a "problem" into an opportunity or a puzzle to solve, to move from "Oh No!" to "Oh Boy!"

This isn't just Pollyanna thinking; how we approach a situation can have just as much impact on the outcome as our knowledge or skill. When we adapt to a different mindset, it shows up in our body language and our energy. Another basic, but powerful, reframe is thinking in terms of "puzzles" not "problems." You can either approach the world as if everything is a "problem" or as if there are lots of "puzzles" to solve; one sounds like a lot more fun than the other! It's the whole reason the Seven Games™ are called Games instead of Tasks, Chores or Jobs.

Although there are many more examples I could give of integrating Natural Horsemanship ideas into equine-assisted practices, I'll confine myself to just one more: *"Thresholds."* We've all seen it in horses: you leave on a trail ride, or you start to walk your horse from the barn to the pasture, and for some reason your horse only goes so far before stopping. You've just hit a Threshold, a place where something important has changed or is about to change in the horse's world, enough so that she has to take a moment to integrate that into herself. As with other horse body language and actions, humans often don't even recognize the Threshold until it becomes "Big": shying, rearing, turning and bolting, etc. The reaction of many a horseperson to this is, "Come on, just get over it!" Push the horse through enough Thresholds and you can have a real problem on your hands.

An alternative is to recognize the Threshold by taking a moment to stop, and let the horse (or person) acclimate to whatever change or discomfort she feels, to "take the time it takes" to first get comfortable. Maybe she needs to stand there for a few moments; maybe she needs to approach and retreat a few times. Either way, taking time to acknowledge and allow, which is counter-intuitive for most humans, can go a long way toward resolving a significant issue the first time instead of encountering it over and over again.

Both horses and people have Thresholds. When we push a horse or a person (or ourselves!) through a Threshold, we effectively push her into the deep end and expect her to just learn how to swim. It's the origin of multiple unhealthy coping behaviors for horses and humans. As humans, we are often taught to blow through our own Thresholds and the Thresholds of others, to "Just Do It." Inviting the client to observe and honor Thresholds in the horse can initiate the process of recognizing and honoring her own Thresholds, replacing unhealthy patterns with a healthy alternative.

In setting up a Thresholds activity for EAP, we might invite a client to take the horse for a walk around the arena or around the farm, and observe any Thresholds encountered. We'll meander along with her within earshot, inviting her to observe and reflect on the following: Where are Thresholds for you? Where are some Thresholds for your

More than a Mirror, by Shannon Knapp

horse? Are there places you feel comfortable and confident going, and places you don't feel comfortable and confident going? How can you support your horse through those processes? How can you support yourself?

The Parelli-ism "Take the time it takes and it'll take less time" is a phrase we use with many clients. In another manifestation of our direct-line, predator mindset we often see clients go for the quick fix, the fast solution. This mindset only serves to create frustration because the quick-fix shortcut usually doesn't save time at all in the long run. When we encourage a client to slow down and "take the time it takes," things are usually resolved the first time, resulting in saving time.

The phrase "Be firm and fair without getting mean or mad" often accompanies any discussion we might have around Phases: can the client utilize Phase 4 pressure without getting emotional? In our earlier discussion of the Phases, we talked about helping clients find both ends of the pendulum before finding center. We also work on utilizing the Phases effectively without automatically bringing emotions into the picture. The process of invoking Phase 4 in this way can be extremely difficult for predator/humans to do, and a great opportunity for skill building practice.

Think of the mother destroying the chair in the earlier example: she had to first find Phase 4 and then explore an emotionally-charged "Phase X" before she could comfortably and reliably go to Phase 4 without a destructive emotional charge. In that example, we used a plastic chair, but we have also had clients tie the halter and lead rope to a fencepost.

"Expect a response but be ready to correct; not more one than the other." This, too, is a powerful concept from Parelli™, which also evokes the additional concepts of "An Attitude of Justice" and "Make No Assumptions, Teach No Assumptions." As I explained in a previous chapter, I

experienced this dynamic in my own horsemanship in doing a classic "follow the rail" activity at a clinic. After my horse repeatedly stopped at the gate, I began to anticipate my horse stopping, so I began encouraging him on before we even got the gate. That was the point at which the instructor invited me to let him make the mistake before correcting it.

This concept helps highlight how often we anticipate responses without giving the people (or horses) around us the benefit of the doubt; how often do we micromanage rather than allow someone the chance to make a mistake first? If you correct a mistake before it happens, there is no learning.

One of the most important concepts we implement with clients is "It's not about the _____ ." It's not about the trailer, it's not about the jump, it's not about your kid's curfew or taking out the trash. It's about the relationship. This is a key concept for moving clients from a place of focusing on the surface of a situation to focusing instead on the deeper problem. It also allows clients to make connections to the "regular world"; what you do here that affects the horse affects other people in your life, too.

Parelli Ideas as Skill Cards

I mentioned earlier that many of our *Horse Sense* Skill Cards were inspired by Parelli™. Each of these cards contains skills and elements—from the Seven Games™ and elsewhere—that enable clients to practice with a horse before engaging the skill in their own life. From reading the cards we can set up activities that allow them to see and kinesthetically feel the process of learning, from concept to action.

The "Touch-and-Go" card, for example, is inspired by the Squeeze Game™ and designed to help the client navigate situations without overwhelming him emotionally with a particularly difficult or paralyzing issue. There's a card dedicated to helping people recognize the Phases and understanding the differences between Phase 1 and Phase

4. We have a Skill Card specifically on Right Brain and Left Brain behavior and their characteristics; we utilize those with clients when reactivity is an issue. We also have a Skill Card called "Setting Yourself up for Success" which has to do with framing and planning for all sorts of challenging situations which the client might face. We often use the "Approach and Retreat" card for fear issues and relationship issues. All of these come from my time in the Natural Horsemanship world and in studying Parelli™.

Opposition Reflex and Brace

Being an "Ambassador of Yes Rather Than Minister of No" is an important Parelli™ concept we use when helping our clients develop awareness of Opposition Reflex and Brace, in themselves and others.

Opposition Reflex is an instinctual behavior, in both horse and human, usually observed as an automatic impulse to do the exact opposite of whatever pressure is being applied. Since the horse is a prey animal, and the human is a predator, it is in the horse's nature to oppose whatever the human thinks is a good idea. A predator's "good idea" is often not a good idea from the prey animal's point of view! Therefore, the horse automatically chooses the opposite of what the human is asking. This is also the case with clients presenting with Opposition Defiant Disorder and Conduct Disorder.

With people, as with horses, often there's a really good reason for choosing to do the opposite of whatever the authority figure has suggested. The idea of illustrating Opposition Reflex in horses can be introduced to clients as something they may recognize in themselves.

Brace, on the other hand, is what happens over time when no release from pressure is provided (often resulting in what many call a "hard-mouthed" horse). If release is what signals the desired behavior has been given, pressure without any release fails to teach. A horse will learn to brace or push back against hard hands or pressure. Brace is a more thoughtful response than Opposition Reflex. To illustrate: Opposition Reflex is a *"can't"* response: "I can't do what you're asking." Brace is more of a *"won't"* response: "I won't do what you're asking." The difference between "can't" and "won't" is enormous, requiring a different response from us as horsepeople and facilitators.

For many of the youth coming to us with diagnoses of Oppositional Defiant Disorder (ODD) or Conduct Disorder (CD)—and I would argue, all youth to some degree—testing the boundaries of authority in their world is a very, very natural response. Horses do it all the time, with humans and each other, because they're asking, "Can I trust you to be the leader? Are you fit enough mentally, physically and emotionally to be the leader?" Youth, when they get to a certain age, are often asking the very same questions of parents and other adults in their world.

Both horses and youth might also ask, "Can I get you emotional? Can I get you to become emotionally charged?" Or they may ask, "Can I pull you off your game? Can I change the game enough so that you lose focus and it becomes what I want it to be about?"

Once the horse (or the client) succeeds in pulling the human (or the treatment team) into an emotional reaction, they get an answer to the most basic question: "Will you turn 'predator' on me?" Their actions suggest that they might think, "I knew it; I knew you were a predator. I was just testing to see if you would go predator on me and you did!" The same parallel testing of leadership and trustworthiness can be seen in relationships between youth and their parents or other authority figures.

When working with the concepts of Opposition Reflex and Brace with clients, we talk a lot about Right-Brained and Left-Brained behavior. First, we help clients learn how to recognize where they are—Left-Brained or Right-Brained—while helping them regulate that behavior more appropriately. If they're operating more from a

More than a Mirror, by Shannon Knapp

Right-Brained perspective (more "can't" than "won't'"), how can they become more Left-Brained and less oppositional or instinctual? If they're more Left-Brained, how can they get back into a little bit more of a Right-Brained space with less "won't" behavior?

Clients can often develop this skill by helping to move a horse from Left to Right or Right to Left. Then, they practice it on themselves. Our clients might describe Right-Brained behavior as "going off, losing it, or snapping" and learn to recognize the signs of Right-Brained behavior as instinctive Opposition Reflex.

We knew we were successful when one of our clients reported, "I just went Right-Brained on this kid..." While we weren't happy with the behavior, we were actually pleased with that answer, happy that he was able to identify the behavior and characterize it as about his own survival and not about "won't" behavior. Our question to him was, "What would you do if a horse went Right-Brained on you?" He had been with us long enough to know that one way to move a horse from Right-Brained to Left-Brained was to ask for backwards and sideways movement. So the question for him became, "What does backwards and sideways look like in you?" In the course of his time with us, he had learned how to stop, breathe and check in with his body. He identified these skills as helping him go "backwards and sideways" so he could move from Right-Brained to Left-Brained in his own behavior.

As a treatment team dealing with a lot of both Opposition Reflex and Brace, one of the things we ask ourselves is, "How can we set up a pattern of 'yes' responses rather than a pattern of 'no' responses?" If every question we ask a client invokes a "no" answer, it becomes a pattern (and we should know better as a team than to ask yes/no questions anyhow!). We need to set up a pattern for a series of "yes" responses. The more "yes" we get, even about things that are "off-topic," the more likely we are to get a "yes" pattern started, both with a horse and a person. As Parelli says, how can we be "ambassadors of 'yes' rather than ministers of 'no'?"

CLOSING THOUGHTS ON NATURAL HORSEMANSHIP & EQUINE-ASSISTED PRACTICES

Isolate, Separate and Re-combine

When either horse or human have a multitude of issues that keep them from being productive members of society, there needs to be a definitive process of prioritizing and tackling those behaviors. One of the biggest challenges both for horsemen and equine-assisted professionals is to slow the learning process down and refrain from overwhelming the learner by stepping in to tackle everything at once. If you try to fix everything at the same time, you end up with a mess.

This is one of the challenges I see regularly for equine-assisted professionals who are in the early stages of their development. Indeed, we struggled with it ourselves at *Horse Sense*. Borrowed from Parelli™ in particular and Natural Horsemanship in general, the concept of "Isolate, Separate, and Re-combine" was an over-arching framework for us when we started to work with rescue horses. Programmed in "survival mode" for such a long time, many rescue horses come to us in a highly reactive state. They don't have the wherewithal to handle basic requests—like having their ears touched or walking through a cluttered aisle. Asking for something complex overwhelms their system. So it becomes necessary to distill each issue down into its most simple components, and then separate the issue further into micro-components. We work in small increments, tiny steps, toward progress.

We often have to do the same for clients. Early on, our treatment teams were inspired by the many great ideas that developed during session and the great metaphors we saw that we wanted to share

More than a Mirror, by Shannon Knapp

immediately with the client. We just couldn't shut up, and risked overwhelming the client every time.

It became a helpful mantra for us to remember to Isolate, Separate and Re-combine. What is the puzzle we need to figure out with the client? What are the pieces of that puzzle? How can we address each piece? Then, how can we put everything back into one whole? It's "Isolate, Separate, and Re-combine" in human format.

The Parelli™ Promises

When I'm wondering how to proceed with a client, the Parelli™ Promises quickly help clarify my direction and purpose. These promises are useful for helping sort out my priorities on any given day; they become a backbone philosophy for many Parelli™ students. I find I use them with horses and humans equally:

- "Put the relationship first." Equine-assisted therapy and leaning are about relationship: relationship to our environment, relationship to ourselves, and relationship to others. In Natural Horsemanship, putting the relationship first takes precedent over our goals, expectations, and agendas. When we put the relationship first, the most important part remains intact.

- "Foundation before specialization" means putting the basic skills in place first. Again, this might slow progress or feel like you are taking the long way around. But our clients often come to us missing some of the basic emotional and social skills to help them function successfully in life. If we build a program so that the basic skills are addressed first, then more advanced skills can stand on a solid foundation that won't fall apart in the first storm.

- "Never-ending self-improvement" is, for me, as much about "Beginner's Mind" as it is about continually seeking to improve my skills, my mind, my relationships with others and more.

Besides, how else can we know how it feels to be a client? That's something I never want to lose sight of in the process of working with others.

Hopefully, I've explained how the numerous tools, concepts, and processes of Natural Horsemanship in general, and Parelli™ Natural Horsemanship in particular, work in equine-assisted practice at *Horse Sense*. As many Natural Horsemanship practitioners learned early on, what we learn in our work with horses provides keys for what we need in life. Horses expose those aspects of ourselves that we need to develop for living productively in our own lives. At *Horse Sense*, our exposure to Natural Horsemanship via Parelli™ gave us far more than we knew. For us, applying these tools to equine-assisted practice has become totally natural.

From the Outside In

THE SCIENCE AND THEORIES IMPACTING EQUINE ASSISTED PRACTICE

Now that we've formed a baseline understanding of the "classic" or typical client progression through equine-assisted therapy and learning at *Horse Sense*, it's time to dig deeper and explore some of the concepts at work when clients interact with horses. There's a Robert Cooper quote I think is significant as we explore the dynamics of client-horse interaction, "The dinosaurs of tomorrow will be those who keep trying to live and work from their heads alone." (2002, p.17) This quote embodies the essence of why horses (and animals in general) excel at being present to their environment. They live and experience life with their whole body, not just their heads.

We tend to treat the concept of the horse and his/her congruency to both the present moment and the environment from a simplistic point of view, and it is simple. But that doesn't mean there still isn't quite a bit going on. Increasingly, the concepts we utilize in our work with EA practice—like congruency—are no longer just theory. Neuroscientists are busy documenting the multifaceted components which serve to help integrate the social, emotional, and physical into our lives. Science is defining concepts like attunement and social intelligence at a whole new level and helping us better understand how humans can become more functional (and less dysfunctional) in their lives.

In developing my own understanding of the science at work in our practice, I've spent quite a bit of time over the past years reading more science and neuroscience as they focus on cognitive and behavioral aspects. Through this process, I've come to understand more about what is happening when we're helping clients. I think it's beneficial to examine and understand some of the scientific theory surrounding these concepts. Although many ideas I'm going to reference in this chapter are considered controversial or not as yet completely proven by science, I'd like to promote discussion on these ideas as they impact equine-assisted practices.

EMOTIONAL AND SOCIAL INTELLIGENCE IN EQUINE–ASSISTED PSYCHOTHERAPY AND LEARNING

In his books *Emotional Intelligence* and *Social Intelligence*, Daniel Goleman defines the four core competences for emotional and social intelligence:

- Self-awareness
- Self-management
- Social awareness
- Social facility

As you can see from this list and from the preceding discussion of an average series of sessions in EAP/EAL, this is largely what is happening throughout the equine-assisted psychotherapy and learning process. With this in mind, a deeper examination of emotional and social intelligence is in order.

There are multiple resources that discuss the components of emotional intelligence. According to the model first developed by Peter Salovey and John Mayer, emotional intelligence is the ability to monitor one's own and other's feelings and emotions, to discriminate among them, and to utilize this information to guide one's thinking and actions. Another definition states that emotional intelligence is the ability to notice, understand, and draw on our emotions in order to have a range of options and choices in any given moment or interaction. I believe that many client issues have their basis in emotional/social intelligence components.

Next, let's look at each of these competencies in an equine-assisted psychotherapy and learning context. As we discuss what happens in the arena with the horses, I don't mean to suggest these processes—of moving a client through self-awareness to empathy, skill building, and other elements—are one hundred percent linear. We move from where the client is currently into the areas that need attention. An early goal for many clients is present-tense self-awareness, or mindfulness. In fact our first two activities, Observation and Meet and Greet, are key, primarily because of their ability to increase clients' self-awareness.

Throughout this first section on emotional and social intelligence, I'll refer by name and by number to the corresponding *Horse Sense* Skill Card we might utilize when working with a client. You can find a complete list of our Skill Cards, by number, in the Appendix.

Early Client Goals: Building Self-Awareness

The first core competency of emotional intelligence—internal self-awareness—entails being aware of and naming one's own emotions, thoughts, impulses, and physical sensations. It also includes gathering information about internal drivers that may be influencing our behavior and decisions. The capability to pause and ask, "What is motivating me in this moment?" requires the ability to listen without managing, analyzing, or judging ourselves. In other words, internal self-awareness is the ability to read our own emotions and recognize their impact on us.

For many people, reacting without thinking is a prominent default pattern. This is often referred to by mental health professionals as "impulse control." With equine-assisted practice, we help a client examine the available choices between stimulus and response. To paraphrase Viktor Frankl, there is space between stimulus and response, and in that gap is power and freedom. In EAP, we seek to help clients extend the space between stimulus and response, to make a more informed choice. We want clients to examine the options in front of them and choose the option that will bring them what they seek.

If a client has no awareness of self, they have no options from which to make different choices. The first and greatest opportunity to help them is to become more cognizant of the forces, driving emotions, and concerns motivating their actions. Sometimes self-awareness is over-arching and must be brought back into balance, as with a client who virtually cannot move for fear of implications or repercussions from her actions. And sometimes the client has absolutely no awareness of her impact on the world at all. Our focus then becomes how we can help a client to better access self-awareness of the physical body and the physiological reactions to changes. As a starting point, we'll invite him/her to notice where sensations take place in the body, and to draw connections between the body and experiences.

Humans are "pattern animals." I doubt you woke up this morning thinking about trying out a new, unique and different way to brush your teeth. For the most part, we don't seek out new ways or new pat-terns of doing things, even when our current patterns may not serve us. What happens in equine-assisted psychotherapy brings these habit-ual, repeated patterns into focus through the client's interaction with horses. We encourage clients to take time to listen and to notice these patterns, whether they be physical, mental, or emotional. For this rea-son, our first three Skill Cards are: *Observing my Environment, Knowing What My Body Is Telling Me,* and *Paying Attention to My Thoughts.* We encourage clients to disengage from any emotional charge and notice the pattern itself without managing, analyzing, or judging what they are noticing about themselves or the horses. Which door to walk through first—mental, emotional, or physical—will depend on the client. Once the client has a sense of her own pattern, we may move to Skill Card 30: *Learning When Not To Do What You Have Always Done.*

We set up this dynamic very early on for clients through the manner in which we encourage them to "see" the horses: Skill Card 1: *Observing My Environment*. We spend time inviting the client to share her observations of the physical behavior of the horses rather than asking her interpretation of the horse's behavior. A client might say, "That horse is angry!" I might respond, "As evidenced by...? What do you see in the horse's body that tells you she is angry?" Or I might say, "If I were a Martian who just landed on earth here in this arena, what would I see in the horse's body that would let me know he/she is angry?" Many times, clients can't articulate what they are seeing or sensing about the horse, or they will point out what they see in the moment, not being sure themselves if that represents "angry" or not. As mentioned in the previous chapter, at this point we'll invite the client to become a detective during the course of the session or throughout their entire time with us: "See if you can notice what the horse is doing with his body each time you feel or think he might be angry." We've set the client up to be attentive observers, first of the horse, and ultimately of himself/ herself.

That doesn't mean the client's interpretation isn't relevant. But first we want to provide an opportunity for the client to "see" the horses, to examine the horse's body language. After we introduce the idea of "clean viewing"—a phrase which owes its genesis to David Grove, founder of Clean Language—which I define as viewing as free of bias and subjective interpretation as possible, we can then invite the client to examine where she finds evidence of her assumptions. This process starts to disclose how quickly the client moves from seeing a situation to interpreting it. Interpretation can reveal a great deal about the internal state of the client, but the impulse to interpret, regardless of evidence, and the pattern of that impulse, provide a great teachable moment as well. This also creates disengagement from the emotional charge of the observed behavior which, when done first with the horses, allows clients to then better disengage from the emotional charge in their own lives.

Self-awareness in EAP is about asking the client to slow down long enough to listen and notice, to find the correlation between patterns in a session and how those patterns play out in the client's life. We provide the client with space to notice, to become aware of self and others. Sometimes it is easier to start observing others and then apply those skills to self. It's also not unusual for a client to interpret the world from a place deep in the past. We'll continually draw her gently back to more recent experiences, and then to the present moment. We listen and pay attention to the interpretations, even as we invite clients to look past them and/or question them.

Suspending judgment and simply observing, rather than pushing quickly into interpretation, helps the client begin expanding the space between stimulus and the ability to choose her response. As Frankl eloquently states, "In that space, there's the opportunity to find a different understanding, and then to make difference choices." This is also part of developing self-awareness.

Responding vs. Reacting
DEVELOPING SELF-MANAGEMENT

Self-management is the next step toward developing core emotional intelligence competencies. Once the client starts becoming more self-aware in identifying patterns and thoughts, emotions and impulses become less likely to hijack the client in any given situation. He can begin disengaging from automatic pilot; the client can listen for the important information his emotions contain, and begin responding rather than reacting. The client gets to take back awareness, then control the response. Some of the Skill Cards we might use to highlight these ideas include: 33: *Responding to Fear*, 34: *Touch and Go*, and 35: *Approach and Retreat*.

Self-management encompasses responding and adapting one's emotions and impulses to the circumstances, and horses often provide a great opportunity to work with this issue. So many people are enthralled by horses and afraid of them at the same time; there's a huge learning opportunity for self-management in this circumstance alone (Skill Card 15: *Learning Zones* applies here). Clients who show up with fear issues around horses can play with the edges of their emotions and impulses in a safe environment. Do they want to turn tail and run (flight)? Do they shut down to the point where they can't move (freeze)? Or do they come out swinging (fight)? An appropriate Skill Card might include 33: *Responding to Fear.*

Self-management is especially important in tense and emotionally-charged situations when one's default, auto-pilot mode is reactive to any and all stimulus. If clients had the balance and the time to engage the thinking side of their brain, they might recognize they're not in a fight-or-flight situation.

Because they are prey animals, horses can be a model of this same flight/freeze/fight reaction. A horse will choose to flee if possible, though certain introverted horses will freeze first. And, if horses don't have the opportunity to flee, some will fight. Giving clients a chance to visually see this process in a horse provides a great opportunity to see themselves in the horse as well. Skill Cards 37: *Moving Through Anxiety,* and 34: *Touch & Go,* might apply here.

In clients where fear is a dominant emotion, we explore self-management by engaging them in Approach and Retreat activities. Every time they notice something shift in their body when approaching the horse, we ask them to stop and describe what they're noticing. Because many clients have no idea where in their bodies they feel certain emotions, this exercise is a valuable starting place. If appropriate, they can retreat a few steps until the sensation shifts again. In fact, we have a Skill Card called *Approach and Retreat*; many people have never learned this as a strategy to overcome fear.

As before with awareness of the client's body language and the horse's body language, identifying the slightest response to our approach in the horse, such as an ear flick in our direction, can affect a client's ability to notice the smallest change in his own body, such as a hesitancy in his step.

Our bodies provide a great deal of information. People who have experienced repeated trauma, for example, can become highly reactive to certain body language. As pattern animals, humans can develop patterns of behavior that become inappropriate and detrimental. Ultimately self-management comes down to recognizing different pieces of information and making grounded, rational choices about how to respond to the information coming in, including knowing what is driving clients' behavior and how it may or may not apply to the situation in front of them.

Social Awareness: Building Empathy and More

As we build on internal self-awareness and internal self-management in our client sessions, we begin turning our attention to social intelligence, comprised of social awareness and social facility. Social awareness is the ability to sense and understand others' emotions; social facility is the ability to make informed choices utilizing this awareness.

Daniel Goleman (2006) describes social awareness as, "A spectrum that runs from instantaneously sensing another's inner state to understanding her feelings and thoughts to 'getting' complicated social situations" (p. 84). This particular quote reminds me of the many clients who live on the autism spectrum, where social awareness is very much an issue. The inability to "get" social situations, understand others' feelings and thoughts, or instantaneously sense another's state, is a constant challenge. In many ways, we've been building social awareness while also building self-awareness, through observing and responding to the horse's body language, behavior and more. The skills for self and social awareness are much the same; the subject of those skills, however, is what shifts.

Goleman (2006) breaks social awareness down into four categories:

- Primal empathy: Feeling with others; sensing nonverbal emotional signals
- Attunement: Listening with full receptivity; attuning to a person
- Empathic accuracy: Understanding another person's thoughts, feelings, and intentions.
- Social cognition: Knowing how the social world works. (p. 84)

Developing empathy is a common issue we face in our work with youth involved in gangs or in the juvenile justice system. Goleman (2006) describes empathy as "feeling with others; sensing non-verbal emotional signals" (p. 84). To support the development of empathy, we'll examine the body language of both horse and human to explore the various meanings one can ascribe to a posture. For example, what does it mean if a person crosses his arms, sticks out his hip, and cocks a leg? Maybe it means the person is mad. Maybe it means the person is cold. Maybe he is tired of standing! We ask the client to explore multiple options to explain the body language. What else could that behavior mean? We might also invoke the analogy of reading one body part being akin to reading one word in a sentence and expecting to understand the entire sentence based on just that one word. We invite the client, either by embodying the behavior himself or by extrapolating, to figure out what that body language might mean in the person exhibiting it.

Another method we've used to develop empathy is to invite clients to groom the horse and notice each shift in the horse's response. We often give them a groom bag full of implements and ask them to try each item at least once, seeing if they can figure out what gets used where and to what end. We invite them to try each implement on themselves first, to see if they can ascertain what body part it might be useful for grooming. What does the horse seem to really like? Not like? How can the client tell? This provides a great opportunity for discussion about reading others, starting with horses. Our motivation is to help clients start recognizing what it feels like to be in someone else's shoes (or hooves, as the case may be). And, again, they begin to recognize that not everything another person or being does is related to or a reaction to him.

We also explore the correlation between the client's actions and the impact of those actions on the horse. When we invite a client to "move a horse from one side of the arena to another," some may pick up a handful of grass and try to move the horse that way; others may pick up a foam noodle and begin waving it behind the horse. Either way, we'll likely call a pause or a time-out, inviting the client to reflect on the impact of that action on the horse, and also how what is happening impacts his relationship with the horse (Skill Card #29).

According to the work of Paul Ekman and his study on facial expression, emotion, and deception, the physical markers (the facial muscles used) for key emotions are universal. *Emotions Revealed: Recognizing Faces and Feelings to Improve Communication and Emotional Life* (2003) by Paul Ekman are excellent references on this material. Further, emotions themselves are contagious. Goleman, Boyatzis, and McKee discuss this concept in the book *Primal Leadership* (2004), calling it the "open loop" principle. Goleman suggests that we have a profound impact on each other's emotions and even on each other's physiology. This open loop function is a design of the limbic (or emotional) brain that regulates inter-personal actions.

The open loop function is what allows us to have a profound impact on each other. It's akin to what causes a school of fish to change direction almost simultaneously, and to what causes a herd of horses to run as a group from danger. Empathy (Skill Card #7) allows us to feel the emotions of others. The degree to which we are open-looped, and therefore open to suggestion from others and outside, will inform how we show up in the world. If emotions are contagious in humans, it is no surprise that horses, with their extreme sensitivity to their environment, pick up on them, too.

The next "level" of social awareness, according to Goleman, is empathic accuracy. Empathic accuracy consists of understanding another person's thoughts, feelings, and intentions. Just as a client can become trapped in one mode of reacting, he can also become trapped in one mode of interpretation and this greatly impacts his empathic accuracy. At one time, we had a client who kept walking into the personal space of a particular horse who enjoys and encourages others to respect his Personal Space (Skill Card #39). Although the horse would object each time the client approached him too closely, the client continued to do so. When we chatted briefly with the client about what was happening and what the horse was doing, he indicated he knew the horse was going to push back and might perhaps hurt him in the process, but that this was okay with him. He'd been traumatized in many ways, including being shot, and hadn't yet made the connection that just because such a violent event had occurred, that didn't mean it had to keep occurring. There was an enormous "Aha!" from him, as he transformed his learned helplessness into new behavior.

In sessions we see issues of empathic accuracy manifest when a client continually mistakenly assigns negative interpretation of the horse's positive behavior towards him/her (or the reverse!). Whether positive or negative, at some point after the Discovery Phase, we're going to start challenging the accuracy of those interpretations. For example, if a client continually reads a horse's behavior as loving and gentle when we know the behavior to be otherwise, we help the client translate and comprehend that information more accurately. Horses who tend to test boundaries and test leadership can be very, very useful in this process, helping clients become aware of whether they're reading the situation accurately in the present or whether they're reading the situation based on their previous patterns.

We often see this in the numerous adult women clients who have been involved in abusive relationships. These women often interpret problematic behaviors from the horses as, "The horse is loving me," or, "He's expressing his affection," when in fact, that is not the case. Horses are great at testing boundaries—flapping a lip on a client's arm, for example, which then turns into rubbing his/her teeth on a client's arm, which can then become slightly catching skin with the teeth—all behaviors which, if not checked, might lead to an all-out bite. Helping a client read that behavior more accurately will often follow a period of realizing that how she sees and interprets the world is perhaps less than factual. If she can begin practicing a more accurate interpretation, this can then translate into better accuracy in her personal relationships and the outside world in general.

Finally, social awareness is also about "social cognition," or knowing how the world works. We start working with clients on this concept by explaining the social world of horses. We invite the client to make comparisons to the social world of humans. Knowing that horses live in herds, that there's a lead mare and a lead stallion in each naturally-occurring herd, and that other horses are constantly negotiating their place within the social framework is sometimes a safe, non-threatening way to approach the issue of social cognition. As with the other concepts, we'll then begin helping the client extrapolate the parallels between the horse world and the human world.

External Relationship Management: Developing Social Facility

A client's ability to successfully negotiate the spectrum of social awareness concepts does not guarantee fruitful interactions. Just because they get what someone's thinking or intending doesn't mean they're able to react appropriately or effectively. Social facility is needed to build on social awareness to allow smooth, effective interactions. Knowing and correctly interpreting what's going on is only the first step; social facility takes us through the rest of the interaction.

According to Goleman (2006), the spectrum of social facility includes:

- Synchrony: Interacting smoothly at the nonverbal level
- Self-presentation: Presenting ourselves effectively
- Influence: Shaping the outcome of social interactions
- Concern: Caring about others' needs and acting accordingly. (p. 84)

Much of the work in EAP-EAL takes place in the realm of synchrony, or its opposite, dyssemia, a deficit in our capacity to read non-verbal signs (Goleman, 2006, p.91). We often see dyssemia in the form of a "social blind spot" with autism/autism spectrum disorder (ASD) clients; I suspect we'll see it more and more as clients lose opportunity for face-to-face communication and hence have less practice in reading non-verbal signs (email, texting, and chatting require no non-verbal skill!). Synchrony, on the other hand, is as simple (and complex) as successfully shaking another person's hand. Have you ever felt "off" in your timing when you've offered your hand to another? Have you ever thought someone was reaching to shake your hand when actually he wanted to hug? Have you ever felt the other person hold your hand too long? That's all about synchrony. Nearly all equine-assisted psychotherapy and learning engages in examining synchrony or dyssemia in clients, offering an opportunity to talk openly about these ideas.

Any of the EAP/EAL activities offer the chance to observe and build synchrony. (Synchrony is also important for co-facilitators in session!) Since we often have a sense of what the client is attempting to accomplish, we can see whether she is acting and interacting with the horse effectively at a non-verbal level. We can usually see this from the very first session, in the Meet and Greet. As the client approaches the horse and the horse responds with a tail swish or an ear flick, does that impact the client's actions and body language? If a client is struggling with self-management, she might observe this horse's body language and think she should stop approaching the horse, but still be driven by hidden motivators inside her to keep walking. A client working with synchrony, on the other hand, would observe that body language and it would impact her actions, perhaps causing her to step back, slow the approach or change the angle of approach. (Skill Card 40: *Boundaries*)

Self-presentation, similar to energy management which was discussed in the previous chapter, is about being able to exhibit competence and confidence in front of other people. Self-presentation allows us to influence the world around us. Inviting clients to be aware of how they present themselves to the horse, and whether that presentation encourages positive interaction and a willing and cooperative response, is one way we begin refining this skill through session work. Again, any of the EAP/EAL activities will offer fertile ground for a discussion of self-presentation. What needs to be teased out during session is surety that self-confidence isn't the issue (which would be more in the realm of emotional intelligence), but that, instead, the issue is about the exhibition or demonstration of confidence, a social intelligence skill. This highlights something we talk about often in EAP: Do your insides match your outsides? Does the confidence a client feels in a certain situation actually show up in his/her body? (Skill Card 12: *Be Assertive*)

Concern is the fourth social facility skill, and it's about caring for others' needs and acting accordingly. We've had clients who, noticing a cut or a nick on the horse, or noticing bug bite welts, ask if they should proceed with session. We're delighted when this happens, because they are demonstrating concern for the horse and awareness of the impact of the situation on the horse. When this occurs, we might have that session focus on cleaning the wounds of horses, feeding and watering horses, and the like. The key distinguishing question that differentiates this concern as a social intelligence issue and not an emotional intelligence issue is: "Is the concern appropriate to the issue?" If the concern is overwhelming the client, then we're probably dealing more with emotional intelligence. If the concern is measured and appropriate to the situation, we're in the realm of social intelligence. (Skill Cards 7: *Empathy* and 46: *Self-Care*)

Emotional and social intelligence are the cornerstones of the skills that clients are getting hands-on, in-the-moment practice in through engaging with horses. Indeed, horses make these skills come alive!

COGNITIVE NEUROSCIENCE & MINDSIGHT

There are a host of sociological, scientific, and neuroscientific theories wrapped around the inner workings of the brain and how it relates to the external environment, all of which have meaning and impact for our field of equine-assisted practices. Cognitive neuroscience, the study of how psychological and cognitive functions are produced by the brain, is a rich and fast-growing area of study with much significance for EAP/EAL. Mindsight, a term coined by Dr. Daniel Siegel, a clinical professor of psychiatry at the UCLA School of Medicine, also has enormous significance for the field of EAP/EAL. Siegel (2010) describes Mindsight as "the ability to look within and perceive the mind to reflect on our experience....mindsight is our seventh sense" (Kindle Locations 156-157). Before we dive into Mindsight and how it impacts EAP/EAL, let's first discuss some basic aspects of the brain, as well as some other ideas that impact EAP/EAL.

Left-Brain, Right-Brain

As discussed in previous chapters, largely in relation to horses' brains but true of humans as well, there are two "sides" to the brain, each in charge of different aspects of function. The left brain controls the linear, logical, linguistic, and literal, as well as explicit and semantic memory. The right side is more holistic: it controls autobiographical memory, implicit memory (memory that helps us accomplish a task without conscious awareness), the sending and receiving of non-verbal information, and the location for our "integrated body map"—how we perceive ourselves in physical time and space. When we're in the arena with a horse attempting to solve a puzzle, we invite integration of the left and the right brain, and/or bringing the brain more into balance.

As an aside, it's important to know that, in the neuroscientific world, using the terms left-brain and right-brain is controversial, as brain scans have shown no key difference between the two sides. I find the distinction helpful for myself and for my clients, and so continue to use it here and in session.

Mirror Neurons

Another fascinating concept in relation to EAP/EAL and the brain is that of mirror neurons, first discovered in research with primates in the late 1990s. According to Marco Iacoboni (2009), a professor of Psychiatry and Biobehavioral Sciences at UCLA, "By helping us recognize the actions of other people, mirror neurons also help us to recognize and understand the deepest motives behind those actions, the intentions of other individuals" (p. 6). Put simply, if you smile at me, the neurons in my brain mirror you and I smile. This is how I understand the concept that a smile can be contagious, as well as a yawn!

Meg Daley Olmert (2009), author of *Made for Each Other: The Biology of the Human-Animal Bond*, further illustrates the impact of mirror neurons:

> In humans, mirror neurons also resonate with the thoughts, intentions, and feelings of others. Thanks to the reflective power of mirror neurons, our brains, at a glance, can understand if a person picking up a glass is going to drink from it or throw it across the room in anger. They help us feel that anger as well. (p. 6)

Olmert's (2009) *Made for Each Other* focuses on oxytocin and its effects on humans and animals, drawing a line connecting mirror neurons and oxytocin: "When we see a smiling face, our own smile muscles are activated involuntarily. The mirror neurons that perform this internal response can release oxytocin and its calming, socializing sensations" (p. 228). A deeper examination of oxytocin will follow.

Mirror neurons, theoretically, are linked with the capacity to understand the actions of other people, hence suggesting a potential connection of mirror neurons to autism, where there seems to be a lack of empathic accuracy and understanding of another person's thoughts, feelings and intentions. It's my suspicion that mirror neurons are at play in the arena with the horses, the clients and the facilitators, and are part of the learning and change process.

Mindsight

Mindsight, a provocative and useful concept developed by Dr. Dan Siegel (2010), posits that "...[T]his capacity to see the mind itself—our own mind as well as the minds of others—is what we might call our seventh sense," what he calls Mindsight (Kindle Locations 1692-1694). Siegel further states, Mindsight is "creating well-being—in our mental life, in our close relationships, and even in our bodies," and "is a learnable skill" (Kindle Locations 171-172). It appears Mindsight is what is being developed in the arena with horses. Let's take a deeper look at it.

Siegel's book *Mindsight: The New Science of Personal Transformation* (2010) has been extremely helpful to me as I've considered and tried to identify what is happening in the arena between clients, horses, and facilitators. Just as emotional and social intelligence concepts helped me understand and better articulate the "soft skills" that are being developed in the arena, Mindsight has helped me articulate more in regard to the science of what is happening, and how we are supporting clients in their move towards wholeness: "With Mindsight we are able to focus our mind in ways that literally integrate the brain and move it toward resilience and health" (Siegel, 2010, Kindle Locations 190-191).

FUNCTIONS OF THE PREFRONTAL CORTEX

By now, it's common knowledge that, "How we focus our attention shapes the structure of the brain" (Siegel, 2010, Kindle Locations 175-176). In the horse arena with clients, we turn our full attention to the moment and the issue at hand, a benefit and byproduct of the experiential process of equine-assisted therapy and learning. It's not easy to lose focus on the moment and worry, say, about your grocery shopping while you are in contact with several thousand-pound horses. Siegel (2010) refers to the nine functions of the prefrontal cortex and their impact on well-being. They are: "1) bodily regulation, 2) attuned communication, 3) emotional balance, 4) response flexibility, 5) fear modulation, 6) empathy, 7) insight, 8) moral awareness, and 9) intuition." As he indicates, "These nine [functions] would top many researchers' and therapists' lists of the elements of emotional well-being" (Kindle Locations 630-633). While we won't dive into each of these nine in relation to EAP/EAL, we'll take a look at a few of the key functions EAP/EAL clearly supports.

The first is Bodily Regulation, part of virtually any therapeutic intervention, but one highlighted in experiential practice more so than in traditional "office-therapy":

> Bodily regulation: The middle prefrontal region [of the brain] coordinates the activity of a part of the nervous system that controls bodily functions such as heart rate, respiration, and digestion. This "autonomic" nervous system has two branches: the sympathetic, which is often compared with a car's accelerator, and the parasympathetic—the brakes. Balancing the two allows us to drive the car of the body smoothly, so that we lift up off the brakes when we press the accelerator, and vice versa. Without such coordination, we can burn out, revving up while trying to slow down. (Siegel, 2010, Kindle Locations 637-638)

Rather than talking about how one feels or how one felt when both the gas and the brakes were being pressed at the same time, EAP/EAL allows for observation and intervention in the moment this is happening, allowing the client the opportunity to observe himself/herself in the process. As Siegel states, in attuned communication

> ...we allow our own internal state to shift, to come to resonate with the inner world of another. This resonance is at the heart of the important

sense of "feeling felt" that emerges in close relationships. (2010, Kindle Locations 640-642)

Although we'll explore the concept of Attunement in greater detail later in this chapter, we'll be speaking about it primarily in relationship to attuning to and with the horse and the therapist. This attuned communication that Siegel describes above points to attunement as a skill individuals can develop and practice themselves, in addition to something that happens as a result of the therapeutic process with horses and good therapists/facilitators. Siegel elaborates:

> Response flexibility harnesses the power of the middle prefrontal region to put a temporal space between input and action. This ability to pause before responding is an important part of emotional and social intelligence. (2009, Kindle Locations 651-653)

Response flexibility gives a name to the space between stimulus and response discussed earlier (impulse control), articulated in brain science terms. Siegel explains:

> Empathy is the capacity to create mindsight images of other people's minds. These you-maps enable us to sense the internal mental stance of another person, not just to attune to their state of mind. (2009, Kindle Locations 666-668)

I particularly like the idea of creating maps of other people's minds, or horses' minds, however wrong we might be in our lack of true knowledge of the workings of the horse's brain! Being able to posit and recognize a variety of potential responses to an occurrence, and then being able to predict how any one particular person might respond to that occurrence, based on our mind-map of him/her, is a particularly challenging and important skill to develop. Beyond attunement, empathy allows us to experience feelings of another being. Oftentimes this is more easily done with an animal like a horse, as the potential responses aren't nearly as varied for animals as they are for homo sapiens! Siegel concludes,

> Finally, intuition can be seen as how the middle prefrontal cortex gives us access to the wisdom of the body. This region receives information from throughout the interior of the body, including the viscera—such as our heart and our intestines—and uses this input to

give us a "heartfelt sense" of what to do or a "gut feeling" about the right choice. This integrative function illuminates how reasoning, once thought to be a "purely logical" mode of thinking, is in fact dependent on the nonrational processing of our bodies. (2009, Kindle Locations 686-690)

In session, we frame intuition for clients—and for ourselves—by suggesting that there are three centers of knowledge: the head, the heart, and the gut, or thoughts, feelings and sensations. Each of these knowledge centers provides a piece of the puzzle. The head center is perhaps most well-known and utilized by our society. The heart center is less well-known and/or trusted, but has become more and more a part of common communication and experience in our times. Yet the gut, or the intuition, is still treated as mysterious and unknowable, and largely disregarded by some scientific communities. But what Siegel points out in his description of intuition is that this knowledge center is physiological, "the viscera": the intestines and/or bowels. In session, if appropriate, we draw attention to this as another knowledge center, and invite the client to become aware of her physical self, her bodily sensations, and how she makes choices and decisions. At the least, we are connecting the client in an intellectual and a physical sense with this third and oft ignored knowledge center.

One of the ways we might incorporate this concept into treatment

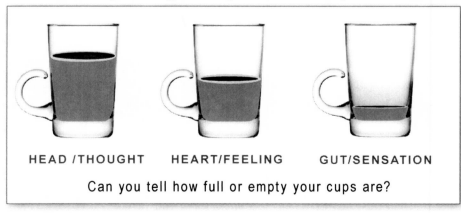

HEAD /THOUGHT   HEART/FEELING   GUT/SENSATION
Can you tell how full or empty your cups are?

Figure 4.1
Visualizing the knowledge centers: Head, Heart, and Gut.

More than a Mirror, by Shannon Knapp

is to invite clients to think of the three knowledge centers as three glasses lined up in a row: one for head/thoughts, one for heart/feelings, and one for gut/sensations. We might even draw three cups on a white board in the horse arena for visual impact. Then, we might ask, "How full is each of these cups for you? Is the 'head/thought cup' full and overflowing? Is the 'heart/feeling' cup only half full? Is the 'gut/sensation' cup almost empty? Where's the opportunity or need for balance?" We might also ask a client to approach an activity primarily from each of these three knowledge centers, and reflect on how different the activity looks as a result.

CREATING IMPLICIT MEMORY

Implicit memory is essentially what we are creating in the arena with horses and clients when we practice EAP/EAL. What is implicit memory? "The kind of memory that enables us to ride the bike is called implicit memory," Siegel (2010) states, "[O]ur ability to recall the day we were taught to ride is explicit memory" (Kindle Locations 2689-2690). Implicit memory, Siegel explains, "harnesses the brain's capacity to generalize from experience, which is how we construct mental models from repeated events" (Kindle Locations 2709-2710). In the arena we create experiences, in the moment with a horse, both challenging and soothing, that help clients generalize outside the arena in daily life. To some degree, we're offering an opportunity to counter past negative repeated experiences with positive repeated experiences.

We can be driven and controlled to an enormous degree by our implicit memories and/or models:

> Our implicit models can manifest as a feeling in our bodies, an emotional reaction, a perceptual bias in our mind's eye, or a behavioral pattern of response. We do not realize we are being biased by the past; we may feel with conviction that our beliefs and reactions are based on our present good judgment. (Siegel, 2010, Kindle Locations 2753-2755)

This is a space in EAP/EAL, when we are convinced "that our beliefs and reactions are based on our present good judgment," when horses offer honest, unbiased feedback, or natural consequences in action, that counter whether this is good or bad judgment. Again, understanding this at an intellectual level can be the easy part of the equation; understanding it on an emotional and visceral level is where horses and EAP/EAL excel.

Integration

Integration, of thought-feeling-sensation, of mind-body-heart or head-heart-gut, is at the core of the difference between traditional psychotherapy interventions and EAP/EAL practices. When we're in the horse arena, much of our job is to help facilitate the client's awareness of his inner and outer experiences, and how those experiences may or may not match. Congruency, an often invoked term in EAP/EAL, involves integrating all parts of ourselves, mind-body-heart together to process information and act. Horses are instrumental, not only in helping us integrate, but in telling us when we get there, when we reach the point of integration/congruency. Practice in integrating leads to congruency, and that practice can happen easily in conjunction with horses.

Dr. Siegel (2010) speaks of integration as part of Mindsight as well:

> Integration enables us to be flexible and free; the lack of such connections promotes a life that is either rigid or chaotic, stuck and dull on the one hand or explosive and unpredictable on the other. With the connecting freedom of integration comes a sense of vitality and the ease of well-being. Without integration we can become imprisoned in behavioral ruts—anxiety and depression, greed, obsession, and addiction. (Kindle Locations 187-189)

Integration involves left- and right-brain activity, too. "When the two hemispheres [of the brain] collaborate, we achieve 'bilateral' or 'horizontal' integration" (Siegel, 2010, Kindle Locations 1982-1983):

> Even to communicate these ideas, I need to use my more conceptual, fact-based, analytical left side—and you need to use yours to understand them. The left hemisphere, being less directly influenced by the subcortical happenings below it, lives in a kind of "ivory tower" of ideas and rational thought compared with its more visceral and emo-

tional right-hemisphere counterpart. (Siegel, 2010, Kindle Locations 1977-1979)

Bringing these two worlds together in the arena gives clients and the facilitation team a chance to see exactly what is happening or not happening for the client, slowing the process down and allowing for examination and integration of external and internal, left and right, head, heart and gut. Which side, or which part needs balancing will vary from client to client and potentially from session to session. Siegel (2010) elaborates:

> Sometimes we need to "name it to tame it." We can use the left language centers to calm the excessively firing right emotional areas. But, again, the key is to link left and right, not replace one imbalance with another. (Kindle Locations 2133-2134)

Just like with the "cups" example of head-heart-gut, balance between right-brain and left-brain is optimal. As StarrLee Heady has observed in conversation with me, horseshoes and EAP are for those in need of balance or support. Many clients come to EAP seeking balance in their lives. Horses are an excellent way to engage the multi-dimensional aspects of humans in that balancing process.

Finally, a related aspect of integration includes the work of Amy Cuddy, Ph.D., a social psychologist at Harvard Business School. In a talk she gave entitled, "Your Body Language Shapes Who You Are", she spoke of the research she and peers have done regarding how our nonverbals govern how we think and feel about ourselves, as well as how they impact outcomes in our lives. In this research, in which she invited clients to either stand in power poses (think Wonder Woman, hands on hips) or the opposite (sitting slouched, legs or ankles crossed, in a small ball), she was able to track significant physiological change in the levels of testosterone and cortisol pre- and post- in participants based on which body posture was assumed. Her conclusion: "Our bodies change our minds, our minds change our behavior, and our behavior changes our outcomes" (TEDtalks Director, 2012). We see this often in the arena when we invite a client to embody what she thinks would be a particular body posture or what someone responding well to a given challenge might look like in her body. Is the horse refusing to stop eating grass when the client wants to move from one arena to another? How might someone who knows how to handle the situation respond physically in that circumstance? We invite clients to play with their postures and nonverbals, inviting them to recall a person from their lives or from history who embodies this necessary quality, whether leadership, or assertiveness, or humility. Clients are often amazed that, even though they don't think they can be "that," their nonverbals can express it nonetheless. A variation on "Fake it 'til you make it," Cuddy posits "Fake it 'til you believe it." This is often the trajectory for EAP clients.

Mindsight, and many, many other exciting books in the field of science are expanding and explaining the ways in which EAP/EAL works for clients. Books like *The Emotional Life of your Brain*, by Richard Davidson (2012), *Buddha's Brain: The Practical Neuroscience of Happiness, Love and Wisdom*, by Richard Mendius (2009), and *The Neuroscience of Psychotherapy: Healing the Social Brain*, by Louis J. Cozolino (2010), all offer insight and understanding. Other books like *Thinking Fast and Slow* by Daniel Kahneman (2011), *Pictures of the Mind: What the New Neuroscience Tells Us About Who We Are*, by Miriam Boylen-Fitzgerald (2010), and the upcoming *Body Sense: The Science and Practice of Embodied Self-Awareness*, by Alan Fogel (2013), and many more will continue to inform and explain what happens in the horse arena for and between clients and horses.

IT'S ALL ABOUT CHANGE
Thoughts and Models to Foster and Support the Process

In the field of equine-assisted psychotherapy and learning, clients generally are coming to us in some form of distress or discomfort. Ours

More than a Mirror, by Shannon Knapp

is not the world of massage or manicures, where clients usually leave refreshed, revitalized, and rejuvenated. The change fostered by EAP is about long-term change, not short-term happiness or satisfaction. In this, we need to be comfortable when others are uncomfortable. That's a big part of being a professional in this field.

Change, for clients, for ourselves, for anyone, is, quite simply, hard. If it weren't, we'd all regularly and routinely solve all our problems just by becoming aware of them and taking appropriate action. But our psyches aren't akin to fixing a flat tire. There are a lot more moving parts, as evidenced by some of the neuroscience literature we've been examining. Flat tires don't often deny they are flat, or think flat is working just fine!

One idea that is becoming abundantly clear is that a system of bribes and rewards to produce change is insufficient and/or flawed. As the title of a book long recommended by EAGALA states, we are often *Punished by Rewards* (Kohn, 1999). The subtitle continues to point the finger at systems that don't work: "The Trouble with Gold Stars, Incentive Plans, A's, Praise and Other Bribes." Kohn posits that collaboration, meaningful content, and choice are much greater methods for reaching lasting change. More recently, Daniel Pink's book, *Drive: The Surprising Truth about What Motivates Us* (2011), continues the discussion, determining that internal motivators will almost always trump external ones. Autonomy/choice, mastery and purpose are more significant in creating lasting change than money or various other carrots. Choice and collaboration are significant elements of EAP/EAL.

There's little surprise in the fact that horse trainers seeking relationship with horses rather than dominance over horses understand the concepts in *Punished by Rewards* and *Drive*. The carrot-and-stick approach, and the limitations of this approach, are represented physically in the Carrot Stick™ Parelli designed. Remember that Parelli tells students that neither the carrot nor the stick is the way; long-lasting development is somewhere between these two approaches. In the world of EAP/EAL, there's a similar lack of surprise that manufacturing positive experiences for clients with horses as a reward for good behavior or to help them "feel better" is more of a carrot-and-stick approach than a true mechanism for change. Experiential approaches to therapy integrate many of the "lasting change" elements identified by Kohn and Pink. As Bettina Shultz-Jobe has commented to me regarding the Natural Lifemanship approach, "It's not about helping people feel better; it's about helping them get better."

Aha! Moments & Clean Language/Facilitation

In his short book *The Brain and Emotional Intelligence* (2011), Daniel Goleman speaks about the process of change through talking about the process of creativity. There is much to connect change and creativity; in fact it may be a deficit in the latter that causes a lack of change to begin with! In EAP/EAL we talk often of "Aha!" moments; speak to virtually any EAP practitioners and they'll report clients have them regularly. What is the brain process of "Aha!" moments? Goleman (2011) explains:

> Brain studies on creativity reveal what goes on at that "Aha!" moment, when we get a sudden insight. If you measure EEG brain waves during a creative moment, it turns out there is very high gamma activity that spikes 300 milliseconds before the answer comes to us. Gamma activity indicates the binding together of neurons, as far-flung brain cells connect in a new neural network—as when a new association emerges. Immediately after that gamma spike, the new idea enters our consciousness. This heightened activity focuses on the temporal area, a center on the side of the right neocortex. This is the same brain area that interprets metaphor and "gets" jokes. It understands the language of the unconscious, what Freud called the "primary process": the language of poems, of art, of myth. It's the logic of dreams, where anything goes and the impossible is possible. That high gamma spike signals that the brain has a new insight. At that moment, right hemisphere cells are using these longer branches and connections to other parts of the brain. They've collected more information and put it together in a novel organization. (Kindle Locations 221-230)

It's no surprise that the part of the brain that interprets metaphor is closely connected with the part of the brain responsible for "Aha!" moments. Whether explicit or implicit, metaphor often inspires and/or informs the process of change. The "Aha!" moment of insight itself is not the change needed, but it is part of the process leading to change. I would also argue that an "Aha!" moment in experiential learning has more impact than in intellectual understanding, because it is experienced in multiple ways: intellectually, in the heart, and viscerally.

But for many, metaphors and symbolism are important elements of the "Aha!" moment in EAP. One of the key facilitation techniques in EAP/EAL as we practice it at *Horse Sense* is designed to help clients find their own metaphors that might move them, a facilitation approach based on the idea of "Clean Language," a specific therapeutic technique developed by David Grove in the 1980s. I like to use the term Clean Facilitation, as suggested by Lisa Baugh in a recent discussion on the EAGALA Members Forum (Baugh, 2013, para. 3). For me and for the *Horse Sense* facilitation team, staying clean about my language is paramount, so as to enable the client to develop and discover personal symbols and metaphors without contamination or distortion by our biases and agendas.

Why this perspective on language is helpful is explained a bit more fully by Wendy Sullivan and Judy Rees (2008), in their book, *Clean Language*:

> Each person knows more about their own challenges than anyone else. Their problem-solving ideas will fit themselves and their problems perfectly—someone else's may not. And their own ideas are more likely to motivate and empower them to take action. Their ideas will continue to work when the advisor is not there to give advice because Clean Language questions encourage people to think for themselves. (Kindle Locations 469-472)

Facilitators using language that's clean make sure they refrain from "leading the witness" or imposing their own words and meaning to influence the client's interpretation. For example, if a client observes that "one horse is standing off to one side of the arena," and the facilitator asserts, "so he seems isolated and angry," the words "isolated" and "angry" belong to the facilitator, not the client, and significantly taint the process for the client. Facilitators, instead, pay particular attention to the words the client is emphasizing and/or repeating, as well as to any unusual words used by clients (Sullivan & Rees, 2008, Kindle Locations 1100-1101). Continuing the process, we will "repeat those words or phrases, particularly those that seem important, back to the speaker," so he has a chance to "see" the images his words are creating, examining them for significance (Sullivan & Rees, 2008, Kindle Location 1104). Imposing our interpretation and language onto the client takes away vast possibilities and serves to disconnect and distance the client from his own experience, and the innate wisdom in clients about how to respond to his own situation or challenge.

Eustress, Distress and Performance

A long time ago, when I was parsing out which "model" approach was the best fit for me (EAGALA? PATH? Epona? EGEA?), StarrLee Heady made the statement that which model I chose to follow depended on what I thought produced change. And, I'm a big believer in change coming about because of being uncomfortable and/or in enough pain to want to do something different. The EAGALA philosophy was an excellent articulation of my thoughts. To paraphrase, people don't change unless they are challenged and they are outside their comfort zone. The most significant change comes when people find their own answers to questions. I thought then, and still feel now, that this is true and best represents how we practice at *Horse Sense* when we offer EAP.

What I didn't know and didn't learn until years later was that there was a term for the "pain" I was talking about: eustress. "Pain" is a layman's term for discomfort/distress/arousal, which I believe are on the same continuum (more on this in a moment). Succinctly put, eustress means "good stress." This stress has less to do with what causes the stress than in how a person responds to that stress. So, what is "good stress" for me might be "bad stress" for someone else: "Eustress refers to a positive response one has to a stressor, which can depend on one's current feelings of control, desirability, location and timing of the stressor" ("Eustress," 2012, para. 3). In the process and the set-up of EAP/EAL sessions, we create a setting of control, dictating the timing and location of stressor: the time of the session itself. The horses provide desirability, a reason to put up with the challenge in the first place. What we're doing in EAP is attempting to shift bad stress to good stress, creating challenges and then reframing the experience and response with more tools, more coping skills, and more support.

Similarly, the Yerkes-Dodson Law also has implications regarding the uses of discomfort in EAP/EAL, helping us recognize how far is too far and how much is too much. This law reflects the relationship between arousal and performance, stating that "performance increases with physiological or mental arousal, but only up to a point. When levels of arousal become too high, performance decreases" ("Yerkes-Dodson," 2013, para. 1).

This is best expressed visually in the Hebbian Yerkes-Dodson model (see Figure 4.2), which "demonstrates the optimum balance of stress with a bell curve....This model is supported by research demonstrating emotional-coping and behavioral-coping strategies are related to changes in perceived stress" ("Eustress," 2012, para. 5).

As Goleman (2011) describes through the lens of brain functioning:

> Just beyond the optimal zone at the top or the performance arc there is a tipping point where the brain secretes too many stress hormones, and they start to interfere with our ability to work well, to learn, to innovate, to listen, and to plan effectively. (Kindle Locations 516-517)

I have certainly experienced sessions in which the arousal was too high and performance for the client crashed; I have also been a part of EAP sessions in which there was little to no "performance" tension, and the impact was mitigated and the session ended up a feel-good petting zoo experience. While I believe in the power of horses just in their presence alone and in contact with them, I believe the power of

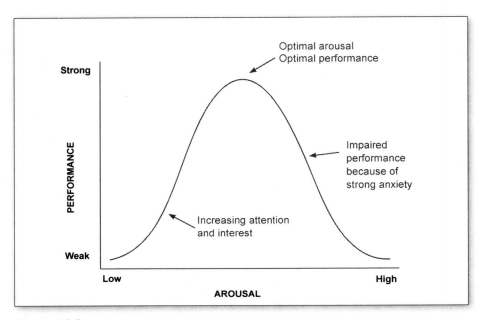

Figure 4.2
Hebbian Yerkes-Dodson Curve (Based on "Eustress," 2012, fig.1)

EAP is about more than just the presence of a horse. Our job as facilitators, though, is to manage the relationship between arousal and performance, creating an environment that is ultimately productive for the client. I've found that when clients spike in arousal beyond beneficial parameters, that's often a good time to move into grooming and other physical contact activities between horse and human, as both experience an increase in oxytocin when that happens, reducing anxiety (again, more on oxytocin shortly!). This kind of intervention will also be appropriate with clients who are experiencing trauma.

I've often felt that excitement/arousal are not far removed from discomfort and distress, that they are on a continuum with each other, or at least are two sides of the same coin. What I have observed in

More than a Mirror, by Shannon Knapp

client sessions is that what is considered excitement for one client is considered distress for another, and that what may start as discomfort and negative regard for the session work for a client can quickly move towards arousal and positive regard. The person who is terrified of horses at the start of a workshop is often to be found hanging out with the horses at the end of a workshop. Helping clients manage their relationship between comfort, discomfort, and fear—the three zones again—is part of the work of EAP/EAL.

Fight or Flight vs. Novelty

Another element we need to be aware of and that needs to be managed by the facilitation team is the Stress Response. When confronted with something new, unique and unknown, which describes most peoples' experience in their first EAP session, people often see the new situation as (at the very least) stressful to some degree and potentially as a clear "threat" (both physically and often emotionally). When clients walk into the arena for the first time, often there is quite a bit of uncertainty: Is this type of therapy going to help me or hurt me? Is this going to change things in my life I don't want changed? Can I do this? We clearly don't want people to be pushed into fight, flight, or freeze mode, although I've seen all of these in session.

But this same unique, unusual situation creates exactly the kind of novelty that can foster positive change. "Among the keys to neuronal growth are novelty, attention and aerobic exercise," Siegel (2010) states (Kindle Locations 2019-2020). He continues:

> We learn more effectively when we are physically active. Novelty, or exposing ourselves to new ideas and experiences, promotes the growth of new connections among existing neurons and seems to stimulate the growth of myelin, the fatty sheath that speeds nerve transmissions. Novelty can even stimulate the growth of new neurons—a finding that took a long time to win acceptance in the scientific community. (Siegel, 2010, Kindle Locations 1574-1577)

There's no doubt that the horses and the experiential learning create novelty for clients seeking change. But this novelty needs to be managed in regard to the stress response. Further, "The observational distance that allows us to watch our own mental activity," Siegel (2010) comments, "is an important first step toward regulating and stabilizing the mind" (Kindle Locations 1754-1755). Observational distance is a significant part of the Discovery Phase of EAP, as in the observation activity and also in the "clean viewing," encouraged by the *Horse Sense* facilitation team. How to use novelty in our favor to support clients without eliciting a fight-flight-freeze response is the role of the facilitation team.

Johari Window

Other useful constructs for me as I practice EAP/EAL include the Johari Window: "A technique created by Joseph Luft and Harrington Ingham in 1955...to help people better understand their relationship with self and others" ("Johari Window," 2012, para. 1). In EAP/EAL, the role of the horses in general and the Equine Specialist in particular, is looking at window #3, the Blind Spot; "things others know about

Known Self	Hidden Self
Things we know about ourselves and others know about us	Things we know about ourself that others do not know
Blind Self	**Unknown Self**
Things others know about us that we do not know	Things neither we nor others know about us

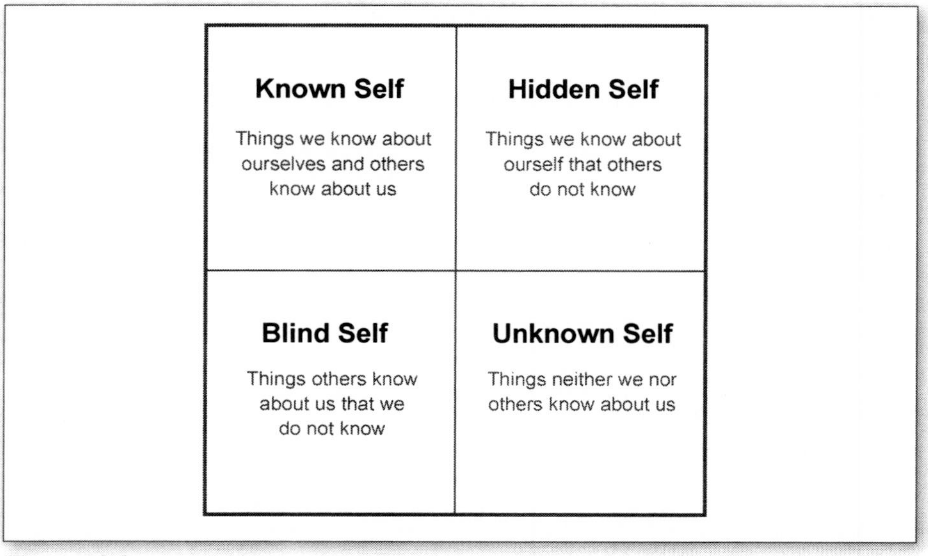

Figure 4.3
Johari Window (Based on "Johari Window," 2012, fig.1)

More than a Mirror, by Shannon Knapp

us that we do not know." (See Figure 4.3) Perhaps this is ultimately true of all therapeutic intervention, but I find it particularly true of EAP. Horses are gifted in expressing what they see about clients' blind spots in a way clients can hear.

4 Stages of Competence

As mentioned in the previous chapter, the 4 Stages of Competence is a construct I find to be a helpful guide in working with clients in EAP, working with interns studying at *Horse Sense*, and in my own experience playing with horses. The first stage, Unconscious Incompetence, entails quite a bit of what is being dealt with in the Discovery Phase of EAP. The second and third stages, Conscious Incompetence and Conscious Competence, mirror what is happening in the Skill-building Phase of EAP. Conscious Competence leading to Unconscious Competence is the goal of the Refinement Phase. (See Figure 4.4)

In session or when planning sessions, I find it helpful to consider the client's stage of competence in regard to a treatment goal or a skill nec-

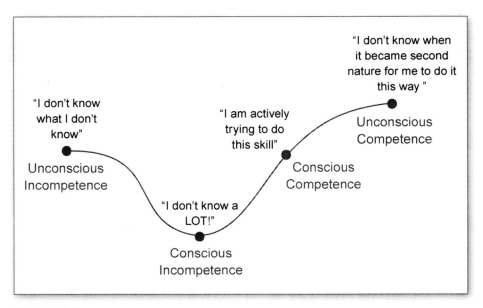

Figure 4.4
The "Four Stages" Diagram (Based on "Four Stages," 2012, para 5-8)

essary to reach that treatment goal. I might also ask: "What can we do, as a facilitation team, to support the client in moving to the next stage of competence?" I also recognize that, to move through the 4 Stages, the client is obliged to do a significant part of the work. This offsets a tendency in myself (and in many others I encounter in the field) to do too much for clients. Remembering the effort I need to put in to move to another level of competence in regards to my own horsemanship helps me recognize what I can, and cannot, do for a client.

The Experiential Learning Cycle

My time at Prescott College, as both a teacher and as a student (of the other students) and other facilitators has greatly improved my facilitation skills, and has given me a language around the experiential process of which I was largely unaware and uninformed prior to joining Prescott College as a Graduate Advisor. Incidentally, it was during my first time teaching an "Intensive" at Prescott on the topic of business building, when I realized that, while I teach to help others avoid making the same mistakes I made (hopefully), I also teach in order to see and to test what I think. Just as writing this book has caused me to get clearer and clearer regarding what I believe about EAP/EAL, I continue to learn as I teach. It's not until I get in front of a class or publish a work and categorically state what I think that I really know what is true for me. Experiential teaching, perhaps?

I've long thought that different kinds of initiatives, like Outward Bound, ropes courses and other experiential education practices, had a great deal to teach EAP/EAL about developing as a field, but I had not done the homework in these fields to understand key underlying principles. Many of the Prescott students I encountered were imbued with experiential learning and experiential education concepts, and frankly could run circles around many EAP folks I'd worked with or observed in terms of facilitation skills. It's a great world to experience, study and spend time in: experiential education, adventure education, adventure therapy, experiential learning. Our field would be well-served if facilitators had more understanding of tenets from The Association for Experiential Education. (www.AEE.org)

As for definitions,

> Experiential education is a philosophy of education that describes the process that occurs between a teacher and student that infuses direct experience with the learning environment and content. The term is not interchangeable with experiential learning; however experiential learning is a sub-field and operates under the methodologies of experiential education. ("Experiential Education," 2012, para. 1)

Experiential learning, however, is "learning through reflection on doing, which is often contrasted with rote or didactic learning" ("Experiential Learning," 2013, para. 3). Experiential learning is often explained by referencing Kolb's Experiential Learning Cycle, recreated in Figure 4.5.

Clients run through all four stages of this cycle in almost every session, sometimes several times a session, in EAP. Then, when they go home, there is "soak time"—time for the experience to sit with them and sink in. Clients usually come back with more experience, if not more information, about what works or what doesn't work, repeating the cycle over and over again with new challenges and activities. Some clients are really good at particular phases of the cycle, like several young boys we've served who were great at active experimentation and "doing," but not so good at abstract conceptualization, or "thinking." Once my therapist co-facilitator and I sat down with Kolb's cycle, we could then tailor activities and create extra support around the process of thinking: How can we provide a structure around abstract conceptualization that would work for these clients?

In addition to mapping out the Experiential Learning Cycle, Kolb also makes assertions about the learner and what he must be able to do:

> However, though the gaining of knowledge is an inherent process that occurs naturally, for a genuine learning experience to occur, there must exist certain elements. According to David A. Kolb, an American educational theorist, knowledge is continuously gained through

both personal and environmental experiences. He states that in order to gain genuine knowledge from an experience, certain abilities are required:

- The learner must be willing to be actively involved in the experience
- The learner must be able to reflect on the experience
- The learner must possess and use analytical skills to conceptualize the experience
- The learner must possess decision making and problem solving skills in order to use the new ideas gained from the experience. ("Experiential Learning," 2013, para. 6-7)

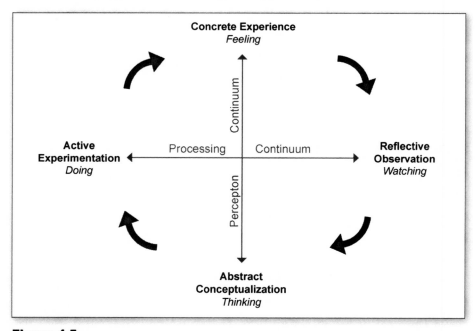

Figure 4.5
The "Experiential Learning Cycle" ("Experiential Learning," 2013, para. 3)

In some circumstances, all of this is true of our clients in EAP. In other circumstances, several of these requirements are not strictly true of our clients; but learning still takes place, to some degree. Our clients aren't always willing participants; some of our clients have little to no ability to reflect on the experience in a traditional intellectual way, and there is no doubt that there are clients with wildly varying degrees

More than a Mirror, by Shannon Knapp

of analytical, decision-making and problem-solving skills. But none-theless, this model and these requirements of the learner do inform and reflect a large portion of the clients served by EAP/EAL, and having the facilitation team aware of and giving the client the language of the Experiential Learning Cycle has definite merits. When the learner doesn't meet the criteria for a learner, as laid out by Kolb, how can the facilitation team adjust and/or compensate the experience?

The Ladder of Inference

As a student of folks like Dr. Paul Smith, Dr. Tracy Weber, and Pam McPhee, one final model/framework I have learned and found useful is the Ladder of Inference. Designed by Peter Senge, et al, as part of *The Fifth Discipline Fieldbook* (1994), I've found the Ladder of Inference to be beneficial in determining where the breakdown(s) is occurring for clients, better allowing the facilitation team to adjust or address these breakdowns (See Figure 4.6).

Although I've worked with clients who have had primary challenges along each of the rungs of this ladder, some challenges stand out as common. For example, many clients' challenge point in EAP occurs during the process of selecting data. Frequently, clients will only see good or positive data in the horse's behavior or, alternately, only see bad or negative data. The amount of data that is selected is usually quite a bit smaller than the amount of available observable data, which is why the team spends a fair amount of time in Discovery Phase trying to help the client scrub clean the data he is observing before applying meaning to it (the third rung of the ladder). Another common challenge point in my experience of offering EAP is in making assumptions, based on the data they have chosen to observe and the meanings they have given to that data. At minimum, the Ladder allows for the existence of a common language between the facilitation team and the client as we move together towards the source of the issues and how to correct them.

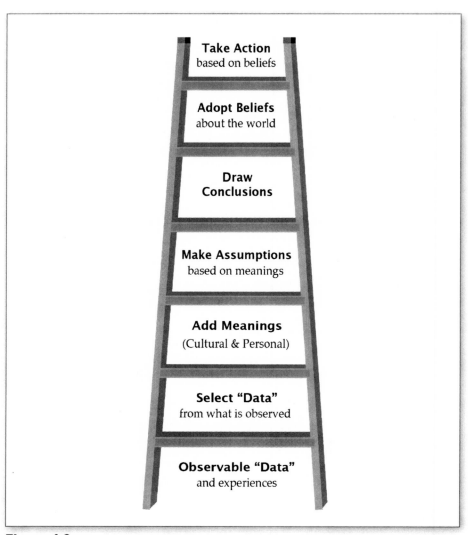

Figure 4.6
The "Ladder of Inference" (Designed by Peter Senge, et al, from of *The Fifth Discipline Fieldbook*, 1994)

Switch

A book that had a great deal of impact on my perception of what causes change is *Switch: How to Change Things When Change is Hard* (2010), by Chip Heath and Dan Heath. Written in an easy-to-read, story-heavy style, *Switch* tackles subject matter similar to what was presented by

More than a Mirror, by Shannon Knapp

Dr. Stephanie Burns years before in the Parelli™ home-study materials of the mid–2000s: If we truly want the change we've identified, why is it so hard to actually follow through? How can we increase the likelihood of making the changes necessary? And how can we, as facilitators, support the client in the cycle of change?

The methodology laid out by the Heaths is broken down into three main segments: Direct the Rider, Motivate the Elephant, and Shape the Path. In the Direct the Rider segment, questions are raised regarding "Bright Spots": Is there any circumstance in which this issue isn't a problem for the client? Is there any time when this issue is working? In this segment, sometimes the issue is as simple as "scripting the critical moves," like drinking water with every meal instead of soda (if the goal is to lose weight). Point to the Destination highlights the importance and the power of focus. In what direction is the client looking? Forward or backward?

The Motivate the Elephant segment discusses "finding the feeling," "shrinking the change," and "growing your people." Shape the Path examines "tweaking the environment," "building new habits," and "rallying the herd." Although largely treated in terms of business and global affairs, the process of change the Heaths examine has implications for the work we do in the arena.

As you may have noticed, I love to use frameworks and charts and lists to express ideas. The Ladder of Inference, the 4 Stages of Competence, the Seven Games™, the 4 Horsenalities—I find these to be helpful mnemonic (memory-assisting) devices that serve me in that moment in the arena when I can't bury my head in a book. None of these are, in my opinion, definitive or the only way to learn or address a concept, nor are they intended to pigeonhole clients or horses. What they are: helpful guides to breaking down what often appear to be big challenges—it's likely we've all worked with extremely challenging horses and clients—into manageable, understandable pieces, creating a pathway for how to proceed.

FACILITATION FOR CHANGE

All the graphs, charts, and models are useless if the facilitator cannot connect with (or get out of the way of) the EAP/EAL client. There are several different approaches and ideas to facilitating change utilized here at *Horse Sense*. One of the most useful tools we use to help the facilitation team get out of the client's way is Clean Language, which has already been discussed. We've also touched on Clean Viewing, which is observation without including "loaded" words. It is preferable to say, "That horse is stomping a foot" rather than "That horse is angry." But, there are a few other helpful ideas impacting change that I'd like to offer.

Mindfulness and Mindful Learning

Mindfulness is the hot topic these days, and this wonderfully worthwhile concept is on the lips of many people, from all different walks of life. Mindfulness, of course, has an impact on EAP, if for no other reason than Mindfulness is about attention. Siegel (2007) explains: "Mindfulness in its most general conception offers a way of being aware that can serve as a gateway toward a more vital mode of being in the world..." (p. 4).

Mindfulness, at its core, is about attention, and there's nothing to grab and hold a person's attention like three horses frolicking ten feet away, or feeling a horse's skin quiver to shake off a fly, or rubbing the soft, silky spot right at the tip of the horse's nose. "Mindfulness in its most general sense is about waking up from a life on automatic," Siegel (2007) states, "and being sensitive to novelty in our everyday experiences" (p. 5). Novelty, getting away from functioning on "automatic", and coming back again and again to the present moment, are all part of the EAP experience.

Mindful learning is also at play in the equine-assisted psychotherapy and learning practice:

> ....the concept of "mindful learning" has been proposed by Ellen Langer (1989, 1997, 2000), an approach which has been shown to make learning more effective, enjoyable, and stimulating. The essence of this approach is to offer learning material in a conditional format rather than as a series of absolute truths. The learner in this way is required to keep an "open mind" about the contexts in which this new information may be useful. Involving the learner in the active process of education also is created by having students consider that their own attitude will shape the direction of the learning. In these ways, this form of mindfulness can be seen to involve the learner's active participation in the learning process itself. Langer suggests that the point of conditional learning is to leave us in a healthy state of uncertainty, which will result in our actively noticing new things. (Seigel, 2007, p.7)

Many descriptors of "Mindful learning" reflect ground we've been covering: offering learning material in a conditional format, inviting the client to keep an open mind by encouraging clean viewing & observation, acknowledging that how we show up affects how we see the horses and relate to our experience in session. In particular, the "healthy state of uncertainty" described above characterizes many EAP sessions, as evidenced by a common response to a classic facilitation technique for EAP. When a group has "gotten the horse over the jump" or "moved the horse from one side of the arena to the other," and looks to the facilitation team for acknowledgement or confirmation of success, the facilitation team will often wait until the clients clearly state that they are done with the exercise before moving on to debrief the experience. This "limbo" time, during which many clients wait for the facilitation team's "ruling," is filled with uncertainty and possibility.

Further,

> Research on mindful learning (Langer, 1989) suggests that it consists of openness to novelty; alertness to distinction; sensitivity to different contexts; implicit, if not explicit, awareness of multiple perspectives; and orientation to the present. (Siegel, 2007, p. 7)

The growing Mindfulness tradition offers many new ideas and strategies, and equine-assisted psychotherapy is already incorporating key components of Mindful Learning into its practices.

Beginner's Mind and the Role of the Horse

The concept of clients working with horses goes beyond simply novelty. The unique opportunity horses offer to clients can be referred to as Beginner's Mind. What a horse brings to a session is largely dependent on what we, clients and facilitators, attempt to achieve. Fundamentally, horses provide a form of feedback allowing clients the opportunity to see how their thoughts, mindsets, and beliefs manifest in real-time, and how those mindsets may be supplanting, ignoring, or overruling different interpretations of the situation.

The presence of a horse presents a client with the opportunity to discern the difference between what she sees or "reads" in a situation and what her mind interprets about the situation (think Ladder of Inference). In meditation practice, observing a thought and watching it rise, attributing it as "thought" without judgment, and letting it flow back out of consciousness is what helps remove us from the ego's undue influence. As humans, we tend to hold onto our thoughts and beliefs tenaciously. Horses quite naturally and, for many folks, literally put humans in "Beginner's Mind," allowing us to view a situation with new eyes and to examine our perceptions by the horse's reaction. Horses help humans match observation with perception.

We also know this: just the experience of being in the presence of a horse elicits response from the client. The form of that response doesn't matter—fear, love, or something in between. Through the framework of the session and conditions set up for moving humans outside their comfort zone, horses evoke response in humans. It's not possible to contain this response as an intellectual exercise; it's an experiential, instinctual, full-body response. It connects the inner to the outer, allowing our neural networks to fully synthesize.

Interoception

Finally, one last tool I'll offer up for facilitating change is awareness of interoception and fostering a client's ability to access this information. Interoception is our own perception of our internal bodily states. Siegel (2010) describes helping foster development of interoception in one of his clients, "Like any skill, focusing his mind on [bodily] sensation would become easier with repeated practice" (Kindle Locations 2060-2061). He continues, "For homework, I had [the client] watch television shows with the sound off. This would engage his right hemisphere's nonverbal perception ability" (Kindle Locations 2074-2075). When I first began working as an Equine Specialist in EAP, I attended a workshop with Patti and Randy Mandrell entitled "Maximizing the Power of the Horse." In that workshop, the leaders recommended we, as facilitators, videotape EAP sessions (with client permission, of course) and then watch the video later with the sound off. This practice not only heightens interoception in the facilitator, it also hones our non-verbal language reading skills. I highly recommend it! Along these same lines, we'll facilitate another activity with groups during observation: invite all the clients to close their eyes while, one at a time, each person narrates what the horses are doing.

By no means is Interoception a skill much recognized or valued in our society, but you'd be surprised at how the lack of it can cause emotional harm, both to the person without it and to the people around him. Siegel shares a case where a client presented as depressed, distant, and dispassionate, and his family worried for him, so much so that they encouraged him to seek out Siegel's help. As Siegel (2010) explains,

> ...finding the words to accurately depict our wordless internal world is a lifelong challenge for many of us. Poets offer us a window into the mastery of this neural skill, but few of us have a poet's gift for translating feeling into words—and it really is quite a feat of a translation, if you pause to think about it. We use our left hemisphere's linguistic packets to ask another person's left hemisphere a question about his experiences or feelings (or to ask ourselves the same question). That

person must decode those signals and send a message across the corpus callosum to activate the right hemisphere, which comes up with the nonverbal somatic-sensory images that are the "stuff" of feelings. He then has to reverse the process, translating the right hemisphere's internal music back into the digital neural processors of the left hemisphere's language centers. Then, a sentence is spoken. Amazing. (Kindle Locations 2114-2121)

Many, many of our clients are initially at a complete loss when we first ask questions like: "where in your body do you feel that?" In the beginning, we expect, and often receive, a shrug or an "I don't know." We encourage people not to try to "come up with" an answer, but to just sit with the question, paying attention to any sensations in their body, both in the moment in the arena and in daily life between sessions.

The Body Scan was a key element of the Epona approach when I was a student of Linda Kohanov and Kathleen Barry-Ingram in the early 2000s. This, and similar tools found in approaches like Somatic Experiencing, can be enormously helpful in connecting a client back with her body and awareness of her own internal state. The arena and horses present a perfect opportunity to practice connecting with one's internal bodily states, if for no other reason than these states are likely to be louder and/or more pronounced in the presence of horses. We will further examine somatic approaches to help with trauma and PTSD a little later in this chapter, but most everyone can use a little help with interoception, and horses are a great way to do this.

When planning and implementing equine-assisted therapy or learning, other more industry-specific models are of use as well. I often find knowing what I'm not doing to be as important as knowing what I am doing. In this regard, Tracy Weber, Ph.D., of Kaleidoscope Learning Center in Michigan has created a wonderful tool. Based on a chart created by Richard Flor in a 1991 article in *The Journal of Experiential Education*, "Building Bridges Between Organizational Development and Experiential/Adventure Education," Weber adds columns to Flor's comparison chart for Equine-Assisted Psychotherapy for Groups and for Individuals, Equine-Assisted Learning for Personal Growth and Equine-assisted Learning for Professional Development, highlighting some of the key differences in focus, practitioner knowledge, methods and more. While I may not agree with each representation within this chart, I think it's an incredibly useful tool for fostering discussion and intentionality around what and how we facilitate psychotherapy vs. professional development. The complete chart is located in the Appendix.

Finally, one last model I like to consider as we're building sessions for clients was developed (and is being refined in her dissertation) by Tanya Bailey, MSW, LICSW in Minnesota. Called the Tri-Balance Model™, Bailey's model highlights the importance of the relationships among and the competence of each component of the model, animal, facilitator, and client, adding in the one element that often gets little attention: the environment. Bailey offers this short explanation of the model below.

— ⌗ —

Animal-Assisted Interactions (AAI) Tri-Balance Model™
by Tanya Bailey, MSW, LICSW

The AAI Tri-Balance Model™ is an illustration of the ever-changing, dynamic relationship which happens during any AAI session. The Tri-Balance Model™ is also a method to provide oversight to the design, implementation and evaluation of AAI sessions.

Components
There are four components present in every AAI session and are represented by the balls in the Tri-Balance Model™ and set the P.A.C.E. for AAI sessions (see Figure 4.7):

- Practitioner—The identified person(s) who plans, leads and holds responsibility for his or her AAI sessions.
- Animal—The identified animal(s) who are assisting and facilitating AAI services.

- Client—The identified person(s) who are receiving AAI services and may be also listed as a participant, student, members of a group, family or individual.
- Environment—The identified location where AAI services are held, as well as the greater environmental milieu.

Connecting Lines Between Components
Each of the four components has a relationship with the other three components—the triad—and these relationships are signified by the lines drawn between each of the components. Although drawn as such in this two-dimensional model, it is important to note this line is not static in its length, strength or consistency and is constantly changing to reflect the connection between each pair of components.

Reciprocal Interactions
The process and results created by the four components in the Tri-Balance Model™—practitioner, client, environment, animal—is called reciprocal because there is a constant give-and-take throughout the AAI session.

Qualities of Competence (QOC)
Each component of the Tri-Balance Model™ brings a level of skill or training to each AAI session and this is called Quality of Competence or QOC. The QOC is represented as a gauge, like the fuel level in a car, with a "plus" sign and "minus" sign, and is not meant to denote "good" or "bad." The greater the competence each component brings to the AAI session, the higher that component is listed on the gauge. Furthermore, some component's QOC can be strengthened or weakened if the relationship it shares with another component is similarly strong or weak.

Balance
The concept of balance in the Tri-Balance Model™ does not mean equality, rather, it is the assessment of each component's QOC and the endeavor to fit components together that complement each other, not produce a deficit in safety, and provide a level of optimal benefit for all involved in AAI sessions.

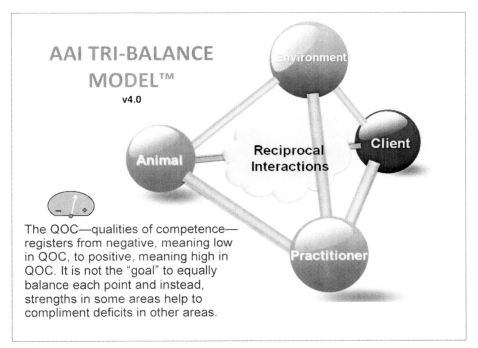

The QOC—qualities of competence—registers from negative, meaning low in QOC, to positive, meaning high in QOC. It is not the "goal" to equally balance each point and instead, strengths in some areas help to compliment deficits in other areas.

Figure 4.7
AAI Tri-Balance Model™ v4.0
(© Tanya Bailey, MSW, LICSW—tanya.bailey1111@gmail.com)

Areas of consideration for each component of the Tri-Balance Model™

- Practitioner—Depending on the overall needs of the identified client, animal and environment, individuals providing AAI sessions may include more than one person and more than one professional discipline. Sometimes, a facility is highly unstable and some practitioners may serve as milieu support. Because they are employed at this facility and can anticipate the slightest changes or concerns, their QOC for the environment is high and this helps to balance the QOC for the other practitioner. Together, both can attend to the animal(s), client(s) and environment with integrity.

- Animal—One size does not fit all; therefore, best practices call for the "identified animal" to have specific training and temperament suited for the goals and objectives of each AAI session. Occasionally, animals who are not identified and who are not trained will become part of AAI sessions. This occurs when observing the larger milieu of the AAI session, especially when the AAI session takes place outside.

This also occurs when working in a setting where multiple other animals reside, like a horse barn or dog training center. Like with practitioners, these animals are considered milieu support and will impact the overall AAI session.

- Client—Whether individual or group, the client has a tremendous amount of leverage in changing the reciprocal interaction of the Tri-Balance Model™. All AAI sessions start and end with the client in mind and it is because of the client's identified and unidentified needs that the AAI session exists in the first place.

- Environment—Examples of "identified locations" may be a horse stall, training center, hospital room, chicken coop or therapy office. The larger milieu of these areas would include the natural world—both indoors and outside—in which each of these locations exist. For example, factors to consider with a hospital room would include how recently was the room cleaned, is the room near a busy nursing station, is the room well-lit or have a window, are there options to adjust the room's temperature.

Applying the Tri-Balance Model™

Case example: A practitioner, Kathleen, has raised and shown horses for 15 years and currently owns three horses she cares for at a local boarding facility. She is currently enrolled in an undergraduate degree in special education. Her required internship matched her with a special education school district that serves a wide variety of students who have emotional, behavioral, physical and cognitive challenges. Over her year-long internship, she assisted five students in their weekly fieldtrip to a working farm where students completed farm chores, groomed animals, and learned basic animal husbandry. This working farm included horses, llamas, sheep, goats, geese and rabbits. The owners of the working farm have also trained the horses and rabbits to make monthly visits to a local nursing home facility. Upon receiving her degree and licensure, Kathleen is hired by the school through which she interned and is given the opportunity to expand the school's current AAI program to include students with emotional and behavioral issues.

Using the Tri-Balance Model™ to develop an AAI session, the practitioner (Kathleen) does a P.A.C.E. assessment in terms of the QOC, the relationships between components, and the resulting reciprocal relationship when all components come together. Items she might consider:

- Practitioner—Her QOC working with a new group of students, non-equine animal species, her relationship with support staff, and her familiarity with the environment of the working farm.

- Animal—Each animal's QOC working with a new group of students, each animal's training and temperament, each animal's relationship with others on the farm, and who is each animal's advocate or handler who will provide the highest level of care and oversight when that animal works in AAI sessions.

- Client—The QOC of a new group of students to receive AAI services: are some members of this new group at risk to themselves or others if taken off-site, what are the known allergies for each group member, and is there any known history of violence or aggression towards animals by any member in this new group.

- Environment—The QOC of the environment at this working farm to host a new group of students to receive AAI sessions: is there a better day in the week for this farm when the routine is more quiet and predictable, and what aspects constitute the word "working" for this farm and are these aspects counter indicated for this new group of students.

If Kathleen decides to move forward with the AAI services expansion, the Tri-Balance Model™ gives her ample checks-and-balances to apply to her new role. She would score a low QOC because she is new as a special education teacher, new in designing AAI sessions, new in working with non-equine species, and working at a new, unfamiliar barn. As she spends more time in each of these areas, receives additional training, and works with these non-equine species, her QOC will also increase. Therefore, to help her "balance" her current level of QOC, she could start by co-facilitating with other practitioners who have more QOC in regards to specific animal species or student population needs. To help her balance her QOC with the animals, she could work with just the horses at this new farm facility as she already comes with 15 years of competence working with horses. However, she cannot assume one horse is just like the next and she must still put in the time and effort to work with each horse individually and build her relationship with each horse. To help her balance her QOC with clients, she could opt to continue the current student group at the farm, and only work with her new group of students on school grounds until she gains competency in this new group's different needs and expectations. By continuing the AAI program with the current group of students at the farm, she also continues to build her QOC in the environment of the farm. Session by session, she will start to notice pieces of the larger environmental milieu and in turn, this helps inform her subsequent practice with a new group of students.

(See Contributor Biographies to read more about this author.)

There are many, many, many ways, approaches, constructs and helpful ideas in the process of supporting client change. I've presented a few that have influenced me, or that I've discovered when seeking out understanding for conditions clients present with. Hopefully you will find value and use in a few of the thoughts presented, to better help you facilitate change for your clients.

OXYTOCIN, ENTRAINMENT AND HUMAN/ ANIMAL BOND

In session, we're observing a variety of concepts playing out: synchrony and dyssemia, social intelligence, empathic accuracy, and others. This interaction between horse and client is even more complex than we realized. Several other aspects to consider in equine-assisted practices include the effects of the hormone oxytocin and the process of entrainment.

Oxytocin is released in all mammals who are in physical contact with one another. It has been linked broadly with our ability to make social connections, as well as with bonding and anxiety and fear reduction. A research project by Dr. Andrea Beetz of Germany, investigating if human-horse interactions have a positive effect on difficult mother-child relationships through measurement of oxytocin levels, stated:

> One of the central common principles underlying relational behavior of humans and non-human mammals is the oxytocin system. Oxytocin decreases anxiety,...reduces and buffers stress. Furthermore, it decreases the activity of the sympathetic nervous system, which results in a lower blood pressure, and increases activation of the parasympathetic nervous system.... the present evidence suggest that oxytocin has important modulatory effects on social behavior (less aggression, facilitation and stimulation of social interaction and communication), stress coping (stress reduction), emotional states (less depression, increased trust in others), pain (reduces pain, elevates pain threshold), and the autonomous nervous system. (Beetz, Kotrschal, Uvnäs-Moberg, & Julius, 2011, p. 2)

In Kerstin Uvnäs-Moberg's *The Oxytocin Factor: Tapping the Hormone of Calm, Love and Healing* (2011), she states:

> Touch and physical contact initiate a reinforcing cycle and produce increased secretion of oxytocin; this makes us more curious and interested in establishing contact, and, this in its turn, releases still more oxytocin, and so on. (Kindle Locations 868-870)

Meg Daley Olmert, author of the book *Made for Each Other* and producer of several documentaries, explores the neurochemical basis of the brain in forging the powerful human-animal bond. Science now recognizes Oxytocin as a factor in social bonding; Olmert's book goes further to assert our close relationships with other species are organically necessary for our well-being, a mutually-beneficial exchange which promotes trust, reduces fear, and increases empathy, all elements necessary for social bonding. This hypothesis is not unrelated to Edward O. Wilson's Biophilia: the "innate tendency to focus upon life and other lifelike forms, and in some instances to affiliate with them emotionally" (Wilson, as quoted in Olmert, 2009, p. 12).

Further findings on the effects of Oxytocin on humans, related by Olmert (2009), include:

> ...oxytocin works within the main brain centers that control emotions and behavior. In fact, oxytocin is central to a mininervous system that can shut down the body's most powerful defensive system, fight/flight, and replace it with a chemical state that makes us more curious and gregarious....Oxytocin lowers heart rate and stress hormones. It

makes people more trusting and more trustworthy. It can even relieve some of the antisocial tendencies of autistics. (Kindle Locations 94 and 109)

In terms of physiology, oxytocin causes:

...a myriad of physiological reactions such as lower pulse rate, blood pressure, and stress hormone levels. At the same time oxytocin promotes the restorative bodily functions like energy storage and growth. The energy conserved by these reactions produces the final stage of positive social interaction—relaxation. (Olmert, 2009, Kindle Location 695)

Further,

Oxytocin is able to calm the paranoid tendencies of the amygdala by activating cells in the center of this nerve cluster that release one of the body's natural tranquilizers, a neurotransmitter called GABA. Its calming influence prevents the amygdala from automatically perceiving new or ambiguous faces, places, or ideas as threatening. It even improves the amygdala's ability to recognize the subtle signs we send through posture, voice, and facial expressions that signal friendly intentions. With GABA's assistance, oxytocin helps the amygdala sharpen our social perceptions and remember those favorable first impressions later.The result is an amygdala chemically tuned to accept social approach. (Olmert, 2009, Kindle Location 730)

Put simply, "oxytocin can quiet the amygdala and allow us to see the world as a less threatening place" (Olmert, 2009, Kindle Location 2400).

The implications for this in the arena and equine-assisted practices is multi-fold. As mentioned earlier, we utilize physical touch in the forms of Sensory Integration (as learned from Rupert Isaacson of *Horse Boy* fame), and in the form of grooming. However it is presented, the effect of oxytocin on both the client and the horse is therapeutic and helpful for many clients. (Although not scientifically proven, it is in this realm that there appears to be the single best support for the idea that horses actually "get something" out of equine-assisted practices with humans.)

Another idea that is relevant to this discussion, Entrainment, is explained by Daniel Goleman (2006) in *Social Intelligence*, and occurs "whenever one natural process entrains or oscillates in rhythm with another" (p. 34). Some studies regarding the horse's electromagnetic field and the impact on humans within that field indicate that humans more quickly reach a state of coherence when in the presence of horses than when not (Walters & Baldwin, 2011). Coherence here refers to "'the quality of being logically integrated, consistent and intelligible,' as in a coherent statement. A related meaning is 'a logical, orderly and aesthetically consistent relationship of parts.'" ("Coherence," n.d., para. 1) For more on this horse-human interaction, see the "Horse-Human Heart Connection" by Ellen Kaye Gehrke in the spring 2010 issue of PATH Intl. *Strides*. See also the Hearth Math Institute, www.HeartMath.org.

As Goleman (2006) says, "When waves are out of synch, they cancel each other; when they synchronize, they amplify" (p. 34). Other studies demonstrate that horses also entrain to us as evidenced by increased heart-rate in horses when there is a similar heart-rate increase in the human at the end of the lead rope or on the horse's back (Zacks, 2009). Yet another study by Katrina Merkies, Ph.D., points to horses being even more relaxed around stressed humans as evidenced by lower heart rates in horses when humans present with higher heart rates. This suggests that "being physically or especially psychologically stressed around horses does not present an increased risk to the humans." (Lesté-Lasserre, para. 8, 2012)

In the arena, I've seen both the horse entrain with the human (especially in the case of an Equine Specialist working with a horse who is unregulated), and I've also seen clients entrain with horses, coming down from an aroused state to a more coherent one. How the entrainment happens and who drives the entrainment—the horse? The client? The facilitators?—is an opportunity for more study. We simply don't have enough measurable scientific evidence to state anything for certain in this regard.

No matter the science, our work in equine-assisted practice allows clients to observe these nonverbal dynamics within themselves. Their interaction with horses provides them the opportunity to practice a host of these and other social intelligence attributes as they play out in the arena. Clients learn how to connect with the horse, with the ability to experiment and practice behaviors while learning the value of qualities like empathy and empathic accuracy.

EAP AND TRAUMA
Attachment, Attunement and Regulation

Trauma and responding to trauma in clients is a very rich area of conversation when considering body-based therapies, including EAP/EAL. When people ask what I do and I tell them equine-assisted psychotherapy, many people are often immediately mindful of how this kind of work might be helpful in resolving/healing trauma; it's a common first connection. Virtually every client we've seen at *Horse Sense* has presented with some kind of trauma; it's part of being human. There are two main categories of trauma I'll reference in this discussion. Peter Levine, Ph.D., the well-known author and developer of Somatic Experiencing™, divides trauma into two main categories, Shock Trauma and Developmental Trauma:

> Shock trauma occurs when we experience potentially life-threatening events that overwhelm our capacities to respond effectively. In contrast, people traumatized by ongoing abuse as children, particularly if the abuse was in the context of their families, may suffer from "developmental trauma." Developmental trauma refers primarily to the psychologically based issues that are usually a result of inadequate nurturing and guidance through critical developmental periods during childhood. Although the dynamics that produce them are different, cruelty and neglect can result in symptoms that are similar to and often intertwined with those of shock trauma. For this reason, people who have experienced developmental trauma need to enlist the support of a therapist to help them work through the issues that have become intertwined with their traumatic reactions. (Levine & Frederick, 1997, pp. 10-11)

I encountered the work of Dr. Levine early on in my EAP/EAL development, reading *Waking the Tiger* in the early 2000s. At that time, I was attempting to understand how horses process trauma, since I was connecting with so many "traumatized" horses through horse rescues and horse welfare organizations. Certainly there is a common language regarding trauma in humans and the language we use to talk about horses, such as predator and prey, and the fight-flight-freeze instinct(s). Horse and humans have default preferences in terms of fight-flight-freeze, which we encourage clients to articulate or at least speculate about for themselves. Levine and Frederick (1997) state: "Unlike wild animals, when threatened we humans have never found it easy to resolve the dilemma of whether to fight or flee. This dilemma stems, at least in part, from the fact that our species has played the role of both predator and prey" (p. 18).

Additionally, I was interested in articulating the similarities and differences between how horses process trauma and how humans do. Levine and Frederick (1997) observe,

> Traumatic symptoms are not caused by the "triggering" event itself. They stem from the frozen residue of energy that has not been resolved and discharged; this residue remains trapped in the nervous system where it can wreak havoc on our bodies and spirits. (p.19)

In years of working with difficult and challenging "rescue" horses, I've seen many horses with responses that suggested a background of abuse and/or neglect: reactivity to men in hats, to ropes, to strange shadows or sudden movements. But what I've only seen once or twice in person and a few times via video (most recently the horse who attacked Buck Brannaman's assistant in the documentary *Buck*, 2011) is a horse who appears to really be suffering from long-term debilitating effects of trauma. Although I've not encountered enough evidence that Post-Traumatic Stress Disorder (PTSD) of some sort or another exists in horses (and am using the term itself to suggest a troubled and unresolved relationship to past traumatic events, not anything clinical), that's part of what I was and am still trying to learn and understand: how is it that humans hold trauma in debilitating ways and horses only rarely do? As Levine states:

> The healing of trauma is a natural process that can be accessed through an inner awareness of the body. It does not require years of psychological therapy, or that memories be repeatedly dredged up and expunged from the unconscious. We will see that the endless search for and retrieval of so-called "traumatic memories" can often interfere with the organisms innate wisdom to heal.
>
> My observations of scores of traumatized people has led me to conclude that post-traumatic symptoms are, fundamentally, incomplete physiological responses suspended in fear. (Levine & Frederick, 1997, p. 34)

I find Levine's explanations regarding how animals "shake off" trauma and how some humans tend to "hold it" compelling, as evidenced by videos of wild animals who, having escaped the take-down of a predator, literally shaking themselves off, like a dog after a bath. In EAP, we use the action of literally "shaking off" negative feelings and emotions and sensations all the time with clients: when we're talking about something really difficult, when the client has been remembering a time he felt trapped or victimized. We'll talk clients through shaking their right hands, then their right arms, then their shoulders....taking them through their whole bodies, shaking off tension or unnecessary energy.

As another leading trauma expert Babette Rothschild states in her book title: *The Body Remembers: The Psychophysiology of Trauma and Trauma Treatment* (2000), and Levine and Frederick (1997) also observe, "Body sensation, rather than intense emotion, is the key to healing trauma" (p. 12). Working with body sensation is, for some of our clients, the very heart of their process with us. I've recently studied a bit of the Trauma Resolution Model (TRM) from the Trauma Resource Institute, which sums up this idea nicely: "We're working on biology, not pathology." (www.TraumaResourceInstitute.com) I think, frankly, that pathology is just plain interesting, and many people want to study and understand that when, in many cases, what needs addressing for the client to be able to function is biology. That's the "here and now" approach in our equine-assisted psychotherapy at *Horse Sense*. It's not that we don't deal with pathology; but in my experience, if we don't also deal with biology, we are missing a great opportunity in serving clients.

But this isn't just biology as sensation or physical affect; we also need to be keenly aware of the brain's development and

MORE THAN A MIRROR: ATTUNEMENT AND HORSES

I find the concept of "attunement" my preferred language for describing what happens when horses connect with humans. I think horses attune to the clients much more than becoming "mirrors" that passively reflect clients. Horses pay attention to what humans do and say about themselves, in mind, body, and spirit. By drawing attention to that, clients learn how to do things in themselves and for themselves by first doing it with a horse. Horses are wonderful at being clean listeners; they can attune and connect to others without losing their own selves, something many people aren't able to do. Horses respond in the moment, so as a client changes the way he/she presents, the horse changes his/her response.

the impact of trauma on the brain. In fact, the two are interconnected: "The somatic processing of trauma is actually changing the brain," according to Shultz-Jobe, "The most recent research on trauma focuses on how trauma affects the brain, which, in turn, affects the body." (Personal communication, Feb 8, 2013) In their TF-EAP training manual, Jobe & Shultz-Jobe state,

> Studies show that functionality of the brain in people who have experienced trauma such as abuse, neglect, combat or natural disasters is often compromised due to disorganization of connections in the brain. These people often struggle with emotion and impulse control, which results in the inability to appropriately handle even minimal stress. (Jobe & Shultz-Jobe, n.d., p. 6)

The two must work hand in hand, creating physical experiences appropriate to the developmental stage of the brain, as well as integrating somatic processing of trauma. Another leader in the field of trauma and brain development is Bessel van der Kolk. I highly recommend becoming familiar with both his and Perry's work to better understand trauma and EAP.

One of the metaphors I use to describe EAP is that it's not "file-cabinet" therapy, in which we go back through all the files from a client's life, read through them, and then help the client create a narrative for moving forward. Instead, we deal with the client who shows up, each and every time. Like the Equine Specialist in session, sometimes knowing less about the client is more productive in helping move him forward. EAP is very much about what's working or not working right now. We've had abundant feedback from Juvenile Justice professionals in our community who report that, in comparison with traditional office therapy, equine-assisted psychotherapy can effect change in clients more rapidly. One of the reasons I believe this is true is that, overall, we're not actively seeking to intellectually resolve past issues. We are instead creating and strengthening new patterns: patterns of thought, patterns of experience, patterns of feeling.

Self-Regulation and Co-Regulation

As we help clients in recognizing, responding to, and reclaiming the body by looking at body sensation, we are essentially in the business of influencing client regulation. What is regulation? Bruce Perry, Ph.D., another leader in the field of trauma, the brain, and human development states,

> The brain is continually sensing and responding to the needs of the body. Specialized "thermostats" monitor our internal (for instance, levels of oxygen and sugar in the blood) and external worlds. When they sense something is wrong (that the body is "stressed"), they activate the brain's alarm systems. These stress-response systems then act to help the body get what it needs.

> Much of this regulation takes place automatically-beyond our awareness. But as we mature, our brain requires that we actively participate in our own regulation. When the internal world needs food or water or the external world is overwhelming, or threatening, our body "tells" us. If we thirst, we seek water; when afraid, we prepare to fight or flee. In short, we "self-regulate." (Perry, n.d., para. 6)

More than a Mirror, by Shannon Knapp

We assist clients using two kinds of regulation: self- and co-regulation. Siegel (2010) defines self-regulation as "sensing [one's] inner world and regulating that world" (Kindle Locations 2435-2436). If we are dis-regulated or feeling out of balance, we can self-regulate again by going for a walk, doing some diaphragmatic breathing, anything that involves repetitive, rhythmic action. Co-regulation is regulating with someone or something else, such as reaching to hold my partner's hand when I am frightened, or in syncing my breathing with a horse's breathing. Some clients know how to co-regulate but struggle with self-regulation. Some clients have never had the opportunity to learn co-regulation. Learning about and addressing deficiencies in regulation is an essential part of EAP.

Dr. Perry has worked extensively with developmental trauma, and has pioneered an exciting and compelling method, a Neurosequential Model of Therapeutics (NMT), for working with traumatized children. His book *The Boy Who Was Raised as a Dog* is required reading at *Horse Sense*. In it, he discusses incorporating "music, dance and massage in order to stimulate and organize the lower brain regions, which contain the key regulatory neurotransmitter systems involved in the stress response" (Perry & Szalavitz, 2007, p. 217). This describes much of what we are trying to affect when offering Rhythmic Riding as part of the Trauma-Focused EAP model (TF-EAP). Jobe and Shultz-Jobe explain:

> [TF-EAP] utilizes the rhythmic, patterned, repetitive movement inherent in riding a horse to increase and reorganize the connections in the brain, thereby increasing the brain's ability for emotion and impulse control. The horse is able to provide the rhythm required to effectively heal the traumatized brain, until the client is able to provide that rhythm themselves. In effect, clients passively learn to self-regulate through the use of the rhythmic, patterned, repetitive movement of the horse. (6)

Attunement

In years of reading about various approaches to therapy and therapeutic practices, one element appears to affect the outcome of treatment more than any other: the therapist. As Dr. Perry states, "Indeed, at heart it is the relationship with the therapist, not primarily his or her methods or words of wisdom, that allows therapy to work" (Perry & Szalavitz, 2007, p. 232). It's my supposition that in EAP, the human therapist is in some cases replaced by (and in other cases supplemented by) the horse as therapist:

> Because of the mirroring neurobiology of our brains, one of the best ways to help someone else become calm and centered is to calm and center ourselves first—and then just pay attention....When you approach a child from this perspective, the response you get is far different from when you simply assume you know what is going on and how to fix it. (Perry & Szalavitz, 2007, p. 245).

Horses do not approach clients as something broken that needs fixing; instead horses respond to the client in the moment. Horses are excellent at responding to danger in one moment, assessing that threat in another and, if appropriate, dropping back down on the physiological alarm scale quickly. Their response to threat is swift and immediate; their ability to be calm and centered is equally quick.

One of the key concepts mentioned to me by therapists when working with clients is developing rapport, which Goleman (2011) breaks down into three key elements:

> There are three ingredients to rapport. The first is paying full attention. Both people need to tune in fully to the other, putting aside distractions. The second is being in synch non-verbally....The third ingredient of rapport is positive feeling. (Kindle Locations 686-693)

The horse is, arguably, better at all three of these elements of rapport than many therapists, which contributes to the success of EAP. Horses engage in "Clean Listening"; they disregard all the distractions which often affect human communication—what kind of car clients drive, what kind of tennis shoes they wear, how their hair is cut, etc. This doesn't mean, however, that a good therapist isn't necessary for the process to be successful. Therapists can still make or break the process for the client, even if the horse is "perfect"!

Horses actually listen to us at a much different and deeper level to the point where they "attune" to us. Goleman (2006) describes attunement as "listening with full receptivity," which horses do without much of the baggage that humans bring to relationship, allowing horses to hear us more clearly (p. 84). Horses aren't always doing this with clients, but it occurs often enough to merit mention. Wendy Sullivan and Judy Rees (2008) call attunement "attending exquisitely" in their book *Clean Language*. They continue, "Being listened to exquisitely is an increasingly rare experience" (Kindle Locations 1116-1118). It's nearly impossible to really, truly listen without one's own self being projected into what is heard. Horses do this more readily than people, allowing for a clean experience for the client.

And it's not just listening. It's about a non-verbal dance of communication between the horse and the client as well. Siegel (2010) explains in terms of humans:

> Through facial expressions and tones of voice, gestures and postures—some so fleeting they can be captured only on a slowed-down recording—we come to "resonate" with one another. The whole we create together is truly larger than our individual identities. We feel this resonance as a palpable sense of connection and aliveness. This is what happens when our minds meet....We sense that our internal world is shared, that our mind is inside the other....stages of protest, self-soothing, and despair reveal how much the child depends upon the attuned responses of a parent to keep her own internal world in equilibrium. (Kindle Locations 367-382).

The horse as therapist can take on the role of the attuned parent in this explanation.

An excellent discussion of these ideas and thoughts appeared in an article from the March/April 2011 *Psychotherapy Networker* magazine, entitled "The Attuned Therapist: Does Attachment Theory Really Matter?" Some compelling ideas from that article appear below:

> Attachment theory seemed to suggest that what mattered most in this clinical relationship was the therapist's capacity for emotional attunement—the ability to hear, see, sense, interpret, and respond to the clients' verbal and nonverbal cues in a way that communicated to the

client that he/she was genuinely seen, felt, and understood. Attachment research had emphasized the psychological core of attunement between mother and child—the continual, subtle, body-based, interactive exchange of looks, vocalizations, body language, eye contact, and speech. Attunement—or "contingent communication" as Daniel Siegel coined it—was really a highly complex, supremely delicate, interpersonal dance between two biological/psychological systems. (Wylie & Turner, 2011, p. 23)

....The right brain/limbic (unconscious, emotional, intuitive) interaction of the psychotherapist and client is more important than cognitive or behavioral suggestions from the therapist; the psychotherapist's emotionally charged verbal and nonverbal, psychobiological attunement to the client and to his/her own internal triggers is critical to effective therapy. (Wylie & Turner, 2011, p. 25)

The article concludes with the following idea: "...the therapist, through the art of a certain specialized form of relationship and attuned connection, isn't just helping people feel better, but deeply changing the physical function and structure of their brains as well" (Wylie & Turner, 2011, p. 48).

Such an enormous number of things are happening at any given moment in the arena between clients and horses: so much that we do and don't know. I've never been a fan of the term "magic" to describe what happens between horse and human in EAP. But I believe that what is often termed magic is that which we can't yet explain or understand: emotional intelligence was coined as a term in the mid-1980s; mirror neurons were identified in the 1980s; neuroscience and brain imaging is very young; Oxytocin is just now really being studied. More and more studies are being undertaken about the horse's physiology and the client's physiology; HeartMath and heart rate variability... what an amazing time to be in this field, as science is catching up to what we've been seeing and unable to explain for so many years, and we are understanding it more and more with each new development.

Section Two

In Section One, I covered some of the terrain I feel vital for understanding the field of equine-assisted psychotherapy and learning: Natural Horsemanship, an overview of key orientations in the field, a sense of what happens in EAP/EAL, both from the inside as a practitioner and from the outside world of science and theory. Yet we've barely begun to touch on two other significant elements of EAP/EAL: the horse and the horse professional/Equine Specialist. What do we ask for and need of horses in this field? Similarly, what important skills are required for a person to serve successfully in the role of the Equine Specialist?

In developing the content for this section, I wanted to access both my own experience and those of other professionals in the field as well. I began in 2010-2011 by conducting a survey of 250 EAP/EAL professionals. Half of the survey questions came from EAGALA-based programs and half from PATH-based participants; some respondents were solely Equine Specialists, others were dually-competent in both horses and mental health and learning. Other feedback came from a *Horse Sense* 2011 EAGALA conference presentation on the role of the Equine Specialist and the horse in equine-assisted practices. This presentation garnered valuable responses from the hundred or so people in the room, responses I recorded and tracked for use in this book, and folded into the survey results. Similarly, I incorporated feedback and thoughts from a PATH conference presentation on the role of the horse in EAP/EAL that I delivered in 2011. In addition to being impressed by the number of people who actively wanted to talk about the roles of the Equine Specialist and the horse (as opposed to programming, grantwriting, etc.—all vital, but different, conversations), I found the answers and thoughts offered in these presentations tremendously insightful.

I designed the online survey to capture a as much of a cross-section of professionals as possible. The survey consisted of a series of multiple choice questions, along with essay questions, about the horse, the horse professional and his/her background and orientation, and more. For the one-on-one interviews, I focused specifically on professionals in the field and/or horse people to whom I regularly turn for advice, support and feedback. Among those I interviewed, many are predominantly EAGALA trainers and practitioners; some are respected PATH practitioners. I also made a point to connect with those who had some sort of specialization as equine professionals. In addition to asking the same baseline survey questions, I conducted a series of deeper discussions with these folks.

Some interview participants came recommended to me as top leaders in the field. These people included Rhiannon Beauregard, Amy Blossom and Carissa McNamara, then vice-president and now-president of the EAGALA Board. Carissa was also the author of an EAGALA article in the *EAGALA In Practice* publication discussing Tom Dorrance, which put her on my radar as someone to interview when it came to EAP and Natural Horsemanship. Patti and Randy Mandrell, and StarrLee Heady, all long-time EAGALA Untrainers, were a part of this interview group as well, both because of their own experience as practicing professionals in the field and because they are consistently in contact with new people entering the field and, therefore, are familiar with the challenges regularly encountered by newcomers. These EAGALA trainers bring a broader perspective of the type of person entering the field of equine-assisted psychotherapy and learning, what skills they possess or lack, and the common challenges they face.

Linda & Don "Z" Zimmerman have been roving practitioners of EAP/EAL for years and bring a true wealth of experience to the conversation; Linda originally worked with Debbie Anderson at Strides to Success, and Z has offered facilitation trainings, workshops and provocative EAGALA conference presentations for years, having also served on the EAGALA Board as Chair. Paul Smith has built wonderful programming at the undergraduate and the masters level in EAMH (Equine Assisted Mental Health) and EAL at Prescott College and

Centaur Leadership Services, and is quite simply one of my favorite practitioners. Thoughtful and inventive, Paul is committed to maintaining respect for the dignity and integrity of the horse. Liza Sapir has been in the EAP/EAL field for years, working in therapeutic residential riding and horsemanship programs and EAGALA EAP, as well as being a life-long horseperson and riding instructor. We were lucky enough to have her as a clinical intern and then a therapist at *Horse Sense* for several years. Tim Jobe and Bettina Shultz-Jobe, both with their own deep, extensive experience and expertise in the field, are now leading the way with a new model of EAP, Trauma-Focused EAP (TF-EAP) through their Natural Lifemanship program. My husband Richard Knapp (Licensed Parelli™ Professional and EAGALA-certified ES) rounds out this group of highly-engaged folks.

As for my contribution to this conversation, I draw from my own decade-plus of personal and professional experience. Through the years since I began *Horse Sense*, I've clocked thousands of hours in client contact with many different mental health professionals, while developing and supervising many different Equine Specialists, interns and more. I piloted every program before training others to partner alongside me or to facilitate in my place. Overwhelmingly, I have worked in the mental health arena and with youth, though I have also worked with many adults as well. My experience includes years of coaching equine-assisted professionals through *Horse Sense* education and development programs, as well as business consultations. Many out-of-town learners have participated in our immersion programs; some stayed for a semester or more as interns. I also bring my experience from working within a private practice model, having operated one of the larger practices of EAP/EAL, engaging with multiple Equine Specialists and multiple therapists. I spent these same years growing and developing my abilities while working with the many horses on our farm, always seeking to improve my horsemanship and partnership skills.

Some of the ground we'll cover in Chapter 5 includes a slightly deeper discussion of how horses, in particular, support the change in clients, what I and others in this field look for in EAP/EAL horses, how we as professionals assess and ascertain a horse's suitability for this work, and how we can best support horses to do the work we ask of them. We'll also consider the impact of working with one's own personal horses in session, a kind of dual relationship that needs to be examined carefully by each of us facing this situation. Finally, we'll take a look at the role of rescued and rehabilitated horses in EAP/EAL, as well as the question of burnout and how this work impacts horses in their "other" jobs on our farms. We'll close with some thoughts about anthropomorphism and its place in our field, in us and in our clients.

I want to emphasize from the outset, however, that my thoughts on horses, horse assessment and many other ideas in this chapter primarily stem from the way in which horses are utilized by *Horse Sense* in practice with our clients. I've been practicing largely within an EAGALA model for many years, and my needs and wishes regarding horses are informed by this foundation. As I've been practicing more and more TF-EAP, with both Relationship Logic and Rhythmic Riding, I find certain characteristics that were not necessary or desirable before are coming to the surface. For example, in Relationship Logic, I am finding that horses who aren't already really good at building relationships are actually a real gift in that process, and that the best horses for this work are those who have not been interacting with lots of different humans for a number of years. Alternately, the horse in Rhythmic Riding (as well as Therapeutic Riding and Hippotherapy) does need to be skilled at filling in for the gaps clients might bring to the session. This re-emphasizes the point that what attributes you need in your horses will always depend on the goals you are working towards and how you plan to get there. There is no one right answer to fit all situations.

In Chapter 6, we'll delve into arguably the most complicated and troublesome element of the EAP/EAL process: the human facilitators.

We'll focus specifically on the Equine Specialist (which I will alternately refer to as the horse professional) as a team member who is distinct from the mental health professional. My expertise is working as an Equine Specialist in a treatment team comprised of this dyad, so I'll confine myself to comments regarding my role as the ES and my role in the dyad. Several of the folks who were interviewed and participated in the conversations through either the survey or the conference presentations offer a glimpse into the mental health perspective. We'll examine the survey data for a sense of how the Equine Specialist fits in today in EAP/EAL, as well as the role of the ES both in and out of session. What should the ES know about horses? About humans and facilitation? What are the common challenges we face as professionals in a still-developing and fairly new field? Where do we find meaningful continuing education to further develop our abilities and facilitation skills?

At certain points in both Chapter 5 and 6, after I've presented my thoughts on a given topic, I'll include quotes from the many interviews conducted on these ideas and questions, in the hopes of providing a representation from different perspectives. By reading these comments, you may find areas of agreement and disagreement, which I'll offer up without commentary (mostly!) or elaboration. These conversations were like oxygen to me, as I sought to connect with others in this field, beyond "what activity do you use when ...." In this section of the book, I hope the many ideas and positions will serve you in your development as they have served me. Finally, we'll close with a few ideas for the newcomer to EAP/EAL, things we wished we'd known when we had first arrived.

All About Horses

Equine-assisted practice is a team effort, but its power comes from one key team member: the horse. It's the horse that drives the client sessions, the horse who possesses the instincts and reactions informing us and the clients, the horse to whom our clients respond.

As we begin talking about the horse, one key idea needs to remain ever-present: "When it comes to the interior life of any other being (including humans)—but particularly beings of another species—there may always be a point beyond which we cannot see or measure or know" (Bekoff, 2008, p. 117). I strive to be clear about my own limitations in understanding horses, knowing that I'm continually bumping up against what I don't know!

PREY ANIMALS

There is one basic concept every Equine Specialist needs to understand about horses: horses are prey animals. Being a prey animal affects everything; it dictates how horses are built, how they learn, how they react to their environment, how they protect and defend themselves, and how they socialize. I repeat this often, in this book and to myself and others, to continue reinforcing this fundamental difference in perspective between humans and horses. Humans are predators, and coming from that predator stance, we often misinterpret horse behavior and actions at the most basic level, and then throw our own anthropomorphism into the mix. No wonder our relationships with horses can become so confused!

It's largely understood that horses survived over time because of their highly-developed sense of perception. They pay constant attention to their environment, acutely attuned to both the physical movement around them and to changes in energy. When they sense change or incongruency in their environment, horses go on high alert and are ready to react. So sensitive is their perception that an entire herd can spook in an instant, seemingly seconds before an event even occurs. Horses don't stand around questioning when change enters their environment; they react first, and investigate later. The horse tunes into this information because he/she has to—it is pre-programmed, for survival.

It's this prey instinct which is a very valuable tool to us in session. Horses pay attention, not to what's coming out of our mouth, but to what we display in our body and in our energy instead, our paralanguage and body language. As herd animals, horses are constantly sensing the emotional temperature of beings in close contact with them, whether human, horse, or other. They're constantly looking to other members of their herd for a sense of what's going on and what needs to happen next.

The manner of response in today's domesticated horse can differ widely from one horse to the next, depending on his/her Horsenality™ (see Chapters 2 and 3 for more discussion on Horsenality™ and how it impacts sessions and clients). It's the task of the Equine Specialist & equine-assisted professional to interpret this response.

When you consider all the elements at play, the complexities of equine psychology, the complexities of social intelligence and other neurobiological factors, we understand that our job as equine-assisted practitioners is much more involved than we initially thought in the first place. I think it also becomes more apparent that the "normal" or "traditional" horse education most of us bring to the field is not nearly enough; it's not broad enough and sometimes it's not even accurate. It is imperative that we search for ways to expand our understanding of horses and their world.

The most critical role of the Equine Specialist is that of interpreting the horse and understanding his responses to the client in session. By

More than a Mirror, by Shannon Knapp

necessity, this requires a deep understanding of horse psychology, as it manifests in body language and by personality type. Like people, the circumstances of the horse's upbringing, the traumas in his past, and the handling by humans over time integrate with an individual persona unique to each animal.

HORSES HIERARCHY OF NEEDS & OTHER BASICS OF HORSES

Parelli™ Natural Horsemanship tells us the first element in understanding horse psychology comes from understanding the horse's basic hierarchy of needs: Safety, Comfort, Play, and Food, often in that order. While the need for Food and Play might be interchangeable among certain horse personalities, Safety and Comfort are core aspects of the equine mind, central to every horse and how he shows up in the world.

A horse responding to a perceived lack of safety is a horse triggered at the most primal level: survival. A perceived lack of safety causes the horse's rawest, most primitive response—namely flight—often heedless of surroundings or anything in his way, making this potentially the most dangerous horse to have in session. On the other hand, a horse responding to the less intense aspect of the spectrum—the need for Food or Play—triggers a different, sometimes less intense reaction.

Knowing where the horse stands within his hierarchy of needs, both fundamentally and on a situation-by-situation basis, becomes a primary aspect in our assessment of a horse and our response to him. This hierarchy should influence how we proceed from his basic care to his development and/or training, and to his suitability and behavior in client sessions.

The professional Equine Specialist, especially, should understand the implications of the equine's hierarchy of needs as it pertains to client sessions, and recognize when a horse's response and body language point to issues of Safety as opposed to Comfort, Food, or Play. The ES needs to know each horse's unique and most probable response as a result of where he might be within the hierarchy of needs at any given moment.

Dr. Robert Miller's book, *Understanding the Ancient Secrets of the Horse's Mind*, is a gold mine for providing many keys to understanding the hierarchy of horses and its implications in our relationship with them. Miller's material is so relevant, in fact, that we'll examine several of the "secrets" to horse psychology as he discusses them:

First among the secrets is the understanding of the concept of flight. The number one, primary response of a prey animal is Flight: run first, ask questions later. If a horse is unable to run, the Flight response can morph into a Fight or Freeze response. A Freeze response is more typical of a donkey or mule, but still a possibility for the average horse. A Fight response is more typical of a highly confident horse, or one who is "backed into a corner," either physically or emotionally/mentally. But, usually, Flight is the more common response.

One of the things that is really helpful and important to know about your horse is the concept called 'the flight line.' A horse, when frightened, is generally going to take off and run. The "flight line" is the relative distance a horse will run before stopping to turn and re-assess the situation. For an Arabian that distance could be several miles, even several hundred miles. The flight line for a common Appaloosa breed might be twenty feet. Horses with longer flight lines have a stronger tendency to flee in the first place.

What's important about the flight line? It's good to have a sense of the flight line for each horse in your herd, and to know that the Appaloosa's twenty-foot flight line indicates just as strong a response as the Arabian's miles. In other words, while we're tempted to think the Appaloosa isn't reacting or responding as strongly because its flight line is appears to be short, it is actually as significant as the hundred-yard response from another breed. Another "secret" of the horse—response time—amplifies the instinct to flee, in that a fleeing horse rarely moves in a slow or plodding manner but, instead, is responding swiftly.

How are flight and response time important in session? If a horse feels unsafe enough to flee, that's a significant marker for me and my treatment team member for what's going on with the client. Flight line is also important for me to know in order to better support the horse in the EAP/EAL process. Subjecting the horse to challenging situations again and again is likely to have some impact on the horses over time. I need to be aware so I can manage this response appropriately, hopefully minimizing the impact on the horses or figuring out another way to reach similar ends. As an Equine Specialist, I also need to be aware of flight and response time to maintain safety for the client and facilitators as well.

Horses possess an acute sense of perception. Horses are perceptive to everything in their environment: people, places, changes, and things. They read all the nuances; they're reading what's different in comparison to what was there before. They look for patterns and any divergence from the pattern. This aspect of horses becomes incredibly helpful in session; we can draw a deep understanding of a situation by utilizing the horse's heightened perceptions to his/her surroundings, including changes in the client from one session to another, or within a session. In short, the horse can offer up information we fail to see or sense.

How horses learn is another "secret" that impacts our work in EAP/EAL. Horses are a precocial species; they are mature and mobile, full-faculty learners at birth. Prey animals have to be precocial learners to react and respond to danger from the moment they are born. Horses learn seven to ten times faster than people do, with the ability for rapid desensitization and acclimatization. Horses excel at learning via repetition. Repeat something three times and it becomes a pattern;

after seven repetitions it becomes a learned behavior. Understanding this helps us understand how best to teach a horse—form a pattern and repeat that pattern so the horse can learn. Be aware and mindful of what horses are learning, intentionally or unintentionally, during session. This secret also presents us with a way to talk with clients about what patterns they have learned, how they have learned them, and how to intentionally overcome negative patterns.

Horses live in a social system based upon hierarchy and competition for dominance, followers looking for leaders. Horses negotiate for hierarchy and their place in the herd every single day as part of their survival instinct, responding more to definitive, assertive leadership and less to emotional, histrionic behavior. Knowing the hierarchy is under continual challenge within the herd as part of the horse's moment-by-moment existence, it should be no surprise that they carry this piece into their relationship with humans as well. While horses tend to allow humans into their hierarchy, they can also test that hierarchy via various levels of play and acts of boundary-setting, just as they do with each other. This is the horse's way of asking questions, or probing another being to determine hierarchy and leadership ability.

That boundary-probing and play look pretty innocuous at first glance, until you understand controlling and influencing movement is exactly how horses determine who's who in the herd. The game goes something like this: he who moves his feet the least, wins. Causing a horse to move his feet, or restricting a horse from moving his feet, is an important part of how the horse understands and interacts with his world.

Upon first inspection, control of movement doesn't really seem to have much application in equine-assisted practice, but it's a key component we need to understand in situations that are both independent of clients and with clients. Knowing a horse is being very deliberate when attempting to get a client's feet to move is obviously important; the horse is, to some degree, testing human clients: their boundaries, their communication, and their leadership. Similarly, when a client is asking a horse to circle or drive, she is engaging with that hierarchal aspect of the horse. It is important for us to be aware of this core issue for horses with and without clients.

Of equal importance to what the horse brings to session is what the horse doesn't bring to session. Although many people speak of the horse being a clean slate, as having no agenda, that's not true in the strictest sense. Of course the horse has an agenda that is present all the time: survival. To assume or assert otherwise is naïve. But the horse doesn't bring what are often the first and foremost considerations for humans: What do you do for a living? Where do you live? Who are your people/your "tribe"? Horses don't generally care about any of that. They don't think about last year's ribbons or ribbons to come or about getting that new and improved pine-scented bedding for their stalls. They are not concerned with what often interests and motivates humans. Instead they care about whether you are safe to connect with at any given moment, and everything else follows (or doesn't follow) from that. This can be an incredible gift to humans who can no longer rely on familiar, and often dysfunctional, ways of relating to others but must explore more unfamiliar, and often more anxiety-provoking but growth-promoting, ways to connect.

What motivated me when I began working in the field of EAP/EAL and continues to excite me is that it's not only possible, but in fact it is desirable, for the whole horse to be invited to the party: mentally, emotionally and physically. So many of the ways we interact with horses in the horse world stifles or suppresses important characteristics of the horse; this isn't the case with EAP/EAL. That's the rich opportunity present in EAP, in which the horse brings the unique gift of feedback by offering a clean, clear response to how humans "show up," or interact with him/her. This provides clients with an opportunity to check perceptions of themselves against the perception of others, in this case, the horse.

THE IDEAL EAP/EAL HORSE

What are the optimal criteria for the "ideal" equine-assisted horse? Many professionals debate the question. Is there a checklist of needs or skills? Should there be a minimum requirements list? For me, I don't think it's a matter of finding horses with certain attributes; I can think of opportunities for all kinds of different horses under all kinds of circumstances. Certainly I can imagine that within certain programs there are very specific requirements for horses, such as in the world of Therapeutic Riding and Hippotherapy. I have preferences for which horses I'm working with in session. But, I think the idea of one checklist being suitable for all programs is unrealistic. What's appropriate for specific clients is a bigger, much broader question that cannot be answered with simply one response covering all who practice.

Since *Horse Sense* is primarily a practice for psychotherapy and learning, interaction with horses as we practice it will involve large amounts of liberty and online work. Thus, horses are not necessarily assessed from a riding perspective (although riding is becoming more prevalent as we begin to offer more TF-EAP in our work). We're less interested in finding horses that fit a checklist than we are in observing their individual responses and propensities and seeing when and where those responses and propensities might be a gift.

We use the Parelli Seven Games™ as a primary assessment tool. These Games™ are so beneficial because each game focuses on a different dynamic of horse behavior. I find that the Squeeze Game™, in particular, reveals quite a bit about a horse. We want to know how the horse responds to varying degrees of physical proximity, to the other horses in the herd, and within her physical environment. Can I squeeze her between me and a fence? Is there a threshold past which she feels too claustrophobic to move? Does she freeze in a squeeze situation, or does she bolt through at ninety miles an hour? For us, each game becomes both an instrument for measuring baseline behavior and for shaping and working with individual behaviors, making the

Seven Games™ an all-in-one, go-to set of tools.

How does the horse respond to physical pressure from different zones of her body? When I refer to zones, I'm thinking of the Zones as explained by Parelli™ in various resources: Zone 1 = the nose and everything in front, Zone 2 = the neck, Zone 3 = the barrel, Zone 4 = the hips, and Zone 5 = the tail and everything behind. (The Delicate Zone is the area around the eyes and ears, basically from where the halter loops over the horse's nose to where it loops behind the ears. Except for work using the Friendly Game™, we avoid the Delicate Zone.) The Seven Games™ are also very helpful in showing us how a horse will respond to different types of pressure, in varying degrees, within each zone. Is she extremely sensitive to touch in certain zones? What about her response to rhythmic pressure? Does she have a hair-trigger reaction or is she extremely tolerant? Since clients are likely to be in any of those zones doing any variety of things, I want to know ahead of time how a horse is going to respond to pressure of any sort from the various zones.

In fact, I have a small chart that I just created recently to confirm that I've played with each horse in each zone, observing the horse's response to an individual playing near or with her in this way, both online and at liberty. Then I use the same chart to check on how the horse responds to these games with groups of people. For example, given the propensity of clients to want to move a horse from behind as a group (for those who have attended an EAGALA training, think Life's Little Obstacles), I want to make sure a horse is accustomed to and relatively comfortable with groups of predators in Zone 5 playing the Driving Game. Although I usually do most of this in my head when observing horses, I have tried to get something down on paper to reflect what kinds of things I'm looking for in a horse. Take a look at the Horse Observation Diagram, shown in Figure 5.1.

Of course what we "need" from a horse will vary from client to cli-

Horse:	Name:		Date:	
Number of People in Session: 1 2–6 7+	Other Horses: Alone–herd nearby With others Alone–herd far away in session		Where: Indoor Outdoor Covered Other:_____	

Left Side	Zone 1	Zone 2	Zone 3	Zone 4	Zone 5
Friendly					
Porcupine					
Driving					
Right Side					
Friendly					
Porcupine					
Driving					

Form Instructions:

Horse: Name of the horse for this session

Name: Your name (or primary person in session)

Date: Today's date

Number of People: Circle the number of people in this observation. Is it one individual, a group of two to six, or a group of seven or more?

Other Horses: Circle if the horse was alone with the herd nearby, alone with the herd far away, or with other horses in session

Where: Where was the observation accomplished? Circle the appropriate location or specify, if other.

Left Side/Right Side: Ensure both sides of the horse are observed.

Friendly/Porcupine/Driving: Use the following scale to indicate how the horse responded:

- '+' – mild   • '-' – moderate   • 'x' – extreme

Figure 5.1
Horse Observation Chart

ent, day to day, so there is never a clear vision of what I want this record of observation to look like. As Paul Smith spoke of in his dissertation, *"The Path of the Centaur: Insights into Facilitating Partnership with Horses to Improve People's Lives,"* one of the "mantras" at Prescott College's Graduate EAMH/EAL program applies here as well: depending on the questions you are asking of the work, you'll get different answers (2012). The questions I might ask of a Natural Horsemanship

More than a Mirror, by Shannon Knapp

horse doing mounted work with veterans, for example, will be different than the questions I ask of an EAP horse working, unmounted, with groups of adults with chemical addiction issues. A "-" in Zones 4 & 5 is acceptable for some situations, such as liberty work. Once a horse is observed for work with individuals (single clients) using this chart, then we'll observe her for small groups and then for large groups.

I'm less concerned about whether we have one hundred percent "+"'s across the board for all zones for the Principle Games (Games 1-3), but that we've asked questions in all the zones. This is no fool-proof formula; it's a starting point. Please note the horse needs to be played with from both sides as well. Horses have more than one side and at *Horse Sense* we play with them on both sides. Clients generally aren't thinking about the "on side," the "near" or the left side of horse vs. the "off" or right side, hence I'm making no assumptions about my horse's abilities to be comfortable with humans interacting with them from any direction. Horses don't usually accept an action from one side if they have only encountered it from the other.

I'm particularly interested in whether a horse is assessed as "solid" before using him/her in session in the Friendly Game™ or the "Extreme Friendly Game." When assessing for these Games™, I pull out all the props and items we might be playing with in session: balls, tarps, cones, jumps, hula hoops, and noodles. Then, I play with the horse to the point where she is responding to the person connected with the item and not the item itself! On a recent drizzly day, I witnessed eight young men dressed head-to-toe in rain slickers approach two of our horses, en masse, in multiple zones at liberty in a pasture. I was curious how our horses would respond to this situation, and was somewhat surprised and particularly pleased when they remained as calm and quiet as the boys, even with all that rain-jacket noise! Had the horses been reactive and spooky to the boys' approach, we would, of course, have held some discussion around it. It was nice to move on to what the clients needed work on, rather than what the horses needed work on!

I also utilize two other Parelli™ techniques—"Undemanding Time" and "Me and My Shadow"—in assessing horses. Both are pretty simple and straightforward processes. Undemanding Time is about spending time with each horse doing absolutely nothing except being with them and quietly observing the nuances of their behavior. Me and My Shadow is about standing beside the horse, usually with a hand thrown over the withers, and mirroring his actions and behaviors. Simple as it sounds, these activities give a powerful glimpse into your horse's world, moment by moment, through his eyes.

It's helpful to know all you can about how each horse might react in different situations. One horse may have a different presentation when he's out in the pasture with a herd, and another, entirely different presentation, when away from his herd by himself. How does each horse behave when he's alone in the arena, both with and without other horses nearby? How is this horse's behavior when alone in the round pen, again with and without other horses nearby? After both Richard and I have spent a fair amount of time with a horse, we'll invite groups of interns and other "stunt clients" over to do mock sessions with any new horse we're thinking of bringing into session. How is this horse with a group? How is this gelding when at liberty with mares? How is this horse when with miniature horses? With the donkey?

It's a good rule of thumb not to try out a grouping for the first time when in front of a client. If I were thinking about doing a session with our Percheron mare, our miniature donkey and our Appaloosa gelding for some reason, I would experiment with that combination in the arena myself before putting that combination in session with the client. Although you never know what behavior is going to show up—it can easily vary from day to day, and hour to hour—putting a certain grouping together a time or two will give you a good sense of the dynamics of that particular herd, and ensure it's not outside the boundaries of safety and propriety, or outside your skill level to facilitate. Also, if a particular group of horses doesn't spend a lot of time together, they may be responding more to each other than to the client. This may be either useful or problematic, depending on the reasons for selecting a particular group of horses in the first place.

This lesson comes from personal experience. Early on in our program, we put our Arabian, a new quarter horse gelding, and my mare Sue together in a session for the first time. Sure enough, unexpected and unwelcome surprises arose. The gelding went hard at the Arabian with stud-like behavior. The ensuing fracas was well beyond being appropriate for the client and, because it was so unexpected, it was close to being beyond my ability to handle. I intervened in the session, and nobody came to any harm, but it would have been far wiser to put these horses together before the session so we could have made intentional and deliberate choices about what might transpire in session, and if it would be useful for the client.

This brings up another important consideration for session work: much of what we do at *Horse Sense* in specific, and in EAP in general, is working with horses in herds. In each session, the grouping of horses you put together becomes a herd for that period of time. Someone will be dominant. Someone will be submissive. Some will just plain not like each other. What is each horse's general answer to a challenge or a request from a more dominant horse? How does each horse communicate fear, dominance, or uncertainty? As much as possible, I want to know what that response is likely to look like from each of my horses beforehand, so I feel able to respond appropriately in the moment and will not be caught off-guard.

One of the reasons why this matters in session: if a dominant horse comes between the client and the non-dominant horse, no intervention is likely to be necessary, as the non-dominant horse will give way to the dominant one. However, if the non-dominant horse is in the middle between the client and the dominant horse, I might change something about the situation so that, should the dominant horse be inclined to push or kick or bite the non-dominant horse, it won't be an action that carries him into or through the client. Being aware of how horses move and react within a herd hierarchy is going to tell you a lot about how to handle these situations. Of course, all this may go quite differently than expected on any given day!

It's also helpful to know what changes for a horse when he becomes unbalanced or unconfident. We have one horse who will probably never work with clients because his Horsenality™ flips really fast and dramatically from "I'm curious and I want to engage" to an attitude of dominance or fear that manifests in an aggressive way. It's the speed with which he moves from ears forward and curious to ears flat back and kicking that will likely keep him from being in contact with clients for a long while, if ever.

I also consider how a given horse handles the pressure of being with a client who's out of balance. This is a lot harder to simulate and to assess up front, but important to learn over the course of sessions. The closest I've come to simulating this scenario is to make a point of visiting with and engaging with a new horse when I'm having a particularly bad day. What kind of response does the horse have to different emotional pressure from humans? How does he behave when the human in the field/arena/stall is clearly out of balance?

I'm often asked how long it takes for a horse to begin actively seeing clients as part of our program. It all depends on the horse. Some horses are able to integrate into the work very quickly, and others might only be suitable or appropriate for limited contact even after a long period of time. Later we'll talk specifically about horses that are unsuitable for this field, and why.

I'm also asked what breed, gender, size or what-have-you of a horse is best for this field. Given our program, I seek diversity in the herd in all ways. The last time I had someone approach me with four hors-es she was trying to re-home, my first thought was that if we needed any new horses, it would be a mare, not a gelding, as we already had a sizeable gelding herd. My next thought was that we didn't have what I call a "flashy pretty" horse at that point, like a paint. We had a lot of browns: duns, chestnuts, etc..., but we didn't have the flash of a paint, which speaks to some clients more than others. So we ended up with Shiloh, our pretty little walking horse, who is also unique in our herd in that she's our only gaited horse.

OTHER POINTS OF VIEW ON IDEAL HORSES FOR EAP/EAL

What do others in the field actively look for in horses for their EAP/EAL programs? This was one of the questions I asked in the surveys as well as in the interviews with leading professionals in EAP/EAL. Here's some of what they said. (For more information and a brief biog-raphy of each interviewee, see Appendix.)

Survey/Conference Feedback

What constitutes a healthy and/or appropriate EAP/EAL horse? The dominant answer from the survey was, predictably—it depends. Many practitioners spoke of horses who are open and curious, calm and cooperative as being well-suited for this field; others required only horses who are breathing (although there have been more than a few I've spoken to who had great sessions that centered around the death of a horse). More than a few said, "It depends on the Equine Specialist" or it depends on the treatment or session goals. Indeed, what horse is appropriate for a session depends in large part on the skills and abil-ities of the horse professional, and what is an appropriate horse can vary with session goals. Many folks also indicated appropriate hors-es being those who were not naturally "mean" or aggressive, as well as taking the EAGALA position of not having horses who are kickers or biters. Quite a few practitioners indicated not having horses who were push-button horses. Many indicated that, in particular, when compared with Therapeutic Riding and/or Hippotherapy horses, EAP/EAL horses could indeed be more spirited, less well-behaved in terms of ground manners, and more opinionated, as long as they were not overly assertive in those opinions.

Interview Feedback

Amy Blossom Lomas: "I like to use all different kinds of horses, depending on the different scenarios. We had a horse that was on stall rest with a broken leg that was still therapeutic for our clients. We had to be mindful to make sure we weren't harming the horse by being in there. If they're sick, then we don't actively use them in our sessions, but we may use that by visiting their stall."

Carissa McNamara: "I really look for a horse that functions well in the herd and what that translates into visually. I like a lot of natural curiosity in my horses and I like a horse that acts and behaves from a platform of kindness. For instance, when I introduce a horse to a herd, I look for signs of what their very first coping strategy might be. There's a big difference between kicking up to let [the rest of the herd] know they're here, and firing and making contact. I look to see if that horse is coming from a healthy place, a trusting place....how high a horse's self-preservation is. And then it's what they do with that. What is their regard for the herd and people when that self-preservation is turned on?"

Liza Sapir Flood: "I really believe a horse needs to have its needs actively met. One example [of such a horse, from my time as a therapist and ES at *Horse Sense*] is Captain, a horse who was very sick and mostly inappropriate for therapy at the end of his days. We had a client who had a real interest in interacting with Captain, so we allowed the interaction. I thought it worked for this reason: while he wasn't healthy, he was receiving an enormous amount of care. And witnessing that care was important for this client. I'm a big believer in having clients help you with that. There is benefit to having a client witness loving care in spite of everything."

Paul Smith: "I would take the position that there's no such this as an inappropriate horse. There are certainly a lot of inappropriate things you can do with different horses, but you can take a dangerous horse and observe that horse outside an arena as part of an equine session about the nature of violence or rage. Think about the emotional impact of being in the presence of power that doesn't know how to contain itself. Would I want to be within 50 yards of that horse? No. But would I have a client within 100 yards? It could be very beneficial. What about putting clients in the presence of a lame or sick horse? There's stuff there to mine. Both examples go way outside the norm of typical sessions but I guess to me, those are the challenges of understanding what a 'session' is."

Richard Knapp: "I like to see a horse that is more natural in responses to things. I want them to be able to think like a horse while also being able to respond. They should pick up that the human client is acting like a predator and say, 'I should leave.' Once the human client acts more cooperative, the horse should be able to respond by acting like a partner with them. I want a horse that is not physically overwhelming—not so much size, but in physical energy. We like horses that are balanced in physical, mental, and emotional stability, able to think through a situation. If they do get unconfident or scared, we would rather have them move away from a situation and then think about what to do instead of reacting violently and causing physical harm. I don't want the horse to behave like a robot, one that looks like they're working on a chain gang. Heads down, broken physically, mentally, and emotionally, they're checked out."

StarrLee Heady: "I think a healthy horse has a healthy herd dynamic. I'm less concerned about their weight, more concerned they have access to fresh water, appropriate feed, and the opportunity to participate in herd membership, with all the active dynamics that require adaptation."

Randy Mandrell: "The appropriate horse is one that's walking. While not necessarily a healthy horse, it can still be a therapeutic horse. I think horses in various stages of health or un-wellness can be beneficial for some clients."

Rhiannon Beauregard: "An appropriate horse is really dependent on the population you work with. Even with a violent population, the horse needs to be predictable, but not so predictable that they're boring. They need to be honest. They need to be emotional without being dangerously emotional. They also can't be so emotional a session will leave them ill, and the horse needs to leave the session in the arena. We take our horses on a three-month trial so we can be sure all these things manifest in practice."

Don "Z" Zimmerman: "I think it's like any other team. You want horses that have their own distinct personalities and areas of expertise. If you put our six horses on a continuum, you have a wide variation without any one specific type of horse. I want a horse that has the same basic skill level, but with their own areas of 'expertise.'"

Michelle Holling-Brooks: "We spend at least sixty to ninety days working with each horse prior to interaction with clients. This gives us time to learn the horse and know what their buttons are. The ideal horse knows how to protect themselves. And I love the ones that are curious. If you can take a fear-driven horse and get them to the point where they are curious, they are healthy and safe. Horses that don't react, those that will sit there and take what the client gives, no matter the situation, are not appropriate. A horse needs to make that differentiation and know when to move away."

HORSENALITY™ & IMPACT ON HORSES IN SESSION

As mentioned earlier, Horsenality™ is an important framework for understanding horses and having an awareness of who they are, in and out of session. Horsenality™ allows us to categorize what we're seeing, both with and without clients. When you see a lot of clients on a regular basis, having a sense of the overall Horsenality™ of each horse is important! Horsenality™ shows us how very differently horses from each quadrant can look, and also speaks to how each Horsenality™ can impact sessions and clients. I think of Horsenality™ not as a way to pigeonhole horses, but a bit like how Don Zimmerman described horses when we spoke recently: each horse has his or her own specialty.

Thinking specifically in terms of sessions and clients, quickly read the following description of the x and y axis of Horsenality™. As you read, think about what kinds of clients would be good fits for each Horsenality™, and what clients might be contra-indicated. (Again, visit the Parelli™ website to download your own copy of the Horsenality™ chart!)

- The left-hand side of the quadrant represents the thinking, responsive Left-Brained horse, a horse who typically exists in a confident state. Left-Brained horses tend to be tolerant, calm and brave, but also dominant.

- The right-hand side of the quadrant represents the Right-Brained horse, one who tends to be more sensitive, submissive, reactive and possibly also nervous or downright fearful. Any horse can become Right-Brained when crossing a confidence threshold, or when Safety or Comfort are compromised.

- The top half of the quadrant represents Extroverted horses. Extroverts are characterized by having more "go" than "whoa," being quick and high energy in general. Extroverts are often more emotional than thinking and tend to be more demonstrative in their bodies. When upset or concerned, Extroverts tend to move their feet a lot. Extroverts also tend to be charismatic and ambitious. Extroverts often make great performance horses, and can be great for our work!

- The bottom half of the quadrant represents the Introverted horse, at times characterized by slow movement and having lower-energy. Introverts need space and time to process information, and tend to move their feet less than their Extroverted counterparts. Introverts are also often described as sweet and content or shy. Introverted horses tend to be very reliable horses, which can make them particularly gifted at things like Therapeutic Riding and Hippotherapy, as well as EAP/EAL.

Digging a bit deeper, Left-Brained Extroverts tend to be very curious, gregarious, and expressive. Right-Brained Extroverts are also expressive, very visibly showing their confidence or unconfidence through movement. Introversion can come across as "willful" or stubborn on the Left-Brained side or expressed as "frozen" or "paralyzed" on the

Right-Brained side.

When a Right-Brain Introvert becomes uncomfortable, the information they present looks more like going inward, disappearing, getting extremely quiet. The quiet is very deceptive; it can look like calm, when in reality this horse has disappeared into a black hole. A Right-Brained Introvert may react to incongruence by becoming more detached, withdrawn, aloof, and distant, but can explode "for no reason." The Left-Brained Introvert's response, in contrast, might look more like pushing or dominance.

Based on the above discussion, one might be tempted to say: "Clearly, I only want Left-Brained Introverts working with clients," or "The best Horsenality™ for equine-assisted practices is the Right-Brain Extrovert." This couldn't be further from the truth. One of the gifts of equine-assisted practice is that there is no perfect Horsenality™ for our field; all horses have something to offer, and what may be perfect for one client may prove counter-productive for another.

Instead of "What kind of Horsenality™ do I want in session?", I'm inclined to ask "How does each Horsenality™ tend to respond to incongruency?" instead. Or, "How does each Horsenality™ tend to respond to aggressive behavior? How does each Horsenality™ most obviously demonstrate unconfidence? How do they express themselves when confident and comfortable?"

Let's say a client presents as incongruent; the Left-Brained Introvert may be more likely to ignore the client, and perhaps even go to sleep. A Right-Brained Extrovert may react to incongruence by taking off and getting as far away from the source as possible. Though very different on the outside, the two responses yield the same possible explanation: the client is incongruent. Too often I see folks in this field (and horse people in general!) conflating a particular behavior of a horse as "always" the result of X or Y, such as a sighing horse is always relaxed, or moving away from a client always means the client is incongruent.

When we try to map this approach onto people, we rather quickly see the limitations: a person standing with his arms crossed isn't always defensive; he might just be cold!

One of my favorite metaphors when describing horse body language is as words in a sentence. Many times, people get focused on reading one single feature of horses, from which they guess the horse's internal state. Some look at ears, some look at breathing rate, some pay attention to the tail. But focusing on any one body part and attempting to extrapolate the horse's internal state from that one element is a bit like picking one word out of a sentence and guessing the meaning of the entire sentence based on that one word. We need to read the whole sentence to understand the statement, not just one word! We need to read the whole horse, and not just one or two key body parts.

MATCH-MAKING CLIENTS AND HORSES

One of the things I guard against, in all this talk of categories and quadrants and such, is thinking that a particular Horsenality™ is the best or only horse for a given diagnosis or situation. I want to guard against match-making the horse and the client. Although I may have suspicions about which horse is going to be a great fit for a given client, I'm almost always going to start out with that horse in a group of horses, giving the client and the horse a chance to determine for themselves what happens next! I'm interested in being open to "mutual choosing," such as happens when the horse and human appear to select each other. If left up to simply my choice of a particular horse for a client, many wonderful learning moments might never have happened. Some of the most insightful sessions have happened when I allowed the horse to choose the client!

THE HEALTHY HORSE AND EAP/EAL

One of the key questions that came up in the process of researching this book and having these conversations is: What is a healthy horse? Young or old, healthy or unhealthy, horses offer feedback when being invited into relationship. We ask them to do all sorts of things, tolerate various forms of sensory input, and even put up with situations involving a great deal of repetition. This is perhaps the more important question one should ask before selecting any horse for session, certainly out of a sense of responsibility toward the horse's well-being, but also because it makes sense that a horse cannot be fully balanced or appropriate for client interaction without being healthy, depending on the kind of interaction. So I'll try to define a healthy horse.

A healthy horse is sound, not just in body, but in mind and spirit as well. She is getting her basic needs met at multiple levels: social, emotional, and physical. Physical fitness is often the easiest and the most obvious of these aspects to address when it comes to health; mental and emotional needs can be more subtle and harder to identify. If a horse is an Extrovert, she needs room to move. If she's Left-Brained, she needs mental challenge and emotional stimulation appropriate to her play drive and energy.

Given our circumstances, an environment that is as natural as we can manage is also the best one for a healthy horse. When I say "natural," I look to emulate what nature has provided to horses. This means being outdoors as much as possible. Keeping horses outside goes a long way toward feeding their emotional and mental health. At *Horse Sense*, we keep our horses in herds, pastured 24/7 except during feeding, in harsh weather or for specific horses with certain health issues. We strive to keep everything—from feed to farrier to vaccination and de-worming—as natural as possible. Our horses receive organic, simple, mostly unprocessed feed. A basic vitamin mixed into grain is also ideal, providing you have the means to afford it. We also feed mixed-grass hay year-round, as necessary, to minimize the risk of colic. We provide free-choice minerals and both red and white salt. We generally don't shoe our horses unless needed for support, balance, or correction of an issue. One of our guides in this regard is Pat Coleby's *Natural Horse Care* (2001).

But, the reality is that not everyone can keep their horses in a totally natural environment. We sometimes have to think creatively to compensate or offset the limitations of any given situation. For those who only have a small area in which to keep horses, Jamie Jackson's book, Paddock Paradise, offers ways for horse owners to set up their property to encourage movement of the herd. There's a multitude of ways to keep your horse mentally engaged even in less-than-ideal environments and situations. Jayna Wekenman wrote her Masters Thesis on this topic at Prescott College. Entitled "Becoming More Equine Centered: A Curriculum to Enrich Experiential Learning Programs and the Equines They Employ," her work is unique in the field for horse people who are serious about examining how the equines in their program are being mentally and emotionally stimulated. Check out Wekenman's new organization, Growing PEAs (find it on Facebook: facebook.com/ GrowingPEAs!). She has condensed some key ideas in the article below.

Encouraging More Equine-Specific Behaviors to Counter-Act the Domestication Dilemma
By Jayna Wekenman, M.Ed.

Many common husbandry practices of the domestic equine encourage atypical (not typical) behaviors and conditions. In equine-assisted programs with therapeutic visions, this causes a dilemma. Sparing all the storybook details, I have developed a passionate frustration for the husbandry practices encouraging atypical behaviors for equines working for equine-assisted programs. Programs excel at "honoring the essence of the (equine)" yet struggle to "create a habitat that enables full physiological distinctive expression" (Salatin, 2010, p. 118). The results: equines showing up in programming reflecting domesticated "horse-ness" (Salatin, 2010) instead of "horse-ness" of the equine species. Conversations are emerging throughout the larger equine-assisted field concerning this dilemma I call the domestication dilemma. These conversations are starters, and equines in the field will continue to show atypical behaviors as long as programs put energy towards a paradigm that supports atypical behaviors.

Not all programs and equines in the field show atypical behaviors and conditions; in fact, behavioral patterns like pacing, cribbing, and learned helplessness may be hardwired in individual equines prior to arriving at programs. In addition to monitoring and managing, programs can actively encourage more equine-specific behaviors by incorporating concepts and techniques like environmental enrichment (FASS, 2010), natural horse boarding (Jackson, 2006), and bio-diverse agricultural systems (Salatin, 1995). By doing so, outcomes in programming may result in all the "horse-ness" of the equine species and other emerging programmatic benefits.

Equine–Specific Behaviors and Domestication

This domestic dilemma is reflective of the larger equine industry. Joel Salatin describes industrialized agriculture as built on "specialization, simplification, routinization, and mechanization" (Salatin, 2010, p. 262). The equine industry (more specifically, equine-assisted programs) create and document special practices and procedures to be followed (turn out, grooming, feed, social interaction), simplify choices of forage (feed: hay, grains, minerals), establish and enforce daily routines; and use tools like feeders, water troughs, halters, stalls daily.

Atypical behaviors (and conditions) are nearly non-existent of feral equines living in more natural habitats (Jackson 2006), yet so common of domestic equines. It seems the domestic equine has been disconnected from feral equine, the same species living on more natural ranges. In domestication, we have expected equines to adapt to restricted environments (restricted in frequency, intensity, and type), allowing limited choice to engage in equine species-specific behaviors. "The difference" between feral and domestic horses, according to Jackson, "lies in how the horses are able to use what nature naturally endowed them with—their mind and bodies" (1992, p. 36). "By wild horse standards, domestic horses are

More than a Mirror, by Shannon Knapp

neither healthy nor sound. They are frail parodies of their wild counter-parts" (Jackson, 2006, p. 12). Programs put substantial amounts of energy, time, emotional, and financial resources towards treating behaviors like cribbing, biting, "burnout," and other stress-related conditions considered atypical to the equine species.

I am not suggesting programs are doing wrong nor is the rest of the equine industry; I am merely suggesting that this "industrialization" in equine-assisted programming is incongruent to personal growth and well-being of individual beings, horse or human. Programs and professionals are at various levels of readiness in exploring modifications of equine management practices; some programs are already doing so, some are ready and waiting, some may recognize the need yet haven't the means to modify, and others may never see the need (energetically or resourcefully). Whatever the situation, individual programs need to decipher what's best for them.

Enrichment and Biologically Diverse Systems

If professionals and equine managers in the field can break away from projections ("that's normal for that horse"), they'll start being accountable for the atypical nature of behaviors and conditions presented (Block, 2008).

I was introduced to enrichment at the Phoenix Zoo. I was both amazed and intrigued by their successes there in treating and preventing atypical behaviors of their animals in captivity. Through careful design and documentation, the Phoenix Zoo has created enrichment programs for each individual animal dedicated to stimulating species-specific behaviors (PhxZoo, 2006). Social enrichment stimulates herd behavior and interaction with various species. Occupational enrichment stimulates fitness-related engagement. Nutritional enrichment incorporates food and foraging. Sensory enrichment offers stimulation of the senses, and physical enrichment describes modifications to the physical surroundings (FASS, 2010). Challenge feeders, scents, sounds, various forages, training, grooming tools, card-board boxes, and construction cones are tools often used in enrichment programming (FASS, 2010 & Tresz, Ambrose, Halsch, & Hearsh, 1997). Natural horse boarding is a concept of designing boarding, turn-out, and work spaces by using track systems and enrichment techniques to encourage typical behaviors of equines regularly (Jackson, 2006).

Joel Salatin advocates for creating agricultural systems rich with poly-culture and diversity of flora and fauna, or biodiversity (Salatin, 1995, p. 47). This creates symbiotic relationships, including humans and program spaces. For example, wooded areas can add natural shelter and habitats for birds and other critters offering social and physical enrichment, manure management, and insect control. In a sense, biodiverse systems honor and intentionally stimulate the "horse-ness of horses," "human-ness of humans," "hay-ness of hay," "water-ness of water," "fly-ness of flies," for effective and efficient ecosystems.

Aim for Opportunities

Once implementing practices to encourage more equine-specific behaviors, I imagine opportunities, specific for programs and equines, to emerge. Programs will exemplify congruence in mission for wellbeing. Equines may exceed proclivity in programming with authentic and conscious feedback, willingness to work, and a highly developed skill of adapting to stressors and novel situations (Jackson, 2006). The time off for equines currently needed in programming may decrease, resulting in a more sustainable number of equines to be cared for and/or more programming to be offered. Programs may save on veterinarian care, medication, property management, and extra time and labor, thus also creating more sustainable practices and remunerative benefits.

I am excited to be part of this conversation. I aim to keep learning and developing my skills and knowledge as I contribute towards this movement. I invite you to join me in exploring. I believe it can be the answer to more sustainable practices, systems of wellbeing, and strengthened relationships amongst all equine-assisted programs. We need not settle for this domestication dilemma any longer and continue to accept atypical behaviors of our equine partners. By doing so, we can both honor and create habitats intentionally developing the "horse-ness" serving participants in programming. *(See Contributor Biographies to read more about this author.)*

References

Block, P. (2008). *Community: The structure of belonging*. Berrett-Koehler Publishing, Inc.: San Francisco, CA.

Federation of Animal Science Societies (FASS). (2010). *Guide for the care and* use of agricultural animals in researching and teaching (3rd ed.). Retrieved from FASS website: http://www.fass.org/docs/agguide3rd/Ag_Guide_3rd_ed.pdf

Jackson, J. (1992). *The natural horse: Lessons from the wild for domestic horse care.* Northland Publishing Company: Flagstaff, AZ.

Jackson, J. (2006). *Paddock paradise: A guide to natural horse boarding.* Star Ridge Publishing: Fayetteville, AR.

The Phoenix Zoo (PhxZoo). (2006). *The Phoenix Zoo: Learn: Animals: Behavioral enrichment. Phoenix Zoo: Phoenix, AZ.* http://www.phoenixzoo.org/learn/animals/behavioral_enrichment.shtml

Salatin, J. (1995). *Salad bar beef.* Polyface, Inc.: Swoop, VA.

Salatin, J. (2010). *The sheer ecstasy of being a lunatic farmer.* Polyface, Inc.: Swoop, VA.

Tresz, H., Ambrose, L., Halsch, H. & Hearsh, A. (1997). *Providing enrichment at no cost. The Shape of Enrichment. 6:4.* http://www.phoenixzoo.org/learn/animals/ProvidingEnrichmentatNoCost.pdf

— ⌘ —

I consider a healthy horse to be confident, responsive, and socially balanced within the herd environment. Our job is not only to provide food and water, but to provide whatever stimulus and circumstances horses need to feed their natural instincts, mentally and emotionally. There are multiple techniques offered by Natural Horsemanship to keep horses mentally engaged and dynamic; it all depends on your imagination and dedication. Parelli's Seven Games™ and the Parelli Patterns™ program are designed to work with the horse's natural curiosity, impulsion, and need for play. When used as a means of mental stimulation, they can be extremely provocative. Too often we rely on taking just a few minutes in the arena, doing the same thing over and over again, to provide that stimulation.

INAPPROPRIATE HORSES & THE EYE OF THE BEHOLDER

When I consider the elements of an ideal herd, there are a couple of different things I actively look for—and several things I would identify as being "inappropriate." But what can be considered "inappropriate" itself is mainly determined on a case-by-case basis, and is largely influenced by what you, the Equine Specialist, see from the horse and how you respond to the horse.

Equine-assisted organizations involved in Therapeutic Riding or Hippotherapy work hard to find balanced, stable riding horses, ones capable of interacting with a variable client population who rides, and whose spastic movement, rigidity, or imbalance can challenge a horse when being ridden. In this scenario, the safety of the rider is a primary concern. The inappropriate horse is obviously one who can't handle those dynamics, or one that becomes easily bored at the repetition of TR or Hippotherapy work.

On the other hand, an inappropriate horse for psychotherapy and learning is one I've often heard described as the "dead broke" or "bomb proof" horse. At first, this seems almost counterintuitive for some folks to understand: wouldn't you want the horse in EAP to be non-responsive, given how challenging working with mental health issues might be? Yet, consider also that one of the most important things we ask the horse to utilize in this work is his/her prey instincts, the same instincts a "dead broke, bomb proof" horse often has re-shaped, or trained out entirely in order to perform in other ways. When these instincts are unavailable or deeply suppressed or modified, it alters the horse's response to stimuli.

One of our staff members went to a farm to look at a horse she was considering to purchase for personal use. With the intention of demonstrating how "bomb proof" her horse was, the owner invited our staff member to go for a ride, then proceeded to jump out of the bushes while brandishing an open umbrella, throwing all sorts of other different, really large stimuli into the path of the rider and the horse. The horse had absolutely no response to this stimulus. The *Horse Sense* staff member was in tears, recounting the way this horse's nature was so altered he could not respond to his world.

We don't necessarily want the opposite either, a highly-reactive horse, but we do want a horse who is fully present and in his/her body. Upon examination, many "dead broke" horses are not "bomb proof" so much as they are completely disassociated or catatonic, especially Right-Brain Introverts who disassociate as a defense mechanism. When we encounter this situation in a rescue horse, it has been possible to bring them back to a more balanced state, which is one of the most rewarding aspects of the rescue and rehab work we've done.

Once we get the horse to the farm and start engaging in Natural Horsemanship activities, these horses start to understand that we're inviting them to be horses, that we want them to be present, not just to carry their body in a certain frame or to run all-out through a barrel pattern. It's rewarding to see a horse respond once she realizes we do want to know her opinion, we do want her to express her thoughts, and that she won't be punished for that. In that moment, it's almost as if the horse asks us: "Are you talking to me? No one's ever asked me what I thought about the situation." Then we get to stand back and see the true Horsenality™ emerge.

In my opinion, young horses are sometimes inappropriate for equine-assisted work. Young horses are by nature very precocious and impressionable; they're absorbing quite a bit of information from us as humans, and our clients are often not the best humans to deliver all those messages. We have a few young horses on our farm right now who won't be utilized in session anytime soon, as we want them to have more of a clean slate than we often get with our rescued/donated horses. We want to help them develop good patterns before putting them with clients.

On the other hand, I think sometimes programs over-rely on senior horses in their barn for equine-assisted work, which can be as much of a problem as relying on horses who are too young. We have two horses in their early thirties who are still actively seeing clients on a regular basis, but they are both quite clear about their boundaries and their "druthers" (I'd rather do this = "druthers"). While this may make some older horses perfect for a given client or situation, some aged horses can start falling too much into the "dead broke" category; the opinions they register are less about responding to the client and more about remaining as comfortable as possible. Can there be young horses and very old horses who are still great at working in equine-assisted work? Absolutely. You just want to be mindful of the potential challenges.

Ill and infirm horses are generally inappropriate candidates if our work with them is going to present hardship, stress, or tension due to their condition. It's also not appropriate for that horse to be in sessions that may involve trotting or cantering. However, we have (and will likely again) utilize an ill or infirm horse within certain situations, such as during rehabilitation, or if caring for that horse can be helpful in the therapy for a particular client. But, mostly, this is done on a case-by-case basis.

On every day that we hold sessions, we work through a check-off sheet:

- Have we examined the horses to be utilized in session?
- Do they appear to be healthy, free of injury, and of normal affect and presentation?
- Have we checked our arenas, horse/client areas and parking areas, to make sure they are free of hazards or safety concerns?

We date and initial this check-off sheet, and keep it on file, where it will be available should there be any need for it later. It's a good practice for any EAP/EAL organization to engage in!

Other Thoughts on Inappropriate Horses for EAP/EAL

In the survey and at the conferences where I've raised this topic, some of the red flags others point to when assessing horses for EAP/EAL include lots of descriptions beginning either with "overly" or "extremely," as in "overly-aggressive" or "overly-passive" or "extremely reactive" or "extremely quiet." The outer edges of behavior seem to be red flags for many practitioners. Extremes of behavior are also commonly mentioned, such as dull, shut down or dissociated on the one hand, or again biting, kicking or rearing on the other. During the interviews, we discussed how to recognize when horses were not appropriate on a given day, rather than about what they seek to avoid in EAP/EAL horses in general.

Inappropriate Horse or Inappropriate Activity Set-up?

Equine-assisted learning and therapy often involves the horse moving and acting at liberty. This requires the horse to have the ability to take care of herself, to get away without being constrained, if necessary. I trust that my horse can get away should she feel the need to, and she trusts I will let her. If she's too old, too infirm, or too ill to do this, I do her a disservice, putting her at the mercy of the work in session, and compromising that trust. We don't want a horse to "stand there and take it"; we want feedback. If that feedback is, "I need to get out of here," then we need to create an environment in which horses are free to do that.

This is why I speak often and somewhat strongly (and negatively) about activities that ask the horse to stand still with a horse professional holding the halter in order for the horse to be handled in a particular way by clients. If that is the activity, then it's not one in which we're allowing the horse to voice all her thoughts about a given client or allowing the interaction between the two. While I can see need for some interactions to be conducted in this manner, I find those to be less about EAP and more about creating a predetermined experience for the client.

To support our horses, we let clients know about the time-out, which anyone can call. Often it is as much for the horse's safety and comfort as for that of the people involved. Clients, as well as facilitators, are allowed to be the voice of the horse should they feel the horse needs a time-out. If time-out is called, and the client happens to have a rope in hand connected to a horse, we tell them to just drop it and move away. Chances are high that the horse isn't going that far. We teach clients that the right response for a time-out is to let go of everything and simply move away.

The "Dynamic" Horse

We have multiple groupings of horses and herds at *Horse Sense*, separated due to physical, mental, and emotional attributes. And, while we can utilize many of our successfully rescued and stabilized horses pretty much any time, several of them still have issues which make them undesirable for close client interaction. Make no mistake, these issues are not isolated to rescue/rehab horses; "normal" horses can present like this just as often. In any event, at *Horse Sense* we call these horses "dynamic' horses," horses who have issues that limit the kind of in session work in which they participate.

In the course of our rescue and rehabilitation work, *Horse Sense* has maintained a few horses whose "dynamic" behavior provides some interesting opportunities for growth and learning in client sessions. One horse was actively beaten and is very reactive to rope and is head-shy; another horse is so confident he'll just step over humans and keep walking. Another horse, who was mentioned earlier, flips back and forth between confident and fearful. It is not a question of never utilizing them, but about when can working with them best serve the circumstance. Dynamic horses are great for observation and passive/reflective-type activities, circumstances in which there is little confinement of the horse and no physical contact between horse and client; the client and horse are separated by a fence, gate or railing of

More than a Mirror, by Shannon Knapp

some sort. The bigger the arena is, the better. These horses can also be wonderful for working one-on-one at liberty with clients in session, with an Equine Specialist who feels confident and comfortable with that horse. Some of the most profound moments reported by clients have resulted from interacting with our dynamic horses. We prefer to set up circumstances in which such horses have choices about whether or not to connect with clients. Of course, the clients also have choices about whether or not to connect with these horses. The Equine Specialist needs to be vigilant when working with dynamic horses, and prepared to end a session or redirect a session at any moment should the situation warrant it—a statement true of any session, whether with dynamic horses or not.

It's also important to note that sometimes horses can become dynamic due to circumstances. We have one horse who becomes a great deal more dynamic in colder weather. He was part of a group of horses left to fend for themselves one winter, without any hay at all. All but one of the horses starved to death; our horse lived. There's no doubt in my mind that this horse has a body memory of this experience and, in general, is much more likely to be dynamic in cold weather. We are ever-mindful of his boundaries and limitations, and expect his rotation time in/out of programming in winter to be different than rotation time in summer.

The other question is: "Why utilize dynamic horses at all?" Is there a good reason for having a dynamic horse in the client's process? Is there some possible learning opportunity available by interacting with a dynamic horse that cannot be be achieved with another horse? Sometimes our answer to these questions has been yes. In a family situation, for example, we chose to integrate a dynamic horse into a generally calmer herd so the family could see the impact on the rest of the herd. Instead of the question, "What's the client going to get out of this" (which is virtually un-answerable), we ask, "Do I have a good reason for why I'm integrating this horse?"

I know I've got an agenda if I start wanting to utilize dynamic horses solely because their responses are grand or large. I call that programming for "big" rather than programming for change. I've met practitioners who go for "big" reactions in every session, every time. If large, dramatic responses are the only motivator for utilizing dynamic horses, that's not a good enough reason for them to be a part of session. Sometimes "big" is a great teacher; oftentimes it's an excuse for poor programming and facilitation. Overall, dynamic horses, while being a bad fit for some clients under some circumstances, can be extremely appropriate in certain situations.

In a conversation with *Horse Sense* ES Lori Araki, she observed how "programming for big" also takes opportunities away from many of our clients to notice and learn from subtleties in communication and behavior, as many of our clients are in treatment with us for "big" behavior themselves (Personal communication, February, 2013). Programming for big also reveals a significant facilitator agenda in the process: why is "big" better, or more useful for a client than small or subtle? Who decides?

SUPPORTING THE EAP/EAL HORSE

A few practices I engage in, specifically to support our horses in EAP/EAL work, include bringing certain groups of people to the farm for our horses to experience. Our horses come in contact with people who are often in a great deal of chaos; if the dominant interaction horses have with people subjects them to that chaos, then it is important to actively counter that experience or pattern. So, I will invite groups of meditators, prayer groups, groups centered on contemplative spirituality and such to have an experience with the horses. We may spend half an hour or so in meditation before doing Observation or Meet & Greet with the horses. It seems these encounters refresh the horses and disrupt the pattern of people = chaos. Although I'd describe most of the *Horse Sense* staff to be grounded and centered, I find the horses' contact with regular *Horse Sense* folks alone to be insufficient to counter this pattern. Horses expect us to be grounded and centered; what I like to provide is an antidote to the horse's regular exposure to others who are read as likely to bring chaos.

On and off through the years, we've also had each EAP/EAL horse have his/her own "person"— either a volunteer, an intern, a member of the broader community, or a *Horse Sense* staff person—who spends special time each week with that one horse: grooming, doing undemanding time, playing the Seven Games™, riding and such. I find this is also a useful antidote for horses spending too much time with people in chaos, with strong needs and energy.

OTHER POINTS OF VIEW ON SUPPORTING THE EQUINE-ASSISTED PRACTICE HORSE

Survey/Conference Feedback

Almost all of the survey respondents and conference attendees spoke of providing pasture time and regular turn-out time to "just be a horse" as being key elements of supporting horses in this field. Many also spoke of time spent in herds, rather than in stalls or in other isolated environments. Some spoke of particular kinds of interventions used to support horses, such as cranio-sacral therapy, reiki, massage and chiropractic care. Many programs paid keen attention to the amount of time the horses spent in session, monitoring that closely and carefully. Many also spoke of listening both to themselves (intuition) and their horses in regards to whether the horse needs a break or a vacation. Quite a few respondents also spoke of horses having outside jobs beyond session work and outside relationships beyond clients as being beneficial aspects of supporting the EAP/EAL horse.

Interview Feedback

Amy Blossom Lomas: "Our horses are outside most of the day, every day. For food reasons, we bring them in at night, and then feed them in the morning and turn them back out. I think horses are healthier outside, both physically and socially."

Carissa McNamara: "I have a deep appreciation for the horse who is enjoying something, and if they're not, letting them choose their way. I look to provide a stimulating environment. I might take a helium balloon out into the pasture and see them respond to it. They might freak out for 15 minutes, then come back and spend an hour playing with it. I look to maintain their autonomy and curiosity."

Liza Sapir Flood: "I think horses need to feel stimulated, both mentally and physically. There are those sessions where a client never gets near the horse, and other sessions where the client is asking for such strange things that it creates a sense of frustration for the horse. I think a horse knows if there's been a successful connection. There's a sense of 'reward'—or release—that feels good. Horses do get bored. There was a point with one of the *Horse Sense* horses where we got the feeling he needed something different to do. So we pulled him out of the program to do things that enabled him to experience a more tangible release/reward. This reinvigorated him."

Paul Smith: "Well, I'm fortunate enough to keep my horses in large, 24/7 turnout pastures. I mix my herd around on a semi-regular basis; I like them to have space and freedom to move and choose. The challenge is for those keeping their horses in a more contained way. Horses build more energy boxed up....The question is: how do you actively enhance an environment, even small acreage, to give a horse access to situations that create more curiosity, and therefore make them be more alive in a session? Just like a person, horses are a lot more interesting and willing to react if you enhance their environment to be more natural."

Richard Knapp: "We keep our herd as naturally as possible. We bring them in stalls when we're using them in session or feeding, but most of the time they're out in the pasture acting like horses. We also play with each horse at least an hour a week, doing liberty, online, freestyle or finesse activities. There is always something going on outside their client session work to keep them fresh."

StarrLee Heady: "All of my horses go out with other horses loose and in big pastures. We feed as little grain as possible, but hay and water are accessible all the time, and they're free to move away from some parts of the herd and closer to others. We might separate a horse from the herd for safety reasons, but even then we only separate them by a fence, they still have contact."

Randy Mandrell: "I've heard people talking about horses taking on the negative energy of the clients. I think horses get tired of doing the same thing over and over all the time, and they start acting out to get relief. What works well at our place is doing a variety of things—they do EAP, they do hippotherapy, they do therapeutic riding, but we also turn them out into the pasture every evening so they can just relax. We try to keep their work load to a minimum so they're not overdone. They're not doing the same thing over and over all the time. Even if it's a job that I like, if I'm doing the same thing every day it's going to get old."

Linda Zimmerman: "Where we're currently working, this is the first time we've ever had horses where they're strictly pasture horses. At first that freaked me out, but I think they're much happier. I like this so much better. Sometimes they come in covered with mud, and we use that in therapy. Everything the horses bring to you, including the dirt, is a metaphor you can use in session. We bring them inside in the winter at least twice a week. We lunge them, we play games, and we love on them. I think it's important. If the only time you bring them in is for a session, it's not good for them; it can produce stress. Ours love to come in because they might be coming in for a session, or they might be coming in to get attention. So I work with them a lot outside of session; that's important."

HOW SESSION WORK IMPACTS/INFLUENCES HORSES

How does session work influence horses? There is no definitive proof that it affects horses in either a negative or positive way. Some studies have shown increased levels of cortisol and increased heart rates in horses in equine-assisted practices, while others suggest that, because of the oxytocin connection, horses do get something positive out of the work with clients. After a review of the scant literature out there on this subject, what is clear is also true of this field as a whole: we need more and better research to answer these questions. Even if we do isolate the positive or negative impact of the work on horses, any definitive study would have to rule out facilitator presence and the relationship of the horse in question with a facilitator(s) from the positive/negative question. Is it the work itself, or the human facilitators that make a difference in whether an experience is positive or negative for a horse?

Yet the question "does this work negatively or positively impact horses" still needs to be answered. As Phil Tedeschi of the University of Denver indicated in his keynote address at the 2011 PATH International conference, we must answer these questions for the field because, if/when we prove beyond reasonable doubt that animal-assisted and equine-assisted practices have measurable positive benefits and outcomes for clients, we will then be obliged to know how much "use" of animals in this effort is too much.

Based on my own observation, many horses are gregarious by nature, and this kind of work appears to suit many horses very well. We see some who really seek engagement with clients while others remain impassive. Through our study of Horsenality™, we've also come to realize that different horses exhibit gregariousness in different ways. Session work seems to influence many horses in a really positive way. If their daily work under saddle is challenging, this is a place they can interact and play while being totally at liberty. For some horses, client sessions invigorate them. It's not a good fit for others, and it ebbs and flows for still others beyond that.

Not this Horse, Not Today: the Question of Burnout

When we see this ebb and flow happening for a given horse, we start watching for burnout. While some of our horses have worked with clients for years without a break and seem eager to start each new day, others need regular periods away from client sessions. We're constantly monitoring what each horse needs and what he/she tells us in session.

We try to have a good feel for how each horse presents when they're balanced, and how that same Horsenality™ changes when the horse becomes unbalanced. When we see the horses' responses shift—maybe they become more muted, or more extreme—we have to determine if that shift is coming from some fundamental change for the horse in general, or if it points to something situational and temporary, like burnout or illness.

Some people argue that burnout doesn't exist; I believe it does. What it presents like depends on the Horsenality™ and whether the horse is/isn't dynamic, but it can show up in a multitude of ways: as hyper-sensitivity, insensitivity (non-reacting), refusing to meet you in the pasture, or refusing to face you in the stall. Again, we base our observations on variance from the horse's typical pattern, and those variances can be extremely subtle. One of our best all-around horses was recently pulled from more traditional EAGALA-type activities because he was simply not engaging at all with clients: he spent days looking over the fence, ignoring all the clients. Since he appears to not want to engage when relationship isn't the focus, we have moved him into the Relationship Logic piece of TF-EAP (as well as the Rhythmic Riding piece). Whether this is temporary or long-term, we don't know yet.

Once we see something occurring, we begin trouble-shooting, starting with the most simple and basic questions, and working toward the more complex:

- What is the variation from the horse's normal behavior?
- Does the variation repeat over a period of days or is it a one-time event?
- What's causing that variation? Is there something different in the horse's environment? We look around to assess what might be different in the surroundings.

Parelli™ has a saying that horses are good at learning "what happens before what happens happens." We need to do the same. We need to pay attention to quality of movement and sequence of actions to reveal the internal world of the horse to us as well as how he is with the client at the moment.

Most certification programs mention in their trainings that horses who often kick and bite are not good fits for EAP/EAL; I agree. Yet, it's important to remember than any horse is capable of kicking and/or biting, with provocation. I've seen horses in session offer to kick and bite when it's been absolutely appropriate to do so; it's reflective of what's going on with the client. Most balanced horses, given a choice, are not going to react in an extreme manner with a person; they will choose to move away from a client instead of making contact. If they do choose contact, they're likely to give a lot of warning beforehand. The challenge is determining if this "appropriate feedback for the client" can be done safely. If there is a suggestion of such feedback from the horse, the horse professional needs to pay very close attention. It's worth repeating—the horse professional needs to remain extremely vigilant and attentive to the first signs from the horse through the final warning before contact is made, calling time-outs, drawing a client's attention to the behavior, and intervening as necessary.

How do you determine if a response is appropriate to the interaction with the client, or if it's an indication of another issue related solely to the horse? If a circumstance occurs with one client, and we utilize the same horse in one or two other sessions that same day or within a few days without incident, it's probably a response specific to that particular client. Does the behavior show up with regular handlers? If the behavior shows up in all three sessions over the course of a day, or over a period of those few days or with his/her regular handlers, it's often the horse. Just like utilizing SPUD'S with a client, we're looking for patterns.

Shutting down or disassociating is another indicator of burnout. Similarly, a physical response, such as a breakdown in physical health, can indicate underlying stress. It's important to remember that these clues can be very subtle or really overt depending on Horsenality™. Likewise, it's important to note that each Horsenality™ has different ways of recovering from burnout. A Left-Brain Extrovert, for example, may seek play and movement. Physical activity stimulates him; he may experience frustration—and eventual burnout—when that play drive is stifled or suppressed. On the other hand, too much mental stimulation is challenging for the Right-Brain Introvert, who needs space and time to think. Too many clients moving too fast and pushing too hard can frustrate and overwhelm. This horse may need more "down time" between sessions to compensate.

There are multiple ways to handle signs of overwhelm, frustration, or outright burnout. First, rule out the physical. We have baseline vitals and weight on all of our horses, and then check for illness and injury (while being aware these often are manifestations of burnout). Consider what might be missing from the horse's diet or daily interactions. Once you verify the state of the horse's physical health, you can act accordingly. You can simply pull a horse out for that session, or for the whole day. You can send the horse out to pasture for a few days of peace and quiet. If a total change of environment doesn't upset his equilibrium, move him to another barn or another part of your property with a different herd. If simple things like this don't quite work, and the behavior persists, do something more significant—give him a month doing nothing but trail riding, or working as a ranch horse moving cattle. There are a lot of ways to give a horse a vacation from his work.

But beyond physical manifestations, sometimes you need to rely on gut intuition to tell you a horse just isn't suitable for session. I've had a horse refuse to approach when I open his stall door. Sometimes my gut says he's just not that into working today, but that he'll be fine in session. Other times, my gut says to leave him out of the arena entirely. I like to err on the side of caution, which is why I like having a larger herd from which to choose. By really observing each horse on a day-to-day basis, you maintain an attitude of genuine curiosity about your horses. I try not to make assumptions about the horse I rode last Sunday, or the horse I had in session yesterday. Paying attention to what the horse is telling me right now encourages me to move my thinking beyond what I assume to be the case.

Finally, I believe it's important to remember how well-equipped horses are to take care of themselves, shedding negative emotions and behaviors with a speed and skill I often wish I had! As we touched on in the "Outside In" chapter, few horses hang onto trauma or unpleasantness in the way humans do; they shake it off much more readily than we think. Similarly, some argue that a beginner attempting to halter a horse without knowing what he is doing damages the horse either by confusing him or setting him up to be unsure of how to respond to someone who does know what he is doing. After much observation, I consider many of these assertions to be unfounded. Horses are much smarter and savvier than these positions represent. They undermine the inherent intelligence of an entire species!

OTHER THOUGHTS ON BURNOUT

Interview Feedback

Liza Sapir Flood: "Sometimes when a horse exhibits a completely unexpected behavior in session, you have to ask yourself if it's a one-time behavior or something more serious. Then sometimes there's the horse that won't even be caught. Is there a reason? Is he trying to say, 'No, not today'? I like what [Shannon] said once about the horse who doesn't want to be caught: we need to work on that issue on our own time, not the client's time. There are days I think I need to work with a horse on a particular issue, but trying to train and do therapy at the same time doesn't work. Making sure we interact with horses outside of session time helps in ironing out those issues, and determining their cause, without impacting clients. It's all about change; you have to know your horses well in order to see a change from normal behavior. How do you know if they're being very unresponsive or overly responsive? I feel strongly that ES's need to spend time with the horses outside of session."

Paul Smith: "If I'm actively managing a horse in order for that horse to tolerate the environment, I think I'm probably getting in the way of the process. If it's taking all my energy and time managing her, if all of my energy goes to the horse, then it's not about the client. I need to step out and get the horse out of that environment. Some horses will sour because they have inconsistent, incongruent people asking them to do things, and there's probably where it starts to tax their temperament. Some horses are more tolerant than others, but vices and behaviors begin to show up: irritation, tail swishing, biting. Some of that you can address by tuning up the horse...but it depends."

Richard Knapp: "Burnout used to appear more [in the *Horse Sense* herd] until we started giving the horses a lot more play time. And if they're kept naturally, they're not as likely to get burned out. They have their time to go out in the field and be horses and shake it off. If they're used too often and don't get enough mental and emotional stimulation, they'll start to protect themselves in ways like nipping or walking away all the time."

StarrLee Heady: "There was a particular time when I went to a training session and I almost felt like we shouldn't have been there doing the training at all. Every horse came out with pinned ears. It didn't matter which horse came out, it didn't matter which person walked near them, they'd pin their ears, grit their teeth, and swish their tails. This was a clear situation where they didn't want people near them. As far as burnout, cranky behavior—acting like an old mare toward everybody—is a pretty good sign of burnout. When I see it consistently with people and with other horses, there's something not balanced in the dynamic. They need to go back out and just have to deal with normal herd dynamics."

Randy Mandrell: "When you're doing therapy, there may be times when you need to allow [cranky behavior] to happen. It's happening for a reason; it's something the humans are doing or not doing that's causing the horses to react the way they are. That's a discussion we have as trainers. When the ES feels like there's an unsafe situation, we really balance it with our goals. What is our objective? Is it beneficial for the client to experience this, or is it not necessary? If we don't really see it as being in the client's best interest, then it's not necessary. We remove the horse. Doing therapy is different from training; what's appropriate in session is different from what's appropriate in training. Horses are like people; they show burnout in different ways. Some will stand there and not move. Some will run and try to get out of the pen, some will get aggressive. When they change, you've got to realize they're starting to get too used to the work, or they're getting sick of it and getting burned out. It goes back to reading what your horse is telling you."

Rhiannon Beauregard: "You really need to know your horses to see burnout. EAP/EAL is very emotional work; my experience with burnout has been seeing a horse run away when you try to catch them, horses shying at different objects, or disengaging completely from the process. I'll also see burnout in the form of horses that hollow out, while others lift their back and stomach when they're tense."

Carissa McNamara: "I think the reason I don't see burnout in my horses comes from constantly doing different things. I think schedule and routine are responsible in large part for the burnout I've seen in other horses. There is no routine for my horses; there is no schedule. I may feed at six in the morning or ten in the morning; my horses have no anxiety around it. My neighbor's horses absolutely come apart when he doesn't feed 'on time.' Doing the same exercises and same things with horses every single day burns horses out. Variety is the spice of life."

Linda Zimmerman: "When a horse shuts down, it's a clear sign. A happy horse is curious, alert of their surroundings. When a horse goes into a corner and isn't interested in what's going on, that's telling you something big time."

Bettina Shultz-Jobe: "I think there is an enormous amount of burnout in horses within the therapeutic riding world because horses are not encouraged to think for themselves and they're not encouraged to be in real relationships. That's not a complaint about therapeutic riding; I love therapeutic riding but the nature of that work is that the horse kind of needs to do what the leader and the side walkers tell the horse to do.

I think burnout happens when horses don't get to think for themselves. One of the things that we've found is that when horses burn out in the therapeutic riding, if they would start participating in some of the mental health work, doing it the way Tim and I do it, we would see horses' demeanors change completely. And burnout looks like nipping, biting, not wanting to be caught, and such."

Tim Jobe: "I was fortunate to learn this from the human perspective first, so the same thing that causes burnout in humans will cause burnout in horses. When you're being controlled all the time, you will burn out. When you are given control of what is happening with you, then burnout is not a very common thing. In what we do, we're not controlling the horses; we're asking the horses to take control of themselves, just like we're asking our clients to do. And when the horses are controlling themselves instead of being controlled by someone, then they're not as likely to burn out.

In the work that we do, we can have horses in session for years without seeing any ill effects because they're constantly learning how to have better relationships and it's hard to burn out when that's what's going on. When you use horses in a way that doesn't benefit the horse, they're going to burn out. If you're doing things that are just going to benefit the client, the horse is going to get burned out if you're not keeping an eye towards whether it's beneficial to the horse. Being constantly aware that everything you're doing is beneficial to the horse—not just to the client, because like I said, if it's not good for one of you then I don't believe it's good for either of you."

Michelle Holling-Brooks: "Burnout is the reason we started our 'two weeks on, four weeks off' rotation program. When you see a shift in attitude from, 'I'll follow you wherever you want me to' to consistently saying 'No!' with multiple clients, that's a sign the horse needs a break. It seemed to happen consistently at the end of two weeks. About halfway through the third week, they would become less responsive to clients. We bring them back [to session work] with play first, then with some of our volunteers, and then with clients so they can recharge."

Cycling Horses and Clients with Attachment Issues

Michelle Holling-Brooks, who has created a distinctive approach with horses and youth with Reactive Attachment Disorder, spoke to me about how she approaches this cycling of horses so rapidly (every two/three weeks), particularly with her clients with RAD. Here's her response:

> We let clients know the first day when they come to visit the farm; we explain that we have different horses for different stages and that our horses do cycle and go on vacation every 2/3 weeks to recharge—that's how we put it. The kids almost look forward to changing to a different horse, because they believe they're moving up a level. And then in the end, they get to pick the horse they want to work with as their "challenge" or stage 3 horse, because at that point, they've gotten to know every one of them. They get to say which horse they want to work with for the last session and we also have alumni days once a quarter, where graduates can come back and love on their favorite horse. They can also bring others out to show them around.
>
> Switching horses helps clients to take the skills that they learned with one horse and apply it to another horse plus applying the skill of re-establishing attachments with horses when they come back in rotation. If the client only really works with one horse and there is a therapeutic reason/goal behind keeping that horse, then we'll look at whether we'll keep the horse working with that client, keeping that horse in a couple more weeks just for that client only. (Personal communication, November 2011)

UTILIZING YOUR PERSONAL HORSE IN SESSION

Many of us are in this field because of our love and affection for horses and, of course, many of us work with our personal horses in client sessions. Based on the survey responses, over half (60%+/-) of practitioners work with their own personal horses in EAP/EAL. This is both a perk of the job and a challenge, as being with our own horses in session constitutes a kind of dual relationship. Dual relationships are most often discussed in the context of the therapist having multiple connections with a client, such as a client who is also a friend, a student, a family member, or an employee, and these are to be strictly avoided. But we horse professionals often have our own personal relationships with the horse or horses utilized in EAP/EAL session, and then we are professional partners in session with that horse(s), our mental health professional and the client. Given my own awareness of this issue and the predominance of horse professionals in the field working with their own horses, it is useful to have a discussion about it here.

As mentioned earlier, I've certainly heard and read that this kind of work can be confusing for horses and poses a problem for them in their ability to assimilate information. One well-known author in the field wrote about beginners who don't know what they are doing haltering a horse and causing the horse stress, and the horse having negative side effects from that kind of experience repeated over time. I think that position significantly undersells the intelligence of the horse, as well as outright contradicts the claims of EAP/EAL in general: that the horse responds in the moment to what is happening.

Yet some pitfalls are present when working with our own personal horses in session. Among those I've either experienced or observed is the issue of focus: where is it? Are you:

- Focusing on your connection with your horse during session instead of the client?
- Noticing faults or perfections in your horse during session? Positive, "hero-worship" of your own personal horse can be just as difficult to surmount as focusing on the negative.
- Thinking about how the current session will impact your horse outside of session?
- Considering where and what you'll be doing next with your partner instead of focusing on the client?

All these take you away from the client and the moment at hand, doing a disservice to all parties.

Another challenge area I find with this dual relationship is making assumptions. Here are some problematic ones. Do you:

- Assume your horse will behave with the client the way he/she does with you? If the horse is the same no matter the person that's with him, then there's not really much value to what we're doing. If your expectation or assumption is that the horse is going to behave in exactly the same way with a client as he does with you, then that's a set-up for you, the horse and the client.

- Have blinders on when it comes to what you see in your horse, based on your past experience with him? This is a bit like making assumptions about a client based solely on his DSM diagnosis or by the back story we're given by parents, school administrators, or the court system. You are seeing everything through that lens without having the ability to step outside of that perspective. That happens a fair amount of the time with people and their horses. That's the gift and the beauty of really paying attention to the horse's body language in the moment—to get outside the story.

- Think the client will love your horse as much as you do, and only say nice and positive things about your horse? This can be a set-up for you both. If you aren't prepared to hear a client talk negatively about your horse, you might need to rethink having your horse in session!

An additional set of challenges around dual relationships with Equine Specialists and their personal horses includes protection. Are you concerned in session that:

- You might break your relationship with your horse if he comes up for a scratch or a pet and you don't engage? I understand that desire and the difficulty in not reaching out to connect with your partner, but if your relationship can be broken by such a simple deferral, how much of a relationship is it? Just like when we ask our clients "not to touch the horse unless he/she touches you first," you might want to consider who that scratch or pet is really for or what it really means?

- Your horse will need saving from a client's behavior? I see this as a problem in the set-up of the session. If you're putting yourself in a position where you have to save your horse in the first place, then maybe something about that set-up needs to be examined. Perhaps there's another way to get into the issue your therapist and you have decided needs to be brought to the surface, or a way to set things up that doesn't compromise the horse in any way. How can you "write"

More than a Mirror, by Shannon Knapp

yourself and your concerns out of the scenario?

Another consideration is if the client finds out the horse she is working with is your personal horse: the client may feel elated to be so trusted to work with your horse, or she may feel manipulated that you've "caused" the horse to respond in certain ways. I believe in transparency as much as possible and as necessary. I don't believe you need to be fully transparent in every moment, but I do believe in being able to be transparent and open about the relationships that are going on in a session. If, for any reason, the client finding out that the horse in session is your "personal" horse makes you uncomfortable, then perhaps that might not be the horse for the job.

Some strategies for overcoming the impact of this kind of dual relationships on you include:

- Not combining relationships too closely time-wise. Although I mentioned it as being helpful to put some time between personal and professional for the horse, it can also be helpful for you to step away from that kind of connection for a bit before going into a session. As anyone who has had a deep relationship with a horse knows, it can be just as heady as human love! Step back and allow yourself to get some perspective.

- Getting what I call 2-D, blending into the background, enough so that the horse loses "me" as part of his world, and circles back to the client. It doesn't always work, and sometimes certain horses will know who gives the best butt-scratches in this crowd and not let you get away. But for the most part, getting 2-D is incredibly effective: not sending them off with gusto, just dissolving into the background. Some people would call this getting out of the electromagnetic field of the horse, so that he's not responding or reacting to you.

- Thinking of your time with your horse in session as being in "neutral." When I'm in "neutral" with my horse when playing the Parelli Games™, the general message I'm conveying is "all is well." While I appreciate him checking in with me, I invite him to keep going back to what he was doing, whether that was following the rail, playing the Circling Game™ or interacting with the client. I don't want to make him feel bad for asking me a question, but the answer to that question won't always be "yes, come in for a scratch."

- Asking yourself whether you are concerned about something happening to your horse or whether you are concerned about something happening to any horse? That might be a helpful lens to look through as you consider if your behavior is guided by your dual relationship or by your responsibilities as an Equine Specialist.

I've also heard a fair amount of commentary about ES's having their horses look to them for what to do/how to respond to a given situation in session, and I think this has its uses and its challenges. It can get a bit more sticky if the horse asking us a question during session is our personal horse. I've certainly had my horses look at me when things were a bit dicey in session with a client, and they could read from my body language whether I was concerned about it or not and respond appropriately. What I don't want to do, though, is think that my horse is always and only looking to me for that guidance. If I've done a good job with him outside of session, he is calm and confident in most situations, and will need only a brief exchange with me to know to "keep calm and carry on."

Perhaps the most important consideration to keep in mind is this: if the only time you spend with your horse is in session, you are likely setting yourself up for trouble. Make sure you have adequate time with your horse outside of session to build your relationship, so that those concerns aren't paramount to you in session.

OTHER THOUGHTS ON DUAL RELATIONSHIP IN SESSION

Interview Feedback

Amy Blossom Lomas: "I think they know the difference when we're 'working' versus when we're not. They've learned they don't come over to me [in session] because I won't pet them. That's not the role that I have out there and they know that I'm not there for them. Now, we've had times they might run near me or behind me in a stressful moment, and I'm mindful of that, but they can take care of themselves. Relationship-wise, I'm different when I'm out there with clients. Now when they're new to the work, I have to be mindful that when they come over by me, I need to not be interacting with them in a way that detracts from the client's experience."

Carissa McNamara: "I have horses that take care of themselves extremely well so I haven't found myself going to that place of 'Oh, I hope he's going to be okay.' I had an experience with one little horse; he's just my best friend in the whole wide world and the snow fell off the roof during session and he was anxious. I just leaned over to my co-facilitator and said 'I'm having a moment. I feel bad for him.' ...I had last year about six months apart, two substance abuse kids hit two different horses of mine. When they talked about it, it was about 'The horse came over to me and he was going to walk away so I hit him before he could walk all the way away.' What was interesting was it didn't bother me at all but my mental health professional was so upset because the horses are these revered animals to her. I said, 'My horses are really good at taking care of themselves and I know they wouldn't have allowed themselves to be hit if it was a truly dangerous situation.' I think they understand intention like we have no concept of. I just have a lot of confidence in my horses that they know what to do so I'm okay with that."

Liza Sapir Flood: "I have worked with my own personal horses in session, and this is back at Aspen Ranch. I think that those sessions sometimes became about me until I became a more mature horse person. I would stress about the clients ruining my horse or would be overly aware of my horse and it was a bit of a distraction. Over time, I realized I needed to give my horse some credit; she knew when she was in session and when she wasn't. I knew I needed to be a stronger horse person in and out of session. I also think it can be really enriching; clients know it's your horse—and I do think there's a relationship between the client and the Equine Specialist and the client and the therapist and both are valuable. When the client knows that relationship between you and the horse in session, sometimes neat things can happen where it's just another therapeutic tool. I do think sometimes over time it comes out and I don't think you should lie about it but I don't think you need to blurt it out."

Paul Smith: "Dual relationships are one of those things that profession-ally there's an allergic reaction to. We have these really strong rules that often get interpreted as somehow dual relationship means 'bad.' I don't buy that; I understand where it comes from and the motivation. I tend to think there's a point where rules are for fools because life is more compli-cated, and that I'm interested in modeling and practicing healthy relation-ships.

So dual relationship with my horse: if the relationship distracts me from the work—if in my example, I'm over-focused on my horse in a way that makes it difficult for me to focus on the client and their relationship to the horse and I'm being kind of protective of my horse, that's a prob-lem. If my relationship with my horse makes me more sensitive to how somebody is around a horse and I can be clear about that, there's a chal-lenge there. And it's not that the dual relationship is bad but if I drop into being over-protective of my horse or showing off my horse, it become a distraction to the primary reason for my being there.

If the client knows it's my horse there's a little bit of 'Oh, this is Paul's horse.' It's a different mystique or aura around that. There are times that I have my own anxiety that my horse needs to be good, or maybe I'll story how this horse is a problem so I can avoid that except that I've cre-ated another story to put on the horse. I notice the difference between the twenty-two horses that aren't mine and the two that are. I'm a little different, they're a little different, they're more attached to me, I'm more inclined to do demonstrations with them because we're partners. It's not necessarily bad; it's different.

Any time I'm with my horse I want it to be about the next time we're together so I'm always interested in doing something that contributes to our relationship being better the next time we get together. I won't sac-rifice my relationship with my horse for a session, so yes, I would hope that working with my horse in session enhances our relationship. It's another place where we show up in our partnership and do a particular thing and then we like it when we get to step away and do something else too."

Richard Knapp: "Sometimes when we're in session and it's my 'levels' horse, the horse I'm taking through the Parelli™ system, when he gets confused sometimes he'll look to me for the answer instead of the client for what's going on. Or he'll walk up to me and want to get scratched and that's a problem; we have a relationship and now that relationship is interfering with the session. I think that happens to other Equine Specialists as well—certain horses that are extremely confident and very comfortable are more willing to just kind of explore their environment. They know who is stable or who is calmer and who is not, so they'll go to the calmer part of the herd.

It usually doesn't negatively affect the relationship I have with that particular horse. As long as I can stop them early enough, keep trying to remove myself from the situation, so if he walks to me and I walk away, and try to let him stay there and then let the client come into the situation. The biggest thing I've seen is sometimes the humans that come as clients are not comfortable or fun to be around, so sometimes that tears your relationship in general with human and horse apart. They don't like that and it takes a little bit to rebuild that relationship."

StarrLee Heady: "I think it does affect our relationship. It's that same 'This is somebody who knows me well and knows my non-verbals.' Possibly my horses and my kids, my family know my non-verbals better than I do. So that can be a really powerful thing in a session because if something begins to happen to me, I can pick it up from the horses that's happening and check myself. It can also be something that can impede their awareness in session because if they're noticing something about me, they may be not noticing something that's going on in the session.

It is a dual thing, good and bad. But being able to trust somebody because you know they know you well I think is a really cool thing. I think it becomes a problem when I want to control that horse's personality or interactions with someone else. And I do see that happen; I see people who physically, even if they're not saying it, cringe when someone shouts at their horse. They can't separate the two. It's triangulation as it is in any other form. It's a judgment about the strength of my bond with my horse and not wanting to intervene and manage it somehow. If you can learn to not let it get in the way it can be really valuable, I think.

One horse in particular I have to watch because I have been doing horsemanship with him. His first experience with people was as an unbroken colt and all his interactions with humans have started with me. And he really clicks into me quickly. I'm definitely a leader and a safety spot; if he gets flustered, if he gets worried, he will look to see what my expectation is. I've even had him come and stand behind me a few times.

So I have to be careful that I'm not walking into the arena with anything personally going on for me that raises my heart rate or my voice higher than normal or makes me more tense because he'll click in on them very quickly and then he's attending to me. And that's not useful in sessions.

I think I've gotten to know my own horses better by working with them in session because my preconceived notions about how they were with people were just how they were with me. So being able to watch them change behaviors and interact with people from a freedom of choice standpoint and see them be able to act very differently, whether it's from attitudes—kind of like 'ears up, pleasant' or 'ears back' or that 'the old horse, I never knew he liked to jump.' I've seen him fly around the arena with a bunch of kids and jump 4-foot jumps and act like it was the best time he's ever had."

Randy Mandrell: "With my personal horses, it's kind of hard to answer. They're allowed to be who they want to be out there and I've got some that are not my personal horses but I still have that relationship with them and I'm the alpha horse and I make a move that tells them to stop, they will. Does it change what I do with my horse? No.

I had some of those issues when we first started; someone was putting a halter on upside down on my horse and I was like 'Holy crap!' but it didn't change the relationship a bit. When I put a saddle on him or ride him bareback he responds to me the same, and he's been doing this work for as long as we've been doing this work. He's 15 now and when we started, I was still training him."

Patti Mandrell: "What I see and hear from a lot of horse people is they love their horse; it's like their baby. I think it's that emotional connection—and it's no different than a child when you let them experience things on their own. It's the same thing with your horse and this 'My horse needs me to survive' mentality. It really is a shift in mindset for a lot of horse people that their horse can handle this and know the difference between this and whatever else they do. All I can say is that I have a whole new level of respect for horses than I ever had.

My horses were my best friends before this work but it's a whole new level of respect after starting in this field—how much I can learn from them, not just how much they can learn from me. And trusting they can handle the situation and be fine with it. The horses, the longer they do this work, the more they realize they can choose to be themselves and if the person does something they don't like, they don't have to stand there."

Rhiannon Beauregard: "I don't do EAP with my personal horses and I can't. I'm way too emotionally attached and I know it. I also think my relationship with my horse is such that he would pay way more attention to me than the client.

We've done EAL work because he's a very special guy and kids gravitate to him. He's very interactive and the EAL work is okay. We have a group of autistic kids on Tuesdays and he waits by the gate for his one autistic kid; he knows his schedule. EAL is okay as long as I'm not teaching it, but for EAP, I'm not comfortable using him.

I've owned him since I was a child, and trained him myself; it's like he's my child. It's not as if I have six horses and operate a barn; it's a much different relationship. If I were to purchase a horse now, I wouldn't be opposed to using it but just not that horse.

I've been starting to think about if I were to purchase my own horses, I would need to walk into the purchase of those horses without an emotional attachment. An established relationship could only hinder this work. It means to be very wary of emotional connections and not using them as your personal saddle horse. I think walking into it you have to know they have a job, and they're not a pet. My personal horse is a pet and I don't think he could handle the real tough stuff."

Linda Zimmerman: "Working with my personal horses in session doesn't concern me. One horse I've had for sixteen years and I just feel like we have a richer relationship in session and off session. I think any time you spend with a horse, you get something back from that horse. I feel fortunate we can use our horses with this because they're good and they all love this work—and we're fortunate about that.

We haven't ridden our horses in about two years and I thought I'd miss that but I don't; I'm with them four days a week enjoying them and am more in awe of them than just riding them. I really enjoy being with a horse, off lead, on the ground and just being amazed at what they can do. You get this healthy respect for them."

Don "Z" Zimmerman: "I think with our horses, it's almost like when you bring them into the arena for a session they think 'Okay, I'm on the clock now'—they don't gravitate towards us; it's like they know they're in there to be part of the session and their prior relationship to us is rarely, if ever, noticed in the arena. If the horse does want to follow us around, we can step to the other side of the arena. They know when they're in the arena and there are clients there, it's about the client. It's just amazing how the horses know that."

Michelle Holling-Brooks: "I do work with my personal horses in session, yes. When I first started doing this, I was not able to do that because my stuff really got in the way. I think it's about that level of comfort; now I'm okay with using my personal horse in sessions and it's easier for me. With my one particular guy, he's so in tune with the client that he tunes me out except for when I want him to look at me and all I have to do is shift my weight.

I was really protective of him; it was that knee-jerk 'That is my child.' If he did anything that wasn't perfect, I was like 'Oh, I didn't train my horse well. He didn't do it!' There was also this other expectation of my training with him. We were to start prelim in eventing and he was showing and doing all that stuff and I was not sure if I wanted to 'mess him up,' so to speak.

I had to get over that and realize that he loves to play with the clients so much he messes with them. For me, he's available to give that to the clients if they can figure out how to ask for it. I finally started to see what a wealth of positive change he can be for our clients. Once I got out of my own way and realized they're not going to ask the way I asked and he was going to be okay—that and he's 17.2 hands, so he can take care of himself. He's not a kid. I think he's okay.

In the beginning I wasn't ready to deal with that with my personal horse but now he has a very specific goal—he works with kids that need to figure out the difference between assertive and aggressive. He also works with survivors of abuse; he's a very powerful teacher for them."

Tim Jobe: "Yes, we use our own horses in sessions—and we're not afraid to do that because everything we're doing in a session is working towards the client and the horse having better relationships with each other. So when I've got people, no matter who it is, working to help my horse understand how to have a better relationship with humans, it's a good thing. And it's a good thing for the horse and the human. We firmly believe if it's not good for both of you, it's not good for either one of you.

I think it's unethical to let something happen to a horse in a session that I wouldn't let happen to my own horse. So we're not afraid to use our horses, because like I said, no matter what horse is in that session, we're working on them understanding how to have a better relationship with humans and we're working at it from both directions. We're working at it with the human too."

SESSION HORSES & THEIR "OUTSIDE" JOBS

I also want to talk a little bit about how equine-assisted work impacts horses who have "outside jobs." Many practitioners utilize their horses for other functions, such as trail riding, ranch work and sport. How does this kind of session work impact their other jobs?

Our survey of equine-assisted professionals yielded varying results here. Some horses are great in therapy and even better under saddle as a result of being able to connect with clients at liberty in session. Because the connection with a client on the ground is so different than the connection under saddle, some horses seem to enjoy the variation.

There may be times during a horse's development when it's not helpful to have multiple jobs; for some horses you may be asking too much, especially if they're young, or if they're in a fragile state of mental/emotional recovery. According to Dr. Robert Miller, "Everything we do with horses either sensitizes them or de-sensitizes them." My husband, Richard, is a Parelli™ Instructor who at one time was working at Level 3 with his horse, Scout. There's no doubt in his mind that session work with clients does affect the horse. When Richard plays with Scout, he works on enhancing Scout's sensitivity and responsiveness. When clients play with Scout, their interaction seems to de-sensitize him. In light of the fact that Scout is a key EAP/EAL horse, Richard treated this as a challenge: how quickly can he re-orient and re-build his relationship with his horse? How quickly can he "sharpen the saw" after a period of dulling?

OTHER THOUGHTS ON OUTSIDE JOBS FOR EAP/EAL HORSES
Interview Feedback

Amy Blossom Lomas: "Horses know which class they're going into based on the bit and the halter on their face and they know when it's an EAP session—they know their different jobs. And I think letting them have that opportunity to be themselves in our EAP sessions makes the relationship stronger because we're allowing them to be themselves. Not that we don't allow them that otherwise, but it's a more trusting thing. We're giving them the opportunity to explore different surroundings and different people and I think that's better for everybody."

Richard Knapp: "Working with clients has slowed my horses down a little bit, yes. If it takes me a week to tune my horse up, it only takes one client session for him to be dull again. It's a fine balance, asking him to be snappier and more responsive on one hand, but then going into session with the client and not being snappy or over-reactive. I constantly play with that horse so he realizes there is a difference when you come in versus when the client comes in. It's another chance to excel."

StarrLee Heady: "Pretty much everybody that we work with has or had an active traditional horse life and I haven't seen that working in sessions has changed the horse's behavior under saddle. I think they're smarter than we give them credit for and when I ask for a response that we've trained on and worked out, they're still there. I've not had a horse get mouthy with people or pushy on boundaries just because a person in a session allowed them to push a boundary. I don't find that has changed them in other areas."

More than a Mirror, by Shannon Knapp

THE QUESTION OF DONATED & RESCUE HORSES

Because the opportunity for great EAP/EAL horses often comes through donated and "rescue" horses, it's beneficial to spend some time on the topic here. As many already know, I'm passionate about utilizing rescue/rehab horses for EAP/EAL, as they are a natural fit for many programs, and have been for us at *Horse Sense*. As I discussed in my first book, *Horse Sense, Business Sense Volume 1*, *Horse Sense* was sparked by a desire to find meaningful work and long-term placement for horses who, for whatever reason, were not rideable. Many of these horses had very little possibility of placement outside the rescue, because of assumptions that an unrideable horse has no value. The EAGALA model's focus on unmounted work was a great fit for the horses we had at the rescue, and adopting these and other horses like them became a win-win-win for the horses, the clients and *Horse Sense of the Carolinas*. But rescue-rehab and donated horses come with a specific set of challenges all their own.

At first glance, a donation or rescue horse sounds like a great idea. They're often free, which can be pretty attractive for cash-starved equine-assisted programs. But, of course, the "free" horse isn't, and that's no more apparent than with rescue-rehab or donated horses. Whether rescue or donation, you should never assume taking the free horse into your practice or program is a clear-cut situation. This is often when people make a lot of mistakes. There are plenty of reasons you might want to think twice about accepting a donated or rescued horse. And, whether rescue or donated, you should attempt to gather a history of the horse in question from as many sources as you can: the owner, the veterinarian, the farrier, etc. Oftentimes, the histories you'll get will be misleading or flat-out wrong, but you still need to do some homework on the matter. Ultimately, it's the horse who will give you all the answers needed about his/her history during an assessment.

Donation horses are those whose owner, for one reason or another, wants to give up ownership of that horse. Many times a donation horse will look like any other horse that's no longer rideable, or might be a rideable horse whose person, for whatever reason, like surgery, financial stress, or divorce, needs to re-home the horse. A donated horse can run the gamut from a retirement or geriatric horse, an off-the-track thoroughbred, or a horse who has nothing to do except be a too-expensive pasture ornament for owners who can no longer afford that. Then, there are the rescue and rehab horses, which are often an entirely different story.

When we are looking to add a horse, we tend to turn first to the other rescue organizations in our community. Horses here are in emergency situations, whereas the conscientious owner looking to donate a horse probably has the ability to find an alternate placement. Donation horses typically aren't in "last chance" situations.

When we're approached to take a horse, the first thing we do is determine if the situation in question is one of those "conscientious owner" situations where you sense there's time and resources to do the right thing by the horse, or if this is a true rescue situation. We have different responses for each. For the donation horse, we'll do everything we can to pass the word along to our network within the horse community and the EAP/EAL community. We'll typically only consider a donation if it fits some specific need in our practice. In a rescue situation, if the option comes down to us or euthanasia (which it has for several of our now happy and healthy herd members!), we'll see what we can do.

But let's start at the beginning. Be aware of the fact some donation horse owners have trouble letting go. We've had some really charged donation situations where the people in question really love the horse and, for one reason or another, were unable to care for him/her. These folks may ask for some accommodation that keeps them connected to the horse, like volunteering at your barn. She may want regular visits or photographs. Or she might be just fine giving their horse away up front, but then try to come back at a later date—say when their financial situation changes—and demand the horse's return.

No matter what type of verbal agreement you might get from a former owner or rescue situation, make sure to get a bill of sale. Even if the sale is only for a dollar, if someone is turning a horse over to you, do not proceed without one. Make sure you have the paperwork in hand, and include a picture of the horse on the paperwork.

When you take a donated or rescued horse, know ahead of time that there may be some time spent responding to the needs of the former owner. We've found it advisable to create a "cooling off" period between the donation and any involvement the former owner might have with our farm either as a volunteer or otherwise. After that, it's important to properly assess the situation. Is the owner having trouble letting go emotionally? Or does she just want to make sure the horse is okay?

The Rescue Horse

Then there's the classic rescue horse. Many equine-assisted therapy and learning programs flourish quite nicely with rescue and rehab horses. But there are multiple implications for taking this horse in. It's a full-time job on its own, with entire organizations dedicated to doing nothing but rescue and rehab.

With rescue horses, there can be many implications for your herd, the first of which are physical. If you allow a horse onto your farm without a quarantine period, any virus or health issue the horse brings with him can have a negative impact on your farm. We've had owners call to say the horse would be taken to us or the slaughter house. We've had another situation where the horse was clearly suffering while the owner refused proper care. We knew there was an equal chance of helping the horse recover or of having to put him down, but we couldn't let the horse linger for weeks on end without treatment. So, he came to the farm. You may not always have control over a quarantine period, but you can still make the decision on a case-by-case basis.

When we started, things were set up as at least a partial rescue operation; we have a rehab barn and pasture, away from the bulk of the herd, specially set up for rescue rehab situations. But there's no guarantee that it's an acceptable distance from the rest of our herd in terms of communicable disease, and there are other horses in the rehab barn who could be put in danger. A rescue-rehab horse's history is often unknown, or the information gathered is unreliable.

Probably the biggest thing most people don't realize is that rescuing or rehabilitating a horse is not something suited to just any person. Once physically recovered, taking the rescue horse the rest of the way through emotional and mental recovery is another thing entirely, often requiring time, skill and experience. People often bring home the mild, meek, starved/abused horse, only to discover a very complicated horse, one who has sometimes explosive behavior, and potentially serious issues.

When *Horse Sense* was first operating, we had fifteen to twenty horses at any given time who were "pass-through" cases. We took them to compensate for an overflow situation at other rehab facilities, or as a holding place for the sheriff's department while they sorted out the owner's situation. If you're going to offer this kind of assistance on a regular basis, you need to get really good at handling the physical abuse situations—recognizing and rehabilitating horses who are physically sick, injured, starved, or challenged in some way. This type of care requires knowing how to handle daily recovery situations: how to treat wounds, how to give shots, and how to re-hydrate and re-introduce feed. There are resources and organizations ready to help you through the process and certainly a good vet is important. Helping a rescue horse recover physically is a delicate task taking weeks, months, or even years.

More than a Mirror, by Shannon Knapp

One last consideration regarding rescued/rehabbed horses in EAP/EAL: there's been an uptick recently of horse programs opening up, adopting five or so horses from a rescue, and planning to do therapy with them, only to fold within the same year while neglecting the very horses they were supposed to be helping. When a new or newly-donated horse arrives, Richard and I are clear that, barring emergency, we are taking on this horse for the remainder of her life. We rarely place horses out that we've taken in and, for that reason, we need to be deliberate and mindful of the consequences of each and every horse we accept. I urge everyone in this field to be aware of the need for long-term, stable homes for horses that might come to you. Finally, the horses are not owned by *Horse Sense of the Carolinas, Inc.* Instead they are owned by the LLC that also owns the arenas, the property and the acreage for the horses. Learn more about that distinction in *Horse Sense, Business Sense, Vol 1* (Knapp, 2007).

The Rehabilitation Process

We break down the process of working with a rescued horse into three different situations: the neglected case, the abused case, and the horse that is both neglected and abused. In my opinion, any neglected horse is an abused horse, but there is a difference between a neglected horse (as in not fed) and an abused horse (actively beaten/harmed). These differences can present different challenges for you, your herd, and your program.

Our first priority when bringing in any new horse is to stabilize the horse from a physical standpoint, which includes treating injuries and establishing a re-feeding process, if necessary. We don't believe in treating a horse in isolation; as a herd animal it's not only cruel to keep a sick or injured horse in complete isolation, it often creates further problems and delays recovery. During the stabilization process, safety is the horse's greatest need. Recovery is delayed if the horse feels isolated from his primary source of safety: the herd.

For this reason, our rehab barn is set up so that there is pasture all around. The horse can physically see and communicate with the rest of the herd without necessarily being in the herd itself. It allows optimum interaction in situations calling for a measure of confinement. Once outside with the herd, the small size of the pasture at this barn prevents overgrazing for the starved horse on restricted intake. Another great way to accomplish this is with a small round pen in a pasture. The horse in that instance can have contact with the world and other horses, as well as remain restricted in terms of intake of grass.

Our observation and assessment begins when we first lay eyes on the horse, but it really kicks in during the stabilization process. One important thing we note is how the horse presents when he first lands on the farm. This may be indicative of how the horse reacts later in extreme, imbalanced, or unconfident situations. Observing the horse while under duress now teaches us quite a bit about what might happen when this horse is in distress later.

What is the fallback behavior of the horse when he's out of balance? For our Palomino, Dreamer, humans didn't even register on his radar screen; he'd been by himself in a large pasture (basically in isolation) for a good portion of his life, and his behavior was quite extroverted when he first saw that he'd have contact with other horses. We've seen many different Horsenalities™ from Dreamer as he developed from a horse in solitary to a horse in the herd.

During this process, we also observe where there might be gaps in the horse's education and foundation. Does he respect space? Does he move away from pressure? We utilize the Parelli Games™ in the process of discovery—the Discovery Phase with horses!—to find and begin closing those gaps. First of all, the Seven Games™ help to establish a system of communication between us and this new horse. We progressively move into deeper areas of discovering thresholds, handling the horse from all the zones and on both sides.

Discovering these gaps is a process; fixing them is another. Not everyone has the skill or resources to train horses. And fewer have the skills to work with a mentally or emotionally compromised horse; it's easy to get hurt and to do more harm than good. Too many people find themselves out-matched. Also consider the amount of time and effort involved in taking on rescue horses. Are you prepared to take on the work involved in rehabbing a rescue while running an EAP practice, for a horse who might never be appropriate for client contact?

We've encountered several "hopeless" horses in our rehab work. One horse experienced abuse being hog-tied and beaten as a yearling, and then was turned loose for ten years untouched by humans, including the vet and farrier, until the owner called the rescue saying, "If you can catch him you can have him!" Another survived an attack by a mountain lion. Our goal with both these horses was solely to give them a safe, consistent and reliable home, and to help them become comfortable and confident again in their own skin. While both are physically fine, both still face mental and emotional challenges. Their rehabilitation has taken years, and continues to this day. Extreme abuse, even with animals who have the ability to "shake off" most traumas, can still affect horses long-term.

In the rescue process, you might encounter the other kind of "hopeless" horse, the one that we know should be put down. Make no mistake, we are always prepared to do what is needed, unsavory as it might be. If we find that there is no other option that serves the best interest of the horse or the humans interacting with him, we will put him down.

Nonetheless, *Horse Sense* has happily functioned for years with predominantly rescued and donated horses. We have wonderful stories of recovery and have been a part of helping horses thrive when others had given up on them as hopeless. It's a great feeling to know you've been a part of the solution for these horses, rather than more of the problem!

LANGUAGE & OTHER CONCEPTS

As we come to the conclusion of this chapter dedicated to horses and their role in EAP/EAL, I'd like to put forward some thoughts on my perceptions and the field's struggle with certain pieces of language as it relates to the horse.

The Concept of Attunement vs. Mirroring

As we sort out the various ways we talk about our work in our field, I want to invite others to consider the concept of "attunement" as opposed to "mirroring." As mentioned in the previous section, attunement to me is a much richer and deeper concept than mirroring. Our field often uses the term "mirroring" to describe what the horse does in client sessions, but I think the process is different than simply "reflecting." When I think of reflection, I think of the mirror, in this case the horse, being subsumed to the process. But the horse doesn't disappear in relationship with us in EAP/EAL; the horse obviously continues to exist.

What does happen more closely resembles a deep, instinctual listening of the horse to the emotional state and the body language of the client, the same kind of deep presence horses seem to exhibit in every moment of their lives. The word attunement rings more true to me in describing this process than mirroring. I've also used the term "Clean Listening" (with apologies to David Grove) to describe what the horse brings to session, which again is different from "mirroring."

My co-worker Lori Araki offered another view of the term "mirroring": "I think of mirroring as the horse's ability to provide a safe forum for clients to discuss issues in the third person. They are not providing a reflection of the client's behavior so much as allowing the client the space to interpret what they see/experience through their own filter"

(Personal communication, February, 2013).When used in this way, I don't object to the term "mirror." But, more often, I see the term used to describe the horse's reflection of the client, which may be what the facilitators see, but is not representative of what I believe is taking place.

Use & Tool

There is much discussion (and wringing of hands) around the term "use" to describe the horse's role in equine-assisted sessions, as in "we use horses to teach people about themselves." I agree the term "use" can suggest domination and objectification, an attitude of viewing the horse as a prop or a tool for our purposes. No doubt, the term can diminish the importance of the horse's role and gifts in the process.

In my experience, not everyone who uses the term "use" is evil or has a patent disregard for the value of the horse as a partner in the therapeutic process. (Interestingly, we are often trying to help clients recognize how they may better "use" their resources.) Many people I know who use the word "use" are incredibly respectful of horses and the gifts they bring to session. I've also seen the opposite, in which many who lean towards the "sentient being" language demonstrate incredible disregard for the well-being of the horse, "using" the horse more blatantly than those who simply speak of "using" the horse.

There are mental health professionals who have deliberately chosen working with horses, as opposed to sand tray therapy, for example, as a means to help the client. So in the strictest sense of the word, they are, in fact, using horses as an intervention. As a professional, I can see how the term "use" crops up in our conversations: horses are one method; they're not the only method to help people learn and change.

When I think of the word "tool," which is another term that is often brought up to point out the objectification of the horse in some EAP/EAL practices, I again understand the sentiment behind the objection without assuming those who refer to the horse as a "tool" are bad. The phrase "make me an instrument of thy peace" comes to mind when I argue with myself about the term "use" and "tool." What is an instrument if not a tool? I personally don't use the terms "use" or "tool" (or I try not to!), preferring instead to use the term "utilize" in my own practice. Ultimately, though, I'm more interested in how I and others treat horses than in how we speak about horses. In a conversation with Kris Batchelor, she stated: "I would challenge all of us to employ the same mindfulness around language that we use within sessions" to this issue, observing that "choice of language isn't always indicative of attitude" (Personal communication, February, 2013).

Horses & Purpose

Other theoretical questions concerning the horse and his/her role in session are raised: What, if anything, is in it for the horse? Does there need to be some purpose for the horse as well as for the human? Assuming these same horses are getting their basic needs met by their barn, equine-assisted work is not a particularly taxing job for a healthy horse, although there can be instances in which burn-out, boredom, mental pressure, and anxiety can arise.

There was a time when PATH International (formerly EFMHA), held the idea that equine-assisted practices should be mutually beneficial for both the horse and the human—the idea that the horse should get as much out of the session work as the humans. I can't say that I know too many horses who wouldn't rather be grazing the pasture instead of in an arena for a client session. But this is true of virtually anything we do with horses: showing, trail-riding, eventing, etc. Some horses will thrive on this kind of work, and others will not enjoy it. We need to be aware of that and the impact of this on our clients and our horses.

ANTHROPOMORPHISM

One of the most fundamental ways we understand, and sometimes misunderstand, the horse is through anthropomorphism, mapping human emotions onto non-human beings. While equine-assisted facilitators ask clients to actively seek metaphor and meaning from the horse's behavior in session, we as equine-assisted professionals need to discourage that same behavior in ourselves.

After so many centuries where society regarded the horse as an object, few of us push back at giving the horse proper credit for her intelligence, gifts, and wholeness as a being. But it's easy to tip that scale in the direction of glorification, and even deification, in our positive regard. I feel this is a great injustice; deification and glorification can be just as debilitating as flagellation and objectification.

Although anthropomorphism is primarily something humans "put" onto horses, I felt a brief discussion of it here in the horse chapter appropriate. At the 2011 EAGALA conference, Lisa Baugh did a presentation called "Anthropomorphism & EAP," and a lively discussion ensued there and later in print on forums and such. What follows is an edited and condensed version of a magazine article on the topic, which appeared in Vol 1, Issue 4 of *EAGALA in Practice*.

Before we dive into this, however, I'd like to share some observations Baugh made at the EAGALA conference that impact our discussion here. In her presentation, she pointed out that Daniel Goleman identifies every act of empathy as projection, and that empathy is a feedback loop between our perceptions and another's reality. Finally, she pointed out that our sense of well being depends on empathy. There is much exciting work being done on empathy and neuroscience, and I'm curious to examine how these works, which I haven't yet read, by Jeremy Rifkin (*The Empathic Civilization*, 2009), Bruce Perry and Maia Szalavitz (*Born for Love: Why Empathy is Essential—and Endangered*, 2011), J.D. Trout (*Why Empathy Matters: The Science and Psychology of*

Better Judgment, 2010), and Jean Decety and William Ickes (*The Social Neuroscience of Empathy*, 2011) will further impact our discussion of anthropomorphism.

— ⚏ —

Anthropomorphism & EAP
Excerpts of Lynn Thomas' interview with Lisa Baugh

It is easy and feels good to assume other species have the same or similar intentions as we do, but how can we really say this is fact? How can we be sure it is not an anthropomorphic projection on our part, just the result of our wishful thinking? I don't think we can. Blatant anthropomorphism is easy to spot, but when it presents itself in less obvious ways, we often have a hard time identifying it, and we may even be totally unaware we're doing it.

For example, there are a myriad of behaviors a horse might engage in when presented with any given client. If someone interprets a horse's behavior as anger, I wonder, what would an "angry" horse look like? How would I know it was anger and not something else such as fear, anxiety, nervousness, joy, or excitement? Is a horse's anger the same as a human's anger? Does it look the same? Does two people's anger look the same? Some say, "People can operate with closeted emotions," but that horses cannot. How do we know this? It's ironic because the very definition of "closeted" implies it is covert, invisible, and undetectable. So if a horse could operate with closeted emotions, by definition, we wouldn't even know! As the expression goes, "absence of evidence is not evidence of absence," or in this case, absence of evidence is not confirmation of an assumption.

Often I see a lot of intention attributed to the horse…as if there is a purposeful, conscious thought process going on for the horse who is "attempting to bring to the surface" or trying to "draw emotions out" of a person. I see assumptions made that horses work to "make a person more congruent," and this is an "automatic process for the horse." For decades scientists and cognitive ethologists have grappled with the concept of intentionality in animals, and despite all the research, it is still a completely unresolved issue.

Whenever I hear or read someone interpreting animal or human behavior and reporting it as fact, a red flag goes up for me. Likewise in EAP, I am always cautious when facilitators claim to definitively know what a horse is thinking or feeling without acknowledging the possibility of projection or anthropomorphism, because in doing so, they are ignoring or denying the inherent tension created by their own subjectivity.

Idealism, or the tendency to see only good qualities while ignoring faults, plays a part. When we idealize, we view things as we wish them to be, rather than as they are. This fits right in with the anthropomorphic assumption of human intentionality in the horse—suggesting the horse is motivated to guide the person to health, that it has a curative ambition, or is consciously attempting to heal the person.

Idealism is so easy to slip into because we all want to see our horses as amazing, powerful, and effective healers. And frequently we witness remarkable changes in our clients as a result of sessions with horses. But all too often I hear EAP explained using wishful, idealized interpretations, in an unconscious attempt to legitimize or prove its value and effectiveness. I call this "EAP Apologetics" and I believe some of it comes from the rift between the hard and soft sciences.

Often we know the words we are using are anthropomorphic, yet we are caught in the limitations of our own human language with no other way to express what we mean. When we are aware of it, it's a more obvious form of anthropomorphism that ethologists call critical, pragmatic, or categorical anthropomorphism. In psychotherapy it is called "active projection" when we consciously use human terms to describe non-human events. Harder to recognize is naïve or inappropriate anthropomorphism. In psychotherapy we call this "passive projection" and it is completely unconscious. We have no idea we're doing it.

In an EAP session it is anthropocentric to conclude that people in the arena cause all the behaviors of the horse. It is anthropocentric to assume the horse must make the person "readable" or a "congruent herd member." Additionally, [we]… assume the behavior of the horse is the direct result of it assimilating the person's emotions, and that it "must" do this for its own safety. However, if we look at alternative scenarios, it is equally possible the horse could care less about the person's emotions. In fact, the horse might not even be aware of those emotions and could be responding to something else entirely, we just don't know. Maybe the person is standing in the horse's favorite rolling spot, or maybe it's reacting to the hat the person is wearing, or maybe it just spent 24 hours locked in a stall and simply wants to move around a bit. And, who is to say that circling around the person in the arena might not be an attempt to expel, rather than integrate the person as a "herd member?"

I might witness the same session…and form an entirely different opinion about what was happening, similar to the alternative scenarios offered above. But this would then be my observation, my interpretation, my anthropomorphism, and my projection! So ultimately, because of the dialectical tension between people and horses, it's impossible to say we know as fact what a horse is thinking or doing. We must accept that our experiences are always going to be tainted by our subjective biases. We should remain suspicious of interpretation presented as fact or risk being overtaken by the illusion of objectivity.

We all anthropomorphize. It's part of our human nature. It's how we relate and connect to the world around us. Evolutionary biologists say it is essential to our survival. We are programmed to see human-like intentions or mental states even where they cannot be. Additionally, scientists believe anthropomorphism is linked to empathy, which is hard-wired for our survival. We naturally resonate with other beings as a way to bond with them and survive in the world around us.

As EAP facilitators, we have to be hyper-vigilant about the language we use and how it can influence a session. Though often we intentionally invite our clients to anthropomorphize (project) by asking questions like, "how is the horse feeling right now?" or "what was the horse thinking?" we actually take away from their experience when we anthropomorphize, ourselves.

If the client attributes the horse's behavior to anger, then a door is opened for them to get in touch with or discuss any thoughts they may have around the topic of anger, if they choose. But this interpretation, and choice to pursue, must come from the client, not the facilitator. The truth is we really don't know what is going on with the horse because we can only speculate (or anthropomorphize!). The only interpretation that counts is the one the client makes. Sure, we can assume something is going on as we point out the behavior to the client, but we cannot say we know for sure what it means, nor should we when facilitating an EAP session.

We want to believe it, so that makes it harder to question ourselves and be skeptical! But when we are, we open ourselves to other possibilities and we are less likely to get stuck on one interpretation which can limit the therapeutic process.

We all anthropomorphize (project), and there's no getting around it. If you are human, you're going to do it! The key is to try to be aware of it, to acknowledge our subjective bias and be open to the possibility of another perspective. And, most important if you are facilitating a session, try to keep your projections to yourself (easier said than done!).

(See Contributor Biographies to read more about the author.) "Anthropomorphism & EAP" originally appeared in EAGALA In Practice *magazine, Vol. 4 No.1. This version edited post-publication by Shannon Knapp, with permission of the author.*

— ⌗ —

As I indicated at the beginning of this chapter, which is "all about the horse" from the perspective of an animal (me) who is not and will never really understand what it's like to be a horse, it's impossible to escape our own subjectivity and ever truly understand another person or another being, especially one who cannot speak to us in language and explain a position. That's certainly been highlighted for me, no doubt, as I've been writing this chapter. As Baugh stated in that EAGALA presentation: "When EAP facilitators claim to definitively know what a horse is thinking or feeling without acknowledging the possibility of projection or anthropomorphism, they ignore or deny the inherent tension created by their own subjectivity." I suspect I've stepped over that line to some degree in this chapter, and trust that I'll learn from my own anthropomorphic impulse as I re-read this chapter and discuss it with others. Curiously, empathy and the impulse to "naturally resonate with other beings as a way to bond with them and survive in the world around us" mentioned by Baugh may be part of what pulls us into this field as facilitators in the first place.

The Equine-Assisted Horse Professional

At this point, we've come to a much deeper understanding about the horse and his/her role within the equine-assisted profession. This chapter brings us to the second part of our equine-assisted equation: the Equine Specialist. With this enhanced understanding of our equine partners, what goals should we strive towards as professionals? As a collective group of professionals, where do we stand today? Where do we need to go as a profession?

This chapter is organized by survey and interview topics, centering around the role of the Equine Specialist. I'll share my experience and point of view on each topic, then review results from the surveys, one-on-one interviews, and conference audience feedback in each of those areas. It's my hope the research and the studies conducted for this chapter help illustrate where today's Equine Specialist stands within the profession, and where we need to go from here.

My questions regarding the Equine Specialist included: How would we describe the current average equine-assisted professional today? What is the self-perceived skill level prior to coming into the field? Are there any theoretical underpinnings that unite us as a group, in terms of horsemanship? Are we all life-long backyard horsepeople? What do the actual numbers look like, in that regard? I wanted to get a better view of the Equine Specialist "forest," rather than of the "trees."

Similarly, I was curious about the role Equine Specialists play once they are working in the field. How many are backyard practitioners? How many are making a living at this profession, or even getting paid? What kinds of certifications do we, as a group, tend to have? And what do we perceive our role to be, both in and out of session? Finally, where are the common challenges and continuing education opportunities for us?

Today's Equine Specialist, Prior to Entering Field
Survey Results

Over 90 percent of the Equine Specialists/horse professionals surveyed are between 30-70 years of age, with over 50 percent being between 51-70 years old; over 95 percent are female. Around 30 percent of all respondents identify as coming from a competitive horse background, predominantly involved in dressage and jumping. More than 50 percent of all respondents identify as English riders; about 30 percent identify as Western, and the remainder identify as "neither/ nothing" or as "other."

Over 40 percent of EAGALA Equine Specialists surveyed consider themselves "Advanced" horsepeople when they began in the field; 35 percent reported "Intermediate," and 10 percent selected "Novice." The remainder identify themselves as "Expert." On the PATH side, 14 percent feel they are "Experts" while 33 percent feel they are "Advanced." Just over 29 percent of PATH respondents consider themselves "Intermediate" and 22 percent classify themselves as "Beginners/Novices."

In regards to how long they have owned horses, EAGALA respondents indicate that 42 percent have owned horses for over 20 years and 18 percent have owned horses 11-15 years. About 33 percent of total respondents are lifelong horse owners, caring for horses in their own backyard. The next largest group, 26 percent, have come back into horses later in life after having been involved as kids. Interestingly, 18 percent were not into horses at all in their youth, but came into it later in life and now have backyard horses. Just over 33 percent of respondents have been involved in the horse world for more than 20 years (without having any personal horses).

For PATH respondents, 45 percent are 20+ year horse owners, 14 percent are owners of 11-15 years, and 12 percent are owners of 6-10 years. Equal in measurement are those who consider themselves "lifelong horse owners" (32 percent) along with those who "got into horses later in life" (32 percent), a much larger number than for EAGALA.

More than a Mirror, by Shannon Knapp

Overall, the profiles of the Equine Specialists coming in via EAGALA or PATH are quite similar.

When asked how many years they had worked with horses before working as an Equine Specialist, both EAGALA and PATH responses were similar in that there was very little middle ground: 29 percent reported they had worked with horses less than 5 years, and the same number (29 percent) reported working with horses more than 20 years, the two largest groupings in the survey.

When asked if they subscribed to a particular school of horsemanship, 36 percent of EAGALA respondents primarily identify with Parelli™, a result no doubt skewed by the *Horse Sense* mailing list, which includes a large number of Parelli™ practitioners. John Lyons and Ray Hunt were next in order; 30 percent of respondents chose "Other" in the survey, and selected from a miscellaneous host of names. Practitioners which could be chosen on the survey included: Tom Dorrance, Bill Dorrance, Ray Hunt, Richard Shrake, Sally Swift, Carolyn Resnick, Pat Parelli, Mark Rashid, John Lyons, Clinton Anderson, Buck Brannaman and Klaus Hempfling. A similar dynamic was present with PATH practitioners; a very large number chose "Other" as their response, with no clear leader in the subsequent identifying field.

Today's Equine Specialist, Specific to the Field
Survey Results

Of all the 250 or so respondents, about half identify themselves as practicing EAGALA EAP/EAL, while the other half are PATH practitioners. When asked how long they have been doing equine-assisted work, almost 50 percent of EAGALA practitioners have 2-5 years of experience, 33 percent have less than one year experience, while only 15 percent have experience of six years or more. For PATH practitioners, 38 percent reported 2-5 years of experience, 19 percent have less than 1 year of experience, while 19 percent have six years or more.

Practitioners with 2-5 years in the field appears to be the largest group, regardless of organization.

The large percentages (33 percent for EAGALA and 19 percent for PATH) of those working less than a year in equine-assisted practice speaks to a significant period in the evolution of our field. When you combine high percentages of inexperienced horse people with large numbers of relatively inexperienced practitioners, it's reasonably easy to assume a high variability in the quality of service we provide, and my experience and the experience of the interviewees for the book bears this out.

Are Equine Specialists getting paid to do this work? A large number—well over half—indicated yes, although an exceedingly small number are doing this as their sole source of income (less than 10 percent). Only 15 percent of the EAGALA folks who answered are not seeing clients, while 32 percent of the PATH respondents are not actively seeing clients at the time of the survey.

How does today's Equine Specialist practice? The choices available for this question included:

a.) My horse, my farm. Sessions happen where I live

b.) Predominantly with one therapist at his/her farm/barn

c.) Predominantly with one therapist at a barn where we rent space and horses

d.) Equine Specialist for hire...I go to multiple programs and serve as ES

e.) Other

For EAGALA, 55 percent answered that they are offering services on their own farm, presumably with their horses. After that, 34 percent did not respond to any categories (Other), but largely listed things like work at a facility with horses that offered the service, like a non-profit or residential program. The next largest category (24 percent) work primarily with one mental health professional, and rent facility & horses from another barn. For PATH respondents, 36 percent live and work onsite, as in response "a" above. Over 42 percent work at a non-profit, and 55 percent listed Other. The take-home message from all this, about the Equine Specialist and the way we are currently practicing EAP? Although a large number of practitioners are practicing in their own backyards, there are as many if not a few more that are practicing in a variety of ways.

A Few Thoughts on Equine Specialists, in General

In my experience, perhaps the most dominant characteristic of the average horse professional coming into this field is a lack of information, or the right kind of information. This leads to a whole host of other problems, including a) not being able to recognize what's happening in session, b) not "maximizing the power of the horse," as Patti and Randy Mandrell call it, c) not being able to communicate with their co-facilitator effectively (if they are working with a co-facilitator) and d) not being able to translate their awareness cleanly.

Many people who are interested in pursuing work in this field enter without either the necessary mental health degrees to work as therapists or the skills to be an Equine Specialist. For many, the Equine Specialist/horsemanship route appears (and is) the easier, faster point of entry. The horsemanship side is broad in terms of credentials, and relies on self-assessment, whereas there's a strict set of skills and credentials necessary to qualify as a mental health professional. Because the bar is lower, many come into the work as an Equine Specialist.

Even amongst "horse people," some enter the field with no formal education or a less-than-applicable education. She could be a lifelong trail-rider, or be showing horses at high levels and still have very little understanding of horse behavior, psychology, and body language. Or she could be a lifelong student of the horse, with a deep understanding of herd dynamics and nonverbal behavior. The playing field is so varied! Herein, I think, is the biggest challenge for our field: there's no true comprehensive curriculum, no way to consistently assess the varied level of education, information, and professional knowledge of those entering the field of Equine Specialist. The backyard enthusiast and high-level dressage rider start on equal ground.

Similarly, Tom Dorrance did not attend a formal "horse" college, nor did Pat Parelli or Mark Rashid; they were students of hundreds of horses. Their wisdom comes from decades of trial and error. There is no university or course of study where some of their insightful concepts can be learned. And the academic curriculums which do exist—veterinary schools, equine management schools and the like—are often providing little information on horse knowledge and psychology, especially the psychology needed by equine-assisted professionals. Prescott College and several other colleges and universities have made a solid start. It is likely to be some time before there is any sort of consensus and standardization of skill for this field, apart from organizations like Natural Lifemanship, PATH and EAGALA (although the recent news that University of Denver has taken Natural Lifemanship as a field of study is promising!).

A potential stumbling block for the new Equine Specialist is either the deification, glorification and mystification of the horse or the complete subjugation of the horse. Regarding deification, there are those in this field who argue that the horse is put on earth to save the world, and holds the key to our salvation. While I love horses much more than your average person on the street, I think this grandiosity speaks more to the people holding these views than to their affection for horses. This scenario reminds me of a dichotomy I encountered back in my days studying women's theory in college and graduate school. In Victorian times, there was a popular concept regarding women, known as "The Angel in the House": the Victorian woman was the center of all that is good, moral and right in human nature, and her job was to become that beacon for men, who were prone to wander from the path.

It was a way of both glorifying women and marginalizing women; by so praising women for idealized characteristics, Victorians managed to put a woman on a pedestal and isolate her in the same breath. I believe much the same thing is happening in the glorification and mystification of horses. On the opposite end of the spectrum are those who promote the subjugation of the horse: "Show the horse who's boss!" Neither glorification nor subjugation is the answer.

The wonderful thing about those coming into the field to operate as professionals is that they—or some part of them—recognize what the horse can do for people; they've seen it happen either for themselves or for someone they know and love. People who come to this practice may or may not have any real horsemanship background, drawn instead by popular movies, books, and feel-good anthologies celebrating the healing power of the horse. The real irony is that it's this healthy aspect of interacting with horses that we promote heavily to draw our clients; the flip-side is that it appeals to those who want to practice as well.

Other Thoughts on Skill/Experience Level
Interview Feedback
Several of the interviewees were loathe to be quoted directly with some of their thoughts on this topic, showing that this subject is sticky and awkward indeed. "Can I take the 5th on that?" one interviewee responded!

Amy Blossom Lomas: "It seems to me like we have more and more college-age students that are looking at this as a potential career path. I see more and more kids who've grown up with horses they've boarded with less actual experience of ownership or care for any long periods of time. There's also what I'd call a sub-group of kids that have gone on to get equine studies degrees and education... then there's also another group of people who have their first horse as adults and they're interested and want to help people and use their horse. I think there's a certain amount of people where they're trying to figure out where their place is because their professionalism is high and this is not generally a full-time job."

Paul Smith: "It really runs the gamut. One of the challenges at Prescott College is we're committed to a model of dual competence—as a mental health professional as well as a horse professional. We're not proposing a single practitioner model; we just believe the lead person needs to be dually competent, and then they have a second person working with them. So still supporting that dual practitioner model for the most part, but looking for each practitioner or the main practitioner to be dually competent if you're going to have a Master's in equine mental health. We're trying to get better at screening—that people need to have a foundation of horse experience and even if someone self-assesses the challenge is you can have someone come in with more horse experience and be less potentially competent at working with horses in a relational way. It's about an attitude and an ability to learn and some basic savvy with other than human beings. So we get the range from people that are full-up horse trainers and often they're more difficult to work into an EAL dual competence model—not across the board, but as a generality, in part because horse training is way of doing that is so much on the surface of the skin. Our students are all over the place. We've tried to identify, what is a baseline competence and what do we want that to be across the board? So what would that mean—what are basic skills, basic aware-nesses, basic safety? Depending on the work someone's doing they don't need to be a horse trainer; they need to be able to read horses effective-ly, be safe around horses, not be projecting all over them, have a realistic understanding in a variety of environments, understand how horses react, and know their own horses. But they don't have to be able to pick up a right lead to be able to be confident in this work, I don't believe."

Richard Knapp: "For those that come into the field with a horse back-ground it's often more of a traditional training as opposed to the natural training; they do things more as the humans see things versus how the horse sees things. There are a lot of people in the program who do not have much horse training at all and are not able to read horse body lan-guage at all, so that really needs a lot of help."

StarrLee Heady: "Some of what I see is a lack of understanding of herd behavior and basic horse psychology—how do horses normally

More than a Mirror, by Shannon Knapp

behave in their herds, their groups—a lack of understanding about herd dynamics and herd behavior. You know, I run into some people I would be happy to work with and not think about their equine background and be comfortable that they're really up on things, but not too many. I have some concerns in the field about that—that people's skills are not even what they say they are or believe they are. They're not really prepared for what I see as the normal range of horse behavior; they're prepared for the normal, quiet, well-broke horse in a familiar environment but not normal horse behavior coming in off 40 acres and running and playing with each other in their normal environment, when you turn a bunch of horses loose. They're not reading those little behaviors that lead up to bigger behaviors. They understand if there's a big blow up; when that happens, they see it but they're not seeing the smaller behaviors of the herd inter-actions that lead up to that, so it seems to come to them as a surprise when those are things they should've been prepared for."

Randy Mandrell: "We see a lot of people who don't have a lot of hands-on experience in dealing with the horses themselves or dealing with a variety of horses. When you train horses and work with horses like I used to, we'd have to take a couple horses to work with a day— there's one ranch I worked on that was 5,000 acres and in the middle of summer, if you don't know how to read what their body's telling you, you'll kill them. And then when you take in colts, everybody's different and you've got to learn to read the horses.

I don't think people do that very well because their experience is lim-ited to their horses. They've got this horse and it's like 'But I've shown horses all my life'—really, if you've got a horse you're showing and winning on, you're not really going to change that much. They just don't know how to read the horses that well. They're just out there saying 'The horse is telling me this'—sometimes I wonder if they know."

Patti Mandrell: "I've been around horses all my life but I don't con-sider myself a horse professional. Would I qualify for one? Yeah. But not until I started this work did I really seriously pay attention to their body language. A lot of that experience was as a child and my perspective was the horse was there to do a job and to have fun; we were great buds but it was about me. I don't think I really got good at observing cues until I came to this field. This is such a different way to look at horses from what we normally do in our riding. Unless you've had some training or worked with someone in your past, you don't—most people haven't looked at their horses this way."

Rhiannon Beauregard: "Going through the EAGALA world and thinking of the EAGALA model of an Equine Specialist, some Equine Specialists have incredible skills with people, some have incredible skills with horses and the ideal would be both. Some people get this model, they get the work, they get the clients and some just don't. All of the certifications and trainings aside, I've worked with so many Equine Specialists and it's something that you can't teach—the sameway a therapist, there's something inherent in ourselves that make us good at the work. As far as the skill level, their confidence to ask questions I don't find very strong. I also don't find their ability to work with horses very strong—it's very hit or miss and it depends on their commitment. I think also that Equine Specialists need to be creative in this type of work, and that's very hit or miss too. This is a very experiential form of therapy and to be a part of it, there has to be that bone in your body, especially when constructing activities or that type of thing.

Equine Specialists need so many skills and a lot of them you cannot train—you can't train someone to be creative, you can't train someone to have a good work ethic and that's someone I need. I think that for me I've had such a blessed opportunity to work with ten Equine Specialists and know what works for me. I really find that the skills I look for is a strong work ethic, a commitment to the field, knowledge of horse behavior and especially when horses are under stress, a creative bone and a passion for people.

If you don't care about people—and I think horse professionals often forget about the people aspect—you're not going to be a very good Equine Specialist. It's also really important to be confident in their life. You've got to be a healthy person to do this work. You need to know the model and stick to it as you come into the field. You can't start by being fancy. And a big one is the understanding that they're not therapists, but they do need to have an understanding of therapy. They're there to fulfill a role in the process."

Linda Zimmerman: "I'll have to tell you I don't have a feel for that because we do our work up here and I'm not in the loop with the people that are coming into the field. I feel like I was so lucky to be doing the work I did and have the opportunities I had because I think it's hard for people to get in the field, get the experience and mentor with somebody who is good. It would be hard for somebody to mentor with us because of HIPAA, so I don't have a feeling for that. But I do have a feeling that it's probably hard for people to get the right experience with the right people.

I think it's such a process; I'm doing stuff now that when we first started, I never would've done. It's really about understanding more what the horse has to offer. I rode for many years and didn't know that the horse was a partner, you could have a relationship with them and so on—I had to make that shift for sure and it wasn't easy. It took me a couple of years."

Don "Z" Zimmerman: "My experiences have been attending the EAGALA trainings or the EAGALA conferences. I think it's like any other professional field—you attend the workshops and eavesdrop on the conversations and you're either 'Oh my God, they really get it' or 'They don't get this at all.' I think one of the biggest difficulties is that whether you're the mental health person or the Equine Specialist, it does require a significant shift in how you look at therapy or how you look at horses.

I think for some equine individuals it's a huge shift because it's looking at a horse in a different way than they've ever looked at a horse before based on their equine background. If you have an equine person who's seen horses only in a certain way, it is hard for them to make that shift. I think some do that easier and for some, it's hard to let go of that safety concern or fear concern. But it's a real challenge to make that shift for some equine people.

The other part for us is that we work with 6 horses and we know our horses really well and they know us; that makes that confidence level a little bit easier because you develop this team with the horses you work with."

Tim Jobe: "Well, I think the most important thing you can know about horses to do this work is the psychology part of horses. I see a real big lack of knowledge about that in this field. I see most of the horse professionals in this field come from a background of having always worked with really well-trained horses that they probably didn't train themselves and don't have a real good knowledge of what it takes to get a horse to that point. I think the most important part of this work is how you build that relationship with the horse, and I'm afraid there's not a lot of Equine Specialists in this field that have a very good grasp of how you build that relationship."

Bettina Shultz-Jobe: "I suppose the other thing I would say is that, in this field, when somebody says they're an Equine Specialist, we don't really know what that means. Right now it seems that many people feel the Equine Specialist simply needs to keep clients safe around the horses. I've heard therapists call the Equine Specialist the "horse handler" and indicate that the baseline requirement is to keep clients physically safe. Safety is definitely important, but for this to be the *only* responsibility of the ES is, in my opinion, an enormous disservice to the clients, the horses, and this entire field of practice."

Equine Specialist Standards
ORGANIZATIONAL STANDARDS

What do the training and certifying organizations say on the subject? Here are the standards for EAGALA, PATH International and Natural Lifemanship.

EAGALA Equine Specialist Professional Standards
(www.eagala.org)

1. Professional must have 6,000 hours (equals to approx. 3 years full-time work) experience with hands-on work with horses.

2. Professional must have completed at least 100 hours of continuing education in the horse profession. Some of this education needs to include topics covering:
   - Ground work experience
   - Horse psychology knowledge
   - Ability to read horse body language/nonverbal communication

3. 40 hours of the continuing education listed in Item 2 must have

been completed in the last 2 years.

While I have seen problems with these standards since they were instituted, I still feel they are a good starting point for anyone wanting to be a professional in the field. How this proficiency is tracked and demonstrated in a meaningful way to others, however, remains a challenge.

PATH ES Standards *(information provided by Kris Batchelor, a PATH Certified Riding Instructor as well as both PATH and EAGALA Certified Equine Specialist.)* PATH International currently has a single level certification available for the Equine Specialist in Mental Health and Learning. There are several requirements that must be met prior to application, including sixty (60) hours of experience in a mental health or special education setting, twenty (20) hours of education in equine psychology and behavior, an online test and recommendations from professionals in the field. Candidates must then attend a three day instructional workshop, which is taught jointly by a mental health professional and Equine Specialist. Through both lecture and experiential format, the workshop explores the finer points of vital ES skills like curriculum development, creation of a therapeutic environment, the art of co-facilitation and the importance of equine welfare and CPR First Aid within this field. On the final day of the workshop, following the didactic portion, participants may elect to take a horsemanship skills test that allows them to demonstrate basic proficiency in safe horse handling. Certification as a PATH ES is subject to annual compliance requirements, including eight (8) hours of documented continuing education and commitment to the PATH code of ethics.

TF–EAP ES Standards *(information provided by Bettina Shultz-Jobe, co-creator of TF-EAP)* Currently, Natural Lifemanship is a training, rather than a certifying organization. In order to effectively utilize TF-EAP, it is imperative that the Equine Specialist have extensive knowledge and an intimate understanding of Natural Lifemanship relationship-building principles and horse psychology. These core competencies will be outlined as Natural Lifemanship continues to develop a field of study through The Institute for Human-Animal Connection at the University of Denver.

What Should an Equine Specialist Know About Horses?

Obviously I've spoken about this at some length already but, in summary, an equine-assisted professional should have a grounding in basic horse care requirements: feeding and nutrition, grooming, de-worming, vaccination, farrier needs, and monitoring vitals and general health. She should know the signs of colic, lameness, and other issues. She should be competent in handling the horse and maintaining a sound facility and environment suitable for horses.

The next tier of knowledge has to do with understanding horses from a psychological perspective. And it's here that things get tricky. There are many horse people who may know what to do when interacting with horses but they don't understand why the horse does what she does. Or, if they do understand, they only understand and interpret the horse from a limited point of view, i.e., the horse is stubborn, the horse is spooky, or even the horse is stupid.

I feel it's pretty important for every equine-assisted professional to take a step back from anything and everything they've ever learned about horses, and re-evaluate its completeness. Ideally, each horse professional develops a never-ending "learner's mind" toward horses, a mindset that always questions the traditional ways while exploring and examining new ones.

From the basics of individual horse physiology and psychology, I think Equine Specialists need to have a thorough understanding of herd dynamics. Horses are a social species, and how they interact, and what they need in a herd environment is very specific and ever-changing. Spending a substantial amount of time watching herd dynamics

More than a Mirror, by Shannon Knapp

and how horses interact with each other, how they use their bodies to move each other, is one way to glean huge amounts of information about horse dynamics. What influences them? What do they choose as motivation—do they move each other over food, do they exert influence to move someone out of a choice shady spot? What are the things that matter? In the process of noticing these nuances, a horse professional can start to notice what matters to horses—both collectively and individually.

When it comes to other equids, such as mules and donkeys, it would be nice for the Equine Specialist to have a basic understanding of their unique traits, not so much from a zoological point of view as from a psychological point of view. How do mules and donkeys interact with horses? How do they differ from horses in response to stimulus, how do their "default" settings track as a species, as well as their individual...muleanalities?

As far as specific breeds go, it's important to be aware of breed tendencies without also making clichéd assumptions. Many people stereotype horses by breed—Arabians, Thoroughbreds, Paso Finos—and have significant biases and expectations. The breed may tend toward being very extroverted; they may have a long flight line. But there are individual exceptions to these tendencies. And one should never rule out how breed perceptions are sometimes the result of breed-specific training methods that can corrupt the basic psychology of the horse.

Equine psychology and body language then lead to the next level of important knowledge: handling skills from the ground. People who understand horse psychology and body language know that ground skills are not about pushing/pulling and more about influencing the horse, from catching and haltering, to safely extricating the horse from the herd, to leading them in from the field, to being comfortable and safe handling the horse from the ground in every situation. We can execute all of these basic functions more effectively when we come from a better foundation of understanding.

At *Horse Sense*, one of the first things we encourage employees and volunteers to do is stop using words around horses. As humans, we tend to rely more on words and pay less attention to our own body language. By inviting people to reverse the two, we invite them to become more aware of both their body language and the horse's.

This understanding can be cultivated in volunteers as well as professional staff. They should be able to ask any horse to yield his hind quarters, yield his front end, put his head down, give to pressure, and follow the feel on a lead rope. Everyone handling horses should have an awareness of how to do these things so that they can learn the individual idiosyncrasies of the horses they handle. They should know a) how to determine if they and the horse are communicating effectively, b) if a given situation is safe or unsafe, and c) what to do to help the horse when communication isn't working or the situation is becoming unsafe.

What Should an Equine Specialist Know About People?

The horse is only one part of the equation in equine-assisted practice. We can't discount the reality that we also work with people, which is what this entire chapter is about. Equine-assisted professionals must have an understanding of people, and of facilitation.

At the most practical level, the professional Equine Specialist should have basic, competent social skills in being around people in general. They should be comfortable undergoing a background check if they will be working with any youth. They should also know emergency procedures related to their facility, and have CPR and basic first-aid certification.

The longer I work in equine-assisted practice, the more I feel the Equine Specialist should also have, at the very least, a college-level understanding of human psychology, including a baseline understanding of common diagnoses. For some of us, work as horse people has never really included a formal understanding of human behavior. We shouldn't go into practice without having some basic skills. And, just as in stereotyping horse breeds, the Equine Specialist should learn to recognize and avoid her personal stereotypes when it comes to biases toward age, ethnicity, or those differently-abled.

I've also come to feel that, because the horse professional is not obliged to spend some amount of time working with a mental health professional on her "own stuff," the horse professional is often in a challenging position with regards to keeping the work clean. Many mental health professional programs require that the prospective therapist do her own therapy, to become more aware of her issues and how those issues might impact work with clients. Currently, this is not a requirement of horse professionals. I really like to have horse professionals who are cognizant of their main "buttons." I don't want an Equine Specialist who doesn't have issues (do those folks even exist?); I want an Equine Specialist who is aware of his/her issues, can call them out in the moment, and take appropriate steps to address these issues should they become an impediment to clients in session.

On occasion, I (personally) and some of my Equine Specialist co-workers have become too involved or invested in a particular group of clients—those with addictions or eating disorders, for example—or with individual clients, so much so that I pulled myself and others out of contact with that client population until more balance was possible. It is the hallmark of a good Equine Specialist if she is able to appropriately remove herself from such a situation. Sometimes that balance is simply not attainable around a particular issue or circumstance. This is not a problem for me if the Equine Specialist is aware of it and able to speak to it; sometimes a break from a certain population allows the Equine Specialist to gain perspective. However, I caution against setting up scenarios in which newly-recovering clients are called upon to facilitate this work for others. Too often, it can end up a sticky, ugly mess, which in no way serves the client.

I recommend engaging in some form of ongoing education in human behavior, perhaps alongside the mental health partners in the practice, as well as ongoing personal discovery. Most mental health professionals are required to have continuing education classes to maintain their licensure. But these classes aren't restricted to mental health professionals; the Equine Specialist can access a multitude of wonderful continuing education opportunities around many of the common and uncommon diagnoses. Similarly, I encourage both the Equine Specialist and the mental health professional to put themselves outside their comfort zones, regularly. It serves to be in touch with the risks and challenges you routinely ask your clients to take.

I've always been a fan of cross-training both the mental health professional and the Equine Specialist. Because of how the horse-human dynamic intertwines in client sessions, knowing only half of the equation is often not enough. Just as the mental health professional should be moderately proficient with horses at ground level and have an understanding of horse psychology, the horse professional should be moderately fluent and aware of the key elements around the client diagnoses with which they hope to work. There are certainly characteristics for each type of client that prove useful; having an awareness of what your horse is likely to encounter, and what issues will be likely brought to the forefront in a session, serves everyone.

And obviously, in any form of equine-assisted practice in which the horse professional is the only facilitator, the educational skill level of that professional needs to be that much higher to adequately serve the client. In fact, it's how inordinately high so many skills need to be—with horses, with humans, in social and emotional intelligence—that only a precious few solo practitioners can serve clients as well as a two-person team. I've met a few of these folks and am in awe of them. But, for a number of reasons, I prefer the two-person model.

Paul Smith and the folks at Prescott College argue, quite convincingly, for dual proficiency for all the facilitators in session work. This doesn't mean that, without a mental health license, an Equine Specialist can't practice; it does mean that both facilitators need to have some skill and training in horses, facilitation, client issues and/or diagnoses and the impact that diagnosis or issue might have on the horse. It wasn't until I spent quite a bit of time around the folks at Prescott College, specifically their undergraduate students who were facilitating large groups in activity and doing it really well, that I realized there was a wealth of information to be mined in the world of "experiential education" that went hand-in-hand with what we were doing in equine-assisted practices. Paul Smith, Pam McPhee, Tracy Weber and others I encountered had flat-out amazing facilitation skills, without having mental health licenses. I must say I had been conflating mental health licensure with facilitation skills (despite experience to the contrary!)—and had found many mental health professionals lacking!

The "philosophy" of EAGALA itself points to key components of experiential education: that, in general, people don't change unless they are challenged, and are outside their comfort zone. The most significant change occurs when people find their own answers to questions. EAGALA itself sprung from the kind of facility that tends to incubate and hire, quite regularly, the kind of amazing future facilitators I was encountering at Prescott College. So, I'm now an advocate of Equine Specialists being schooled in concepts of experiential education as well as horses, and I myself continue to be a student of the amazing "field staff" facilitators we have been working with at various residential treatment facilities, such as the folks out at *SUWS of the Carolinas*.

I encourage new (and experienced!) Equine Specialists to attend workshops and events sponsored by the Association for Experiential Education (www.aee.org), and to spend time with some good books from the field. But, at this point, I would expect the Equine Specialist to have familiarity with basic facilitation skills, both for individuals and groups. Among those facilitation skills should be an awareness of how to de-escalate situations (in partnership with their mental health professional or alone), and an awareness of the different possible learning styles for people. There are also skills to be learned in order to structure the "classroom/group" setting and to optimize the client experience. Many groups ultimately require these basic "classroom" management skills. Although I'm very aware of professionals today who do just fine without being studied in these areas, I also know those same professionals have cultivated an ability to tune in to their client groups and discern their differing needs.

So now that we've got the basic human skills ironed out, it's time to look at the more advanced concepts I believe the Equine Specialist needs to know. This is where my particular insistence on skill in reading both horse and human body language comes into play. Both Equine Specialists and mental health professionals would benefit by having some education in non-verbal communication for both species, an awareness of the multitude of ways humans and horses show up in and out of session. I'd like Equine Specialists to read the whole human as well as the whole horse, and to possess a curiosity about how non-verbal congruency compares to verbal congruency.

I look for the treatment team members to pay attention in session to how a client responds non-verbally to the words of the therapist or other treatment team members, to gauge how the client absorbs and responds to comments, observations, or questions. Just like with horses, the team is looking for patterns of behavior in how clients respond physically, as many clients have little vocabulary for "sensation," as opposed to thoughts and feelings. On a number of levels, it's also important that the facilitators not assume they know how a client feels based on body language alone.

One colleague of mine has made interesting discoveries utilizing her Equine Specialist skills as a staff member at a psychiatric hospital.

She's found a crossover between the ways clients show up physically and how she can connect with them most effectively. She has been successful in applying horse/prey psychology to make progress with clients and to de-escalate situations in ways where traditional human/predator approaches don't help. She finds herself applying more and more horsemanship skills to her daily situations, trying to discover the impetus or cue for certain behaviors and speaking to that dynamic rather than trying to "fix" the behavior itself.

A profound moment for me, both in terms of working with horses and with people, occurred during a Parelli™ Summit Performance by Linda Parelli in Pagosa Springs, Colorado in 2005. Linda was giving a demonstration working with Replica, a particularly challenging horse who was having extreme difficulties calming down and becoming present in any way. The horse was extreme right-brain extrovert, which often presents as an inability to stop moving the feet, and Replica was certainly doing that. Replica was brought into the arena and placed in a round pen, and didn't disappoint: she was fast-flying around the round pen, reactive and unconfident. Linda talked us through her approach to helping Replica. She began by mirroring Replica's movements from the outside of the round pen. As Replica turned and trotted in one direction, Linda did the same. When Replica turned and trotted in the other, Linda mimicked. This went on for some time, until, by almost imperceptible degrees, we began to see Replica notice Linda—that Replica became aware of this other being alongside her in her movements. Linda didn't attempt to change or force Replica out of this behavior, she simply joined her there. After a period of time, Replica began slowing down, and the path she had worn on that one side of the round pen began to get shorter and shorter. Linda again mimicked Replica's behavior. Then, after a bit of time, Linda began the shift: she began to lead the behavior. As they made their way to one side of the round pen, Linda would stop a bit shorter than Replica and turn. Soon, Replica was following her lead, rather than Linda following Replica. By this time, it was safe for Linda to enter the round pen, and Replica began following Linda around through sharp turns, stopping and starting together. At the end, Replica had her head down and was deeply connected to Linda, trusting that Linda knew what she felt and would not try to force her out of her feelings and perceptions. The demonstration, which was probably slated to take no more than an hour, became a marathon session and lasted through the lunch break, as Linda wouldn't leave the horse in an unsatisfactory state, not even for a crowd of over a thousand.

What I learned from this is that we need to re-train ourselves on how we respond to humans in the same way we re-train ourselves on how we deal with horses: meeting "resistance" with force is rarely a positive or productive long-term fix. The "mirror neurons" in our brain can mimic the resistant client and respond with the same almost instantaneously: I certainly have been in situations where I've met resistance with force with clients (in a non-physical way) and found myself in conflict long before I remembered actually choosing that path! We need to know how to de-escalate a situation, not just in an intellectual way, but in a physical way as well. As my colleague at the psychiatric hospital and Linda Parelli have demonstrated, there is much to be understood about horses and people by joining them where they are.

It is just as necessary for the Equine Specialist to have curiosity about humans and human behavior as it is for them to have curiosity about horses and horse behavior. I'm not sure how ideal it would be to have an Equine Specialist who has no strong empathy, compassion, or curiosity toward the human component of equine-assisted practice, although I know folks who appear to have little regard for the human. Equine-assisted work is probably not the ideal field for the Equine Specialist focused solely on the horse.

The Equine Specialist In Session

What is the role of the horse professional in session? At *Horse Sense*, one of the key responsibilities includes making sure the horses, clients and facilitators are safe and able to communicate their needs in a way that causes harm to no one else. The Equine Specialist is responsible for being attentive, aware and ready to intervene for the sake of safety at a moment's notice. This includes making sure that, if there are props or restraints of any sort used with the horse (restraints such as a halter or lead rope), the horse still has a way to indicate disagreement or dissent without hurting others. This also includes being able to either redirect the clients out of potentially harmful situations or being able to step in to redirect the horses out of the same.

At *Horse Sense*, the horse professional is usually responsible for the "safety talk" at the start of each session and as necessary throughout the session. The "safety talk" at *Horse Sense* is documented in Chapter 3. Oftentimes the horse professional will ask the client(s) what kind of horse experience they have had to date, to determine a level of confidence with horses, but usually we'll also ask the client to rate, on a scale of 1-10, how nervous or anxious they feel about interacting with the horse(s) (again, this is documented in Chapter 3).

After the client is "in" with the horse(s), the horse professional monitors the horse(s) and the client(s) activity, monitors the herd activity and interaction, and monitors the physical space and the environment, alert for disruptions or challenge. This is done not so much to change anything as to seriously consider the impact on the horse and client. At this point, the horse professional is also using Clean Facilitation with clients about interactions with the horse(s), asking questions or making observations about the client and/or the horse to the mental health professional, and/or doing the same with the client, as appropriate.

When it feels appropriate, or when invited by the mental health professional, the horse professional may share the horse's background, history or a general horse fact, such as how horses respond to pressure or threat, or how they process trauma (to the best of our current ability to understand). Depending on client and treatment goals, the Equine Specialist may demonstrate an action or respond to a request for help by the client. In the event of an incident or emergency, the Equine Specialist secures the horses and responds to requests of the mental health professional.

At the start of each day or at the start of a session, *Horse Sense* horse professionals also complete a checklist for the facility and the horses. I request that Equine Specialists at *Horse Sense* have a pocket knife, a small length of rope (likely a Savvy String), and a cell phone on them at all times. The knife is to quickly extricate a horse from any entanglements which might arise (a standard practice for horse people on our farm, regardless of whether they are Equine Specialists or not); the length of rope is so that, should a horse get loose, we don't have to leave the session in order to get a lead rope to secure that horse.

Other Thoughts on ES in Session
Survey/Conference Feedback

In the surveys, the overwhelming consensus was that safety of the horses and the humans is the focus of the Equine Specialist. Next in the list of primary responsibilities for the ES is offering observations and/or feedback to the mental health professional and/or the client, in session. Other comments of interest include assigning journal topics to support clients in processing the experience, setting up and explaining the activity, and creating awareness of nonverbal communication between the horse(s) and the client(s).

Interview Feedback
Carissa McNamara: "I think the primary responsibility while you're in session is be flexible, supportive and keep an eye on the big picture. My role changes dramatically depending on the group, the dynamics and where we are. At the end of the day, that ability to be flexible and take

a step back is my role. I don't feel obligated to hold it together; that's what the clients are there for. There are some times I might ask 5 or 6 questions and times I might ask 1. And really it's a check and balance with the mental health professional. Yesterday we did a session 'Raging River' where we had addiction on one side and sobriety on the other. You've got to get all of your guys and these horses to the other side without touching the water. The two mental health people, when they came back in, said 'Who has seen a raging river? Has anybody seen a picture of a raging river? Has anybody heard a raging river?' I pulled her off to the side and asked her why she was so worried about the river. She really wanted them to understand the gravity of the situation, where it may or may not have been relevant."

Liza Sapir Flood: "I really like a lot of sharing of responsibilities—at *Horse Sense*, I was lucky enough to work with people who were either therapists or had really good intuition about clients. I do think one thing that the Equine Specialist should do is be a source of creative inspiration in terms of their observations and how they can relate their horses' skills and behaviors to the client's general issues—what you know about the client's history. Horses are constantly providing all these cues about what they're thinking and feeling, etcetera—it's about connecting what you're seeing in the horse with what you're seeing in the client. I say 'creative' because it takes a lot of creativity. It's like 'Wow, this horse is sensing their fear' and I know the client is dealing with a fear issue in their life. The Equine Specialist has to weed out all the horse behaviors that are less relevant; the Equine Specialist has to have that creativity and knowledge of the client to say 'That's relevant now.' It's something to distinguish from the tendency to point out horse behaviors. I think you have to do more than just say 'This is what I see'—unless it's lead by the client, and that changes everything.

The other thing I think is the role of the Equine Specialist is to bring in the exercises that naturally fit with the horse's agenda and the farm's agenda without being contrived. This is something Richard [Knapp] is really good at—and about finding interesting, creative exercises for them to do. I think the clients loved the stuff you guys are doing because it's real stuff.

I learned at Aspen Ranch really early that I was letting my ego get in the way and back in those days I was less confident. [My boss had] this tendency to be like 'Let's get the kids to call the shots' or 'Let's have the kids do this'—I felt myself in those days thinking, 'I want to do that' and looking back, I realize that was about me, instead of being confident in my own skills and sharing all these really rich things that need to be done on a farm. Kids get so invested because they know they're contributing. I think you have to let go of yourself as the horse professional and share some of that. I bring this up because I sensed it in my own interactions with Equine Specialists sometimes; they would claim horse tasks as their own and didn't want clients to have their hand in it because that task was very attached to their own identity."

Paul Smith: "A dedicated set of eyes not just to safety but the nuances of the role in place and presence of the horse in session. They're tracking the client as well. The more understanding they have of the client in process the better, but their primary focus is what's going on with the horses, and on a safety level, making the judgment on whether they need to step in or not. Also being able to make horse selection for specific activities, advocates for the safety and health of the horses—one that says 'I'm not comfortable with this' or 'Buddy's not the best horse for this activity.'"

Richard Knapp: "The role of the Equine Specialist is to read the horse's body language and take care of the physical situation of the environment. We provide that feedback to the therapist and most of the time they will process it through their filter and then move it towards the client. There are times when we question the client directly, but almost everything goes through the therapist or mental health professional first.

There are times when I'll be in the middle of an activity and I'll see an opportunity open up for either a similar activity or an extension of the activity that they're doing, and I might talk to the therapist for a little bit, get some feedback, and then change the direction of the session in that way."

StarrLee Heady: "I think it's not just one thing. I think bringing in deep understanding of the horses is the biggest role. If they can come in with understanding and knowledge about horses, then they have the ability to assess what's going on for the horses in that setting, and how what's happening for the horse may affect the flow of that session. So physical safety is one of the roles, but more than physical safety is a real understanding, a dynamic understanding of the horse's world and that has to be there.

It's critical to the team that somebody knows what's going on, just as somebody has to know what's going on if a client with a mental issue has something happen. I think it has to be there to be a team member. We've kind of gotten away from defining roles tightly, 'Okay, you're going to set up the session' or what not. I think a good team has strengths and weaknesses and it's up to that team how it's going to be played and how things are going in the moment. I think the primary responsibility is a heightened awareness and understanding of the horse's world."

Randy Mandrell: "My role is number one, safety; reading cues to tell me if a possible unsafe situation might arise. I'm interpreting what the horses are telling us and if they're telling me, 'I'm uncomfortable with this,' then it's my time to say 'Hey guys, let's talk about what's going on.' I don't want the clients to get hurt or the horses to get hurt. That horse is my partner; I have a mental health professional but I also have the horse. I think that's the primary role."

Patti Mandrell: "And the more skilled your Equine Specialist is at doing that job, the more options and more doors you open up as to what you can do in therapy. For instance, when Equine Specialists first begin, they'll be quicker to step in on a situation that's unsafe, whereas the more you do the work—what we see, the more skilled the Equine Specialist is in reading those cues, the more the Equine Specialist can do their job subtly without affecting the flow of the session. I'd say it's also the Equine Specialist's job to be the alpha in the herd at all times in the arena."

Rhiannon Beauregard: "The physical safety of the horses, and bringing the horses' behaviors and interactions into every aspect of the session. I really rely on their role as redirecting the therapist. For people who are just mental health professionals, reminding them what it's all about in a team-oriented way is key. One of the most valuable roles is that Equine Specialists are not therapists and they can be themselves. They're authentic and genuine and bring a non-therapeutic side to therapy.

I'll give you an example; I had a session where the father had been unemployed and was finally getting an interview and feeling good. The

Equine Specialist on the way out said 'Good luck on your interview, sir'—and I was so caught up in payment and rescheduling and that, I forgot about the human aspect of it. That's what I love about Equine Specialists. I really want to stress that while the roles are very clear, I love the Equine Specialist just being another human being. We get caught up in the robotics of being a therapist that we forget to be a human."

Michelle Holling-Brooks: "There are two main things—one is to ensure safety, but to me, ten percent happens in session and the other 90 percent happens in your relationship with your horses outside of session. And then the other thing is to ensure your observations of your horses and what they're doing and how they're playing with clients is translated into the processing and also with the clients so that clear observation can happen where the clients can put their stories on top of what's happening with the horses and with themselves. Those are the two main things I see as the role of the Equine Specialist."

Amy Blossom Lomas: "Everything is a team approach from the facilitation of the actual session—the Equine Specialist is there to mindfully choose which horses to have in that session with input from the therapist. Being able to work towards treatment goals without having a set agenda, being willing to work with the mental health professional so that both of them are staying true to the model.

Of course, other things include watching the horses and what they're doing and noticing about the things the horses are doing that relate to what the client is saying—bringing those to the attention of the mental health professional. There are so many different responsibilities for the horse person; the Equine Specialist has multiple roles in that room."

Tim Jobe: "From my point of view, the role of the equine professional is to understand what's happening with the horse in relationship to what's happening with the client. Just seeing that the horse is starting to get upset doesn't help you a lot if you don't understand what's making him feel that way. Also, there's a lot more subtle stuff to that and understanding just when a client's working with the relationship with the horse, helping the client understand the little things that they're doing that are affecting that relationship in either a negative or positive way.

Of course, safety is a big concern to everybody but I think it's primarily the equine professional's role to make sure that the client is learning to keep themselves safe, not the equine professional's job to keep the client safe. I know that can be a very thin line to walk, but I think everything as an equine professional that I do for a client robs them of the ability to do that for themselves. When I take on the role of keeping the client safe, I think that stands in the way of the client learning the things they need to learn."

Bettina Shultz-Jobe: "The equine professional role, I think, is to have a grasp of what is reality—what is really going on with the horse. We do allow clients to put their own meaning on what's happening, but it's important that we do have a grasp of the real deal. I know there's a lot of discussion in the field about anthropomorphizing and all of that. The horse professional should be able to tell the difference between when a horse is angry, scared, mad, glad, happy and some of those things. We do have clients who say 'Oh, this horse loves me' but the horse is clearly pinning his ears and backing his butt up to the client. The therapist decides where you go with that, but the horse professional should have a grasp of what's actually going on with the horse."

Linda Zimmerman: "For the session, I feel like I'm responsible for setting up a safe environment—not safety that everybody gets hung up on, but setting up the activities. In the session I've always felt very fortunate working with Z because when you go in, you can't bring your ego in there and you can't bring 'Oh, I'm just the horse person.' I hate to hear that and I hear it every once in a while at conferences. You're part of a team and you have to blend all of your skills together and you have to have such a trusting relationship because when you get into the arena, things change and the horse says 'This is a better idea.'

As a team, you have to recognize that—all three of you. As a horse person, you can't be so rigid but you also have to understand that I'm not a mental health person. I may be asking questions but the mental health person is the one that finesses things; I'm certainly there to support and the two of us clue each other in. It's so much about a team, but I think if you're going to be a good Equine Specialist, you have to be very secure in yourself. You have to walk into that arena and have some self-confidence there that you're offering an opportunity to the client and you're part of the team that offers that opportunity."

Don "Z" Zimmerman: "I would reiterate some of the things that Linda says, and most important, I don't think the mental health person or the Equine Specialist can bring their ego into the arena. I think Linda and I are fortunate and unique because as a husband and wife team, I think people could come in and observe us and not really know which is the horse person and which is the mental health person.

I do rely upon Linda a great deal for the horse knowledge. That takes some pressure off me—I'm also watching the horses too, but Linda knows the horses so well and knows their body language, and I also rely on her for the facilitating skills in the process.

I think one of the things that make us unique is that we're married, and because we're together that gives us a lot of time to process a session prior to the session and also process the session afterwards. That's a situation where a lot of teams don't have that advantage. You have to leave time to debrief yourself in terms of what went well and what you want to do differently; I think a lot of teams don't have that opportunity."

Linda Zimmerman: "After a session there are many times that Z and I will ask each other: 'Why did you go there? Why did you ask this question?' It's important for the horse specialist to know that if they don't understand something, they need to do that. When something doesn't flow, the Equine Specialist needs to ask why. Talk to your team member and find out things and don't just think 'I'm the horse person so I'll put up the horses and clean up the activity.' There's a lot more to it than that."

Equine Specialist Outside Session

Aside from the more obvious of the roles the Equine Specialist plays outside of session here at *Horse Sense*, such as bringing horses in, care and feeding in between client sessions, maintaining stalls and taking horses back out, the key role of the Equine Specialist out of session is developing and refining relationships with horses who are, or might be, involved in EAP/EAL session-work. This includes a whole host of activities discussed in the previous chapter.

Further, the Equine Specialist is constantly looking at and assessing the herd available for contra-indications or concerns for particular horses engaged in particular ways. For example, we currently have several horses who are part of the work in observational activities or liberty activities, but are not yet ready to engage with groups of clients or with clients at all in certain physical spaces. Finding those edges for each horse is part of the outside work for the Equine Specialist.

The Equine Specialist is also developing activities suitable for each client and each session, usually in conjunction with the mental health professional and always with regard to treatment goals. The activity or the treatment goals may point to a particular horse for a session, or a particular location for a session, such as round pen, arena, pasture or stall. The selection of which and how many horses is usually done primarily by the Equine Specialist, again in conjunction with the mental health professional and with regard to treatment goals.

All this communication with the mental health professional, before and after session, is another part of the horse professional's role outside of session. There is the expectation for pre- and post- session communication, including general debriefing, ideas for the next session, and discussion of what went well or what was challenging.

Equine Specialists at *Horse Sense* do write notes for every session, at least for a period of time when they first join *Horse Sense*, to facilitate reflection and the mentoring process in their development. These notes do not live in client folders, and contain no identifying information of clients. The mental health session notes are the ones that go in the client files. But the Equine Specialist also has notes to write up, both on the horses and on himself/herself. Should we be collaborating with therapists from an outside organization who do their own treatment notes and maintain the client files offsite from *Horse Sense*, the Equine Specialist often writes out a session note for our records.

Other Thoughts on ES Role Outside Session
Survey/Conference Feedback

The surveys and other feedback consensus indicated that creation of activities and selection of horses was key to the role of the Equine Specialist outside of session. For those who practice as a team, consultation with the mental health professional was also a regular part of the process. Many Equine Specialists—almost three-quarters—are moving horses to and from pasture, and are responsible for the care and feeding of the herd, at least during session days and times. A significant number of Equine Specialists write notes separate from the mental health notes, and a significant number are participating in marketing and other business aspects of their program as well.

Interview Feedback

Carissa McNamara: "Healthy horses. At the end of the day, I think that's the most important thing—the mental and physical and emotional well-being of the animals you keep and being sensitive to that. I had two horses that were born twenty minutes apart and it was weird because we bred the mares three weeks apart. They were pasture brothers and one colt ended up dying in training of colic and the little horse, I've never seen grief of that gravity. I called my mental health professional and asked if we could put together a play date to have fun with these horses. He needs to be around some fun. He would wait at the gate and he would trot right over for these little kids. But he needed something that I as an individual couldn't provide."

Liza Sapir Flood: "Obviously know your horses, and I think that means interacting with your horses outside of session. I'm a really big fan of having projects going on with your horses. At the Biltmore where I taught riding lessons, I needed to engage in projects with my horses without the students around—and these projects were seemingly unrelated to their lesson work. Opportunities like that help you to really get to know your horses and they increase your own scope, your bag of tools and experiences that you're always pulling from in session. Obviously I think in all the best scenarios the Equine Specialist is part of the general care of the horses, even something as simple as taking horses to the pasture after a session or getting them before session. I'm glad that I did that and it wasn't the barn hands' job. I needed that time with the horses."

Paul Smith: "Ideally I see them as a co-facilitator, so I think of them in terms of if I'm working with an equine professional, I want them to be a gifted facilitator and have good human skills, which is a hard combo sometimes. But they're not a silent partner; I would want them to be active in debriefing or asking questions outside of a session, reflecting on what worked, what didn't work, what's going on with the horses. If the mental health person is not a horse person, then it changes the role of the horse professional. Then I think it's even more important for the horse professional to be dually competent. One of the two needs to know the bridge between the worlds. If the mental health person provides that bridge, I think you can have a horse professional and a mental health person who's providing clear leadership. If you've got a mental health person that thinks this is interesting, likes horses and has been to an EAGALA training but has no real clue about horses, then I think it's increasingly important for the horse professional to understand facilitation and goals and group process to help be the bridge."

Rhiannon Beauregard: "Well, I really like to collaborate out of session with activities. If I have an instinct towards an activity, I will say, 'This is what I'm seeing in my head. What can we come up with to create an activity?' I like that my Equine Specialist is making sure the horses are safe, they're trying out herds ahead of time—I have walked out into a barn and said: 'This is not a safe situation for my clients to be in!' I think also ethics and confidentiality is such a huge problem for me; I know they offer information about this at the conferences. Last conference, I asked all the Equine Specialists I knew to attend the session [about confidentiality] and only one did, and that was my partner. I said. 'I need you guys to be aware of what we're up against. You cannot share these stories.'

I feel that therapy takes preparation and I think someone who's coming from a riding background to a therapeutic background, it's not just that you show up for an hour and leave. If you as an Equine Specialist want to walk down this path, there's an investment you need to make in this work and it's ensuring you can do the job to the best of your abilities."

Michelle Holling-Brooks: "Out of session is that other ninety percent that we talked about earlier, what needs to happen in order to ensure that session, that fifty minutes with clients, can happen appropriately. Out of session, the Equine Specialist's role is to maintain that healthy relationship with the horses—to make sure your horses are happy, healthy and mentally able to do this job, to make sure their safety is ensured, and the biggest thing is to make sure that relationship piece is there. Without that, you'll never be able to get through a session with clients."

Amy Blossom Lomas: "Well, again everything is a team approach, a shared responsibility where the Equine Specialist is to work with the mental health professional with anything that relates to that client on their case load. Obviously the mental health professional has more say in how that goes, but when they work together I think they can build a better product. Getting here before the session, setting up, deciding which horses to use and anything that has to do with getting the horses ready for a session, setting up any equipment, and of course marketing and public relations with regard to our organization and being an ambassador for EAGALA.

Then after the session, it's making sure the horse is put away in the right way; if the horses need to be fed, that's part of the responsibility of everybody who was here working—and, even noticing anything unusual that needs to be addressed, whether it's a potential hazard or something that's not working or something that needs to be replaced. Also the Equine Specialist is responsible for the treatment team and making sure they're staying focused—it's the responsibility for both the Equine Specialist and the mental health specialist, but making sure everyone is doing their part to keep with the mental health plan, keeping good records, and so on"

Richard Knapp: "Equine Specialists usually plan for the session, look at the previous one, figure out what activity they were doing and then maybe plan activities for the coming session, make sure the horses are available and ready to go. Not necessarily groom them because some-times the clients like to do that or bring them in—sometimes the clients also need to do that."

StarrLee Heady: "Checking to make sure the horses are okay. You know, we're putting them into an environment that puts stresses on them that's not in their normal environment, so being able to evaluate them as to whether or not they're having changes based on coming out of a session— are they behaving differently? Are they showing signs there's something out of sorts for them in the way they're dealing with their world now? How's that affecting them? If their behavior is different, then we need to look at a particular session; did certain things happen in a session or is this happening all the time? I have a responsibility that they get their own time to be who they are without human interpretation or needs."

Tim Jobe: "Of course just the overall care of the horses but I guess basi-cally when I've got a horse that's been through a session where there was no resolution to some of the feelings the horse is going through, it's my role after the session to take that horse back to a place where it's got its mind working in the right direction so the horse can feel comfortable and relaxed in the sessions and still be the contributor to the sessions that it needs to be, but where it's not leaving the sessions in a place where it's feeling disjointed or that the session was a failure for it.

I think the equine professional has a responsibility to the horse, just like the therapist has a responsibility to the client, that they're not leaving the session and melting down until the next sessions—that the horses is able to contain the emotions and the feelings its had throughout the session and can find some kind of closure to that session, whether they find it with the client or not. If they haven't, then as an equine professional it's my role to provide that for them.

Bettina Shultz-Jobe: "I think the equine professional is responsible for the emotional health and well being of the horses—the physical, of course, if that's part of the farm. Tim is responsible for the emotional well-being of our horses."

Kendall Smith, former Clinical Director at *Horse Sense* and a wonderful mental health professional to work with, wrote up a description of what a mental health professional generally looks for in an Equine Specialist. I thought the point of view was an important one to consider, as we discuss what makes a good Equine Specialist. I know that at *Horse Sense*, we're finally in a place as an organization and I think as a field in general where we can start expecting more polished job applicants now. We weren't there ten years ago, but I think now we're in the position where we can start to ask for a baseline and start to have an expectation around that.

— ⬚ —

The Ideal Equine Specialist
By Kendall Smith, LPC

Working in partnership with someone is no easy task. The divorce rate statistics remind us of this every day. And, although you won't be marrying your Equine Specialist (usually), you do need to find someone who you can connect with on many levels and whom you trust. Here are the three characteristics that I find essential to evaluate before you sign up for long-term contracts with an Equine Specialist partner.

At the most basic level the Equine Specialist needs to be just that, an expert in horse behavior and psychology. This person must have an extensive background of working with horses, ideally in a variety of settings. As a therapist the flow of your session depends greatly on how much you trust your Equine Specialist to keep everyone, horses and humans, physically safe, while simultaneously not interrupting the session when the risk is relatively insignificant. This ability to intuitively sense what is going on with the horses in the herd comes as a natural gift to some, and after years of practice and observation to others. Either way, when I step into the ring with my Equine Specialist I trust him/her completely in the realm of physical safety for all. When I see something that makes me anxious, which I have at times, I check in nonverbally with my Equine Specialist, and I have faith in his/her decision of how to proceed.

In addition, I have had the good fortune of working with Equine Specialists who are skilled enough to often be in the position of communicating with the horses without drawing much attention to what they are doing. It is extra helpful if your Equine Specialist has the skill of making subtle requests to the horses and being respected.

Another point on this matter is that your Equine Specialist devote the time and energy to know the herd that you are working with in sessions. It is not enough for an Equine Specialist to have years of experience if they don't seem invested in learning the unique Horsenalities™ of the ponies you will be playing with. All of this comes down to your Equine Specialist being passionate about continuing his/her professionalism in the equine field. Someone who not only loves horses but also loves learning and truly makes equine work their life's goal is the foundational quality in a brilliant Equine Specialist.

The second characteristic is commitment to personal growth and development, not only in the professional realm as outlined above, but in the mental, emotional, physical, and spiritual realms. This is not about religion or subscribing to any particular brand of self-improvement. This is about stepping into the arena with people who are struggling and accepting them where they are without judgement and with positive regard. Mental Health Professionals go to school to learn many skills, including how to filter their own personal experience so that it does not interfere with the client's process but instead utilizing it to elevate the power of the therapeutic experience. Equine Specialist folks do not have the clinical background to support them when a client triggers their own 'stuff' (as the EAGALA model has defined it in SPUD'S™). Any individual who is not invested in looking at their own 'stuff' when it comes up will be challenging to work with in the arena. To be clear, the time to delve into the issues is not in the arena with clients, it is in the debriefing and then on the Equine Specialist's own time.

At some point everyone who works in mental health will be triggered; it is the gift of being human. The Equine Specialist is especially vulnerable to this experience because he or she has not been professionally trained on how to handle such situations. For this reason it is imperative that the Equine Specialist you choose to work with be willing to work with his/her own issues. How to judge whether or not someone is likely to be willing?

During your interview process, bring up this dilemma of the work: Equine Specialist folks are subject to the same potentially stressful/traumatic (or enlightening and encouraging) experiences without the support of clinical training. How does the person you are interviewing plan to deal with the possibility of being triggered in a session? Talk through what the person already knows about as potential triggers (comments about the health of a horse, domestic violence perpetrators, child abuse issues etc.) and discuss ways of communicating about the effect of such experiences.

My final quality of evaluation is the potential for positive communication and productive feedback exchanges. It is extremely challenging to be an effective treatment team when communication patterns between the Equine Specialist and therapist are dysfunctional. You may at times have success, but overall you will not be providing your clients with the most fruitful experience possible. Also, your partnership is less sustainable if you cannot offer and receive feedback with one another. Many Equine Specialist and therapist teams were friends first; this is not necessary and can even lead to greater challenges in the working relationship. We have certain expectations of our friends that we do not hold our work colleagues to. Be aware of how whatever prior relationship you had with your Equine Specialist influences your current communication. It can be an excellent match to partner up with a friend; just move into that work partnership with consciousness, discuss how working together brings up different issues, share concerns as well as areas of excitement, plan for what to do when you meet a work-related stress. For folks that are brand new to each other, begin with sharing how you best receive constructive criticism, what kind of positive reinforcement or feedback works for you. This sharing will also allow you to know more about how introspective and self-aware the potential Equine Specialist is. If someone is not able to identify how they prefer to be approached with constructive criticism it does not mean you shouldn't hire them; it is simply information and an opportunity for growth. However, if you do not ask these questions, you don't know where the areas of growth are, and perhaps neither does the individual you are considering partnering with. Also, no surprise here, not all therapists are completely in tune with the way in which they struggle to have positive communication patterns. It is the therapist's responsibility, in my opinion, to lead the way with self-inquiry and the desire to better know oneself through experimentation and practice. The therapist should help to make explicit the parameters of the professional relationship that make it safe to grow and develop individually and as a team.

Short list of skills to look for in an Equine Specialist:

- Horse experience
- Being able to communicate with horses without expending a lot of energy
- Personal development
- Boundaries
- Relationship
- Communication
- Intuitive sense of what is going on with the horse based on extensive exposure to horses in a variety of settings

(See Contributor Biographies to read more about this author.)

Common Challenges for the ES

Some of the more common ways Equine Specialists at *Horse Sense* have gotten "off the beam" in equine-assisted practice, myself included:

- Getting attached to client success with an activity
- Having too much of an attachment to a particular activity for a client or session
- Having attachment to our own view or interpretation of an event or situation such that we neglect to hear the client

Quite a bit of the above elements can be boiled down to the idea of being comfortable with others being uncomfortable, and being mindful of how our attachment to any one outcome can be detrimental. The impulse to fix and tend and care is hard-wired in many of us, to the point where others' discomfort becomes our own. This is some of what I've seen get in the way for the horse professional in equine-assisted practices, both at *Horse Sense* and elsewhere.

Another sticking point for Equine Specialists includes knowing the difference between when to step in to skill-build with a client and when to allow the process to continue. The mental health professional is a key guide in this decision. I tend to see people jump in either too quickly or not at all; both can be problematic for clients. Similarly, knowledge of horses and horse psychology, or the lack of it, contributes to many unforeseen and unfortunate challenges for Equine Specialists.

Other concerns include getting too prop-heavy or rule-heavy in an activity and talking too much during session, which includes the Equine Specialist playing therapist, getting out of his/her depth and/ or forgetting the horses. Similarly, effective co-facilitation between team members in a client session is a key skill for both mental health professional and Equine Specialist, as is having awareness of when to speak and what to share. I've always found that, when in doubt, don't say anything, or ask your mental health professional first. The Equine Specialist co-facilitating with a mental health professional—having a team approach, and being a true partner with that person, in addition to being a partner with the horse—involves having to listen equally to multiple points of view. This is a tall order, a challenge I've encountered myself. In my consulting work, I hear more angst around the mental health/Equine Specialist relationship than I ever hear about the human/horse relationship, making it one of the most common problems.

Finally, one of the key challenges I see for Equine Specialists is playing by someone else's safety rules. Instructions for how to keep all participants safe in an EAP/EAL session is beyond the scope of this book, and I'm not sure it could be communicated in writing at all. But the harder part is realizing that what is safe for one is unsafe for another. I've been to many training sessions in EAGALA and in other schools of thought where I felt the horse situation was so completely out of hand that I would not be comfortable facilitating. And I was absolutely right. If I feel the situation is beyond my skill and safety level, then I shouldn't be practicing in that way. Similarly, I've had interns, students and consultation clients who have said: "I can't imagine allowing X to happen with horses in a session and not intervening," in regards to something I've demonstrated. And they are also absolutely right. The biggest danger is not when you are practicing at the edge of your safety comfort zone; this is challenging, and I encourage knowingly stretching boundaries. But when you try to play by someone else's rules entirely and ignore your own wisdom, you are compromising your ability to be effective. Mapping someone else's safety comfort zone onto your own, without it being true to who you are, is a recipe for a dangerous situation.

One more special circumstance that relates to this topic: Folks often ask me about how I manage the personal side of working with gang-involved and incarcerated youth. They ask whether I have any concerns or trepidations about having these clients on the farm—at my home—working with my horses. There was a period of time when I had lengthy discussions with myself on where I stood on all of these issues. My sincere advice to others is: If you feel it's going to get in the way of how you show up, then it will negatively affect the session, the horses, and the clients. The clients will pick up on it and there will be a detrimental effect on your program. If you can't be at peace with the potential larger ramifications of what you are doing, I advise against doing it!

If you choose to work with challenging populations such as this, either on your farm or offsite, you need to be in dialogue with yourself (and potentially others) concerning these issues. It is more about knowing yourself and knowing your own limitations regarding what you're able to handle and then setting boundaries around what you can't handle. I counsel Equine Specialists to program around their weak points, until they can either claim those spots or let them go entirely.

There is a specific situation that happened to a colleague of mine that ended badly (a person was kicked by a horse) and I'd like to dissect this a bit, as an "accident analysis." It involved a training situation, with outside trainers working with someone else's horses. Those horses were my colleague's horses. Here's the story, from the point of view of the horse owner:

> The activity had no release. When you're choosing the activities, there has to be some way the horses know they've done something the clients wanted. [The facilitators/trainers] did a variation of Life's Little Obstacles. In this variation there were two jumps in the middle of the arena, and the directions were to get as many horses you want to jump over the obstacles as many times as you want. That was the first step wrong in my observation. There was no release; there was nothing that said to a horse 'Good job. Go back to chilling in the corner.'
>
> That was the first step that created this perfect storm. The second step was that the clients themselves were very assertive, crossing the line into aggression and nothing was done to stop that. The third step was the horses willingly did the job and, when the horses were showing body language that they were done, the clients followed, pushed them into corners, and physically started to hit them. This all happened with the horses taking it and finally one horse did a kick. There were many places this could've been shut down or redirected. The horse had no choice but to take that control back.

I find this to be a helpful example and reminder of the many ways situations in real time can get beyond us, and that when they get beyond us with horses, they tend to get there quickly. But there were several warning signs in this example, giving us important questions we can ask of any activity we have in mind:

- Where is the horse's release, either in the design of the activity or after the activity is "completed"? If there is no natural release, can one be built into the activity? After the activity, is there any release for the horses, or does the pressure continue? How can we redirect that behavior in a way that helps the client "see" what we are doing and gives the horse a break?

- When/Is it appropriate to comment on and/or redirect aggression towards horses in clients? How can I do this so as not to shut down a teachable moment and retain the dignity and integrity of the horse? In watching a demonstration of Life's Little Obstacles at an EAGALA conference one year, my husband Richard observed that the clients were being encouraged and rewarded for becoming "better predators." Doing nothing was detrimental to the clients and the horses. I want to be clear, though, that I believe there is a difference between "telling" a client he/she is being aggressive and shutting down the learning, and facilitating the client to help him/her see his/her behavior in a new light.

Finally, there was another part to this incident that happened prior to the horses and clients ever entering the arena. My colleague explains:

> We have horses that have different jobs; we have our therapeutic riding horses that will stand there and take anything. If I put an aggressive EAP client with that horse, that's abuse and that's not the appropriate horse to use with that client. Then we have our other horses [who do EAP] that are going to flee if something is not right. I told the guest facilitators: 'This horse does not like to be prodded multiple times. She does not like to be chased or feel cornered.' It was a large group which was to only be 4 and it ended up with 12 people.
>
> My discomfort was voiced through the whole entire session and about two minutes before the horse kicked somebody I said 'If you don't stop this now, she's going to kick somebody.' I was deferring to the outside facilitators, which I will never do again. I did let down my horses in that situation and it was a lesson I learned. I have never had a horse kick someone. It just doesn't need to get to that level.

This adds several more questions to the discussion:

- Do I have the right horse selected for this client and situation and activity?
- Did I trust my gut and act when I felt it was appropriate, practicing within my own safety comfort zone, or was I allowing someone else's safety comfort zone to trump mine?
- Do I trust that another facilitator will honor my knowledge of my horses and respect my requests in this regard, whether they agree with those requests or not?

This last one is particularly tricky, as we all bump up against our safety comfort zone.

So, in short, here are the questions I invite us all to consider as we design and implement activities in session with clients (using the previous story as an example). I've also incorporated a few of my own standards in these questions as they relate to activity design and selection:

- Where is the horse's release?
- How will we respond to aggression towards the horses by the clients?
- Do I have the right horse(s) selected for this client/situation/activity?
- Do I trust another facilitator to honor my knowledge and requests with regards to my horses (when applicable)?
- Does this activity pass the "bale of hay" test? i.e., could a bale of hay be substituted for the horse, without any meaningful impact on the activity? If so, why do I have a horse as part of this?
- Does this activity address the treatment goals of the client?
- Does this activity in any longterm, meaningful way sacrifice the horse in service of the client?

One of the most impressive interactions I've ever witnessed at a horse clinic was between a horse and Mark Rashid. Mark was interacting with a woman's horse in a round pen, and was coming up against some of the horse's defenses. When he attempted to correct the behavior, the woman became upset and asked him to stop. He did, and praised her courage in speaking up and voicing her concern. He said something along the lines of "it's not appropriate for me to do something with your horse that you feel is abuse; you get to tell me to stop that behavior." The biggest challenge comes in knowing when the intersection of circumstances is such that the horse can't respond, and stepping in.

Other Thoughts on Challenges for Equine Specialists
Survey/Conference Feedback

The survey responses were varied and numerous, although I was surprised to see relatively few folks mentioning safety in regards to challenges (aside from getting over the traditional safety paranoia of horses and people!).

Among the most-often voiced concerns in regards to the human co-facilitator were lack of communication, incompetence, co-dependent/rescuing behavior towards the clients and a lack of respect for the Equine Specialist. In regards to co-facilitation, some articulated challenges in learning how to work in a team and/or how to trust the team member, and merging the differing roles of the two facilitators in a team.

Within the role of the Equine Specialist, quite a few respondents mentioned the challenge in knowing what to say and when to say it, knowing how to offer feedback or how to phrase questions, letting go of "training the horse" or "teaching the client" mentality, and not overthinking or overmanaging sessions (i.e., letting go of expectations about how sessions are supposed to look). Only a few folks articulated problems in dealing with particular kinds of behaviors from clients, such as the client who simply won't engage or participate in the process.

Interview Feedback
Amy Blossom Lomas: "Most of the time when things don't go as planned it's from not trusting your own instincts. Or when there are too many distractions; that's when things happen. It's about having the focus—and the experienced eyes—to see the difference between a new path opening up in the session, and a session that's going completely off course. It takes experience for the Equine Specialist to understand that. Mostly I see the need for practice and experience, especially practice letting go of control in the arena. The experience level of the mental health professional in relation to horses also impacts the session, including their comfort level allowing horses loose in an arena with their client. There's no such thing as having control when two living beings are out there interacting."

Carissa McNamara: "I don't know if I've had anything really go wrong, but I've had opportunities to talk to people when things 'go wrong.' The common theme seems to be that the perception of it was wrong. I have a quote: 'If humans didn't exist, the horse would never be wrong.' I firmly believe we are the ones who assign that right or wrongness to the horse. The interesting thing is that when horsepeople try to 'save the day,' that's when things get chaotic. It's really wrapped around wanting to have control or trying to show the client how to do it right. It seems to be manifest, or made worse, by the people."

Liza Sapir Flood: "Poor communication with the therapist is probably the biggest culprit. That, and being uncomfortable with being uncomfortable. When things get crazy in a session and you're uncomfortable, that's okay; you have to be able to own it publicly. Here's the thing: anytime you're not telling the client, the horse knows anyway. And that's a problem; the horse is then responding to you. When things go wrong, I often wonder if the Equine Specialist needs to be okay with naming and owning his or her own discomfort publicly, aka with the client. It's a form of disclosure that needs to be understood before changes are invoked."

Paul Smith: "There are the 'misreads' and then there are the 'I missed something.' If the energy is at the level at which you really need to intervene, I feel like I've probably misread something going into the set-up. It means I wasn't paying attention. Then it's a little bit of 'my bad' which involves stepping in and taking responsibility. I've also seen a group really escalate a set of horses, which is a misread on the level of activity and responsibility given the group. If I have a bunch of people in with loose horses, and the group's energy is big and loud enough to put the horses into high energy and get out of hand, I might not have misread the horses but I misread the group. I trust horses to take care of themselves. As much as I know things can go wrong, and can get big, people and horses can all survive; there's real learning to be done at those edges. But I don't program for big pushing people fairly deep, or far past their comfort zone.

There are some equine professionals that come from a more highly-managed equine environment who might be incredibly competent horse people but they've never seen two horses turned out in a paddock together. There are others who are a little more cavalier who maybe identify with horses because of the energy of it. If these folks see hors-

More than a Mirror, by Shannon Knapp

es in session just standing around grazing, they think something's gone wrong. They love horses because they love the energy of it, so they're programmed towards big energy and I think there's a danger of an 'entertainment' value there that's not therapeutic or educational necessarily. For them, the stretch would be trusting simpler, calmer moments."

Richard Knapp: "It could be a physical issue where something happens where they miss the horse giving warnings—they miss the body language saying what's coming. The human easily sees the big reactions, but they miss all the other stuff. Or sometimes there's just too much energy; maybe the wrong horses are in the session. A second issue would be taking the conversation in a direction we don't need to go; that's why we run things through the therapist first to make sure we stay on track and act as a team and not go different directions. A third issue would be not adapting to the situation. Sometimes a client will show up totally different one day than they did the previous session. Not adapting the plan to fit the client might be detrimental to the scope of the session. A final one: Equine Specialists bringing their stuff in and thinking about that versus what's going on in front of them."

StarrLee Heady: "When I hear about things going south, it's usually from the Equine Specialists who are inexperienced. What I hear is they're not accepting the horse's behavior; they're thinking about 'making a mess' and worrying about it causing problems in a session. If a horse jumps up and happens to step on somebody, I don't see that as a big thing. People that are newer to horses, they think it's gone to hell in a hand basket. That kind of stuff is going to happen. Honestly, I think there are too many mental health professionals trusting Equine Specialists that aren't knowledgeable. On the other side, there are horse people who don't have that level of comfort so the least little thing tends to frighten them and they think they have to over-correct or over-control."

Rhiannon Beauregard: "One thing that goes wrong is making assumptions and being judgmental about your client. You cannot put your own judgment on the client; that comes back to your own health and wellness. In therapy you have to be accepting. There are people that want to do this but have so many unresolved issues; you can only take your clients as far as you've come yourself. Other issues I see: an Equine Specialist who doesn't say anything or contribute to the session or the Equine Specialist who over-steps boundaries and interjects opinion. And sometimes they don't remember the sessions. An Equine Specialist should have their own set of notes. Therapists are trained to this, but Equine Specialist often aren't keeping notes from one session to the next."

Michelle Holling-Brooks: "Stuff can go wrong when the horse's voice isn't being heard or acknowledged. If the Equine Specialist does not find a way to release the pressure from that situation, then something can go wrong. Some facilitators might get lost in 'whatever the horses do, the horses do.' That doesn't mean there should be a free-for-all. There needs to be a purpose to the activities and that's where the mental health therapist states their treatment goal and the Equine Specialist knows what horses will best meet that goal.

Liberty is also an important part of Equine Specialist work; if the Equine Specialist doesn't safely know how to handle their horses at liberty, they don't know what they can and cannot do. The basic at liberty piece is just not there. People don't play with their own horses enough to really know them from the ground, which is essential. It's what we do in session."

Linda Zimmerman: "It's taken me several years to really believe in my heart the intuitiveness of the horse, because that wasn't how I started with horses. To really believe that and let the horse be part of the session, I think, takes years if you didn't start out that way. I think people have to start out giving themselves the grace that maybe they're not going to feel comfortable for a couple of years."

The following exchange between Tim and Bettina on the topic I believe best sums up this section about challenges for the Equine Specialist. It's a particularly rich discussion:

Bettina: "One of the things we say all the time is that if it's not an issue for the client or it's not an issue for the horse, it's not something we address because it's my issue. Tim hasn't worked with other horse professionals but I've worked with lots of other horse professionals and I do find that when things really go wrong, it's because we start working on the horse professional's issues. They're freaking out about a safety rule that's a rule no matter what horse you're using, so the focus becomes on a safety rule instead of on the emotional health of our client and our horse."

Tim: "And the interaction between the client and the horse. And sometimes getting in the way of that interaction as a horse professional, it's kind of easy to justify doing that, but I think you have to know your horses well enough to understand when the interaction is becoming unsafe for either the horse or the client—not when it's becoming uncomfortable for you. There's a big difference in that, and understanding the difference is probably the hardest part of being a good horse professional."

Bettina: "And the other thing I've seen is, as a therapist, most therapists have a lot of training in professional boundaries and the ethics of confidentiality, and I've seen it be more of a problem with horse professionals—horse professionals who give riding lessons, there's a very different emotional boundary with clients than there is in therapy sessions. Over the years I've found that I've got to get my horse professional training that helps them understand some of those professional boundaries and confidentiality and all of that, because they're not bound by it in the same way the therapist is."

Educational Opportunities/Continuing Education for Equine Specialists

We'll begin this topic by covering some of the initial educational opportunities (as opposed to continuing education) out there for becoming a horse professional, and then move on to more thoughts about equine-assisted practice-specific trainings. Although I touched on what I call "the big three" in Chapter 2—PATH, EAGALA and TF-EAP—I'll comment on some of the other popular organizations and individuals out there, and what they have to offer.

Certainly, the traditional equine studies major is available, which often help people learn a lot about barn management, horse management, breeding, and the like. Anyone wanting to be a horse professional in this field would not go wrong to take this route, although I'd make some effort to determine if the program is traditional or progressive in its approach to horses and horsemanship. For a less formalized education, groups like Pony Club and 4-H are available, and their value varies from group to group, state to state. There are riding instructor trainings and certifications that are popular and offer quite a bit of value, especially if you are considering a riding-based application of equine-assisted practice. A really good riding instructor is worth his/her weight in gold, in my opinion: an instructor who invites the client to be a part of every aspect of the horse, not just a "tacked & ready to ride: hop on" kind of experience. I also think lifelong horsepeople, who've owned and cared for horses, day in and day out, can have all the baseline horsemanship experience I'd want in a professional. That is why, when I was on the EAGALA committee that discussed the current Equine Specialist standards, I wanted to make sure that the backyard horseperson wasn't left out of the equation.

Of course, I would also say getting a baseline understanding of horses and horsemanship is important; you would not be misplaced to approach and study any of the horsemanship methodologies out there. I'm certainly a big fan of Parelli™ for a number of reasons, but I don't think time would be ill-spent with anyone who places emphasis on horse psychology and groundwork. Mark Rashid, Buck Brannaman, the works of Tom Dorrance, and more have a great deal to offer the equine-assisted professional. And you can learn something from just about any horseman or horsewoman out there—good or ill.

Other practitioners of interest are: Klaus Hempfling, Alexander Nevzorov, Michael Bevilacqua, Sally Swift, Linda Tellington-Jones, and Carolyn Resnick, just to name a few. Stormy May's "Path of the Horse" video is of particular interest because her personal decisions are based on her study. As a result of her examination, she no longer rides. Because of that, I think that encourages her to move in new directions in awareness of liberty work. And then there's www.HorseConscious.com: a forum for people who are coming together to talk about different ways of being with horses and different ways of learning how to be with horses. Provocative indeed!

Regardless of your "flavor" of teacher, where I'm finding the biggest disconnect is that many of the equine-assisted practice training programs out there expect that people are proficient with horses prior to coming to their trainings, and that simply isn't true. Many people don't have that foundational information and just get a lot of neat and sugary icing, but have no cake! Again, this hearkens back to language found in Parelli™: "foundation before specialization." In general, I've found that many Equine Specialists lack the horse foundation before seeking the specialization of equine-assisted practices.

The more time spent in conversation with your horse, other horses and herds of horses—meaning watching, listening, learning, and then trying these things out—the better. That's probably the single place I would encourage people to spend time. Apprenticing—and by apprentice, I mean almost daily hands-on contact with horses, for a period of months, if not longer—is also a great way to get plenty of experience with a variety of horses. We have apprenticeships at *Horse Sense* for folks who stay anywhere from three months to a year with us, spending a great deal of time with Richard and our herd of approximately twenty horses, tending to their daily care, feeding, training and development (and scratches!), before digging into facilitation theory and practice, study of human body language and mental health, as well as working with clients in session. Mares and geldings, drafts and minis, a blind horse, "dynamic" challenging horses, young and old. It's quite an educational experience!

Finally, I would also recommend taking psychology courses and studying facilitation, in whatever delivery method or format is available to you. One course recommended by Kris Batchelor of Triple Play Farms near Charlotte, NC is a Mental Health First Aid Certification, which sounds particularly helpful (www.mentalhealthfirstaid.org). Similarly I'd recommend all non-mental health professionals have a basic training in HIPAA and confidentiality, not unlike the kind of training someone who works the front desk of a doctor's office might undergo, to fully understand the needs and expectations of client confidentiality. Many folks who want to be Equine Specialists would be well-served to dual-major in Equine Studies and Psychology or Education. Increasingly, there are more and more colleges and universities with specializations in animal-assisted therapy and equine-assisted therapy, including Prescott College, Carroll College, University of Denver and more.

For those who are ready to pursue specialized training in the field of equine-assisted practices, organizations to check out are EAGALA and PATH International, as well as the newest offering from Natural Lifemanship—TF-EAP—which I find to be the best of both worlds, mounted and unmounted. If you can attend all three trainings, I strongly recommend it, as each organization has gifts and ideas to offer.

EAGALA has more of a track record for the Equine Specialist who focuses mainly on ground work and on mental health interventions. They have defined that specific role as part of their team for over a decade—a role that's distinct and separate from any other role a horse person has historically played at other organizations. PATH, on the other hand, has the longest and most proven track record for the side of the equation that covers mounted work, and really has set the standard for working with differently-abled clients, in mind and body.

In addition, you'll find many individuals out there offering extraordinarily expensive development and continuing education courses, apprenticeships, certifications and the like. There are probably more of these programs than there are functioning and sustainable equine-assisted programs. Those programs that are doing big business are generally doing train-the-trainer programs, which produce "professionals" for what is currently a very small (but growing) market. Buyer beware; do your homework. Find out exactly what kind of *actual client experience* these individuals have working in the field before plunking down your cash. Generally speaking, any program that asserts they can give you all the horse knowledge plus all the facilitation skills you'll need in order to work for an equine-assisted practice (and in less than six months of hands-on experience, no less) is blowing smoke.

What continuing education programs specific to equine-assisted practices are available once you are working in the field? Again, the best source is hands-on experience with horses, although those opportunities are seldom available. Other EAP/EAL-specific trainings come and go, but EAGALA-approved continuing education providers have some really interesting, provocative and useful trainings. As of this writing, there are several programs on the topics of military work and EAP, "Maximizing the Power of the Horse" (with a horse focus, obviously!), and one training on the 12 Steps and Recovery. Annual conferences are educational; attendees can view a cross-section of the kind of work being done all over. Look for PATH in the fall and EAGALA in the spring of each year, with locations changing each year, as well as Prescott College's Best Practices Conference, usually in Arizona each May. *Horse Sense* generally offers two conferences a year, one on Parelli™ & Equine Assisted Practices and another on Youth & Horses. We also present a virtual conference to support the business side of our work as well. There are also PATH regional conferences and EAGALA Networking groups that provide support and assistance on a more local level. Finally, I continue to attend and re-attend trainings by these organizations over and over again. Models that are continually developing interest me!

Other thoughts on Continuing Education
Survey/Conference Feedback
By far, the most popular response to the question of how current

Equine Specialists continue their education is through reading, followed by auditing and participating in horsemanship clinics. Quite a few respondents mention the trainings specific to the field of EAP/EAL and, of course, watching videos on horsemanship is quite popular. There was some mention of continuing education on the human side of the equation, both in understanding clients and in wanting more opportunities to examine their own self-awareness and self-arousal, in terms of having their own buttons pushed, including how to recognize, respond to and manage such occurrences. The lack of available hands-on apprenticeships was widely lamented.

Interview Feedback

Amy Blossom Lomas: "More continuing education in any kind of horsemanship is an opportunity to learn more about horse's natural behaviors and behaviors that have been created as the result of their environment. Any opportunity you can have to learn from somebody who's been around the field. My experience has been a lot of people want to come into the field and do the work and get paid for it but they don't want to do all the learning that needs to happen first.

The working student is kind of a thing of the past. I don't know if that's regional in our area but it seems like students need to want to learn to be better and that usually comes, as with anything, with a price. You either have to pay somebody who knows what they're doing to teach you or go to school to learn. It doesn't seem like people understand that."

Carissa McNamara: "For me, I'm big on business leadership retreats, women's retreats—anything I do to stretch and be aware constantly of where I am in my environment makes me the best horse person. Horses demand awareness and you'll be a great horse person if you can step into that world. I think you have an obligation to work on yourself for your horses and the people around you."

Paul Smith: "We've been playing with the language of Relational Horsemanship at Prescott, so regardless of someone's background or discipline or orientation, how can they pursue their horsemanship in a way that focuses on relationship, partnership, collaboration, and listening and is less dependent on artificial aides. While it can be connected to performance and training, it's typically this other way of being, so to do really intense versions of Me and My Shadow, or truly sit in the paddock with horses for forty-five minutes once in your lifetime or three or four times a day, I think it's huge to step out of the 'doing; and into the 'being' to slow it down. And then to also get people exploring communication from the ground."

Richard Knapp: "I've been told to cross train and study some of the mental health professional side, and I've also read a lot of books on body language, reading the micro-expressions a la Paul Ekman. There's another book series about how to spot a liar and it's not that you're necessarily trying to call them out on anything but being able to tell when the body language of the human is starting to stray and show that kind of stuff.

Continuing in horse training, being able to read the horse's body language, the Parelli™ Horsenality™ to understand which horses are appropriate or not appropriate for sessions; constantly thinking of new activities or extensions of activities or slight tweaks to get the most out of each session. A final idea would be the environment: don't be restricted to just being in an arena. Don't be afraid to play in a large pasture, or in other locales. Sometimes that's appropriate too."

StarrLee Heady: "A great improvement actually comes from spending time with loose horses in a herd environment. And I understand that's difficult for people to do sometimes, but because of the way this field is developing, I think it should be mandatory—that people be exposed to herds of horses loose, so that you're actually seeing the horse's behavior rather than a training response. I think finding a place to do that is absolutely critical, whether it's big breeding farms or a zoo that keeps horses. I don't care where you get that, but I think you need to do it.

And a lot of times I think it needs to be guided by a seasoned horse professional to answer questions like 'Where did that behavior come from?,' or 'Did you see that just happen?' I think there's some mentoring that needs to happen. I think I've had that opportunity with people who work with horses every day for a living. I don't think it's something you're really going to get unless you deal with horses every day. I think they need time with natural horses and people who already understand that.

I don't think peoples' equine skills are going to improve by re-attending equine-assisted practice-specific trainings. I think to improve equine skills people are going to have to go into the equine world—horse trainers, horse farms. Whether you're an advocate for Parelli™ or John Lyons or some of the European guys, any of those that spend all their time with horses, that's where people should go. If you can't afford to pay, then work at a breeding farm—some place where you yourself have to pay attention to herds. Put the time in."

Linda Zimmerman: "There are certainly enough PATH-based facilities that you can get wonderful experience in. You could volunteer at lots of therapeutic riding centers and more and more, they're going to ground activities; it's not 100 percent riding like it used to be. You just can't get that experience easily if you're doing therapy, but any place that's doing learning—I'm a big believer, when we were doing the school groups, nobody could just come watch. They had to volunteer or participate.

I think that really is a big dilemma right now. If I were starting out right now, where would I do that? Where are the opportunities to get experience? I don't know."

Don "Z" Zimmerman: "What I would add to that is there are several national CEU providers that I get flyers on, but I got one the other day that was on building your skills in group psychotherapy—I know Linda has gone to a couple of workshops with me years ago on the autistic population. I think there are opportunities for the Equine Specialist to learn more about the mental health process or the particular population you might be working with.

Even workshops on marriage and couple therapy skills or family therapy; I think it's beneficial for both the mental health person and the Equine Specialist to attend those workshops; that gives the Equine Specialist more of an idea of what the mental health process is all about."

Rhiannon Beauregard: "I would recommend that Equine Specialists do their own therapeutic work and I would recommend experiential work. It comes back to my point about that you have to be healthy to do this work. We recommend it in our own therapeutic world as far as mental health professionals.

Also attending mental health conferences with your mental health professional. EAGALA Part 1, Part 2, and Advanced is the standard but

I think Equine Specialists need to do more than those. Training in ethics and confidentiality; we require that here—and again, talking with your mental health professional about magazines or journals to get so you can keep up with the issues. My number one point, though, is doing a course of experiential therapy themselves."

Tim Jobe: "Well, the best place to learn any of it, I believe, is the place I learned most of it and that's out there in the round pen with the horse. And letting that horse help you understand what's really going on and what really works and what you're doing to get in your own way of being successful. There are people that can help you along that journey; like Bettina said, her greatest learning in all this was in that pen with that horse, even as a therapist.

I can tell you all about how it works but I'm not as good at telling you about it as that horse is. I think for horse people to be constantly getting better, not only with their own horses, but I think horses that they don't know, that they don't already have a relationship with, and learning what it takes to build that relationship with the horse that doesn't already know how to do that. I think that's probably the most effective way to learn any of it. And if you've got somebody who will guide you through that process, I think it's even more powerful, but I don't really think you can learn this without being in the pen with that horse—with somebody that understands enough to help you figure out what's going on."

Bettina Shultz-Jobe: "I think everybody learns differently and Tim didn't actually have somebody to teach him a lot of that stuff; there weren't a lot of clinics when he first started.

Tim has also gone to a ton of stuff that's just for therapists, that's not horse-related at all. The horse professionals I've worked with that are really good at this are people that are willing to learn the therapy side as well—that there's a little bit of dual training going on.

And I will say in this field, CEUs are a challenge. I think finding them is a challenge. Eventually you get to a point where you need something beyond EAGALA Part 1, Part 2, and the Advanced training. I do think that you get training anywhere you can and if you do, you're going to be a better horse professional, rather than just picking one way of doing it and sticking to that."

Michelle Holling-Brooks: "For me personally it's attending horsemanship-specific clinics that deal with, for me, the natural horsemanship side—whether it's Parelli™ or one of the other clinics. Also riding and maintaining on your own, playing with your horses on your own, and if you're into riding, making sure that you're always up to date. I think that's a key thing that's outside of the Part 1 and Part 2. You will not get that in the EAGALA model training; it has to be something that people seek outside."

Liza Sapir Flood: "A therapist will go and do CEUs that's just therapy and that enriches what they bring to therapy; I think Equine Specialists need to do horse training. An example would be some of the really neat exercises that Richard was able to bring to our sessions from his Parelli™ work—principles that I never heard of but they were so appropriate because I think in natural horsemanship it's about relationship and leadership and reading body language. It's a lot of the same stuff that therapy is about."

Randy Mandrell: "I'm not real sure as far as what's going to help people. What helped me to speak with people has nothing to do with horses. Patti and I were teaching a marriage prep course at church and we had to get up in front of about forty people—my ears were just red. That's what helps me—to get up in front of people and talk about what I know about. It was getting out of my comfort zone and doing what I needed to do. Another helpful thing is to go to seminars that are mental health seminars where you learn the lingo and you know what your mental health professional is talking about."

Patti Mandrell: "And for Randy, 'doing what he needed to do' was focusing on the area that he needed the most growth—the speaking in front of people and counseling aspect, even though that was a class, it was a class of people working through their stuff to get married. And he was working with his therapist also to do that; being his wife, it also helped us to get better at working together and trusting each other and going back and figuring out the team stuff."

More than a Mirror, by Shannon Knapp

Thoughts for the Newcomer

What are my closing thoughts for the newcomer coming into this field? Well, that's one of the reasons I wrote this book! To boil it all down, I would strongly encourage spending an enormous amount of time and energy being a student of your horse and horses in general. Be a student of more than just your horse if you've got one or two key horses. I think we so easily fall into patterns with the horses we think we know. It also serves to be a student of your clients. In much the same way that I seek to learn from my horses, I look to my clients as well.

Spend as much time as possible reading the works of, studying the videos of, really examining these natural horsemanship folks. A good dose of "head study" and a lot of experiential study, trial and error, practice and more practice—experience all these different ways to really be a student of the horse. In Florida, when I had attend Parelli™ trainings for a month or so, I would really get into a groove of doing my "feeling" in my body and in my hands and heart during the day and doing my "thinking" at night, almost the reverse of the normal routine for most folks. It was such a pleasure to be able to spend that kind of dedicated, concentrated time "feeling with" the horse, rather than a few hours here and a few hours there. Pat talks about "feeling of the horse, for the horse and with the horse." There is no better teacher.

Other Thoughts for the Newcomer
Interview Feedback
Amy Blossom Lomas: "What I usually tell students who are interested in becoming Equine Specialists is what I'd do to be able to have this kind of career. I tell them to go to school or stay in school, get a degree in psychology or equine studies—I personally wish I'd gone through and gotten my Master's so I'd be a therapist with a horse background. You get a lot more flexibility. For me, I would have more flexibility. And I would recommend to them to learn anything they can about psychology, mental health, horses, the different theories of training horses. We do a lot of in-service training here, we send folks to conferences and I go too; it's

important to keep learning on both sides of things. It's important to learn a variety of methods and philosophies. One of my favorite classes in college was Theories of Personality; it allowed me to take what was most applicable to my own philosophy, and a lot of that ties into the horse training theories too.

Really, never stop learning. Every EAGALA training you go to, you learn something new. Also, consider the mental health track. Don't take this job as an Equine Specialist as a shortcut. And be willing to work in exchange for knowledge. That's one of the best experiences I ever had. I think working as an apprentice under somebody who knows what they're doing is worth so much. It's worth every minute of effort. You learn those kinds of lessons from people who have been through it before, and I think it's also good not to just learn from one person. I think people need to think about what it is they like about this work and then think about whether the mental health track is something to consider."

Carissa McNamara: "Work on you. I think at the end of the day, have a good sense of self and where it is you're coming from. Be prepared for it to never be about you. If you have any kind of ego or anything like that, then you're going to be disappointed because this work is about the connection of these other people with these horses in a world that exists totally outside of you. You're giving them an opportunity to be around healthy role models and be a healthy role model; I think that is the most important gift that you can give. If you're not working on yourself outside of session, then it's difficult to be a healthy role model to other people and other horses.

It's interesting because my young horses—I have two young horses that are getting ready right now to be integrated into the 'big kid' herd and I rely heavily on my alpha gelding and my alpha mare. I call them the 'kind king' and the 'fair queen.' You can't put a dollar amount on them and God bless that I have them. They're firm with those colts but never mean, they never come from a place of unkindness and they serve as really great role models. Then I've got three colts that are eighteen months old that have been in cutting training for sixty days. They're getting ready for a break and when they come home for their break, their immunity is down, their self-esteem is down—it's hard work and it wears on you. It's overwhelming; there's a lot of stimulus, a lot of information.

More than a Mirror, by Shannon Knapp

So these young colts I put back in with the ones that are eight months old because they're now the alpha and they'll stay with those young colts for ninety days and serve as a role model for them, just to build them back up. If you dump them right back in, you're not setting them up for good mental health.

I think we should behave the same way as people; when you get to that place, surround yourself with really good role models and do what they do. Surround yourself with happy people. The more work you do on you, the better the horse person you're going to be. I think that is important."

Liza Sapir Flood: "I would say that, one, you need to be a damn good horse person. You could say 'I can do that' and just make sure no one gets bitten; to do it well, and that's your responsibility, you need to be good. It's a growing field and is growing in popularity and it's not acceptable to be an okay horse person. When the therapy works, the horse person is really strong. That's one thing.

Another thing—and it's funny to say 'What do I wish I knew?' because in some ways I was coddled because I got the best of the best trainers. I also would say study everything you can. I remember Linda Parelli at some point was like 'I'm going to study some dressage and see what I can learn'—and that's the thing. When you're a therapist, you get out there and learn these different approaches and then bring the tools back. I think it's the same for the Equine Specialist.

And then maybe something about you—I needed to be fulfilled in terms of my own horsemanship outside of session. I couldn't rely on sessions to feel like I was getting the horse time I needed, I think. And it worked for me—I got to focus on my horsemanship at the ranch and the farms where I worked; when I was in session then, it was easier to just be.

Then the last thing is know your horses. Really well."

Paul Smith: "I guess as the field develops more, I want people to know it's not a matter of inventing it from the ground up and it's wide open. The danger of it being established is that people begin thinking there's one way to do it. It's really just wide open, as opposed to 'This is just what you have to do.' I think there was that sense of that ten, twelve, fifteen years ago and as it becomes more established, the benefit is that people have more resources to call on. But the danger is people think 'This is the only way you do this.' I would want every person coming into the field to understand—here's my imprimatur—depending on the population you're working with, the goals for that population, your background and philosophical orientation and skills, you are asking a different question of the work than somebody else is. And if you're asking a different question than I'm asking, it's really important that you be willing to get a different answer. It doesn't mean that my answer is wrong; it means I asked a different question.

As you enter the field and you go and see people doing things that might be totally different, I would encourage you to be curious about 'Wow, what is the question they're asking of the work? How does this answer make sense? Does it have anything to offer or inform the question that I'm asking?' But hopefully you're asking your own question, not somebody else's."

Richard Knapp: "I wish I would've had more horsemanship training; the better we are mentally, physically, and emotionally the better we're going to be with our horses and the better we're going to be with our clients. The best way is with the horse, natural horsemanship like Parelli™; it's not just horse training—it's training people with horses and it makes a huge difference. It teaches us to be smarter; we learn to think more like a horse. We're less chauvinistic, we're not better than the horse, we're just different. We don't demand things. And we're not so anthropomorphic that we try to push our feelings on the horse. Sometimes we do too much, we get in our own way of thinking and seeing things. I wish I would've had more horsemanship training before I started this."

Linda Zimmerman: "I guess what I'd really like to tell people coming into the field is that this is the most rewarding work I've done in my entire life. Whatever it takes to get there, go ahead and do. It's going to take a couple of years to feel like you're there; it's a profession—it gets better as you go along. It's a wonderful profession to be in and I feel good about myself doing this work. I guess just words of encouragement because it's kind of discouraging at first because you can't find a team, you can't find a barn, you have to get money for programming; you have to go through all these building blocks before it comes together, but do it—it'll be worth it."

More than a Mirror, by Shannon Knapp

Don "Z" Zimmerman: "I would reinforce all that. The only thing I would add is to encourage the Equine Specialist that they are a team member and they are bringing in a necessary level of expertise and to recognize that. Recognize you are bringing in this wealth of knowledge, but don't trip over it."

Michelle Holling-Brooks: "First, to trust your own judgment when you're in sessions. And then the other piece is to not put your stuff onto your horses; I think that's the hardest piece for an Equine Specialist— bringing those clean observations into what you're doing. I think that's a key to how you honor and bring your horses into this field. And then also to really practice how you bring that into your sessions.

I think what makes equine-assisted activities such a powerful modality compared to other experiential models like art therapy or play therapy is all of those are based on the clinician's interpretations of what the client is doing and coaching the client through what they're seeing them do, at least as I understand them. The horse has given us a way to step out of our stuff and if we honor that and if we're clear about bringing in what the horse is doing, that's the key. I wish somebody had told me that when I started because it would've saved me a whole lot of figuring it out on my own.

Another piece is the at liberty work is so immensely what this work is; if you only play with horses fifteen minutes before clients get there, you don't know your horses and they'll never be able to do their job well enough to the point where you can get to the next level of healing for your clients. It really takes a lot of work to know your horses."

StarrLee Heady: "Immerse yourself in horses and herd behavior and equine knowledge before you expect to be part of a team and manage it in a mental health setting. If you don't have the expertise or just wish you did or are worried about it, go get it. Go hook up with a trainer, let him or her know what kinds of things you need to know. Don't necessarily take riding lessons. If you're not going to be riding, riding lessons won't do you any good in there. If you don't understand horse behavior, you can't change it or intervene for anybody's safety."

Patti Mandrell: "My thought is practice, practice, practice. You can go to clinics and workshops and sit in lectures, but it's not going to come until you're getting out there, whether it's real clients or EAL kinds of scenarios. It's getting out there with the horses and as an Equine Specialist, spending time with horses and not on their back so much—just moving them around and interacting with them and stuff."

Randy Mandrell: "I agree. For some people, what they need to hear is equine-assisted practice really works. It really works. I think some of them come in and they're just coming to a training and think 'Well, this therapist wanted me to come and check it out. What's your take on this deal?' My take is that it works and if it didn't, I wouldn't waste my time doing it if it wasn't helping people get better."

Conclusion

As I mentioned at the start of this section, the single most complicated part of the EAP/EAL process is the human part: the Equine Specialist, the mental health professional, the human facilitators. The horses are the easy part!

There is a great deal to know in order to be a good—much less a great—Equine Specialist. Horses and horsemanship are only a part of that, albeit a significant part. But the challenge is: how do we get at the horsemanship skills that are key to this field, and how do we support those skills? Supporting Equine Specialists in effective activity design and implementation is another area in need of attention. In addition, facilitation skills, along with personal growth and development, simply can't be discounted. How can we integrate that into the standards for today's Equine Specialist? Is the answer in college curriculums? In independent courses of study apart from universities and higher education? Is this a community college degree or a Ph.D.? *Horse Sense* has been engaged, in theory and practice, in the process of answering those questions since opening. Many, many people wanting to be professionals in this field have come to our doors, and we've attempted to serve them to the best of our ability. The new *Horse Sense* Equine-Assisted Horsemanship™ program is the result of that work to date.

I hope this discussion has pointed out areas that need to be looked at in order to improve this path for others coming into the field. I also hope I've illuminated, to some degree, who is already showing up today to be an Equine Specialist, and how we might influence that group in a way that serves the field as a whole. Because it's in serving this field that we serve clients and horses; for me, these are the two areas of greatest importance.

Conclusion

I began the design and writing process for this book in the summer of 2010, although the idea of writing this started much earlier. It's been a long time from start to finish, and I'm grateful for all that has transpired during that time to make this the book you have before you. Changes at *Horse Sense* and in the field abound, in services, programs, products, clients, horses, and more; each piece was essential along the journey.

In terms of services, *Horse Sense* has added Therapeutic Riding and Hippotherapy, bringing in a small but consistent revenue stream, as well as a whole new group of clients. We've learned a great deal about what is needed for these practices in terms of staff, facility and horses, and how these needs differ from traditional EAP/EAL practice as we've engaged in it since 2003. We've also added Trauma-Focused EAP to our services, including both Rhythmic Riding and Relationship Logic, learning the unique needs of this model for staff, facility and horses.

During this time as well, I've deepened my connections and enriched my learnings with several organizations, including PATH, Prescott College, Natural Lifemanship™ and Parelli™. I was involved in exciting work as a task force member for PATH International's Equine-Facilitated Psychotherapy and Learning Membership Group, authored a small section in a PATH EFP manual on business, presented at several PATH conferences (national and regional), and learned a great deal from my colleagues in all these capacities, both for EFP/EFL and Therapeutic Riding/Hippotherapy. This work put me in contact with wonderful people for rich conversations about the requirements for offering EAP/EAL, both for the horse and the horse professional. Many more such people and conversations presented themselves as I had the privilege of teaching multiple intensives at Prescott College as part of the Master's program, alongside StarrLee Heady, Richard Knapp, Paul Smith, and Tracy Weber. I benefited greatly from the non-denominational approach to EAP/EAL of Prescott, from the diversity of practitioners who show up there, and from the freshness and eagerness of the students.

Natural Lifemanship's TF-EAP™ has been a blessing to the field and invigorated our practices here at *Horse Sense*, and our new position as the SouthEast training facility for TF-EAP will afford us the opportunity to learn from, support and grow alongside Tim, Bettina and this model for many years to come. As Richard achieved his first star-rating as a Licensed Parelli Professional™ during this time, we began to offer trainings and programming specifically about and for those passionate about Parelli™ and EAP/EAL, learning as we taught—my favorite combination—how to integrate and help others integrate these complimentary practices. We are excited to have offered the first ever Parelli & Equine-Assisted Practices Forum, bringing together professionals from both walks for connection, and look forward to many years of hosting this gathering. I'm grateful to be a supporter and committee volunteer for the Parelli Education Institute™, a new non-profit, with many exciting developments afoot. Collaborating with Pat and Linda Parelli to write a segment instructing mental health professionals on what they needed to know about horses to offer EAP/EAL was an honor. I also officially passed my Parelli Level 2!

All these experiences, combined with the clients and horses who've crossed our path at *Horse Sense*, have brought about the book in your hands. It's been both about the process and the goal: the process of writing and all that has happened during that timeframe, and about the goal of finishing and publishing. Every moment along the way has certainly broadened my understanding of the many approaches, perspectives and opinions about this work.

We have also nearly completely restructured *Horse Sense* during this time, from primarily having mental health professionals on staff serving alongside our Equine Specialists to collaborating with many "outside" mental health professionals at residential facilities and programs in our region. After spending eight years with hundreds of youth and thousands of hours working with the Department of Juvenile Justice and Delinquency Prevention, the North Carolina Governor's Crime Commission and many other organizations working with adjudicated youth, we've broadened our client base beyond primarily government and grant-funded populations, working more and more in the private sector. We've simplified and streamlined, as well as brought our evolving values into the day-to-day operation by building a beautiful outdoor labyrinth and pavilion, allowing us to offer a whole host of Mindfulness and Contemplative Practice programs, with and without horses, partnering with Massage, Yoga and Meditation professionals in our community.

And I've continued to learn from the many organizations and individuals I've consulted with about their EAP/EAL programs, from individual back-yard businesses to multi-campus residential centers all over the United States and everything in between. Serving as an EAGALA Business Mentor and supporting EAGALA in whatever way I'm called to continues to be a part of our identity here at *Horse Sense*. I've also continued to learn from the horses in the *Horse Sense* herd, as always, and am looking forward to spending more time with them, upon completion of this book!

My goal upon starting this book was to examine my thoughts, beliefs and practices in offering EAP/EAL, and to have deep and rich discussions with others in the field around the role of the horse and the role of the horse professional in typical equine-assisted psychotherapy and learning sessions. I often don't know my own mind in regards to our practice until I try to articulate it to others, so this has been a wonderful learning opportunity for me, to consider, reconsider, challenge and engage myself and others about how and why we practice the way we do. It was my intention in this process to raise the level of discussion and the professionalism of those in the field. I hope this work has done so.

Appendices

APPENDIX 1
The Cambridge Declaration of Consciousness

As I was in the later stages of writing this book, the following declaration was made. I thought it germane to reprint in full.

The Cambridge Declaration of Consciousness

On this day of July 7, 2012, a prominent international group of cognitive neuroscientists gathered at The University of Cambridge to reassess the neurobiological substrates of conscious experience and related behaviors in human and non-human animals. While comparative research on this topic is naturally hampered by the inability of non-human animals, and often humans, to clearly and readily communicate about their internal states, the following observations can be stated unequivocally:

- The field of Consciousness research is rapidly evolving. Abundant new techniques and strategies for human and non-human animal research have been developed. Consequently, more data is becoming readily available, and this calls for a periodic reevaluation of previously held preconceptions in this field. Studies of non-human animals have shown that homologous brain circuits correlated with conscious experience and perception can be selectively facilitated and disrupted to assess whether they are in fact necessary for those experiences. Moreover, in humans, new non-invasive techniques are readily available to survey the correlates of consciousness.

- The neural substrates of emotions do not appear to be confined to cortical structures. In fact, subcortical neural networks aroused during affective states in humans are also critically important for generating emotional behaviors in animals. Artificial arousal of the same brain regions generates corresponding behavior and feeling states in both humans and non-human animals. Wherever in the brain one evokes instinctual emotional behaviors in non-human animals, many of the ensuing behaviors are consistent with experienced feeling states, including those internal states that are rewarding and punishing. Deep brain stimulation of these systems in humans can also generate similar affective states. Systems associated with affect are concentrated in subcortical regions where neural homologies abound. Young human and non-human animals without neocortices retain these brain-mind functions. Furthermore, neural circuits supporting behavioral/electrophysiological states of attentiveness, sleep and decision making appear to have arisen in evolution as early as the invertebrate radiation, being evident in insects and cephalopod mollusks (e.g., octopus).

- Birds appear to offer, in their behavior, neurophysiology, and neuroanatomy a striking case of parallel evolution of consciousness. Evidence of near human-like levels of consciousness has been most dramatically observed in African grey parrots. Mammalian and avian emotional networks and cognitive microcircuitries appear to be far more homologous than previous thought. Moreover, certain species of birds have been found to exhibit neural sleep patterns similar to those of mammals, including REM sleep and, as was demonstrated in zebra finches, neurophysiological patterns, previously thought to require a mammalian neocortex. Magpies in particular have been shown to exhibit striking similarities to humans, great apes, dolphins, and elephants in studies of mirror self-recognition.

- In humans, the effect of certain hallucinogens appears to be associated with a disruption in cortical feedforward and feedback processing. Pharmacological interventions in non-human animals with compounds known to affect conscious behavior in humans can lead to similar perturbations in behavior in non-human animals. In humans, there is evidence to suggest that awareness is correlated with cortical activity, which does not exclude possible contributions by subcortical or early cortical processing, as in visual awareness. Evidence that human and non-human animal emotional feelings arise from homologous subcortical brain networks provide compelling evidence for evolutionarily shared primal affective qualia.

We declare the following: "The absence of a neocortex does not appear to preclude an organism from experiencing affective states. Convergent evidence indicates that non-human animals have the neuroanatomical, neurochemical, and neurophysiological substrates of conscious states along with the capacity to exhibit intentional behaviors. Consequently, the weight of evidence indicates that humans are not unique in possessing the neurological substrates that generate consciousness. Non-human animals, including all mammals and birds, and many other creatures, including octopuses, also possess these neurological substrates."

The Cambridge Declaration of Consciousness was written by Philip Low and edited by Jaak Pankseep, Diana Reiss, David Edelman, Bruno Van Swinderen, Philip Low, and Christof Koch. The Declaration was publicly proclaimed in Cambridge, UK, on July 7, 2012, at the Francis Crick Memorial Conference on Consciousness in Human and non-Human Animals, at Churchill College, University of Cambridge, by Low, Edelman, and Koch. The Declaration was signed by the conference participants that very evening, in the presence of Stephen Hawking, in the Balfour Room at the Hotel du Vin in Cambridge, UK. The signing ceremony was memorialized by CBS 60 Minutes.

APPENDIX 2
Pat & Linda Parelli Biographies

Portions of biographies reprinted with permission from http://www.parellinaturalhorsetraining.com/pat-and-linda-parelli-natural-horse-trainers/.

Pat Parelli

Born in California's Bay Area, Pat Parelli was obsessed with horses at an early age. When Pat was just 13, a horseman and trapper named Freddie Ferrera of Livermore, California, recognized Pat's talents with horses and took him under his wing. During the summers he would teach him valuable lessons about how to be more natural with horses, dogs, cattle, and nature itself.

Pat's horse career began with working in stables at age 9. If there were horses, Pat would be there, enthusiastically helping with whatever he could, ears open for every drop of information. He even started to develop his own ideas about raising foals and training horses, an unusual thing for a young boy.

At the age of 17, Pat launched himself into rodeos, his favorite event being the bareback riding. A natural, with a good coach in John Hawkins, Pat won the Bareback Rookie of the Year title in 1972, his buck-off average just 4%. Watching many rodeo athletes trying to move on, Pat was determined to find life after rodeo. A career in training horses seemed logical and he started a business that concentrated on starting colts. However, like many trainers before him, it wasn't long before the pattern of equine and financial frustration set in and Pat found himself on the verge of getting out of horses altogether. He also resisted the idea that horse training should treat horses like inanimate objects.

Then three significant events changed his life:

- He met Tony Ernst from Australia, who was a student of the horse, a disciple of Kung Fu martial arts and a master musician;

- He began to work under the tutelage of Troy Henry, a master horseman from Clovis, California, who specialized in training and developing both horse and rider for competition using psychology and communication;

- He took an interest in developing mules to be able to perform like horses.

Through Tony Ernst, Pat learned about inner power and the Kung Fu principles of discipline, body control, and mind-body mastery. Troy Henry opened up a whole new world to Pat by helping him understand horses' mental and emotional processes as prey animals as well as the true dynamics of horsemanship and how they applied to performance horses. The mules taught Pat the importance of reverse psychology, the principle of safety and comfort as the only real incentives, and developed in him more savvy on how to get a prey animal to "want" to perform. They also taught him about patience! In 1980, Pat founded The American Mule Association.

Being an intense student of horses and horsemanship, Pat had begun to develop his own style of teaching and expanding these principles. He also became interested in showing reined cow horses and was successful in reining and cutting events with both horses and mules.

One of the greatest frustrations Pat experienced in training horses was handing them back to their owners who often had a noticeable lack of skill and understanding. He found that if the rider didn't have enough savvy, the horses would regress. After much soul searching he finally decided that he couldn't go on just training horses, he had to find a way to help people become more savvy with horses. Pat Parelli discovered that he had a natural talent in finding the right words to explain what he understood about horses. So he turned his attention to helping people instead of horse training. He began to give "lessons" but had no idea that one day he would be able to help people on a much larger scale.

In 1983, while performing bridle-less at the California Livestock Symposium, Pat met three men who significantly contributed to his horsemanship knowledge: Tom Dorrance, Ray Hunt and Ronnie Willis – all masters who became Pat's mentors. A few years later the world's leading equine behaviorist, Dr Robert M. Miller, observed one of Pat's bridle-less demonstrations and recognized that Pat's concepts aligned strongly with his own philosophies on influencing the horse's mind and on foal imprinting. He predicted that by the time Pat Parelli reached age 40, he would have become one of the best horsemen and teachers the world had known.

Temple Grandin describes Pat and his ability with horses in her recent book, *Animals Make Us Human:*

> A few years ago I saw Pat Parelli, one of the natural horsemanship trainers on the circuit, give a demonstration at the Rocky Mountain Horse Expo in Denver. He rode a beautiful sleek black horse bareback without a bridle or a halter. The horse went through all the gaits— walk, trot, and canter—and turned right and left at Pat Parelli's signal. If he wanted the horse to go faster, he leaned forward. If he wanted the horse to go slower, he leaned backward a little. If he wanted the horse to stop, he leaned back a little more. When he wanted to turn right, he turned his head to the right; if he wanted to turn left, he turned his head to the left. When Pat turned his head, the horse felt a faint directional signal from his legs. This was a beautiful, calm horse. No tail flicking, no skin quivering—totally peaceful. That's what positive horsemanship looks like. I hope someday all horses can have such a beautiful relationship with a person. (2010, p. 136)

Linda Parelli

Linda Parelli was born in Singapore and was enamored with horses from the first moment she can remember. When she was twelve, her family moved to Australia, where she began her long love affair with riding and jumping. As an adult she was introduced to dressage and it became a special passion. At the time she met Pat, she was advancing in the competitive world with an ex-racehorse name Siren, but the gelding was becoming duller and duller. Her other horse, a hot Thoroughbred named Regalo, was out of control and dangerous. Her fateful visit to the tack store [where she encountered a video of Pat that changed her future] was to purchase yet another gadget to help her control her horses. (Miller, 2005, p. 63)

When people hear Linda Parelli's story, they always want to know how in the world a dressage rider ended up studying with a cowboy like Pat Parelli. She explains, "Had I not owned a horse who brought me to the 'end of the road,' I would never have gone to Pat Parelli for advice. But, there I was struggling for two years with a Thoroughbred that I was advised to 'sell to a man' or 'put a bullet in his head.' I tried all kinds of devices to control him: chambons, martingales, draw reins, nose bands, all different bits. But this horse would still go crazy—bolting, rearing, and freaking out. Are you getting the picture? It was just miserable and dangerous every time I rode."

Then Linda Parelli—who at the time was Linda Paterson—saw a video of Pat riding bridle-less. Something told her that "this cowboy was my last chance." So she registered for a Parelli Horse Training Clinic and showed up with a list of problems in her hand.

But she never got to show Pat the list because within five minutes, she had learned that horses were prey animals who lived by their instincts and when they felt threatened, trapped or unsafe, they would do whatever it took to escape. She suddenly understood that her horse was not being "bad"—he was simply following his instincts. Linda says that that Parelli natural horsemanship clinic "changed everything between me and my horse."

To this day Linda Parelli can ride that horse without a saddle or bridle... and remember, this was a horse who couldn't be stopped even with $200 worth of gadgets on his head!

APPENDIX 3: HORSE SENSE SKILL CARDS BY NUMBER

1. Observing My Environment
2. Knowing My Body & What It Is Telling Me
3. Paying Attention To My Thoughts
4. Problem Solving
5. Awareness of Triggers
6. Changing Negative Thoughts
7. Empathy
8. Deep Breathing: Knowing How To Chill
9. Brainstorming Options
10. Weighing the Pros and Cons
11. Idenitifying Feelings
12. Be Assertive
13. Dealing With Anger Before It's Too Late
14. Participating In Enjoybale Activities
15. Learning Zones
16. Thinking, Feeling, and What We Do
17. What is Depression?
18. Are You Dealing With Depression?
19. "I" Statements
20. Stages of Grief
21. Stages of Grief: Denial
22. Stages of Grief: Anger
23. Stages of Grief: Bargaining
24. Stages of Grief: Depression
25. Stages of Grief: Acceptance
26. Muscle Relaxation
27. Good For You!
28. Challenging Distorted Thoughts
29. Relationships
30. Learning When Not To Do What You Have Always Done
31. Diversity
32. Right Brain vs. Left Brain
33. Responding To Fear
34. Touch & Go
35. Approach & Retreat
36. Missing Out On the Good Stuff
37. Moving Through Anxiety
38. Phases
39. Personal Space
40. Boundaries
41. Barn vs. School vs. Home
42. Self Respect
43. Respect For Others
44. Respect For The Environment
45. Setting Up For Success
46. Self-Care
47. Balance
48. Good Listening
49. Standing Up For Yourself
50. Change

APPENDIX 4
Experiential Education Grid, by Tracy Weber, PhD.

	Experiential Education	Organizational Development	Equine Assisted Psychotherapy – Individual
Focus	On individual-group experience	On Organization	On individual experience
Program time	Short-term, intense program	Long-term relationships with clients	Short-term, intense program
Individual vs. Systemic	Individual "takes home" new perspective or skills that empower them to better live in a system which is not necessarily seen as changing	Change must occur in the system (or sub-system) to support change in the group or individual.	Individual "takes home" new perspective or skills that empower them to better live in a system which is not necessarily seen as changing
Knowledge	Need to know individual and group psychology	Need to know organization psychology and culture	Need to know individual and group psychology
Assessment	Informal process of assessment prior to planning course program	Formal needs assessment of organization and subsystems done in prior planning	Formal needs assessment of individual and subsystems done in prior planning
Methods	Espoused methods of change more "normative" in nature, i.e., "we know what they need, more challenge, risk-taking, etc."	May be "normative" or "situational" in nature; i.e. "what is needed depends"	Espoused methods of change more "normative" in nature, i.e., "we know what they need."
Type of training	Tends to be "off-the-shelf" training	More "customized" training	More "customized" training
Group Type	Works primarily with newly formed groups or strangers	Works primarily with existing groups or co-workers	Works primarily with existing groups or families
Prospective	Staff often see self as different from client, especially corporate clients, rather than seeking and acknowledging similarities; sometimes leading to a "we-they" perspective	Planning actively involves the client, collaborative nature	Staff often see self as different from client, rather than seeking and acknowledging similarities; sometimes leading to a "we-they" perspective
Follow-up	Little or no follow-up evaluation	Follow-up and evaluation built into action plan	Follow-up and evaluation built into action plan
Control	Little or no control over system which customers live and work	Role of facilitator as change agent, ability to influence organizational at systems or structural level	Little or no control over system which customers live and work

First two columns are taken from Richard Flor's November 1991 article in *The Journal of Experiential Education*, "Building Bridges Between Organizational Development and Experiential/Adventure Education."

Equine Assisted Psychotherapy – Individual	Equine Assisted Psychotherapy - Group	Equine Assisted Learning – Personal Growth	Equine Assisted Learning – Professional Development
On individual experience	On group or "family"	On individual experience	On individual- organization
Short-term, intense program	Short or long-term relationships with clients	Short-term, intense program	Short or long term relationships with clients
Individual "takes home" new perspective or skills that empower them to better live in a system which is not necessarily seen as changing	Change must occur in the system (or sub-system) to support change in the group or individual.	Individual "takes home" new perspective or skills that empower them to better live in a system which is not necessarily seen as changing	Change must occur in the system (or sub-system) to support change in the group or individual.
Need to know individual and group psychology	Need to know individual and group psychology	Need to know adult learning, neuroscience	Need to know organization psychology, neuroscience, and culture
Formal needs assessment of individual and subsystems done in prior planning	Formal needs assessment of family and subsystems done in prior planning	Informal process of assessment prior to planning course program	Formal needs assessment of organization and subsystems done in prior planning
Espoused methods of change more "normative" in nature, i.e., "we know what they need."	Espoused methods of change more "normative" in nature, i.e., "we know what they need"	May be "normative" or "situational" in nature; i.e. "what is needed depends"	May be "normative" or "situational" in nature; i.e. "what is needed depends"
More "customized" training	Tends to be "off-the-shelf" training	Tends to be "off-the-shelf" training	More "customized" training
Works primarily with existing groups or families	Works primarily with existing groups or families	Works primarily with newly formed groups or strangers	Works primarily with existing groups or co-workers
Staff often see self as different from client, rather than seeking and acknowledging similarities; sometimes leading to a "we-they" perspective	Staff often see self as different from client, rather than seeking and acknowledging similarities; sometimes leading to a "we-they" perspective	Planning actively involves the client, collaborative nature	Planning actively involves the client, collaborative nature
Follow-up and evaluation built into action plan	Follow-up and evaluation built into action plan	Little or no follow-up evaluation	Follow-up and evaluation built into action plan
Little or no control over system which customers live and work	Role of facilitator as change agent, ability to influence organizational at systems or structural level	Little or no control over system which customers live and work	Role of facilitator as change agent, ability to influence organizational at systems or structural level

Contributor Biographies

Tanya Bailey, MSW, LICSW

Tanya is a licensed clinical social worker with over 20 years' experience providing Animal-Assisted Interactions (AAI) in mental health, wellness, and learning programs for individuals, families, school districts, and human service organizations. She is the Animal-Assisted Interaction Program Specialist at the University of Minnesota's Landscape Arboretum, and a consultant to the U of MN's Center for Spirituality and Healing where she co-facilitates a graduate course in AAI. Tanya is a Pet Partners® team evaluator with Pet Partners (formerly known as Delta Society) and committee member for the Pet Partners Curriculum Development Team; a TTEAM Practitioner-in-training through Tellington-TTouch; and task force member for PATH International's Equine-Facilitated Psychotherapy and Learning (EFP/L) Membership Group. Tanya focuses on engaging people in the journey towards balance and as a multi-species practitioner, works with her registered therapy chicken, an amazing herd of horses at the U of MN's Leatherdale Equine Center, and goats, llamas, and donkeys at program sites in the Twin Cities.

Kris Batchelor, BA

Kris founded and runs *Triple Play Farm, LLC* (www.tripleplayfarm.com), a premier center for equine facilitated learning and therapy just outside of Charlotte, North Carolina. She began as a PATH Intl. certified therapeutic riding instructor and was so inspired by the emotional and behavioral benefits experienced by her riders that she chose to transition solely to the mental health field. She is fortunate to have a wonderful four-legged staff, including several Norwegian Fjords, that work with clients of all ages who are interested in learning about themselves by partnering with a horse. She is a PATH Intl., EAGALA, and OK Corral certified Equine Specialist who is always seeking ways to expand the farm's programming and elevate the EFP/L field. She is also a Level 2 graduate of Parelli Natural Horsemanship and is constantly humbled by all that horses choose to offer us.

Lisa Baugh, LMFT

Lisa is a licensed Marriage and Family Therapist in private practice in Wellington FL. She is EAGALA Advanced Certified and has owned and shown horses since she was 6 years old. She provides traditional psychotherapy for individuals, couples, children and families, with an emphasis on serving the local and international equestrian community. She provides EAP services through her private practice and for local substance abuse and mental health treatment centers, as well as offering personal growth and corporate team building workshops.

Rhiannon C. Beauregard , LMFT

Rhiannon is a Licensed Marriage and Family Therapist and is EAGALA Advanced Certified. With over 23 years experience in horses, she is dually qualified as a mental health professional and equine specialist. She is also an AAMFT Clinical Fellow, AAMFT Approved Supervisor, an EAGALA Mentor, and a PATH International Therapeutic Horseback Riding Instructor. Rhiannon is currently the New Hampshire 4-H Animal and Agricultural Science Education Program Coordinator for the University of New Hampshire–Cooperative Extension, melding her passion of positive youth development and animals. She also maintains a small private practice in New Hampshire specializing in sexual trauma, relationship and couples counseling, and sexual issues.

Liza Sapir Flood, LPC

Liza started working in wilderness therapy with at-risk teenagers in 2000. Inspired by this population and the promise of alternative healing, she was soon led to equine therapy. She worked for two years at Aspen Ranch in Loa, UT, where she and her partners integrated the principles of EAP and natural horsemanship into their work. In 2004, she moved to Asheville, NC to pursue degree in counseling, and completed an internship at *Horse Sense of the Carolinas* as part of her clinical training. Liza was then employed by *Horse Sense,* first as an equine specialist and later as a therapist. There, she co-authored Running With Mustangs: Equine Assisted Cognitive-Behavioral Therapy with Court-Ordered Youth with Valeria Krall, and facilitated a research project that tracked recidivism rates and mental health outcomes for program graduates. During this time, she was also a horse trainer and instructor at Biltmore Equestrian Center. Liza is now pursuing a graduate degree in ethnomusicology at the University of Virginia.

StarrLee Heady

StarrLee is a lifelong equestrian and a certified riding instructor. She grew up in Wyoming and Montana. StarrLee and her husband currently own and operate *PX Equine Enterprises Inc.* in Green Cove Springs, Florida. She is involved in the everyday operation of the barn and training as well as maintaining a private practice in Equine Assisted Psychotherapy as a Licensed Mental Health Counselor. StarrLee has been consistently facilitating groups since 1985. She was initially trained in Group Facilitation through a U.S. Military Navy program and The University of Arizona, (NADSAP & PREVENT). She has since trained in group work at the Master's and Doctoral levels and currently works with active duty Military groups, couples and families.

Ms. Heady first utilized horses and equine assisted programming in 2000 and has continued to combine horses and psychotherapy models in Military programming, parenting training, youth at risk groups, substance abuse and recovery groups, independent living programs and corporate training as well as other equine and mental health programming. Ms. Heady has served as a board member for EFMHA (Equine Facilitated Mental Health Association), and as a board member of TRAVERSE Inc. She is a past Clinical Program Director of EAGALA (Equine Assisted Growth And Learning Association) and currently contracts to facilitate EAGALA training and mentoring. She is a member of the EAGALA Military Task Force and will continue to provide Equine Assisted Psychotherapy and Learning to our U. S. Military and others. StarrLee provides both EAGALA programming and non-EAGALA programming such as Horsemanship For Health™ and Equi-Learn™ programs. She also provides continuing education and consultation in equine assisted work in multiple areas.

Leif Hallberg

Leif is a pioneer and leading expert in the field of equine interactions and her book, *Walking the Way of the Horse: Exploring the Power of the Horse-Human Relationship* is used as a teaching text across the United States and internationally. She has been an active volunteer for PATH Intl. as a past board member of EFMHA and chair of the PATH Intl. EFP and EFP membership task force. Her 16 years of practice includes clinical directorships at the San Cristobal Ranch Academy, a residential treatment center for men 18-25 and the Esperanza Center, a community-based experiential growth and learning center, as well as an assistant professorship in the psychology department at Carroll College and on-going teaching opportunities at Prescott College. Leif has worked extensively with American Indians teaching equine and nature-based skills and has worked in jail and correctional facility settings with highly at-risk populations. Leif travels extensively, consulting, teaching and lecturing both nationally and internationally. She maintains a private practice in Portland, OR.

Ashley Edmonds Hayes

Ashley is the Founder and Executive Director of *Shepherd Youth Ranch* (www.shepherdyouthranch.org), a faith based 501c3 non-profit organization located just outside of Raleigh, NC. Since 2004, Ashley and her team have served over 3000 youth and families in need through EAL, EAP and Parelli Natural Horsemanship™ based equine assisted skill building programs. Ashley received her Master's of Arts degree in Christian Counseling and is an EAGALA certified Therapist and Equine Specialist as well as a Parelli One Star Instructor trainee. Today, Ashley is growing a phenomenal equine assisted youth ranch program for youth and families in need as well as a traveling demo team (Savvy Shepherds) who like to show off their relationships with horses! In addition, Ashley writes curriculum and programming for Equine Assisted Practices and provides educational workshops, training and consultative services to organizations who want to start similar ministries. For more information about consultation services and training, contact shepherdyouthranch@gmail.com

Michelle Holling-Brooks

EAGALA Advanced ES, EAGALA contracted Mentor for ES's, PATH certified Instructor and ES in Mental Health & Learning. With over 12 years of experience in the EAAT field and working with at-risk populations from court systems, residential facilities to out-patient, Michelle is currently the Virginia EAGALA networking group state coordinator and founder of *Unbridled Change*, an out-patient EAAT non-profit organization serving the greater Roanoke Valley area in VA. She is a lifelong equestrian and professionally trains jumpers and 3-day eventers.

Tim Jobe

Tim is truly one of the pioneers in this field. The Natural Lifemanship model of Trauma Focused Equine Assisted Psychotherapy evolved from Tim's work of over 40 years training horses, and more than 30 years using horses to help youth and families overcome adverse life circumstances. He has worked full-time in this field while developing an innovative way to help both children and horses, resulting in thousands of hours spent in therapy sessions. He is one of the founding board members of the Equine Assisted Growth and Learning Association, on whose board he served for 10 years. Natural Lifemanship relationship building principles are unique in that they were specifically designed to apply equally to horse and human relationships, resulting in deeply therapeutic work in the mental health field. Tim continues to train horses and work with a variety of clients at *Spirit Reins* in Liberty Hill, Texas.

Elizabeth Kendall, PhD

Dr. Kendall is a professor and research psychologist at Griffith University and the Centre for National Research on Disability and Rehabilitation (CONROD), She focuses on adjustment and self-management following acquired disability and chronic illness. She also examines innovative health service models that are responsive to diverse populations and the creation of healthy contexts (family, work, community, service systems) to accommodate disability, prevent injury, and/or promote health. She has nearly 30 years of experience experience in rehabilitation for people who have acquired brain or spinal injury and has a particular interest in developing community-based services that respond to the context in which people live or draw on the natural supports in people's environments. She has spent many years advocating for policy and practice changes that can improve services. She has a long-standing role in the development of Riding for Disabled in Australia.

Richard Knapp

Richard spent seven years in the US Air Force, spending part of that time as a flight instructor. After a stint doing contract software development in Dallas, TX, he and Shannon moved to Marshall, NC where they bought a small ranch for their two horses. Fast forward a few years and they now share their ranch with twenty two horses and Richard has become a Licensed Parelli Professional.

Amy Blossom Lomas, BS

EAGALA Advanced. Amy is the Executive Director and founder of *Reins of Change, Inc.* in Elgin, Illinois. Reins of Change is a private stable and mental health center, dedicated to providing Equine Assisted Psychotherapy, Equine Assisted Learning, personal growth and corporate training workshops, EAGALA trainings, and other educational opportunities for clients of all ages.

Amy is a past Chairman of the Board of Directors for the Equine Assisted Growth and Learning Association (EAGALA),a non-profit 501(c)(3) organization developed to address the need for resources, education, and professionalism in the field of Equine Assisted Psychotherapy. She currently works as a trainer for EAGALA. Blossom has been trained and certified by the Equine Assisted Growth and Learning Association since 1999, and is internationally recognized as a program developer, presenter, trainer, and leader in the field of Equine Assisted Psychotherapy.

Harriet Laurie

Harriet is the founder of *TheHorseCourse*, a UK charity which delivers an Offending Behaviour Programme at four UK prisons using Parelli trained horses to provide motivation, feedback and reward to help high risk violent offenders learn mental and emotional self control. Referrals prioritize those who are disengaged and difficult to reach and who have been thrown off or deemed unsuitable for accredited interventions because of their attitudes and behaviour. Harriet is a law graduate, was for 20 years a designer and communications consultant. She has ridden from childhood and has studied Parelli Natural Horsemanship since 2005, taking a special interest in "difficult" horses. She has studied various schools of thought regarding the drivers of human behaviour and change. These two disciplines contributed to Harriet's idea of using horses and horsemanship to influence behavioural change in so-called "difficult" prisoners.

Patti Mandrell, M.Ed., LPC

EAGALA Advanced. Patti is cofounder of *REFUGE Services*, a Christian non-profit organization that provides outpatient EAP services in Lubbock, TX that serves over 150 clients per week. She serves as director of therapy services supervising other therapists, horse professionals, volunteers, and intern students. Prior, Patti served as a program director for a residential treatment center for girls with eating disorders in south Texas. Patti was the first professional counselor to be nationally certified in Equine-Assisted Psychotherapy (EAP) in the state of Texas, and she and her husband, Randy, were among one of the first group to reach advanced certification with EAGALA in the country. She has been incorporating EAP for over 14 years and a therapist for over 15 years. She is a trainer and mentor for EAGALA. Patti received her master's counseling degree at Texas Tech University. Patti has been spotlighted and interviewed in numerous local, state, national and international publications and television broadcastings promoting the use of EAP when working with families and children. She wrote the first textbook in press used around the world about EAP: "Introduction to Equine Assisted Psychotherapy."

Randy Mandrell

EAGALA Advanced. Randy is cofounder of *REFUGE Services,* a Christian non-profit organization that provides outpatient EAP services in

Lubbock. He is the Director of equine services, managing Refuge's 40 acre equestrian facility with over 20 horses. Prior to this, Randy was the equine director for a residential treatment center for girls with eating disorders in south Texas. He was the first horse professional to offer Equine-Assisted Psychotherapy (EAP) services on an outpatient basis in partnership with professional counselors in the state of Texas. Randy has been practicing EAP for over 14 years working with adolescents, adults, families, couples, and groups of all types. Having 36 years of experience with horses, 22 years experience as a professional horse trainer and farrier, Randy was recognized by EAGALA as "Outstanding Horse Professional" in 2001 for his superior work with clients and collaboration with other therapists in his community. He is also a trainer and mentor for EAGALA.

Annick Maujean, PhD

Annick is a post-doctoral research fellow in the Griffith Health Institute and the Centre of National Research and Disability and Rehabilitation Medicine at Griffith University in Brisbane, Australia. She is a registered psychologist who has completed her PhD in Clinical Psychology. Her research focuses on how to use non-traditional interventions (i.e., non-clinic mechanisms) as therapeutic tools to engage young people who have disengaged from school and/or the community. Her research have helped several non-profit organizations to deliver appropriate services to disengaged young people who have not responded to traditional interventions. She has developed, delivered and evaluated several types of equine psychotherapy programs for people with disabilities, young people with mental illnesses and those who are disadvantaged in society. She has published research articles about equine therapy and continues to deliver successful programs.

Laura McFarland, M.Ed.

Laura is a doctorate candidate at The University of Texas Department of Special Education and serves as a board member for Spirit Reins. Spirit Reins is a not-for-profit that transforms the lives of children and families through trauma-informed therapy services, training, and research. They offer a variety of innovative professional counseling services, but specialize in Trauma-Focused Equine Assisted Psychotherapy (TF-EAP) in serving children who have experienced abuse, neglect, or other traumatic events.

Carissa McNamara

Carissa graduated with a Masters Degree in Public Administration and Nonprofit Management from The George Washington University. While in Washington, D.C., she worked for The George Washington Law School Office of Advancement. She also worked and interned on several projects for The George Washington University including how technology addresses Homeland Security, as well as the impact of the implementation of legislation related to No Child Left Behind. Upon her return to Utah, she took the position of Program Director for a residential treatment facility for women and children with substance abuse issues. She eventually left the treatment communication for an Executive position with the Mayor's office.

Carissa has 14 years of solid horse experience in the Quarter Horse industry, and her continued commitment to horses and alternative treatments for PTSD brought her to EAGALA. She started and runs BX Ranches which provides outpatient EAGALA EAP/EAL services, and also serves as the Program Director for Ascend Recovery in Highland, Utah—a residential drug and alcohol treatment center where EAGALA sessions are provided to the clients.

Cami Murnane, MSW

EAGALA certified MHP. Cami has over 12 years of experience working with at-risk youth and working in the alternative school system as a therapist. She is Unbridled Change's lead therapist and has worked with UBC for 5 years. She is a lifelong horse lover and enjoys the opportunity to combine her passion for working with clients and horses together.

Lillan Roquet

Lillian has been involved in Parelli since attending her first tour stop in 2004. She was 15 years old and decided *this* was what she wanted to do with her life. Despite this dream, she also wanted to graduate from college, and thus help to achieve Pat Parelli's goal of raising the level of professionalism in the horse industry, so she began at Linfield College in 2007 from where she would graduate a year early in 2010, with honors and a Bachelor of Science in Psychology. Since then, she has worked directly for Pat Parelli at his barn, as a Horse Developer at Atwood Ranch in California, and directly for Linda Parelli at her barn. This past year, she was asked to manage the Parelli barn on the Horse and Soul Tour, as well as being a featured performer. 2011 found her in Queensland, Australia where she was privileged to be a part of the Horse Play program, using her knowledge as a Parelli Instructor to help at risk youth. She looks forward to continuing to expand the relationship between Parelli and youth therapy.

Bettina Shultz-Jobe, LPC

Bettina has 10 years of experience utilizing Equine Assisted Psychotherapy, having done EAP with hundreds of traumatized clients. She is a licensed professional counselor and licensed clinical mental health counselor. She is EAGALA and PATH certified, and trained in the use of expressive and experiential therapies, play therapy, neuro-biofeedback, the Neurosequential Model of Therapeutics, Trauma-Focused Cognitive Behavioral Therapy (TF-CBT), and Eye Movement Desensitization and Reprocessing (EMDR). It is her passion and mission to utilize horses to do evidence-based practice, which has contributed to the Natural Lifemanship model of therapy in which every aspect of the horse is very intentionally used to help adults and children heal from various forms of trauma, abuse, or neglect. In 2004 she conducted a seminal research project on EAP which continues to be cited in ongoing research projects, utilized in grant writing, and is required reading at several universities throughout the country. Bettina continues to work with a variety of clients at *Spirit Reins* in Liberty Hill, Texas.

Kendall Smith, LPC

Kendall is a Licensed Professional Counselor. She currently works as a Staff Counselor at a small liberal arts college. Kendall earned her masters degree in Transpersonal Counseling Psychology with an emphasis in Wilderness Therapy. She fell in love with horses while working at a ranch in Colorado and volunteered at horse rescues and therapeutic riding programs while in graduate school. Kendall studied equine assisted psychotherapy as part of her degree and completed her internship at *Joder Arabian Ranch* in Boulder, Colorado. After researching EAP programs all over the United States Kendall moved to North Carolina to pursue employment with *Horse Sense of the Carolinas*. Her efforts were successful and she was delighted to become a member of the *Horse Sense* team in 2008. During the academic year Kendall provides individual and group therapy to undergraduate students, including yoga therapy and somatic-based interventions for anxiety and depression. In the summers she returns to Appalachia and works with the *Horse Sense* herd whenever possible.

Paul Smith, PhD

Paul serves on both undergraduate and graduate faculty for Prescott College and as the Executive Director of the college's equine program, Centaur Leadership Services. Having worked for over thirty years in the field of experiential education with a variety of populations, Paul actively seeks out opportunities to explore, support and facilitate the development of positive human potential. As a leader in the academic training for Equine-Assisted Learning and Equine-Assisted Mental Health, Paul has effectively partnered with other leaders in the field to support what several colleagues appreciatively refer to as a "non-denominational approach" to EAL and EAMH. In addition to his work in Arizona, Paul facilitates education and leadership trainings around the country; working with business and corporate executives, social workers, educators, people living with cancer, veterans, and student in the fields of Experiential Education, Leadership, and Equine-Assisted learning.

Lynn Thomas, LCSW

Co-Founder and Executive Director of EAGALA. Lynn received her Master's of Social Work from the University of Utah and has over 16 years experience working with adolescents, families, individuals and groups in various settings including youth corrections, wilderness and ranch programs, private practice, and mental health agencies. As Executive Director for Aspen Ranch, a residential boarding school for troubled adolescents, she developed a program integrating horses as the primary treatment component. Lynn additionally served as Executive Director for the Aspen Achievement Academy, a wilderness therapy program. In 1999, recognizing the efficacy of the experiential learning approach, the intense impact of the equine relationship, and a need to professionalize standards for this new modality, Lynn formed EAGALA, a non-profit 501(c)3 association. With the help of an energized and dynamic team, Lynn developed the organization's training and certification program and ancillary training manuals. Today, she continues to spearhead operations both domestically and abroad as EAGALA augments its global presence.

Tracy Weber, Ph.D.

Tracy created *Kaleidoscope Learning Circle, llc.* (KLC) to combine her passions for horses and helping people. Kaleidoscope's clients range from internationally known companies to small teams or individuals seeking experiences which provide learning opportunities for personal and professional growth. KLC believes in a learner-centered model and program designs that are based on the most current research in neuroscience, systems thinking, human behavior. Through both her faculty experiences and equine collaborations she has facilitated learning experiences or courses in Dubai, Croatia, Dominican Republic, Puerto Rico, and several US states. Tracy is recognized as one of the founders of some EAL principles as she was part of the initial EAGALA EAL committee and held the first-ever associate Education EAL faculty position at Prescott College, distinguishing Dr. Weber as a recognized leader in EAL, higher education, and organizational development.

Jayna Wekenman, M.Ed.

Jayna graduated from Prescott College's Masters of Arts Program in Education: Equine Assisted (Experiential) Learning and has been affiliated with various organizations and associations in the Equine

Assisted fields. Jayna recently created Growing PEAs—a mobile organization with a vision of Growing Possibilities in Experiential Education and Agriculture. As Growing PEAs evolves, environmental enrichment and other animal husbandry concepts will continue to be a focus; presentations, trainings, program development, and implementation of such are offered. Jayna currently resides in Michigan.

Don Zimmerman, Ph.D.

Dr. Zimmerman has over 30 years' experience in the mental health field working with agencies, children, adolescents and adults. He is a licensed mental health counselor and a licensed clinical social worker. He received the 2007 Indiana Mental Health Counselor of the Year Award. He is also Board Certified in Emergency Crisis Response, serves as a clinical director of the Indiana Crisis Response team, and has responded to a number of national crisis events. His practice also includes traditional therapeutic services, and consulting with businesses and agencies. His areas of expertise include grief and loss, trauma and PTSD, crisis response, anger management, anxiety, self-injury, eating disorders, and autism and other childhood disorders,

Linda Zimmerman

Linda has over 20 years' experience as an equine specialist. She is a former cardiac nurse and served as a clinical manager of a large cardiac practice. In addition to her EAGALA certification she is a certified PATH instructor. She and her husband "Z" co-founded *Manitou Connections* in 2008 and work together as an EAP team. She is also co-author of four nationally recognized EAL curriculums (*A Horse with a Different View: An Equine Assisted Learning Curriculum for Assisting Students on the Autism Spectrum*; *Cowboy Poetry*; *Journey of the Spirit Horse*; and *Marvelous Minis*).

References

Association for Experiential Education. (n.d.). *What is experiential education*. Retrieved from http://www.aee.org/about/whatIsEE.

Baugh, L. (2013, Jan. 7). *Staying "clean" versus using "clean language"* [Members forum]. Message posted to http://community.eagala.org/forum/members_forum/staying_clean_versus_using_clean_language.

Beetz, A., Kotschal, K., Uvnäs-Moberg, K., & Julius, H. (2011). *Basic neurobiological and psychological mechanisms underlying therapeutic effects of Equine Assisted Activities (EAA/T)* [HHRF grant—Public report]. Retrieved from http://www.horsesandhumans.org/.

Bekoff, M. (2008). *The emotional lives of animals* [Kindle version]. Available from Amazon.com.

Cooper, R. K. (2002). *The other 90%: How to unlock your vast untapped potential for leadership and life* [Kindle version]. Available from Amazon.com.

Equine Assisted Growth and Learning Association. (2012). *Fundamentals of EAGALA Model Practice: Equine Assisted Psychotherapy Certification Program (7th ed.)*. Santaquin, UT: Equine Assisted Growth and Learning.

Espinoza-Sokal, S. (2010). *A Parelli Perspective on Teaching*. Savvy Times, August, pp. 52-54.

Eustress. (2013). In Wikipedia, The Free Encyclopedia. Retrieved February 6, 2013, from http://en.wikipedia.org/w/index.php?title=Eustress&oldid=535103700

Experiential education. (2012). In Wikipedia, The Free Encyclopedia. Retrieved January 16, 2013, from http://en.wikipedia.org/w/index.php?title=Experiential_education&oldid=528072493.

Experiential learning. (2013). In Wikipedia, The Free Encyclopedia. Retrieved January 16, 2013, from http://en.wikipedia.org/w/index.php?title=Experiential_learning&oldid=531775937.

Four stages of competence. (2012). In Wikipedia, The Free Encyclopedia. Retrieved January 11, 2013, from http://en.wikipedia.org/w/index.php?title=Four_stages_of_competence&oldid=523091577.

Frankl, V. (2006). *Man's search for meaning* [Kindle version]. Available from Amazon.com.

Goleman, D. (2006). *Social intelligence: The new science of human relationships* [Kindle version]. Available from Amazon.com.

Goleman, D. (2011). *The brain and emotional intelligence: New insights* [Kindle version]. Available from Amazon.com.

Goleman, D., Boyatzis, R. E., & McKee, A. (2004). *Primal leadership: Learning to lead with emotional intelligence* [Kindle version]. Available from Amazon.com.

Grandin, T., & Johnson, C. (2009). *Animals make us human: Creating the best life for animals.* New York, NY: Houghton-Mifflin Harcourt.

Iacoboni, M. (2009). *Mirroring people: The new science of how we connect with others* [Kindle version]. Available from Amazon.com.

Institute of HeartMath. (n.d.). *Coherence.* Retrieved from http://www.heartmath.org/research/research-home/coherence.html.

Johari window. (2012). In Wikipedia, The Free Encyclopedia. Retrieved January 11, 2013, from http://en.wikipedia.org/w/index.php?title=Johari_window&oldid=527427808.

Lesté-Lasserre, C. (2012). *Study: horses more relaxed around nervous humans* [Members only]. TheHorse.com, (Article # 20354). Retrieved from http://www.thehorse.com/articles/29455/study-horses-more-relaxed-around-nervous-humans.

Levine, P. A., & Frederick, A. (1997). *Waking the tiger: Healing trauma* [Kindle version]. Available from Amazon.com.

Low, P. (n. d.). *The Cambridge declaration of consciousness.* J. Panksepp, D. Reiss, D. Edelman, B. Van Swinderen, P. Low & C. Koch (Eds.). Retrieved from http://fcmconference.org/img/

CambridgeDeclarationOnConsciousness.pdf.

Miller, R. M. (1999). *Understanding the Ancient Secrets of the Horse's Mind.* Neenah, WI: Russell Meerdink Co.

Miller, R. M., Lamb, R., & Downs, H. (2005). *The revolution in horsemanship: And what it means to mankind.* Guilford, CT: Lyons Press.

Olmert, M. D. (2009). *Made for each other: The biology of the human-animal bond* (Merloyd Lawrence Books) [Kindle version]. Available from Amazon.com.

Parelli, L. (2010, April 24). *Way more than horsemanship* [Web log]. Retrieved from http://parellihorsemanship.wordpress.com/2010/04/24/way-more-than-horsemanship/.

Parelli, P. (1999). *Introduction & theory: The partnership program.* Pagosa Springs, CO: Parelli Natural Horsemanship.

Parelli, P. (2000). *Introduction & theory: The harmony program.* Pagosa Springs, CO: Parelli Natural Horsemanship.

PATH International. (n.d.). *NARHA/EFMHA integration FAQs.* Retrieved from http://www.pathintl.org/images/pdf/about-narha/Integration-FAQ-web.pdf.

Perry, B. D. (n.d.) *Keep the cool in school: Self-regulation–The second core strength.* Retrieved from http://www.scholastic.com/teachers/article/keep-cool-school-self-regulation-second-core-strength.

Perry, B. D., & Szalavitz, M. (2007). *The boy who was raised as a dog: And other stories from a child psychiatrist's notebook--What traumatized children can teach us about loss, love, and healing* [Kindle version]. Available from Amazon.com.

Senge, P., Kleiner, A., Roberts, C., Ross, R., & Smith, B. (1994). *The fifth discipline fieldbook: Strategies and tools for building a learning organization.* New York: Currency Doubleday.

Siegel, D. J. (2007). *The mindful brain: Reflection and attunement in the cultivation of well-being* [Kindle version]. Available from Amazon.com.

Siegel, D. J. (2009). *Mindsight: The new science of personal transformation* [Kindle version]. Available from Amazon.com.

Stable Life Inc. (n.d.). *History of therapeutic riding/equine assisted activities*. Retrieved from http://www.stablelifeinc.org/historyEAT.html.

Strides Therapeutic Riding. (n.d.). *Riding through history*. Retrieved from http://www.strides.org/history.html.

Smith, P. C. (2012). *The path of the centaur: Insights into facilitating partnership with horses to improve people's lives*. (Unpublished doctoral dissertation). Prescott College: Prescott, AZ.

Sullivan, W., & Rees, J. (2008). *Clean language: Revealing metaphors and opening minds* [Kindle version]. Available from Amazon.com.

TEDtalksDirector. (2012, Oct. 1). *Amy Cuddy: Your body language shapes who you are* [Video file]. Retrieved from http://www.youtube.com/watch?v=Ks-_Mh1QhMc.

Uvnäs-Moberg, K. (2011). *The oxytocin factor: Tapping the hormone of calm, love and healing* [Kindle version]. Available from Amazon.com.

Walters, L., & Baldwin. A. (2011, March 15). *Horses, humans and the frequencies of connection* [Web log]. Retrieved from http://equusatoriwp.nathanstrong.com/?p=206.

Wylie, M. S., & Turner, L. (2011). *The attuned therapist: Does attachment theory really matter?* Psychotherapy Networker, March/April, pp. 18-27, 48-49.

Yerkes–Dodson law. (2013). In Wikipedia, The Free Encyclopedia. Retrieved January 11, 2013, from http://en.wikipedia.org/w/index.php?title=Yerkes%E2%80%93Dodson_law&oldid=530715767.

Zacks, N. (2009). *Horses react to human heart rates, study finds* [Members only]. TheHorse.com, (Article #23697). Retrieved from http://www.thehorse.com/articles/23697/horses-react-to-human-heart-rates-study-finds.

Index

C

Equine Assisted Growth and Learning Association   397

Equine-Assisted Growth and Learning Association, see EAGALA

Equine Assisted Learning, see EAL

Equine Assisted Psychotherapy, see EAP

equine-assisted therapy   iv, 67, 99-100, 159, 161, 178, 289, 354

Equine Facilitated Mental Health Association, see EFMHA

Equine-Facilitated Psychotherapy, see EFP

Equine Guided Education Association, see EGEA

equine psychology   24, 54, 61, 230, 315, 317

ES (Equine Specialist)   v, vii, x, 61, 63, 72, 78, 84, 121, 126, 218, 224, 229-30, 232-3, 256, 261, 303, 305, 307, 315-16, 318-20, 322, 324, 326, 341-2

ethics   60-3, 125, 315, 335

eustress   71, 188-90, 397

experiential   51, 63-4, 74, 78, 81, 178, 187, 191, 194-6, 202, 204, 321, 380, 397

F

facilitators   64-6, 74, 78, 99-100, 187-8, 190, 199-200, 203, 227, 260, 266, 300, 320-2, 345, 381

facility, social   162, 168, 172-3

FASS (Federation of Animal Science Societies)   252-4

Fear Zone   52, 86-7, 108

fight   167, 191, 211, 215, 218, 232

flee   19, 167, 215, 218, 232-3, 345

flight   167, 191, 211, 231-3

Flood, Liza Sapir   244, 264, 270, 279, 327, 334, 348, 360, 363, 384

Flor, Richard   204

G

Goleman, D.   169-71, 173, 186, 189, 213, 220-1, 398

groundwork   15, 26, 28, 69-70, 74, 76, 352

H

Hallberg, Leif   59, 386

Hayes, Ashley Edmonds   iv, 133, 140, 386

Heady, StarrLee   183, 188, 225, 245, 264, 271, 281, 286, 310, 328, 337, 349, 357, 365, 369, 385

HEAL Model (Human-Equine Alliances for Learning)   73

Hippotherapy   56, 59, 256, 265

Holling-Brooks, Michelle   124, 246, 273-4, 284, 330, 336, 350, 360, 365, 387

Horse & Human Comfort Zones   39

Horse Observation Chart   238

Horse Play   130-1

Horse Sense Business Sense   v-vi, 291, 401

Horse Sense of the Carolinas   viii, 10-13, 36, 42, 55, 76, 160-1, 217, 226, 236, 250, 260, 287, 291, 318, 371, 401

horsemanship skills test   62, 315

Horsenality   iv, 26, 32, 37, 47-9, 120, 133, 135, 139-40, 149, 199, 230, 242, 246-8, 266-7, 269

horses

abused   291

appropriate   243, 245, 345

humans teach horses   13, 37

I

impulse control   70-1, 127, 163, 179, 217, 219

interpretation   vi, 65, 89, 95-6, 98, 165-6, 171-2, 187-8, 202, 300-1

J

Jayna Wekenman   251, 394

Jobe, Tim   67, 120, 226, 273, 284, 313, 330, 337, 359, 387

Johari Window   192, 398

Journal of Experiential Education   204

K

Kendall, Elizabeth   130-1, 387

Knapp, Richard   iii, 12, 122, 245, 264, 271, 280, 285-6, 310, 327-8, 336, 349, 353, 357, 364, 369-70, 388

Knapp, Shannon   iii-iv, 270, 401

L

Ladder of Inference   197, 199, 202

Laurie, Harriet   140, 388

learning zone   52, 86-7

Left-Brain Extroverts (LBE)   135, 137, 269

Left-Brain Introvert (LBI)   37, 49, 112, 136-8, 140, 248

Left-Brained   46, 156-7, 250

Liberty and Horse Behavior course   12, 47

life skills   ix, 102, 105, 120, 135, 140-2

Lillan Roquet   iii, 130, 391

Lomas, Amy Blossom   244, 263, 278, 286, 309, 330, 336, 347, 356, 361,

unmounted work 76, 287

V

vision 34, 94, 395

volunteers 57, 61, 128, 263, 273, 289, 318

W

Waterloo Horse 1

Weber, Tracy 75, 197, 204, 321, 369, 394

Y

youth iii, 75, 91, 93, 130, 133-7, 156, 169, 226, 274, 304, 318, 370, 385, 401

Z

Zimmerman, Don "Z" 225, 246, 284, 313, 332, 358, 365, 395

Zimmerman, Linda 225, 265, 272, 283, 312, 331-2, 350, 358, 364, 395

About the Author

Shannon Knapp is founder and president of both *Horse Sense of the Carolinas, Inc.*, and *Horse Sense Business Sense*. *Horse Sense of the Carolinas* is a national provider of Equine Assisted Psychotherapy and Learning services, and a leading resource for equine-facilitated therapy professionals worldwide. Learn more at www.HorseSenseOtc.com. *Horse Sense Business Sense* (www.HorseSenseBusiness.com) provides equine-assisted programs with the practical resources, information, and tools they need to build a successful business.

Shannon has played with horses and people for over thirty years. After ten years teaching in college, she left academia and began working with abused and neglected horses. She began pairing "rescued" horses with people in 2001, and Horse Sense was formed soon after. Since 2001, Shannon has logged thousands of hours with hundreds of clients with many different issues, specializing in working with youth and addictions/recovery. She and her husband Richard continue to work with horses through horse rescue organizations and local humane societies and law enforcement.

✱

Shannon is EAGALA Advanced Certified, a Parelli Level 2 graduate and is the author of the book, Horse Sense Business Sense, Volume 1, *an introduction to starting and running your own Horse Therapy & Learning practice, as well as numerous other resources for Horse Therapy & Learning programs. In addition, Shannon is a Graduate Advisor for Prescott College's Equine Assisted Learning Masters concentration program, & offers consulting services to those interested in starting their own Horse Therapy & Learning business;. She also offers educational workshops and trainings. Shannon and Richard live in Western North Carolina with their twenty+ horses, four dogs, and multiple cats.*

CPSIA information can be obtained at www.ICGtesting.com
Printed in the USA
BVOW04s2247030414

349478BV00002B/3/P